SEVENTH EDITION

ADOLESCENT PORTRAITS

ANDREW GARROD

Dartmouth College

LISA SMULYAN

Swarthmore College

SALLY I. POWERS

University of Massachusetts, Amherst

ROBERT KILKENNY

Simmons College

D1262213

Boston   Columbus   Indianapolis   New York   San Francisco   Upper Saddle River
Amsterdam   Cape Town   Dubai   London   Madrid   Milan   Munich   Paris   Montreal
Toronto   Delhi   Mexico City   Sao Paulo   Sydney   Hong Kong   Seoul   Singapore   Taipei   Tokyo

Executive Acquisitions Editor: *Jeff Marshall*
Editorial Assistant: *Michael Rosen*
Marketing Manager: *Nicole Kunzmann*
Marketing Assistant: *Jessica Warren*
Production Manager: *Meghan DeMaio*
Editorial Production and Composition Service: *Hemalatha / Integra Software Services*
Creative Director: *Jayne Conte*
Cover Image: *Rebekka/Shutterstock*
Cover Designer: *Bruce Kenselaar*
Printer/Binder/Cover Printer: R. R. Donnelley & Sons

Library of Congress Cataloging-in-Publication Data
Adolescent portraits : identity, relationships, and challenges / Andrew
Garrod ... [et al.]. — 7th ed.
   p. cm.
 Includes bibliographical references.
 ISBN-13: 978-0-205-03623-3
 ISBN-10: 0-205-03623-6
  1. Adolescence—Case studies. 2. Adolescent psychology—United States—
Case studies. I. Garrod, Andrew
HQ796.A3343 2012
305.235—dc22   2011017352

10 9 8 7 6 5 4 3 2 1 RRD 15 14 13 12 11

PEARSON

ISBN-10:   0-205-03623-6
ISBN-13: 978-0-205-03623-3

CONTENTS

CASES CATEGORIZED BY THEME

The seventh edition of *Adolescent Portraits* includes four new cases and four new reflections by earlier contributors on their lives since writing their stories. In choosing new cases and removing others, we have considered feedback from faculty and students using the book and our own understanding of the important issues facing adolescents in the first decade of this century. We welcome further comments on the usefulness of particular cases and the varied ways in which you may use them in your courses. We particularly value suggestions about critical adolescent themes that are not yet addressed in our text.

This seventh edition is accompanied by an online Instructor's Manual, which includes further suggestions for teaching strategies and assignments to be used with the cases. An expanded review of films also appears in the Instructor's Manual, along with a sampling of cases from the first four editions, which we thought were important to keep available to instructors: "Working through My Adolescence," "Running Hurdles," "To Be the Best," "Guilt Was Everywhere around Me," "No 'Boring Little Friends,' " and "Love Me for Who I Am." In addition, we have included the following five cases from the fifth edition: "A Step in the Only Direction" (and follow-up), "Courting Danger" (and follow-up), "At Least We Got One Right" (and follow-up), "Loving Women," and "Pa Jam Decourajer"; and the following cases from the sixth edition: "Things Began to Click," "In Search of My Voice," "Falling for Someone," "The Family I Have," "Beyond the Euphoric Buzz," and "Color-Blind." The Instructor's Manual can be accessed at http"//www.pearsonhighered.com by clicking on the Instructor Resource Center (IRC) link. Access to the IRC is password protected and for instructors only. Instructors may contact their Pearson representative for help with accessing the Instructor's Manual.

ACKNOWLEDGMENTS

The cases in this book are the words of college students who have taken our courses, individuals who were willing to share their life experiences with many outsiders. Although we cannot thank them by name, we wish to acknowledge their personal strength as well as the time and energy they invested in this project. In addition, we want to recognize the many students who worked with us on cases that have not been included in the book; they, too, gave tremendously of themselves as we worked to shape the final manuscript. We are grateful for the support of Amy Miner, University of Massachusetts, Amherst, in the preparation of the revised Instructor's Manual that accompanies the seventh edition of *Adolescent Portraits*. We would also like to thank the following reviewers for their comments and suggestions for this edition: Richard Brody, The College of St. Rose; Julie M. Hupp, Ohio State University, Newark; Charles P. Resavy, Wilkes University; and Wendy J. Steinberg, Eastern University. The manuscript has been put together with the assistance of the following highly competent Dartmouth students: Tien-Tien Jong, Trevor King, and Victor Lekweuwa. Most of all, I would like to acknowledge the absolutely invaluable help given by Dennis Zeveloff, who was responsible for the final formatting of the manuscript.

OVERVIEW

■ ■ ■ ■ ■

THE STUDY OF ADOLESCENCE

The way in which we view adolescence depends, to a large extent, on our perceptions of human nature and the relationship of the individual to society. Current researchers draw on past perceptions but also bring a new set of lenses to the field. Many have begun to realize the diversity that characterizes their individual subjects and the difficulty in generating a theory that captures the experiences of all adolescents. Using the lenses of class, ethnicity, race, gender, and sexual orientation, researchers work to describe and explain the complexity seen in adolescent thought, behavior, and relationships.

Twentieth-century understanding of adolescent development has some of its roots in earlier studies of human development (see Elder, 1980; Lesko, 2001; Moran, 2000; Sisson, Hersen, & Van Hasselt, 1987 for additional information on historical trends in the study of adolescence). The first consideration of adolescence as a separate stage of life is often attributed to Plato (1921) and Aristotle (1941), both of whom described the adolescent as unstable and impressionable. They advocated schooling for girls and boys that would shield them from society and help them develop the self-control and reason that characterize a mature individual. In the Middle Ages, the prevalence of Christian views of human depravity and of knowledge as external to the individual led to a less developmental perspective. Children and adolescents were seen as miniature adults who needed to be socialized into acceptance of adult roles, values, and beliefs (Muuss, 1996).

John Locke and Jean-Jacques Rousseau helped to restore society's belief in the qualitative difference between children and adults. Rousseau, in particular, emphasized a process of development during which innate knowledge and character unfold throughout childhood and youth. In *Emile*, Rousseau presented his view of this process and the role of society in nurturing and schooling young people as they develop into responsible citizens. Rousseau attributed different natural characteristics and social roles to males and females and suggested that, while the process of development is similar for both, schooling toward the end product should differ as a result of their divergent natures and responsibilities (Martin, 1981).

In the nineteenth century, several social and intellectual movements influenced perceptions of human nature and adolescence. Charles Darwin's *The Origin of Species* included humans as part of the natural world, providing a more biological and evolutionary view of human development and growth. The industrial revolution led to a gradual de-emphasis on the family's role in socialization for work and relationships and a growing discontinuity in an individual's experience of home and work. Accompanying movements such as child labor laws and compulsory schooling contributed to society's perception of a phase of development between childhood and the assumption of an adult role in society, a phase which G. Stanley Hall named *adolescence* in 1904 (Moran, 2000).

Hall (1904) described adolescence as a key stage of life in the evolution of the mature individual. Drawing on Darwin's work, he postulated a scientific theory of recapitulation in which the individual develops through stages that parallel those of human civilization. Like Rousseau, he saw development as a natural, largely innate process that could be guided and supported by society. Hall characterized preadolescence as the "savage" stage in the life of the individual. Adolescence followed, a transitional period to adulthood filled with contradictory emotions and behaviors: selfishness and altruism, sensitivity and cruelty, radicalism and conservatism. Through the struggle of adolescence, the individual is reborn and a new self is created, ready to assume a role in modern society.

Hall's work influenced the study of adolescence through the twentieth century, but it has also been modified and challenged over the years. While Freud and those whose ideas developed from his work (e.g., Blos, 1962; Erikson, 1968; A Freud, 1946) continued to focus on biological imperatives and their influence on the individual's psyche in the process of development, others began to take a more sociological perspective on adolescence. The work of Margaret Mead (1958) and Ruth Benedict (1950) suggested that society determines the behaviors, roles, and values of its adolescents. Others focused on the effects of social disorganization, social class, and social institutions on the life of the adolescent, documenting the role of environment in the shaping of experience (e.g., Havighurst, Bosman, Liddle, Matthews, & Pierce, 1962; Hollingshead, 1949). In the 1950s, studies of adolescence tended to emphasize the role of the peer group and the uniqueness of the adolescent experience; adolescence was seen as discontinuous with both childhood and adulthood. Adolescents had their own culture, comprised of a unique language, patterns of interaction, and beliefs.

While the events of the 1960s contributed to this perception of an adolescent subculture, they also led those who study adolescence to focus on the intersection between the life course of the individual, the age cohort, and the historical context within which the individuals act (Elder, 1980). Some researchers and theorists, following Mead's emphasis on cultural influences on adolescence, focused on the social-historical context of adolescent development. They challenged Hall's view of adolescence as necessarily stressful by examining continuity and change in adolescent behavior over time (e.g., Modell & Goodman, 1990). Others began to reexamine the period of adolescence within the context of an individual's life span (Arnett, 2004). Research in child and adult development and in ego, cognitive, and moral development led to an understanding of adolescence as one of a sequence of life stages during which the individual addresses key issues such as identity, autonomy, attachment, and relationship. The emphasis in this work has been on phases or stages of development that cut across social, historical, and cultural boundaries (e.g., Erikson, 1968; Kohlberg & Gilligan, 1972; Piaget, 1972).

Some of the most recent work in the study of adolescence has challenged approaches that emphasize either sociocultural determinism or universal developmental theory, suggesting that understanding adolescence involves a consideration of how social categories such as race, ethnicity, class, sexuality, and gender interact with processes of individual development (e.g., Gonzales & Cauce, 1995; Leadbeater & Way, 1996; Martin, 1996; Savin-Williams, 2005; Way & Chu, 2004). The historical and cultural context is important in understanding adolescent experience, but it may not be sufficient to explain an individual's behaviors, beliefs, and sense of self. Stage and phase theories of development tend to overgeneralize from small, nonrepresentative samples and often ignore key variables such as race, class, gender, and sexual orientation that have a profound impact on an individual's experience and identity. The study of adolescence, then, has become more inclusive in terms of who is studied, what questions are asked, and how experience is analyzed. It has also become more complex, as we take a range of variables and contexts into consideration when examining individual development.

Research in the past thirty years has also refuted the "storm and stress" model of adolescent development that grew out of Hall's work. This approach sees adolescence as a time of severe turbulence, during which relationships disintegrate as the individual rebels against internal and external value systems (e.g., Blos, 1962; A. Freud, 1946, 1958). In contrast, more current work in the field emphasizes continuity and renegotiation as processes that characterize adolescence. "Normal" adolescent development encompasses a wide range of experiences, including a variety of family structures, sexual experimentation and orientation, and ethnicity and racial exploration. Although some adolescents may experience more environmental stresses than others, these challenges occur within a meaningful personal and social context for that individual. Researchers have come to accept many variations within their definitions of normality in adolescence.

Even as researchers and teachers try to understand the multiple aspects of each individual's identity, the context within which American adolescents develop continues to change, further complicating the picture. Adolescents in the late twentieth and early twenty-first centuries are growing up in a society that takes technology and global communication as givens. On a large scale, this adolescent cohort's historical and cultural context is one in which international shifts and conflicts mean changing relationships between the United States and other countries. Increased international communication continues to change our knowledge of relationships with others around the world. Closer to home, these adolescents experience a society that is working toward greater acceptance of diversity—one in which women and minorities strive to defend and work toward their goals while simultaneously trying to change society. Although they are growing up in decades of change and progress, today's adolescents also face persistent political and social problems: educational systems struggling with declining enrollments and shrinking resources; urban, suburban, and rural communities focusing on teenage drug use, school violence, and the spread of AIDS; and continuing racial and ethnic questioning and occasional conflict. The social questions and issues that surround them demonstrate to today's adolescents that society does not have all of the answers and that it often seems to lack the direction and commitment needed to find them.

THE CASE STUDY APPROACH

Those of us who teach courses in adolescent development continue to search for materials that address our students' lives and illuminate emerging approaches in the study of adolescence. Such materials help students learn what past and present theorists and current research have to say about the adolescent experience and engage students in asking questions about those theories and approaches as well as their own lives. We want our students to be thoughtful and critical participants in the study of adolescence, contributors to our growing understanding of how this phase of life relates to the larger life cycle.

The authors of this book found this kind of material in a book called *Experiencing Youth*, first published in 1970 by George W. Goethals and Dennis S. Klos. We all used this book in our own study of adolescence and initially incorporated it into the courses we taught. *Experiencing Youth* (1976) is a set of first-person accounts written by undergraduate and graduate students (the latter appear primarily in the second edition) that highlight key issues in adolescent development: autonomy, identity, and intimacy. These cases demonstrate how powerful narrative can be as a way of examining individual lives within a framework of theory and research on adolescence.

By listening to the voices of individual adolescents, students and teachers of adolescent development can gain a greater understanding of the issues facing some of today's adolescents. Case studies illustrate the complexity of the individual experience and the interactions among an individual's needs, ideas, relationships, and context. Each case, taken alone, helps us begin to know one more adolescent and his or her experience; taken together, the cases provide a rich overview of the field of adolescence. Through them, we come to a greater understanding of key theories and current research findings in the field of adolescence as we examine patterns in their lives and the lives of others. We are indebted to Goethals and Klos for helping us and our students learn the value of the case study.

In this book, we build on the model provided by Goethals and Klos, bringing together the voices of students in our own classes and some key theories and approaches used in the study of adolescence. Each case in this book was written and revised by an undergraduate or very recent graduate, most of whom have taken a course in adolescent development.

   Although it is never possible to be completely representative, we chose students and cases with the goal of achieving a cross-section of ethnicities, class backgrounds, and experiences. The eighteen case writers include adolescents who are white, African American, Native American, Latino, and Asian American. The writers include men and women who are gay and straight, and those who are questioning their sexuality. Case writers come from around the United States as well as the Caribbean, India, and Vietnam; from urban, suburban, and rural environments; from more and less privileged backgrounds; from single- and two-parent homes; and from situations that have stimulated reflection and those that have allowed the writer to develop without thinking deeply about the implications and meanings of his or her actions and ideas. Although we have included each case under a major topic (as listed in the Contents), each case addresses a number of issues. The chart at the front of the book provides a guide to the themes present in each case, as do the abstracts at the beginning of each case. See the Instructor's Manual (available for download at: http"//www.pearsonhighered.com) for further suggestions for using the cases in this book in a variety of classroom settings.

PART I

IDENTITY

THEORETICAL OVERVIEW

The eight cases in the Identity section of this book show a pattern of a struggle for meaning and a quest for wholeness. Within the categories of values and ideology, the self in social context, and sexuality, the adolescent writers wrestle with important choices—who they want to be, how to relate to others, what values should guide them, and what their place is in various spheres of their lives. Though the content of the autobiographies may differ from case to case, the reader will see that the writers share common explorations and preoccupations with the self: the self in relation to others and the self in relation to the broader society. We offer here a framework for approaching the cases in this section.

Erik Erikson (1968), who has helped shape our understanding of identity, proposed a detailed and widely applied psychosocial theory of identity development. Convinced that the study of identity is as crucial to our time as the study of childhood sexuality was to Freud's, Erikson forged a radical rethinking among psychoanalytic theorists about ego structure and the role of culture and environment in personality development. His writings have, over the last decades, been expanded (e.g., Marcia, 1967) and debated (e.g., Gilligan, 1982) by a succession of theorists, some of whom have significantly broadened and challenged his theory's applicability.

When asked to describe his adolescence, one of our students recently wrote: "I don't know where it started and have no more idea if it's ended. Something inside of me tells me I'm in transition between something and something else, but I don't know what." In transition between two "somethings," this young man is not at all sure where he has come from and even less sure of his destination; he is Kurt Lewin's (1939) "marginal man," uncertain of his position and group belongingness. As an adolescent, he is in a stage of his life in which pressures, both internal and external, to define himself become simultaneously impossible to ignore and impossible to satisfy. He is working to establish a self-concept while at the same time realizing that this concept is changing as rapidly as he can pinpoint it. Like Lewis Carroll's Alice, he may well reply to the question: "Who are you?" posed by the Caterpillar, by saying "I, I hardly know Sir, just at present—at least I know who I was when I got up this morning, but I must have changed several times since then." In Erikson's terms, the adolescent has entered a psychological moratorium—a hiatus between childhood security and adult independence.

Adolescence is a critical stage in the individual's development. Adolescents are intensely aware of how they are seen by others—aware, as V. S. Pritchett (1971) observes, that "other egos with their own court of adherents invade one's privacy with theirs." It is a time in which the values and perspectives of others become clearer to the developing mind. The adolescent must first attempt to evaluate his or her different options—different ethical positions or religious beliefs, acceptance or rejection of societal norms, attitudes toward sexuality, ideological stance in relation to family, friends, and community—before he or she can choose among them. In this sense, the search for identity is not only the process of molding an image of oneself—it is also the attempt to understand the fundamental components of the clay that will be used.

The identities of childhood, strengthened by identifications with significant others and by growing mastery of the tasks of school and family life, may no longer hold; the challenge for the adolescent is a creative synthesis of past identifications, current skills and abilities, and future hopes—all within the context of the opportunities the society offers. This challenge is made immeasurably harder because of the technological society we live in, in which multiple roles and careers tantalize us with choice. Mead (1958) suggests it might be easier to live in a society in which roles are inherited through birth or decided by gender! Yet the critical task of the developing adolescent is to balance the imposition of identities provided by his or her position in the social structure, the family, and the community with an agentic sense of who one is, what one stands for, and how one relates to the world.

Theories of identity development focus on themes of separation and individuation of the emerging individual *and* themes of connection or relationship between the adolescent and significant others in the process of renegotiating the childhood self or selves. Theories of separation stem from the work of Freud (1953) and Erikson (1968) and focus on how the individual rejects prior identifications in the search for a separate, unique, and unified sense of self. Theories of connection (Gilligan, 1982; Miller, 1991; Stern, 1989) explore how individuals come to know themselves through relationship; adolescent identity development is a process of refiguring one's relationships to account for new psychological and social needs and expectations. More recently, studies of adolescent identity have focused on how adolescents draw on aspects of both separation and connection in negotiating the multiple identities they construct and perform in this stage of life and into adulthood.

Erikson's theory of ego identity formation focuses on the concepts of ego identity, the identity stage, and the identity crisis. He defines identity as "the capacity to see oneself as having continuity and sameness and to act accordingly. It is the consistent organization of experience." Erikson held to the epigenetic principle of development in which "anything that grows has a ground plan, and that out of this ground plan the parts arise, each part having its time of special ascendancy until all parts have risen to form a functional whole" (Erikson, 1968, p. 92). The stages are not merely passed through but instead add cumulatively to the whole personality; Erikson saw the quest for identity and the crises that it often produces as the defining characteristics of adolescence. His psychosocial stage theory is founded on the belief that life is composed of a series of conflicts that must be partially resolved before the developing individual can move to the next stage. He proposes eight general stages of conflict: trust versus mistrust, autonomy versus shame, initiative versus guilt, industry versus inferiority, identity versus identity confusion, intimacy versus isolation, generativity versus stagnation, and integrity versus despair (Erikson, 1968). Following psychoanalytic theory, these stages appear in sequential order but are never completely resolved. Erikson saw the quest for identity and the crises that it often produces as the defining characteristic of adolescence. The formation of ego identity does not take place only in the identity stage, however; the degree to which one satisfactorily resolves the identity crisis is heavily dependent on the resolutions to the challenges of the first four stages in Erikson's eight-stage life-cycle theory. Each item exists "in some form," Erikson tells us, before its decisive and critical time normally arrives (Erikson, 1968, pp. 93, 95). That is, there are identity elements in all preceding stages just as there are in the succeeding stages, and if the conflicts in these earlier stages are concluded satisfactorily, the healthy development of the ego is more probable. If the conflicts are resolved unsatisfactorily, negative qualities are crystallized in the personality structure and may impede further development.

The psychosocial moratorium—a time of deferred choice—is the period in an adolescent or young adult's life for resolving the identity crisis. It is a time when role experimentation is encouraged and where there is little expectation that the individual will commit to permanent responsibilities or roles. The identity crisis "is precipitated both by the individual's readiness and by society's pressure" to separate from childhood identifications and find a coherent individuated identity (Erikson, 1980, p. 130). The age at which the identity crisis occurs may vary "according to such social structure factors as class, subculture, ethnic background, and gender" (Côté & Levine, 1987) or socialization factors such as child-rearing practices and identification with parents (Jordan, 1971). The moratorium must end, with the experience of role experimentation complete and the achievement of a resynthesis of positive identifications. These achievements enable the individual to find "a niche in some section of society, a niche which is firmly defined yet seems to be uniquely made for him" (Erikson, 1968, p. 156). The niche is dependent on the adolescent's feeling that commitment in the areas of values, vocation, religious beliefs, political ideology, sex, gender role, and family lifestyle are accepted, settled, and expressions of personal choice. Other more critical theorists, Jackson, McCullough, and Gurin (1981) for example, have suggested that the option of having a moratorium and being in a position to choose in the area of commitment are limited by social, political, and economic structures and dominant ideologies.

Allied with Erikson's faith in ego identity is his understanding of the difficulty involved for adolescents in creating and maintaining this identity. Identity confusion, and the resulting identity crisis, results from the individual's inability to understand the "mutual fit of himself and the environment—that is, of his capacity to relate to an ever-expanding life space of people and institutions on the one hand, and, on the other, the readiness of these people and institutions to make him a part of an ongoing cultural concern" (Erikson, 1975, p. 102). Feeling pressured by society and his or her own maturation to choose between possible roles even as personal perspectives are rapidly changing, the identity-confused adolescent experiences a confusion that challenges his or her ability to form a stable identity.

Erikson believes that the success with which the adolescent resolves these crises is extremely important for the eventual achievement of intimacy with others. It is only through the commitment to sexual direction, vocational direction, and a system of values that "intimacy of sexual and affectionate love, deep friendship and personal abandon without fear of loss of ego identity can take place" (Muuss, 1996, p. 54). Identity achievement, as opposed to identity confusion, allows the individual to move smoothly from preoccupation with the inner core of identity to exploration of the potential roles this self will play in intimate relationships with others.

Erikson's construct of identity versus identity confusion has been expanded by James Marcia (1966, 1980). Marcia, whose work on the ego and identity development began with his dissertation "Development and Validation of Ego—Identity Status" (1966), establishes two concepts already mentioned by Erikson—crisis and commitment—as the determining variables in identity achievement. "Crisis refers to times during adolescence when the individual seems to be actively involved in choosing among alternative occupations and beliefs. Commitment refers to the degree of personal investment the individual expresses in an occupation or belief" (Marcia, 1967, p. 119). Using these variables as the determining standards, Marcia breaks Erikson's fifth stage down into four substages: identity diffusion, identify foreclosure, moratorium, and identity achievement.

The identity-diffused individual is characterized by having neither an active involvement in the search for identity roles nor a commitment to any of these roles. He or she is not questioning alternatives. At this point, the adolescent is like James Joyce's Stephen Daedalus, "drifting amid life like the barren shell of the moon." Identity foreclosure is characterized by commitment without crisis; that is, the individual has chosen a set of values or ideological stance, most often that of his or her parents or valued others, without examining this value or searching out alternatives. In moratorium, on the other hand, the individual is in the midst of a crisis, actively questioning and searching among alternatives, without any commitment to one option. In achievement, the individual has experienced the crises of moratorium and has successfully made a commitment. Identity achievement is most often attained in the college years, with moratorium and diffusion characteristic of earlier adolescence (Santrock, 1990). It should be pointed out that differences exist between societies and between groups and individuals within societies in the length of the sanctioned intermediary period, the psychosocial moratorium (Manaster, 1989). Also, those not afforded the time or opportunity to engage in identity seeking may well not undergo an identity crisis in adolescence or young adulthood.

Some theorists, among them Miller (1991) and Surrey (1984), have suggested that adolescent identity development (like childhood development that precedes it and adult development that follows) is more a story of connection and relationship than one of separation and autonomy. Early theorists in this field argued that adolescent boys seem concerned with separation and individuation while adolescent girls create identity more in connection to peers and members of their families. Carol Gilligan (1982) writes of her reservations about Erikson's theory in *In a Different Voice*. Gilligan points out that Erikson recognized sex differences in identity development and discussed how for men identity precedes intimacy and generativity in the optimal cycle of human separation and attachment, but for women these tasks instead seem to be fused—the woman comes to know herself through relationships with others. Erikson nevertheless retained the sequence of identity preceding intimacy. The sequencing of Erikson's second, third, fourth, and fifth stages, Gilligan suggests, little prepares the individual for the intimacy of the first adult stage. "Development itself comes to be identified with separation, and attachments appear to be developmental impediments, as is repeatedly the case in the assessment of women" (Gilligan, 1982, pp. 12–13).

In contrast, more recent theorists explore how the challenges of adolescence—brought on by puberty, a more active role in the social structure, and changing cognitive abilities—are negotiated within and through relationships by all adolescents. Both adolescent girls and boys explore who they are through interaction with families (Hill, 1987; Taylor, 1996; Ward, 1996) and peers (Chu, 2004; Savin-Williams & Berndt, 1990), and through the other social groups and networks that are important in their lives (McLaughlin & Heath, 1993). While finding a separate, unique identity is important, that process occurs within and through negotiating the self in relation to other individuals and social groups. This relational perspective also allows us to examine how adolescents form multiple identities that differ to some extent by context and need. The adolescent in school, experiencing certain demands and opportunities, may differ from the adolescent at home, where alternate relationships and expectations influence actions and values (Ferguson, 2000; Flores-Gonzáles, 2002). The adolescent must learn to balance the search for a coherent, separate identity with the multiple identities, negotiated through relationship, that characterize his or her sense of self.

The process of adolescent identity formation may also vary in accordance with the ethnic and racial background of the individual. A number of theorists have presented stage theories of ethnic or racial identity development (e.g., Cross, 1991; Kim, in Ponterotto & Pederson, 1993). These frameworks of analysis suggest that nonwhite adolescents tend to begin the process in a stage in which they either identify with the white majority or are unaware of the role of race or ethnicity in their experience. They move, often as the result of a series of events or encounters in which their race or ethnicity becomes salient, into a stage of awareness. In this stage, individuals become more conscious of their position in the society and begin to question who they are in relation to their own racial or ethnic group and in relation to the dominant culture. In a third general stage, adolescents identify with their racial or ethnic group and often immerse themselves in an exploration of that group's historical, cultural, political, and social position in the society. The final stage in most of these theories is a stage of integration and internalization, in which the individual incorporates his or her identification with a racial or ethnic group into a more comprehensive identity. This more inclusive identity may allow individuals to identify with their group and interact successfully in the dominant (white) culture. Ponterotto and Pederson (1993) provide a similar framework for examining white racial identity development. The stages they posit parallel those previously described and include preexposure, conflict, prominority/antiracism, retreat into white culture, and redefinition and integration. Stage theories of racial and ethnic identity development have their limitations, however. They tend to assume that all members of a particular group experience the process of identity development in the same way and that the process itself is both linear and progressive. More recent examinations of the impact of race and ethnicity on adolescent identity development focus on the various ways that individuals and groups engage in explorations of who they are in relation to racial and ethnic groups and to the dominant culture. Mary Waters (1996), for example, examines a number of ways in which Caribbean American teens respond to others' expectations of who they are and their own sense of self. Stacy Lee (1996) explores the multiple identities taken on by Asian American students in an academically demanding high school. And Nilda Flores-Gonzáles (2002) describes how Latino students from the same neighborhood develop different identities based on their relationship to school and their community.

In her examination of black identity formation, Fordham (1988) considers the phenomenon of "racelessness." She explores the relationship between group (black) identity and academic success and concludes that black adolescents follow one of two paths. Some respect an "individualistic ethos," disregarding their mandatory membership in the black group—a path that may lead to academic success. Others consider this to be "selling out" and espouse the "collectivistic ethos" of their minority group in order to avoid becoming "nonblack," although they sacrifice academic success in the process. More recent research challenges Fordham's conclusions and demonstrates, again, the multiple ways in which African American students integrate their racial, gender, and academic identities. Mickelson and Velasco (2006), Annette Hemmings (2006) and Prudence Carter (2006) provide case studies of groups of African American students who negotiate school, gender, and racial identities in a range of ways. Ward (1989) examines identity formation in academically successful black female adolescents and discovers that racial identity formation is compatible with academic accomplishment. Considering not only the factors of beliefs, values, attitudes, and patterns of family socialization but also "the girls' own subjective understanding of the role that race plays in their lives" (p. 217), she concludes that racial identity must be considered in order to gain a complete understanding of identity formation. Cases in this edition that focus in particular on adolescents' experiences of ethnic and racial identity are 1, 3, 4, 5, 6, 7, and 18.

Other recent areas of exploration in identity development are gender and sexuality. Gender is an aspect of identity that is socially constructed, or performed, within available discourses and institutional structures (Connell, 2000; Walkerdine, Lucey, & Melody, 2001). Adolescents explore their gender identities often within a binary framework of stereotypical masculinity and femininity (Kimmel, 1994; Martin, 1996). They make choices within these frameworks, sometimes challenging the norms and sometimes functioning, consciously or unconsciously, within them. Adolescents also begin to explore their sexuality and sexual identities. While Freud (1953) sees this as a natural part of the developmental process, Mead (1958) suggests that cultures impose a heightened sense of sexuality on adolescents. While past theorists have, again, posited developmental stages of sexuality development (e.g., Troiden, 1998), more recent researchers focus again on the role of relationships and interactions with others in a variety of contexts in their examination of adolescents' active construction of a sexual identity (Martin, 1996; Savin-Williams, 2005). While many cases in this book include adolescents exploring aspects of gender and sexual identity, Cases 2, 3, 8, 12, 13, and 17 in particular allow us to examine these issues.

Other authors have explored the interactions among the multiple identities adolescents actually contend with during the process of identity formation. James Sears (1996), for example, has examined the experiences of adolescents who are both gay and African American, and Alex Wilson (1996) probes the lives of those who are gay and Native American. In Leadbeater and Way's book, *Urban Girls* (1996), researchers report on studies that investigate the experiences of male and female adolescents juggling issues of gender, race, ethnicity, and class as they figure out who they are. Maria Root (1999), Theresa Williams (1996), and others have contributed to our understanding of the complexity of racial and ethnic identity development in their studies of multiracial individuals. Their work suggests that the process of racial and ethnic identity is multifaceted and complex and an inherent part of identity development for all adolescents.

Alternative perspectives on the process of identity development in adolescence, then, focus on the examination of the individual in context. Development is seen as a process of renegotiating relationships, redefining oneself in relation to individuals and social groups (family, racial or ethnic group, class, and gender) of which one is a part. In the Identity section of this book, we include cases that address several aspects of identity development—values and ideology, the self in social context, and sexuality. In most cases, the writers are, themselves, engaged in exploring multiple identities. We encourage the reader to examine these autobiographies through a consideration of the following questions. What roles do issues of trust, autonomy, initiative, competence, and identity play in each person's case? Within what contexts does the author define himself or herself? What relationships and connections contribute to his or her sense of self, and how are they changing?

Whatever theoretical perspective one adopts, and we suggest an eclectic approach, the essential components are a simultaneous discovery and creation of the self leading to a deepening self-understanding. We believe the cases in this section capture that process in both tone and substance. In each case, there is a greater sense of understanding and acceptance of oneself at the end than at the beginning. Each author makes clear that the process continues, but they seem here to have reached a plateau from which they can look back and survey their progress. Readers may do well to suspend somewhat their theoretical assumptions while reading a case, lest they miss the sheer spectacle of lives unfolding. Though different identity theorists provide a useful framework for interpretation of these cases, the best of them are but a scaffolding for understanding. We should try to listen first to each author in his or her own terms, to see the authors' evolution through their own eyes. In the unique and intimate details of their individual lives, we can discern the outline of a universal struggle to identify our true selves. Your readings here should influence your understanding of theory at least as much as theory influences your reading.

SOMEDAY MY ELDERS WILL BE PROUD

This Native American woman recounts her experience of living in two worlds. Jean describes how her mother raised her and her three brothers after her father abandoned the family when she was quite young. These circumstances, along with abuse at the hands of her uncle, leave lasting emotional wounds she will not address until much later. While firmly rooted in and proud of her Native American culture, Jean becomes a scholarship student at an elite secondary school. Her family's relative poverty and the condescending attitudes of her classmates further feelings of self-doubt, low self-esteem, and ethnic inferiority. Her transition to college does not succeed; she turns to heavy drinking, fails academically, and returns home. She gets a job working with troubled Native American adolescents, and through helping the self she sees in them, she finds a purpose in returning to college.

I grew up in Bismarck, North Dakota. My parents met through a relocation program. Relocation attempted to assimilate Native Americans into urban life from their reservation or tribal communities. The goal of the program was for an individual to gain economic self-sufficiency by means of a vocation or technical school education. My parents were in just such a program in Denver, Colorado, where they met and married. That is where my three brothers and I were born. My mother, a Cheyenne, was 22, and my father, a Blackfoot, was 21 when they had me. I am the oldest.

My father ran back to his reservation in Montana before my youngest brother was born. I must have been almost four years old. I have no concrete memories of him. My mom says that he taught her how to take care of me, because she didn't know that much about babies. He began drinking when I was born, and he was a womanizer. Soon his drinking got out of control. Despite her problems with our dad, Mom would always tell us how he loved my brothers and me and that he was a good father to us. Whenever he came home, we would run and crawl all over him. We never saw him again after he left Mom and us behind. Dad died on the reservation when I was seven years old, from alcoholism. He was only 28. I don't remember exactly when Mom told us, but it held no meaning. It seemed that he had already died when he left.

By the time I was six, my mother had moved to Bismarck, where many of her relatives and immediate family lived. We did this because family was important to her tribe, and they would help us as much as they could. Initially we lived off welfare and the help that our relatives could give us. My mother decided she didn't want us to live like that forever. She wanted to be a good example for the four of us, so she worked during the day and went to school at night to get her bachelor's degree in social work at the state university. We grew up in a single-parent family with the benefits of an extended family.

Mom worked through temporary services at factories and we got some monetary help from our father's social security benefits after he died, food stamps, and AFDC. We were very poor. We went to garage sales, Salvation Armies, and Goodwills for most of our clothes, furniture, and toys.

During those years when my mother pushed herself, my brothers and I were watched by one of my mom's younger brothers. She had no choice; he needed a place to live, and we needed a baby-sitter. I think he was in his twenties. He stayed with us from the time I was in first grade until I was in the sixth grade. He was always there after school when we came home. He taught us good things, like to stick up for each other when we used to get chased home from school by the white kids and not to be afraid of fighting for ourselves.

However, our uncle was an alcoholic and had a violent streak in him. We became convenient scapegoats for him when he was sober or drunk. Even though my mom forbade him to drink in her home, he still did. There are lots of stories about how we couldn't wear shorts because the belt or switch marks were too vivid. He never hit us when Mom was home. When he did whip us, he'd say to us after he was finished, "You'd better keep your mouths shut and not tell your mother." And we stayed silent.

It was for stupid reasons that we got whipped. Who moved his magazine, who messed up the kitchen, who lost his sock and where was it? Who did it? Guilt, innocence, truth, right, wrong, what did any of that matter? It meant nothing. We could have been perfect children but that wouldn't have changed anything. We learned to clean the house as soon as we got home, and maybe it was good enough, maybe it wasn't. We learned to hide in our rooms until Mom got home. We used to be mean to our dogs and sometimes to each other. He made everything seem our fault.

Why didn't we say anything? I don't know. I remember one time how our uncle picked up my brother Lance by the hair and Lance was screaming. I never felt so helpless. I was mad, but I was afraid too. I knew it was all wrong, but I was glad in a way too, because it wasn't me. Mom kicked him out finally when I was in the sixth grade. All that mattered to us then was that he was gone. I still remember the relief I felt.

Why so long to get him out? Mom had to know. All I can think of is how her tribe is strongly patriarchal; men rule the home, and women must listen to and abide by what their brothers say. You never tell them that they're wrong; it would be disrespectful. In the traditional way, uncles are a second father to their nieces and nephews. Alcoholism ran through her side of the family and our dad's. I know that our two uncles had a violent father and uncle too. Those behaviors were probably passed on and were allowed to continue because men have so much power to do what they want. Mom hadn't quite broken out of that mind-set when our uncle was living with us, and she tried so hard to make our lives better at a cost to hers. I couldn't really be angry at her because I remember how she tried to make us happy.

When I first started actively remembering everything that our uncle did to us, I hated him. I was glad that he couldn't hold a job, that he had a rotten marriage, that his own kids were uncontrollable and spoiled, that his drinking gave him critical liver and heart problems. But I tell you, it's strange. He loves us. I'm not going to live fueled by hate, and so I tried to understand what there was in him and his life that let him beat four little kids. He never had it easy himself, and he is the one who has to live with what he's done. He doesn't need another person who hates him or another part of his life to make him more bitter.

Many of our relatives on my mother's side lived in Omaha. Lots of these relatives were members of the newer religion, Native American Church. NAC integrates Christianity, adapting to urban life by getting an education or keeping a job, and being aware of what's good and beautiful in life, in other people, and in yourself. At least that's what it means to me.

An NAC meeting lasts throughout a night; you pray for whoever the meeting is for, including your family. You get no sleep, people sing "hymns" that are in the native language, and you eat a bitter-tasting cactus called peyote. The old school relates the Bible to life, and others talk about what their elders told them about being good people. People talk about how to cope with problems, talk about why things are the way they are, how you can look at your misfortunes, and how we must appreciate and recognize the good that we have. They talk about humbleness and realizing that so much of what we deal with will pass in time. It was there that I felt awe for wisdom and reasoning.

We drove back to Nebraska frequently for NAC meetings and for traditional religious ceremonies, where we prayed and made offerings to the gods and spirits, holding feasts and dances to honor what was being done for the people. We used to travel around the surrounding states for powwows—intertribal gatherings where dancers and singers from different tribes got together to dance and visit with one another. We also stayed with close relatives with whom my mother's generation had grown up. They told us stories from long ago, and they fed us and took us along with them in their areas. The four of us liked going out of town; our world was not defined by the city.

When I finished sixth grade at the public school, Mom had me tested for a private school that an uncle's wife highly recommended. They wanted me to go to a school better than the public junior high. I was accepted and given a scholarship, and when seventh grade came around I went there. At the time, I didn't want to go. I wanted to go on with my friends to the public junior high.

I remember feeling that I didn't fit in and being apprehensive. It was an affluent Episcopalian college preparatory school, grades K–12. It wasn't race that made me an outsider, though there were undercurrents of it. If anything, it seemed to be worse in grade school, where my brothers and I had come home crying, until they told us to fight and stick up for each other. I'd say that poverty made me an outsider.

The first day an English teacher had us write essays on the furthest place in the world we had been. After we finished, we placed them up on the bulletin board. I wrote about Nebraska, and when I looked at the other essays, I saw people saying, "I've been around the world on a cruise ship." A larger majority than I could have imagined said countries in Europe, California, all over. Showing off seemed to occupy a great deal of time at school.

Kids were mean there, not physically, but with their words. "*Who* does your shopping for you? You've *never* been to the Calhoun Club? *Where* do you get your clothes from? You mean you *haven't* been out of the U.S.? You *rent* your home? You mean you don't get an *allowance?*" I couldn't have what they had or really understand the importance of it all, and I felt it acutely. There were the times when I would be talking with someone and instead of listening to whatever it was I was saying, they'd be staring at my clothes.

It wasn't anything that my family or relatives understood. We all knew that it was a good thing for me to go to school there. They wanted us younger kids to be able to work at the jobs we wanted and not struggle like they had. Being poor was awful, the bills were too many and too much. I knew all of that in a vague sense way down and I suppose that's why I stuck it out. But still, it didn't help me in dealing with the daily questionings or scornful looks from my peers. When they did that, I just looked away or down, shoulders slumped, because I felt self-conscious.

Learning the stuff from the books wasn't ever really hard; it was just memorizing most of the time. So I'd memorize and forget everything later. Mom made sure that I did homework when I was home. She always used to say to us how important school was, because if we had it, life wouldn't be as hard for us as it was for her generation. If anything, the material was boring. I noticed that the kids were highly conscientious about doing their work. Grades mattered to them in a way I never really understood. Mom never said to me, "Jean, I want you to get As," and she never acted disappointed when I didn't get an A. All Mom ever said was, "Did you try?" and that was enough. The other kids did their work because they wanted a good grade. For me, it was a way out.

The only way I could figure out to make things better was to bug Mom incessantly about clothes. She tried her best, but it wasn't good enough in my eyes to catch up to the other kids. So I started stealing from stores and from unlocked lockers at school. And then it happened; I got caught. I felt hunted, and I knew the other kids would really talk. "Can you believe what she did?" Most of all, I knew that I would hurt Mom. That's what mattered the most to me. I got suspended for a couple of days. When my mom and I came in to talk to the middle school director and I was asked "how come?" I ended up crying and talking about how people called me names, looked at me funny, and that I couldn't take feeling bad about myself anymore. I hadn't realized that those things preyed on my mind, that they hurt, and that's why I was stealing.

So Mom and I went home and she talked with me. She said that it was wrong to steal and that it reflected on me and the kind of upbringing I had. She said how it was easy to steal, it was cheating, and that it was hard to tell the truth and live by it. She said that we all make mistakes and that it was all right. "Just learn something good from this." And then she talked to me about the things that I had been called. "They're wrong and cruel and do not know you or your strengths. They're just a bunch of kids." I knew what I had done and felt ashamed about myself, but she made me believe in her love and in myself. From Mom, I learned to be compassionate.

I think I learned that I couldn't be myself at that school. I had to be like the other students to be happy there; I had to be rich and snobby. Because of my family's poverty and our tribal gatherings, I couldn't be like them. Not really anyway. Most of the time I was bored, or distracted by home. So what if the football team lost? So what if you're pissed off because you can't talk on the phone past 8:00? What kind of problems are those?

I felt that I had to put on airs or have a dramatic life that people would be interested in, otherwise I was a lonely person. I needed to find a niche somehow, somewhere. So for about two years, somewhere between eighth and ninth grade, I became a liar. I made up the death of a relative, talked about things like drinking, or weed. I told people that I was part Greek. I quit when someone asked about my Greek grandmother. I knew what a lie it was, and I thought to myself, what about your real grandmother? Why can't you be proud of her and everything back home? It was like I had erased her life, said it was nothing by making up another woman who never even existed. I knew something was really wrong with me then. I cringe at the pitiful person I was. I see why I did what I did, but still… I decided that never again would I lie like that because it takes away from the truth of my life. It's "cheating." Parts of my life were ugly, and not understood, but it was mine. My life was no less important than my schoolmates'. Life can't be for everyone what it is to the affluent or sheltered, and none of that makes them better than those less fortunate or different.

By this time I realized how hard it was for my mom to support the four of us on her own. I know the bills and our teenage wants that got more and more expensive were getting to her. She would lash out at us about "never being satisfied" or about not helping enough around the house. She used to point out our faults to us, not in a nice way, during those times. For myself, I cowered during those times when she lost her temper. I couldn't help it. But it wasn't anything like those times with our uncle when we were kids—I understood why she was frustrated and yelling. Even so, Mom always came through for the four of us. She would tell us how smart we were and how strong we could be. If we did something wrong, she would understand what drove us, but always tell us to learn from it all.

There were other times when we went to an NAC meeting, powwow, lodge feast, or a meal with the relatives. I loved all those things. I didn't think about why I felt that way, all I did was feel good. I remember being back at school in the ninth grade after one weekend when we'd been to a powwow. I was in math class, looking around and listening, but my attention kept fading. I kept staring out the window, remembering. We had been to Canada, and the powwow was by a huge network of lakes. During one of the breaks, my brother and I had gone out onto the lake on a motorboat. He killed the engine in the middle of the lake and we were drifting; we could see the powwow ground and all the campers, smell the fires, hear the singing, see dancers walking around in bright colors, shawls and bustles and people laughing.

We tried to start the engine, but it wouldn't, and we had forgotten to bring oars along. We were drifting farther and farther away to the opposite shore, and right before we got tangled in the reeds by the shore, we tried one last time to start the engine. It started, and we were laughing, and the wind whipped our hair back as he gunned the engine. We sped around for a while like that, and when we got back, we had a good story to tell.

People were always teasing each other about something. That's what I liked, laughter. At night you could see all the stars; coffee tasted the best when it got chilly after the sun went down. The smell of a wood fire was always around too, and you were up late and probably tired, but you were having a good time, so it didn't matter. Out of the four of us, I liked to dance the most. When I was small, I used to dance until I had blisters, and they would make me rest for a while.

No one at school, though, would know what in the world I felt good about, or why. I felt caged. What did I care about a logarithm? I was disgusted when I kept hearing three girls across the aisle talking about the teacher, how nerdy she looked, and wasn't John hot, he just broke up with his girlfriend.

Reconciling school, our trips, and home life was hard. Keeping up with us and the bills was hard on Mom, and she was alone. Even though she finished up at college and got her degree, $18,000 a year didn't go far enough for the five of us. Mom was always stressed, and then there were the four of us being adolescents going through all of our stages. Sometimes I wasn't the nicest person and got mad or upset when I couldn't do something because we didn't have the money. I would act like it was all Mom's fault. My brothers Rick and Lance were starting to hang out with the crowd at school that smoked weed, skipped school, and acted tough. Lance tried to run away one time when our uncle who used to live with us threatened to beat him up if he kept on smoking cigarettes.

My youngest brother, Bill, went to school with me. My other two brothers went to the public high school. They also tested for our school when they finished sixth grade, but there weren't any scholarships for them. By the time they were offered one, Mom couldn't swing it. As it was, the school was always hounding her to pay up. If she had paid on time, we would have gone without food, and probably heat and electricity too. Most of me wishes that my other two brothers could have gone to school with us, but part of me feels so glad they didn't. Basically, I didn't want them to feel bad about themselves. I know life would have been "easier" for them, but do years of ridicule have to go along with it?

By the middle of the ninth grade, I developed some friendships. I found it easier to talk to other new students. For the first time in two years, I had friends. Most of the time our talks revolved around classes, boys, how hard track practice was. I liked it.

I think that high school for Bill and me was a time where we numbed ourselves to being poor and to forgetting the Cheyenne and Blackfoot ways. It was easier that way. It seemed that we had to learn to be one way at school, and another at home; but it was hard, how are kids supposed to do that? I went unwillingly to family functions. My family didn't see that much of me the last two years of high school. I was involved in sports, stayed over at friends', or talked with them on the phone incessantly. I didn't want to hear about how far we were behind in bills anymore. School was easier because it was shallow. I could handle talking about classes, but I couldn't do anything to help Mom or not make us poor.

By the time I was a junior, my brother Bill was in the upper school, too. Only thing is, I didn't like him that much because I saw things about myself from his behavior. He looked down on our family for being poor; he was ashamed. School and the people in it were the most important to him. I saw it in him when he brushed my mom aside. She was trying to tell him something, and he answered in a condescending voice to her. I was angry at him for not respecting everything she had done for us. He paid more attention to his friends than family. He said derogatory things to my other two brothers like, "Oh, what do you know?" and after a while they'd say things about our "rich private school." He looked down on them, and I thought, my God, it was only luck that got Bill and me in; it wasn't Lance's or Rick's fault they had to go to public school.

By the time it came around to applying for schools I had a sneaking suspicion that I had neglected something really essential by ignoring as best I could home and the tribes for so long. I applied to colleges because it was what everyone else did. I did fairly well on the entrance tests, had a good grade average, and got recommendations from teachers who liked me. When I applied to school, I applied to out-of-state schools because I wanted to see what it was like elsewhere. The whole process was funny, because I had all these Ivy League schools interested in me. I didn't really care about going to a top school, but most of the other kids did, and a lot of them did double takes when one of my friends teased me loudly about Harvard calling for me. I liked the school I'm at now the most because it had a Native American Society. I knew that I would need some connection to my background to help me out in school without my family or relatives.

Again, my relatives and mother were encouraging. I'll amend that. Everyone but the traditionals were glad for me. As a young woman, I should have been starting a family, not running across the country for four years. They never actually said anything, but when Grandma told them, they'd look away, or talk about something else. In my eyes, going to college wasn't going to make me less Indian, or forget where I came from. If anything, it would enhance it.

It used to bug me sometimes when Grandma would say where I was going, because the way she said it would make other people jealous of me. Lots of people she told this to had kids in state schools or community colleges, and I felt bad because they were just as good as me. I didn't want people to be envious, or think that I was snotty. There were a lot of relatives like that, who were proud of me, but I hated it when they would announce where I was going; they didn't always mention that Sue was doing something really good for herself by going into the Marines, or that Bob was a supervisor in a plastics factory. They weren't any less than I was; in fact, the things they did demanded so much more.

Graduation was boring, and I wasn't crying like most of the other students were. I just remember being glad that school was finally all over with. I wouldn't yearn for my years in high school, and I wouldn't miss most of the people there.

My family brought me to the airport. Mom, Grandma, Grandpa, two uncles, two cousins, and my brothers were there. They took all kinds of pictures of me and my brothers, me and my cousins, me and Mom. I said goodbye to my brothers, and Mom was crying. She tried not to, but I knew she would miss me. And all of a sudden, I knew that I would miss her, too. It startled me. I had tears in my eyes and was biting my lips, and Grandma said, "You're going away to do a good thing. Nothing bad has happened. We don't have to cry." They called my name as I boarded, and I turned as they snapped a picture. I sat in my seat and looked out the window, crying. This man tried to make small talk with me, until he saw me crying, then he let me alone. The plane started to go toward the runway, and I looked at the terminal, and there they all were, standing and waving. I could still see Mom crying. Love. I was leaving love.

I was excited about going to school, partly to be on my own, but I thought because it was college, people would be wise and mature, that there wouldn't be the cliques like in high school. I was wrong. It was freshman week, and most of the people were *just like* my high school peers. I was horrified. I couldn't get into the class spirit, I didn't like my roommate, I didn't like most of the bubbleheads I met. I didn't really feel my purpose in being there—except possibly to meet all the self-important people and party as much as I could. It was a time when I had to stand on my own and rely on my strengths. The only thing was, I didn't know what my strengths were. It didn't feel like I had any.

I was sitting alone one night that first week looking at the stars, like I used to at powwows or in Nebraska. All of a sudden I had a tight feeling in my chest, and I said aloud, "Why am I here?" I felt like walking into the woods and crying, because I didn't want to go through a repeat of being new, like when I started private school.

This is what I did my first term at school: I went to math class for the first week, I went to English for the first half of the term, and to my third class maybe once a week. I drank whenever I could. I remember being three or four papers behind in my English class. I read the books I had to; I just couldn't sit down and say something about the topic questions. I sat in front of a computer and, for the life of me, couldn't think of a damned thing to say about Conrad's imagery in *Heart of Darkness* and its effect on the reader. I went to math for the first three classes and it was all review, from like the eighth grade. The thing is, I always hated math. It was my earliest class, and I didn't feel a compelling need to wake up and go to it.

When I drank too much, I would end up crying and babbling. One time I was at a fraternity, looking at the mob of people dancing, watching people weave in and out through the tightly packed basement to get a beer, and I saw people jumping up and down and crowing with triumph about a beer pong game when a cup got knocked over. I was supposed to be having a good time. I ran out and stood under a pine tree, fists bunched up, crying for my relatives. I was always embarrassed about crying or babbling like that and would act like I had never done it the next day. I was homesick, more than I had thought possible, but I didn't know it. I felt empty and knew something was wrong with me because I should have been having the time of my life. After all, I was young and at college.

People tried to help me. Friends would ask if I'd gone to class, if I'd caught up in math and English. I'd say no, and they'd say, "Jean, you've got to or you're going to be in trouble." I'd laugh, or say nothing. I got called in by my freshmen dean, and he asked how come I was having trouble. I said I didn't know. I was nervous and afraid of what he'd say to me. He said, "You went to a private school, you did well there, you are more than capable of doing well here. You're messing up. Why aren't you doing well?" I didn't say anything. He asked if I was homesick, and almost sobbing, I said yes. He told me that I had to go to classes, and that I could do it. I walked out of there, and composed myself. Crying, what good did it do anyway?

I used to talk with my mom about once every week. She always asked about the people who I was meeting. So I'd tell her about the people I hung out with, what we did or talked about—except the drinking parts. Mom hated to see any of us ending up alcoholic. She asked about classes, and I'd say that they weren't going so well. She'd ask about how I was doing, and I'd say, "I don't know, Mom, not so good." She always said, "You can come home if you want to, Jean. You know that. We want you to be happy."

Somehow I imagined that if I had a boyfriend, everything would be okay. I had met this Native American guy my freshman week. I went looking outside of myself for what I lacked. I liked it that he still had close ties to his tribe, that that was where he drew his strength from. I had spent the night with him a couple of times after parties during the weekend. Platonically, I mean. We spent most of our days together. People were always wondering if we were ever going to get together. I wondered too.

John came up and said he wanted to talk. I had had a knot of anxiety and yearning in me, and it loosened up. He said something about wanting to wake me up with a kiss when I had slept in his room, taking it slow, how he had fun when we were together, and that he respected me. But it was almost like he was dictating a letter to me or something. Maybe I should have gotten up and gone to him when he finished talking. Instead, I said that I needed to go to the bathroom, because I really did.

When I came out, he had gone downstairs, and I felt disappointed. He ended up drinking until he passed out, and then I knew that we didn't have anything. I felt immensely alone, and sad. The next day we studied together, and that was it. He wasn't very talkative. We went back to his room, and he said I would probably hate him, because he had decided to get back together with an old girlfriend and that he didn't want to date someone who wasn't Navajo. I told him I hoped it worked out for him and felt surprised that I meant it. But that was the last straw for me, and I set myself on the path of self-destruction. I just drank whenever I could, tortured myself with dreams of getting him back, and forgot completely about classes.

With the end of the first term came finals. I wouldn't get up to go to my math final. Why go? I was going to fail anyway. I still needed to finish three or four papers, and I hadn't done my term paper for my third class.

I got a call over break, and my dean said that I had been suspended. So when I went back to school it was to pack. Dimly, I regretted it. I had been on my own out there, and I was just beginning to see that there was a lot I could have done, such as pulling my act together, being independent, and maybe learning to loosen up with people my age and have fun.

Mom was supportive of me, as were most of my relatives when I got home. I didn't really know what to do with myself in terms of getting a job or going to the state university. I didn't really feel like doing anything. For about three months I stayed home a lot, cleaned, cooked, and hung out with Mom and my brothers. I tried to escape from thinking about myself and what I would do. The only things I made an effort for were to go to Nebraska with my grandmother and to go to as many NAC meetings and powwows as I could.

I started to drink on the sly. I'd drink when there wasn't anything for me to do, or just to liven things up. One time, I had been slipping into the bathroom to take a shot of vodka every now and then, and I got carried away. My brother Rick told Mom that I was acting weird, and I remember sobbing as she rubbed my back. The next morning I woke up, and I thought, "Oh my God, what have you done?" I felt apprehensive, I couldn't remember anything, and I couldn't really believe that I had gotten stinking drunk like that.

Mom came home, and this is what she said: "Jean, you can't do this to me. This happened to your dad. If something happens to you because of drinking, I'm going to feel really bad. What's the matter? Why are you doing this?" And I didn't know what to say. But I realized that the parents are supposed to die first, not the kids. I saw in her face that Mom knew that she couldn't help me. I had to help myself, and drinking like there was no tomorrow wasn't going to do it. I saw how my not thinking had led me to so many things, and that somehow I needed to make sense of what was bothering me. I said how sorry I was, and for the first time in my life, I meant it.

So I enrolled in a religion and psychology class during the evenings and I got a job tutoring math and English at an inner-city alternative high school for Indians. Most of these students were from the reservation and had come from North and South Dakota, Nebraska, and Montana. Indians flock to Bismarck for jobs or for excitement. Most of us are poor, lots are alcoholic, and many come from dysfunctional families. What smacked me in the face was seeing that abuse was a way of life, the only way of life they knew and accepted. Their education; poverty; alcohol; drugs; emotional, physical, and sexual abuse.

There was a girl named Sharon who did her work and was quiet. When people picked on her, she would cower. When she was called on in class, her voice shook and she wouldn't look up. If I told her she was smart or looked pretty that day, she'd say, "No I'm not." If she had to ask me for some help with some problem, she'd say, "I'm so stupid, I can't do this." I heard Sharon's boyfriend sneering, "Why am I even with you, I could have any woman I want." Sharon said, "I'm sorry, please don't be mad. I'll be how you want me to be." When I heard that, I winced and ran into the bathroom. I tried to block out the echoes of her beseeching him. Those were my words whenever anyone was mad or displeased with me. I knew how that felt in your gut.

They had nothing. So those that still had any fight left in them latched on to being tough, independent, and reckless, all for pride. Everyone needs something. I don't know why the kids talked to me and told me about their lives so much. I don't know why they picked on almost all the other teachers and aides (to their faces most of the time) and left me out of their ridicule. Maybe it was because at 19, I wasn't that much older than them. Or because I was Indian. I liked to laugh with them or tease them when I could. And when they talked to me, I listened, because what they were telling me about was their lives.

All I could say to them was, "It doesn't have to be that way, you know." Those kids are the trapped, the bereft, the haunted. They are the reason I came back to college. I have to find a way to open up a life and world outside of their childhood so that they can at least get through high school and get an adequate education, one that prepares them for college. I have to find a way that doesn't make them feel ashamed about their pasts. I want to change the schools somehow. Schools and your success in them determine what kind of life and career you're going to have. I see so many kids weeded out, and it has nothing to do with their intelligence. Why is the path through high school to college so narrow?

Working helped me decide what to do with myself in terms of college. Since my return, I have done fairly well in classes. I still have problems in making myself go to classes on a regular basis and doing all the reading that I'm assigned. I'm more caught up in my family life and what goes on there than in my studies or the issues at school.

I don't aim for straight As, but for learning what I can that will be useful to me when I go into education or what will help me understand people in general. I also try to learn as much as I can about the culture here, what kinds of ideals and standards motivate the students and professors. It's still a pain a lot of the time, because for all the advantages that most students have here while growing up, and for all their intelligence, there's an incredible lack of compassion or understanding that there are people who live hard, hard lives. Their worlds and lives are closed, too, and it disheartens me lots of times. Sometimes I think that academic knowledge is how they gauge the wisdom and respect of one another. It's something I don't understand, because what does academic knowledge have to do with who we are as people? As far as I can see, wisdom has nothing to do with books and theories.

For a while when I first came back, I joined a coed house, but I found that I still drank a lot to pass the time. I was hungover at least three times a week. I drank so much that I ruined something in my body. Now, when I have more than three beers or mixed drinks, I'm hungover really badly the next day. Luckily, I only get carried away once or twice a year like that. Now, I'll have a beer with dinner once or twice a month, and that's about it. I don't really miss it because I finally figured out that drinking solves none of my problems. It only wastes my time.

Since I have been back, I have been an active member of the Native American Society and have lived at the Society's house whenever possible. It feels like a home. Most of my friends are Native American, not because I'm prejudiced, but because I'm much more at ease with them. I am still really quiet and shy when I first meet people, and I avoid at almost any cost participating in class. Just this past year I decided that I couldn't always be like that, and for now that's enough. I also fell in love for the first time. We were together for two years but broke up three months ago. It was so hard—it still is.

Peter accepted me for who I was, faults and all. He used to say that he wanted the two of us to be able to do what we both wanted and then be able to tell each other about it all. But I didn't know how to accept myself, and I demanded so much from him. It was as if I expected him to make up for things lacking within myself, within my life. Now I know that there's no one in the world that can do that for me but myself. Until I met Peter I was always lonely. With him I learned how to actually reach out to another person instead of being someone who just dreamed about love. He reached out to me and I learned to trust.

One time I went out with a high school friend, and she was talking about how her father went to meetings for abused children and children of alcoholics. She named off all the symptoms that these children have. And you know, as she listed off the characteristics, she described me. I sat there with my mouth open, and it felt like I had been punched in the stomach.

I saw a lot of the abused child behaviors in myself throughout the whole time Peter and I were together. It's like there was a lightness in me after I realized it. Even when I was with Peter I often felt hopeless and depressed. I was always afraid he would leave me. I never understood what he saw in me, so I would try to be what he wanted. I couldn't stand getting into fights with him, and if I was ever mad at him, I'd sulk around and keep it in because I was afraid to express it. I was so insecure with myself. Things would build up, and when we finally got it out in the open, I wouldn't even know myself what I was mad about. Somehow

I felt inarticulate and that I didn't even have the right to be mad. I still have some of these tendencies.

I see how I turned him into a kind of addiction and couldn't give him what he gave me, love and acceptance. When I told Peter about the fact that my brothers and I had been abused, and that I wanted to do something about it, he held me. My voice was shaking, and I could barely get across what I had found out. Peter asked if I felt like crying, and when I said yes, he said, "come here" and hugged me. But I couldn't cry. And when he asked how I felt, I said I felt ashamed. He said, "Oh babe, you don't have anything to be ashamed about. It wasn't your fault." And then I cried.

As time went on, when we were apart, I became more and more insecure. I demanded that he put me at ease and hounded him to keep me a part of his life. I smothered him. Slowly, I lost confidence in myself and in him. Then I knew that I had a long, slow battle to feel good about myself and to not revert to my victim reaction. Oh God, I just wish we had met years from now when I was normal. I wish I had not been abused. But that is not going to change the past. I need to deal with how things are now, and slowly get rid of the things from my childhood. At least now I am aware, unlike many people who never have an inkling about what beneath it all is really bothering them.

Graduation is finally in sight. I plan to go on to graduate school for Indian education. I want to work in curriculum and administration, but I will probably teach first so that I can get some practical experience. I find that because of my experiences away from home I've gotten a lot of perspective that has, in the end, allowed me to appreciate my heritage. I will always do my utmost to keep family ties, NAC, traditions, and powwows in my life. I want all that, or something like it, for my children.

I've learned to think about myself as important and to know that I have strengths. I'm finally starting to be at ease with myself and with other people, and I look forward to the person that I'm becoming. It's been a long, slow haul. When I walk down that aisle for graduation, I want my relatives to be there with me, and I'll walk proudly. I would do everything over again. I wrote this poem that speaks for me and for others:

> *I wear a coat. I wear tennis shoes.*
> *I play a game and I am winning.*
> *I go to school. I feel the worth*
> *in the knowledge of my relatives.*
> *I play the game, I do not live it.*
> *Knowledge from all areas…*
> *My thought, my hope:*
> *someday that all my elders will be proud*
> *respectful of the little ones who follow them.*
> *I dream… to make a way for the small ones not yet here.*
> *The younger ones to play the game in a skillful manner.*
> *In a way that I never could.*
> *It is our wish, it is our wish.*

THE STRUGGLE OF A LIFETIME

Born into small-town life, this college senior describes a lifelong confusion about who he is and what purpose his life serves. The kind of teenager pious adults point to as a "fine young man" who will "make us all proud," Jon conforms to expectations while longing to be a "regular kid." Lacking the ease and self-confidence to develop close friends, he experiences loneliness and isolation from his peer world. A religion of good and evil choices gives comfort and affirms his self-sacrifice and avoidance of typical adolescent pleasures. Beginning college away from home offers Jon an opportunity to recreate himself, but he repeats the lonely pattern of social and sexual avoidance. Through a change in academic focus to theology and involvement in campus ministry, he questions the moral certainties of his Christian beliefs, including its condemnation of homosexuality. He sees his future framed by the struggle of balancing service to others through a religious vocation with the need to be comfortable within himself and accepting of his human needs and imperfections.

My early childhood revolved around a close family, and Sunday dinner after church at my grandparents' house was a weekly ritual. Until I left for college, Nana and Gramps—my mom's parents—hosted a huge homecooked meal for our extended family. There was never enough room on the table for all the different dishes Nana made. Everyone had multiple helpings of mashed potatoes, ham, carrots, and strange things like turnips and parsnips. We would spend the afternoon talking, playing outside, and taking care of their two horses. My dad's parents would join us all on holidays, and since all four of my grandparents grew up in the same town, they loved to sit around the table telling stories about Bedford when they were young—and poor. "We didn't know we were poor," Nana would say. "We thought we had it good."

I grew up in Bedford, too, in the same green duplex as my mom. One of the many little towns in the so-called Coal Country of Pennsylvania, Bedford came into existence around the anthracite mines. All of the mines have been closed for years now, and things are not looking up for Bedford, which is the poorest of the nine towns in our school district. The population is almost entirely blue-collar, working-class families, elderly on social security, or various arrangements of people on welfare.

My family always pointed out the drunks walking up and down the main street, making sure I saw them falling over and looking dumb. I fully got the message when I was 10, when Gramps gave up alcohol for good after years as a borderline alcoholic. He owns a fuel delivery business, which was his father's before him. Now well over 70, Gramps still works six days a week, more than eight hours a day, with no vacations, ever. His business is his life, and I know he'll work until he dies…probably behind the wheel of an oil truck.

Gramps started driving trucks when he was 12 years old, and at 18 he borrowed $1,500 from his mother to buy his own coal truck. Now the business is worth more than $2 million, and he worries about what will happen when he dies. He lives modestly, shares his profits with my mother and her sister, and makes special trips in the winter to deliver oil to people whose tanks are empty, even if they cannot pay. Though not a religious man, he is a kind of pastor to the community. He knows literally everyone and their family histories, and he spends time visiting with people when making deliveries. He buys their homemade pastries and pierogies, lends them money when they need it, and is an advocate for the working people with business and governmental bureaucracies. While growing up, I spent every Saturday working with Gramps, managing his office, riding on the oil truck, filling bags of coal and tanks of kerosene. His mother said he grew up too fast, and I realize more every day how much I am like him.

My own family is a strange one, inheriting from my dad's side the characteristic of not talking to each other. We stopped doing things as a family by the time I was in middle school, and since then my parents, my younger brother and sister, and I have each had independent lives. Trained as a nurse, my mom cannot work anymore because of severe joint problems that keep her in almost constant pain. For a while she was a teacher's aide in special education classes for children with emotional and behavioral problems. What I remember best about mom is her taking food and clothes into school for her kids, who often came to school hungry and without winter coats. I remember how frustrated she got at the administration's apathy. My father is a hospital administrator who hates his job. Work causes him huge amounts of stress, and he usually spends all his time at home watching television, which does not help the fact that he is overweight with heart problems and diabetes. I think he feels locked in a self-defeating cycle.

Though I remember family vacations and playing ball in my backyard, I was never really close with my brother, Luke, who is one year younger than I. Now a junior in college, Luke always felt that he was living in my shadow—he was "Jon's brother." Trying hard to be visibly different, for a while he wore only black clothes, and he still has long, unkempt hair. Now an accomplished musician and very happy with his life, Luke was always the outsider of our family. My sister,

Rachel, is five years younger than I, and I remember helping take care of her as she grew up. Rachel is very different from Luke and me, an outgoing social butterfly who is constantly on the phone or chatting online with her friends to arrange trips to the mall or lament a boyfriend lost.

I was dubbed "the smart one" in my family early on. In elementary school, I loved learning and was excited to go to school. Education was important to my family, but the rest of the town saw it differently. Sports reigned supreme, and the other boys had been on mini-football teams, which their parents coached, since they could walk. My parents never got me involved with them, and though I was on a YMCA swim team for a while, I was awful at sports. Not able to throw a football to save my life, I hated recess and was always the last one picked in gym.

By fourth grade, I was bored to death with school, and my teachers persuaded my parents to transfer me to Bridge Street School for the "academically gifted," located three towns away in a community of upper-middle-class professionals. Students were bussed there from all over our district, but I was the only one from Bedford. At Bridge Street the classes were harder, and for a while I was lost. I got a C on a test for the first time ever, and I didn't win the spelling bees anymore. I was determined to excel again, and by fifth grade I had risen to the top of the class and regained the reputation as the one who always got the highest grade—and who was picked last in gym. Besides my natural shyness, I had a hard time fitting in because I lived in a different town from everyone else, and my parents weren't about to drive me all over. The other kids came from wealthier families, too, and I never had the right brand of clothes or backpack. But life was good, as my parents would remind me. I had a loving family, clothes on my back, food on the table—"some people don't even have that, you know."

For middle school and high school, everyone in the district came to centralized buildings, with heavily tracked classes to keep the "good" doctors' and lawyers' kids in the honors classes with the "good" teachers, and everyone else in the "regular" ones. Entry into that coveted honors group had taken a lot of work for me, and it took even more to stay at the top. I was thankful for making it and felt responsible to do my best. That's all my parents ever asked for, but my best kept getting better and requiring more from me. I felt guilty if I gave less than 100 percent and wondered how other people in my honors classes could totally blow off work.

For me, academics always came first, but in high school I took on a string of activities and leadership roles. Student council, newspaper, literary magazine, and chorus filled up my days, and then there were more and more positions in Boy Scouts, church, and community organizations. I worked constantly, and I was sure it would all pay off. I pressed on, earning the praise of adults and the certificates and plaques that covered the walls of my room. My résumé was growing at a frantic pace, and I envisioned that someday I would be valedictorian, get into a good college—maybe even Harvard—and be "successful." *Then it would all be worth it.*

Toward the end of the summer before my junior year, the choral director from a private school asked me to join his select choir for a concert tour in

France. Jumping at the chance, I ended up singing in Notre Dame, Chartres, and Orléans Cathedrals. The music was spiritually moving, but the people were the most wonderful. Though I avoided going drinking every night with the junior and senior guys in the choir, it was okay. Everyone truly liked me for who I was, and I finally found a group of people that *I* liked. I finally fit in.

That experience made me disgusted with my high school, where no one, including the teachers, cared much about anything. Far from loving learning as I once had, I was now doing the minimum amount of work to get the highest grade, which took less and less effort as teachers and students became more and more apathetic. Overseas, I saw for the first time a whole world beyond my little town. I realized that life could be different from what I saw in high school, and I wanted to know and see and do more, to break out. I was convinced that I would go to college far, far away, probably never to return. Most of all, though, I wanted real school friends like I had found in the choir in France. I finally knew it was possible. When the choir director invited me to transfer to his private school, with a full scholarship, I *really* wanted to transfer, but my parents resisted until I just gave up.

When school started in the fall of my junior year, I felt that I had made the wrong decision and had forever lost the chance to change my life. By that winter, everything came crashing down; the stress I was feeling overwhelmed me. I felt unfulfilled by my work outside of school and hated being in class. More than that, my reputation had taken on a life of its own, and I hated the "Jon Davies" I saw in the mirror. I was supposed to be this responsible, honest young man full of integrity and honor, who would "make us all proud." I spoke at fundraisers, got put on boards of directors as the token youth, and was paraded around as Scouting's poster child. I didn't drink or party, have sex, or smoke pot. I was "trustworthy, loyal, helpful, friendly, courteous, kind…" just like a good Boy Scout. I did what adults think kids should do, but I was torn between the life I was living and an intense desire to "be normal." Why did I care so much what everyone thought of me? Why was this reputation so important to me? Why did I cling to it?

Because it was all I had to cling to. It embodied all my successes and the praise of adults. It was the source of my self-worth and pride. Now it was falling apart underneath me, and I was alone. For the next few months, I spent hours crying and talking to myself in my room, agonizing over my desire to go to that new school and start over sans reputation. I lamented my inability to tell my parents forcefully, "This is what I want." But I still am not sure I knew what I wanted—I was running around in circles and had to do something. I realized that I could not live up to that "Jon Davies" image that everyone had for me. For a while I thought I should say "to hell with it all" and go be "regular" like everyone else—get drunk, go on dates, not do any homework, hang out, and just love living life without a care in the world. Forget the stress, forget the responsibility, forget being a leader. I wanted to be a teenager. I wanted my childhood back. I wanted to experience all these things for myself. But a nagging part of me said something different. The sacrifice would have been so high and would have cut off *everything* that made me who I was, however out of control it had become. My experience in France gave me hope that there might be some other choice, and there the story of my faith truly begins.

For most of my life, my family attended Second United Methodist Church, a quaint little place just a block from home. My mom taught Sunday school and my dad was on the board of trustees. There were lots of nice people who cared about each other, especially the children, and I did the typical Protestant things: Sunday school, youth group, Christmas pageants, and church suppers, in addition to the service on Sunday mornings. It was a great place to grow up, but by high school I was dissatisfied. The 45-minute sermons were boring and totally irrelevant to my life. By senior year, all the kids I grew up with stopped coming, and it was weird to lose all my church friends to jobs, girlfriends and boyfriends, and general apathy. I wondered whether church for most of the congregation was not just a social ritual that made them feel good about themselves. And I wondered about myself. What drew me back week after week? Had church, too, become part of my so-called good-person image?

My *own* faith became important after it intersected with that stressful winter of my junior year. For the first time, I questioned the faith I was taught. I did what the adults said to do: I was a good person, I went to church. And look where it landed me: miserable. I somehow knew that turning into a wild and crazy teenager would not work for me, so I turned instead to examining Christianity *for myself.* I thought it might be the way out of my confusion. I began to listen to Christian radio and read free books from evangelical preachers like Billy Graham and Chuck Swindoll. I found a new message of sin and grace, pain and renewal, death and life spoken to people living in sadness and confusion, who did not always succeed, and who were not perfect—something I could identify with.

There was no one time when I was "born again," but that winter saw an important change. I found Bible verses that spoke to my need, especially "Come to me all you who are weary and heavy-laden, and I will give you rest" (Matthew 11:28). I had always had my church, but I had never learned to *be* a Christian. Now I heard a passionate promise of reward for the struggle and ultimate meaning far more significant than anything I worried about. I prayed those "asking-Jesus-into-your-life" prayers, and I felt changed. The radio preachers and book authors were so clear and perceptive, pointing—it seemed—right at me. Most importantly, I found a sense of peace as a real gift from God. My life was mostly the same; I just had a new outlook. Faith was my way out of confusion, the source of ultimate meaning for my life, and a way to deal with failure.

As much as I used faith to get back on track, I still lacked friends. Evangelical talk about purity and walking the narrow path of righteousness made me judgmental of my peers at school. But by the senior awards ceremony, my achievements and ostensible success could not make up for what I was feeling inside. I got more prizes than anyone else, and new plaques joined the collection already covering my bedroom walls: National Merit Scholar, AP Scholar with Distinction, and my Ivy League admissions certificate topping them off. For a long time these honors were a confirmation from the adult community that I was on the right track, that I was the model to follow. But if loneliness was the cost of this kind of affirmation, I felt I had made the wrong choice.

At graduation, I was named valedictorian of my class—the ultimate prize toward which I had worked since sixth grade. But first the principal gave a long speech—to thunderous applause—about the baseball players who had won the state championship earlier that day. Then he quickly announced the valedictorian and salutatorian, offered his congratulations, and had us stand in our place amid the sea of 250 navy and silver gowns just long enough for the yearbook photographer to snap our picture. It was the ultimate hollow victory.

Coming to college, I had huge expectations. The wood-paneled library seemed the essence of the intellectual life I hoped to find. Here would be a place in so many ways far from home, where learning would finally be valued and where I would fit in because I was smart. More than anything, I wanted friends. In the basketball arena with the thousand other new students at our first class meeting, someone gave a speech saying, "Now's your chance to make a new start, to create yourself again, to be the kind of person you want to be." My parents were gone, no one knew me, and I could be just like everybody else. I would stop being shy and just go up and meet people. I would go to fraternity parties and drink, maybe even join a frat. I would get the girlfriend I never had in high school, be involved in sports for the first time ever, maybe try out for crew. I would see movies, take road trips, and hang around. But I never did any of those things. My freshman English professor called me one of the college's "closet intellectuals," and inside I hoped that there were others like me.

Freshman year was a replay of high school. I spent all my time studying, convinced that I had to get an A in every class. I followed college rules meticulously, so thankful to be at a great college. A near 4.0 GPA and two academic citations proved that I could make it, that I was good enough. I planned to double major in Russian and government and then work for the State Department. I decided to spend sophomore fall on a foreign study program in St. Petersburg, Russia, which was supposed to confirm my plans to enter the foreign service. But I was in for a big surprise.

Any illusion of self-sufficiency was gone after 10 weeks in Russia. It was a totally different world. Fourteen students lived in little four-person apartments on the eighth floor of a broken-down dormitory whose stairwells smelled of trash and vomit. Sometimes we had hot water; most of the time we did not. The heat seldom worked right, the windows never closed all the way, our stove caught on fire, and the bathrooms smelled like sewage.

And for the first time I lived close up with people who acted my image of *normal*. My three roommates spent most of their time drinking, drinking, and drinking. They went to bars, clubs, or room parties more nights than not. It baffled me how they could do no work, sleep through class, and never study. How could they waste this opportunity? Most of all, I saw them drunk and hated it. I could never imagine being so *out of control*. Sure, I saw drunk students bumbling around campus and heard stories of random hookups and "booting" in the bathroom. Even though I thought they looked dumb and immature, I had felt I needed to try all this out in order to be like everyone else. Now that I was seeing face to face the hangovers, vomiting, and vulgar drunken conversations, I wondered if I had to do it for myself to avoid feeling regret. I wondered if this was really the prerequisite for having fun and friends.

But it was also in Russia that I began to appreciate simple blessings of life. Beggars were everywhere—on the sidewalk, in the subway, in churches. On a cold November afternoon I will never forget, I was walking into a store to buy postcards, and an old woman in a wool coat and head scarf was standing in the entranceway. Her eyes were cast down, her hand outstretched, and she said "*Pomogitye!*" I knew the Russian word: "Help." Never before had someone cried out for help, right to me. More than a little shocked, I rushed inside but felt horrible the whole time I was shopping. It was the best kind of guilt. My 10 postcards cost 22,000 rubles, a little over three dollars then, and though most people give beggars spare change, I handed her a 20,000 ruble note on the way out. She looked at it, put it into her pocket, and began to cry. "*Spasibo vam bolshoe.*" "Thank you," she said, and she began to pray out loud. She thanked God for me, and prayed that I might have every blessing, love, and happiness. She reached out, and I let her hold my hand. I remember the warmth of her skin so clearly, the tears in her eyes and mine. Over the next month I had many old Russian women pray for me, holding my hand as I looked into their eyes, and I know God heard them all. Their prayers truly changed my life, and all it took was to stop and look them in the eye, to see not a miserable beggar but Christ Himself.

As powerful as my time in Russia was, the routine of college life took over soon after returning to campus sophomore winter. One big change, though, was the resolution of my search for a church home. I spent all of freshman year "church shopping," often attending the United Church of Christ (UCC) in the morning and St. Andrew's Episcopal Church's student eucharist in the evening. The UCC was a lot like my church in Bedford, but I eventually chose St. Andrew's.

Entering college, I had a very evangelical understanding of Christianity: God created the world, sin came into the world by Adam, all are guilty of sin and should be damned, Jesus died to save us from hell, and if you believe in Jesus you will be saved, otherwise you go to hell. That was it: plain and simple absolute truth. Right was right, wrong was wrong, nothing in between. But I also had a passion to learn more about Christianity, especially Roman Catholicism, which was demonized among Protestants back home: "They worship statues, you know." I took religion classes, studied the Bible by myself, read the church fathers and contemporary theologians, only to find a Christianity I never knew before. Truth was hardly as simple as I thought.

At St. Andrew's, I found a church focused on Holy Eucharist and rooted in the historic Creeds. With a new appreciation for tradition and the work of the Holy Spirit, the Church in all its human frailty replaced a literal reading of the Bible as my source of theological understanding. In the parish there are feminist liberals, family-values conservatives, and everything in between. Side by side we share one bread and one cup around the Lord's table. Anglicanism has become my foundation for learning more about God, and I appreciate its freedom of ambiguity.

Soon after settling in at St. Andrew's, I realized that its college ministry, minimal my freshman year, was now gone altogether. Honestly seeking Christian friends for myself, I suggested to the priests that we start something up again, and found myself appointed as the student minister with the task of rebuilding from scratch a campus ministry. With no idea how to do that, I tried hosting dinners, getting speakers, organizing worship services, and a hundred other things, but hardly anyone came. I was working hard, praying hard, but nothing happened. The clergy talked about how I was planting seeds, but I was looking for some fruit.

At the same time, I very much felt the need to be "successful" in other ways: to make a lot of money and/or become famous. Preparing to be an important diplomat who would make a difference in the world, I received a Rotary Ambassadorial Scholarship to spend a year at Moscow State University in Russia. But deep down I knew this was the wrong path. For so long I had lived according to the expectations of others, and being an ambassador or international businessman was never something I actually wanted to do. I remember how my father always talked about hating his job and my mother about wishing she had gone to a music conservatory instead of nursing school. "Do something you'll enjoy," they always said, "don't make the same mistake." So when some typically Russian logistical snags gave me the chance to back out, I chose not to go to Moscow. Though my parents and mentors still are dumbfounded, it was a key decision that set the rest of my life into motion.

During that sophomore spring I had no idea where I was heading, but not going to Russia became the surprising first step toward exploring a call to the Episcopal priesthood. My first taste of ministry came in Scouting, where I led chapel services at summer camp. I loved studying the Bible, selecting songs, and writing prayers. Soon I was asked to do more than chapel services, though. When campers were homesick, they got sent my way. Staff with real problems ended up at my tent. The same happened in high school, when I heard about devastating breakups, arguments with parents, and complaints about teachers. There was nothing I could do to help, but I guess people found me a safe person who would take time to listen to them.

Though being a clergyman has always been on my mind, I never spoke about it to anyone. I was afraid of what people would think of me. I was afraid my parents would think they were wasting their money on my first-class education, afraid that my high school teachers would be disappointed, afraid that my hard-earned status as an intellectual would be in question, afraid that other students would think I was crazy. In this training ground for investment bankers, a future priest was definitely "sketchy."

But my choice of the Anglican church and a call to the priesthood were strengthened in the aftermath of the brutal murder of Matthew Shepard, a gay college student from Wyoming. Since Matthew was a devout Episcopalian, I impulsively contacted my college campus' homosexual advocacy organization about helping with the vigil they were organizing. When asked to make spiritual remarks, I spent hours in front of the computer trying to figure out what to say— how could I offer something meaningful that would touch the souls of people I knew little about?

When it was my turn to speak, I was terrified of offending someone and making the tense situation worse. There were already people planning, in the name of Christianity, to protest Matthew's funeral with "God Hates Fags" signs— and here I was, the guy from the Episcopal Church. Midway through my remarks, which were vague because of the Anglican Communion's conflict over homosexuality and my own confusion about its morality, I knew I was merely making myself feel good that we bothered to show up. So I skipped to the prayer I wrote, and after a moment of very holy silence, began: "Eternal God, unsearchable and unknowable mystery, our refuge from one generation to another. To you we turn with sighs too deep for words."

When I finished, I sat down, and I listened. For the next two hours, students told painful stories about their victimization that to me were unimaginable. I could not empathize, *only listen.* A Native American student, beaten up in a town parking lot for confronting someone about a sexually offensive homecoming T-shirt, a gay student who received death threats, African Americans, Jews, Latinos, all saying that life at this campus was not nearly as comfortable as people made it out to be. And I wondered what responsibility the Church had in causing their pain and the hate and fear that led to it. Do we in our rush to grab hold of and proclaim the truth end up causing evil, sin, and death? In that night of holy tears, I learned a great deal, most of all that God's people are not all like me, and that I have a lot more to learn.

In a Christmas card from my rector, he wrote that that night confirmed in his mind my "true priestly calling." But as I became more of a presence at St. Andrew's and prepared to take the first official steps of the ordination process, I realized the need to deal more directly with the most difficult questions in my life.

Living for so long as a loner, I value the freedom of independence. But my lack of good friends for the last 20 years has taken its toll. At school I was never close with anyone: I never went on dates, never had a girlfriend, and did not go to any of the proms. I came up with lame excuses, maybe because it was easier to make them up than to learn the social skills I lacked but everyone else seemed to have perfected. In high school, the stories of other people's sexual encounters became cafeteria and locker room conversation.

With my Boy Scout values and evangelical Christian sense of right and wrong, everything sexual seemed pretty wrong. The whole issue went unspoken in my family. And as much as I stuck to my beliefs, I began to wonder if I was the abnormal one. At Scout camp, one staff member my age, Doug—a vulgar guy who chewed tobacco—constantly asked me, "You get laid yet?" knowing full well the answer was "No." After a while, Doug made a little addendum to his comments: "If you don't get laid soon, I'll know you're a fag." Was I?

Without real-world experience of romantic relationships, I often sought release from my sexual tension through Internet pornography. High-tech versions of newsstand magazines, what I saw on the computer screen in a dark room by myself was all I knew of sex. Partly *because* it was so detached from reality, it became my reliable outlet. I could distance my public self from my private desires and let them wander and explore, without risking my image. This was better and safer than really having sex, or so I told myself. All along it felt strange, though, and fake.

Sometimes I felt like a hypocrite, masquerading as someone righteous but with a clear sense of the sinful habit I allowed to entangle me. Pornography kept me trapped in a cycle of disappointment with myself, and I wanted for a long time to break out of it by force of will. At other times, I realized that sexuality would not magically go away and that creating another prohibition for myself, or another benchmark for personal moral achievement, was equally self-defeating and missing the point.

For the longest time, sexuality was bound up in my image of the wild and crazy teenager, and later with the "work hard, play hard" frat guy. At first fraternities were a secret world of carnal pleasure that appealed to me as a way to be normal for a change. Later I thought fraternities were the only way I could make friends. Maybe playing beer pong, the college's favorite drinking game, was a necessary rite of passage. So many times on a Saturday night, I resolved to finally go to my first fraternity party. I would get dressed and walk almost up to the house, see the line of people outside, and every single time I turned around and went back home. The yelling and loud music, kegs of beer, people dressed up and flirting, all seemed to say, "This isn't for you." "But what is for me?" I wondered. "Is there another way that won't leave me full of regret or set me up for a midlife crisis?"

I always was a person outside of every group but with a foot in them all, and most of my relationships were one-sided: me helping people. I felt like I was their counselor or mentor, never a friend, but I also wondered how I could help people when I didn't share their experiences: bad relationships, divorces, single parents, drugs, suicidal thoughts, bad grades, and the list goes on. From what people tell me, they talk to me because I am a patient listener, actually care about them, and am a stable person they can rely on or use as an example.

That last part is the trick. In high school I took pride in being that example. As much as I hated my reputation as a "fine young man," I wanted people to believe that I could *really* help them get their lives straightened out, so they would be good, just like me. I constantly wavered between questioning my own normalcy and trying to get the people I was supposedly helping to follow my Scouting ideals and Christian morals, ones that I then believed to be universally true and good.

Giving up that need to make people be like me, admitting that I really need to learn a lot of social skills, and making time to spend with people instead of just working have helped a lot. But there still is more. Dan's question "Did you get laid yet?" and the implicit one, "Are you gay?" would replay themselves in my mind. So many girls in high school and college told me, "You'd make a great husband," but because girls have always been my closest friends, I could never conceive of them as a "hookup" or a "chick" I'd "get with," like the more popular guys did.

But the longer I remained a virgin, the more suspicion I raised of being a closeted gay. And I secretly wondered myself. I never met an openly gay person before college, and even then homosexuality was categorically condemned by evangelical Christianity and Boy Scouting, still my two main sources of moral authority. But my sexual fantasies were about both men and women, and bisexuality was an even more foreign notion to me. I wondered if I was deluding myself by offhandedly excluding a possibility far more dangerous to my reputation than I could imagine.

I got to know a lot of homosexual people in college, and that real-life exposure made me question the outright moral condemnation I had been quick to apply to them—and to myself. I felt locked in between the pressure of those who said "repent" and the ones who said "come out." But both seemed too much like a prepackaged solution. When I was honest with myself, I realized that my homosexual feelings, directed toward heterosexual guys, were essentially envy masked by lust; I most wanted to *have* what they *had:* the muscular body, the popular girlfriend, and physical intimacy.

And so I set about exercising more, taking care of my body and appearance, becoming more emotionally self-confident, and asking myself what I truly imagined for my future. Part of me really longs for a family, but often I wonder if I am called to a more radical service in a life of celibate singleness. Even within my religious tradition, that option is uncommon and strange. And though the mystique of "getting laid" has faded from its earlier importance to me, to others I still appear as a closet gay: a suspicion which has become more problematic as I encounter homophobic attitudes in my church and Boy Scouting. When I came to college I was offended by the term *homophobia*, but I realize now how much the fear of being called gay has interfered with my own life and the lives of other young people.

There is an Ojibway saying that I carry inside my appointment book: "Sometimes I go about pitying myself while all along a great wind is bearing me across the sky." The great wind in my life has been Boy Scout camp, where I have spent every summer since I was 14. There, away from my parents and school, the woods provided an alternative reality, a break from the discouragement and stress of the rest of my life. When I think I have no friends, I remember all of my close relationships on camp staff. We have shared late nights around campfires, deep conversations about the important things in life, the sweat of hard work, and days that never seem to end.

For the last two years, I served as program director of the camp, and my main goal was to create an environment in which the teenage boys who were campers there could be themselves. It would be a place that pushed their limits but supported them when they failed, where people cared about each other and could reveal their weaknesses, where approval was not conditional on fitting stereotypes, and masculinity was not dependent on performing physically, smoking and drinking, or making fun of people. It seemed a near-impossible challenge, but it has begun to work. And all the while I became more free, more confident, more at ease. I became my own true self.

I had just begun to curb the widespread practice of using "faggot" as a put-down, when midway through the season the Supreme Court ruled that the Boy Scouts of America was free to exclude homosexual Scouts and leaders from the organization. So when a camper said to me, "Boy Scouts hate gays, right?" I was at a loss to give him a good explanation without disagreeing with official policy and risking my job.

Can I be true to myself and still be a Boy Scout leader? Can I best advocate for change from the inside or the outside? Those same questions face me as I consider more seriously a call to ordination, which would place me squarely within the institution of a church which has lost its former appeal to me. Hypocritical, irrelevant to daily life, and bound up in bureaucratic infighting, the church seems very distant from the radical way of Jesus as self-sacrificing servant and liberator of the oppressed, which is now the core of my personal faith. Even the sermons of my priests at St. Andrew's, once moving and intellectually challenging to me, now seem like empty words. So what if "Jesus died for you and would do it all over again if you were the only one"? What does that mean? I want to know what *difference* being a Christian makes.

One day a Jewish student asked me, "Do we see God?" I answered with a presentation on the differences between the mystics and the scholars, but he interrupted and asked, "What do *you* say?" I never thought about that before. What *do* I say?

This year, I have begun to spend much of my free time at Royalton Heights, a low-income housing development just a 10-minute drive away and yet worlds apart from campus. As I come to know the children there by name, I see them living in the midst of sexual abuse, alcoholism, illiteracy and poverty, hunger, neglect, and violence. Looking them each in the eye, touching their lives, and allowing their lives to touch mine, I find the moral conflicts of my time in Russia coming back again. How can I spend three dollars on an ice cream cone, when children 10 minutes away are going hungry? How can I worry about a perfect GPA when adults there can barely read?

It is a daily struggle as I think about my future. People who are poor, hungry, in prison, suffering from the captivity of abuse and neglect, these are the ones the homeless Jesus I claim to follow called "blessed." These are the ones in whose lives I find God, yet I know that my comfortable lifestyle depends at least in part on their suffering. I still want to preserve myself, to feel fulfilled, to somehow recapture that part of me that got lost in my growing up. But Jesus says that the only way to find one's life is to give it away for the sake of the world. What will I say?

I don't know. I still struggle with my simultaneous desire for close friends and the freedom to love everyone and avoid any exclusive group. I enjoy being independent but realize that I need a source of stability for myself. I have been working on the social skills I never learned growing up, and I am less shy and afraid of self-disclosure. I have some close friends, male and female, with whom I can freely talk about my life, both the good and the bad parts. I struggle with sexuality, but now it is symbolic of the larger question of how to live out my vocation, as a married or celibate person. Liberated from the burdens of adult expectations and my own academic and moral perfectionism, I am beginning to discover my true self. And while I believe deeply that the Kingdom of God is our true human destiny and that no one will be truly free until all are free from oppression, I struggle to let go of my need for security and live a life of service, with no guarantees. This will be the struggle of a lifetime.

■ ■ ■ ■ ■

IN SEARCH OF A *SANGAM*

*Asha spent her childhood as her Indian immigrant parents' "perfect"
daughter. During her adolescence, she deals with the conflict of being "raised
in one culture under the guidelines of an entirely different one" and tries to
balance herself as both a "dutiful Indian and an independent American girl."
Increasingly, her search for wholeness leads to clashes between herself and
her parents. In college, she embarks on relationships with people from varied
backgrounds. On a trip with her mother to India, Asha comes to see her
search for personal identity through the metaphor of a sangam—an Indian
word for "meetings of bodies, be they geographical, physical, spiritual, intellectual." Ultimately, she comes to see herself as a good Indian girl, "just not
the one my parents have in mind."*

As the plane descended into Indira Gandhi International Airport in Delhi, India,
the chattering of Hindi from my fellow passengers grew louder. I had been anticipating this moment for seven months. It was the fall term of my junior year in
college, and I was going to India to research educational systems through a grant
I received from my college's center for international understanding. It had been
eight years since I traveled to India, and I knew that the trip would be a challenge
for my identity as an Indian American female. Would I be comfortable? Would I be
able to relate to the people? Would I feel as lost in India as I did in America? I had
decided not to force myself into a process of active soul-searching. Rather, I would
open myself up to the culture and accept what naturally occurred.

The moment I walked out of the Delhi airport, the hot midnight air enveloped
me. I felt a distant and singular sense of familiarity. There was a mass of people waiting outside. Family members waving, pointing, yelling excited greetings. This is the
way it is in India. I had forgotten. When loved ones travel, especially internationally,
it is a huge family event. I scanned the crowd and my eyes landed on my *maasi* (aunt),
then *naanaaji* (maternal grandfather), my *mausa* (uncle), and finally my nine-year-old
cousin. They all rushed forward to give me a hug and welcome me home.

I felt like a foreigner for the first few weeks I was there. While I had memories of previous visits and had a connection to the country through my parents, I was detached from the daily goings-on, as if I was only an observer. As this "foreigner," I did not think much about the implications of the culture on my life. After all, I was there to observe schools as an American and my relatives viewed me as an American; that's what made me interesting to them.

Since starting college I had been neglecting my "Indian side," and it eventually became normal to go about my life without connecting to it. I did not participate in the events of the college's South Asian group because I felt they marginalized the culture by perpetuating stereotypes. Their "culture nights" tended to focus on superficial things that would easily entertain, though not necessarily educate: midriff-baring fashion shows, dances from Bollywood films, brainless skits that mocked what they were supposedly celebrating. These were not the things I associated with being Indian. As it seemed there were no outlets to express that side of me, a sort of deactivation occurred. But once I was back in the country of my ancestors, it was not long before I began to feel India in me. For better or worse, the land and people and sights and smells and tastes and sounds could no longer be compartmentalized in the back of my mind. The objective mind-set of an observer/anthropologist was slowly and surely being replaced by the personal subjectivity of a participant. I remember thinking on several occasions, "This country is *me*. This is where I come from." It was overwhelming to feel a sense of place, a kind of responsibility to the land because it had become a part of me.

This does not mean that I love everything about India. On the contrary, there are many things that infuriate me about the way things work there. For example, it is rare for a woman to walk down a street without getting ogled by men who feel entitled to let their eyes and mouths wander wherever they want, embodying the power of the patriarchy. I experienced this everywhere I went. In a small town, a group of young men once followed me, trying to take my picture, as though an Indian girl in a tank top and sneakers was the most incredible thing they had ever seen. Also, corruption is apparent in everyday life, as bribery is a common method of getting things done. And, as expected, the level of poverty and division of classes were extremely difficult to come to terms with. A society structured upon such obvious and ancient hierarchy left me questioning my own biases; how could I judge something I didn't understand? But while I had to accept these things to a certain extent, I was accepting them in an entirely different context than before. I was personally offended by the negative things I saw and proud of the positive, as if I had something to do with it. Limbless beggar children and beautiful ancient temples struck a similar sense of ownership within me. My many emotions—fury, excitement, anger, confusion, and fondness—were heightened and transferred to a part of me that hadn't been tapped in years.

These sensibilities were intensified when my mother joined me about a month after I arrived in India. We traveled together quite a bit. She was hesitant at first, wanting to stay in Delhi with the family, but I insisted that we explore the country, as we both had seen little of it. We touched all sides of India, even venturing into Nepal, and these travels gave us a perspective on the culture and land that we had never before experienced. Every place we went was like a mini-country within India, each with its own language, food, dress, and lifestyle.

We traveled to two places known for their *sangams* (meetings of bodies, be they geographical, physical, spiritual, intellectual)—Allahabad and Kanyakumari. Allahabad is the city that sits on the convergence of the rivers Ganga, Sarasvati, and Yamuna. It is considered sacred because of this *sangam*. Once every 12 years, millions of people travel to Allahabad for the *Kumbh Mela,* a Hindu bathing festival of rebirth. Kanyakumari is the southernmost tip of India. The *sangam* here is again one of water: the Indian Ocean, the Bay of Bengal, and the Arabian Sea—three immense bodies coming together at a single point, creating a breadth and depth of endless blue waves. Breathing the air was intoxicating; all that water, all those different entities from different places that had seen different things coming together to create one being. I felt very connected to these *sangams*. The separate waters are akin to the mishmash of different origins I have felt within myself, never knowing where I fully belong, *if* I fully belong. Being in Allahabad and Kanyakumari gave me some comfort with these issues, made me feel that my own distinct parts were as natural as the bodies of water themselves. My mother's presence personified these challenges of identity and gave me a soothing sense of foundation.

Our travel experiences, combined with spending time with family members (some I'd never met prior to this trip) and being in the country of my heritage, gave me a new take on myself—who I was, where I came from, where I was going. While I did not feel that I could completely identify as an Indian or an American, I became more comfortable with both the distinctiveness and synthesis of these cultures within me. My mother expressed her personal struggle with immigrant identity when I asked about her own cultural identification on our journey back to America. She looked at me with confused eyes and said, "You know, Asha, after living in America for 30 years and going back to India this time, I realize that there are things about each place that I both identify with and don't. Truthfully, I feel kind of lost." That moment was one of the closest between us. Despite our disparate personalities and opinions, and the number of fights we'd had about our battling cultures, I will never forget how well we understood each other then.

That moment of understanding with my mother was particularly meaningful because my parents and I grew up very differently, so we rarely relate to each other's personal cultural experiences. Both of my parents are from India. My father was born in a section of India that is now in Pakistan. He is the eldest of five children from a religious Hindu family. His family was poor, and they experienced terrible hardship traveling to India from newly formed Pakistan during the 1947 Partition of India. They settled in Delhi, where my grandfather started a business that still operates today. My father had to play parent to his younger siblings for much of his youth, as his father was hard at work and his mother was preoccupied with health problems. Despite these hardships, he excelled academically, and in the early 1960s earned a scholarship to an American institute of technology, journeying across the world as the first of his family to come to America. My father later earned a Ph.D. at an Ivy League university. Following his schooling, he returned to Delhi to meet the women his family had selected for him as possible wives. One of these women was my mother, whose story is quite different.

My mother's family quickly grew prosperous after their own struggles during Partition. The eldest of four children, my mother grew up mainly in India, but also in other parts of the world, as her father worked for the United Nations. Her family was very close; my mother's mother was extremely loving and fulfilled her maternal duties above and beyond the expectations of a good Hindu. My mother also excelled in school and was one of the few women at her college in India to study chemistry. She also studied the hard sciences in America, until she returned to Delhi in 1970 to consider marriage.

My mother and father were introduced with the intention of marriage. They went out a couple times and decided they were a suitable match. Six weeks after they met, they married and subsequently returned to America to start their lives together. Four years later, my sister was born. I came along six years after her. My mother did not pursue her love of the sciences after my sister was born, as she chose to devote her life to her family and home.

Upon setting foot inside our house, there is no question that we are an Indian family. Many of our paintings are of traditional Indian scenes. Our living room is full of Indian furniture, painted wooden screens, and sculptures (one of Gandhi and one of Buddha). Small bronze figures of Indian gods and goddesses, a miniature replica of the Taj Mahal, and a large map of India add to the thematic décor, and the scent of *agarbathi* (incense) permeates the air. Most evenings, my mother can be found preparing dinner, usually spiced *daal* (lentils), *chawaal* (rice), *achaar* (Indian pickle), and some form of *sabzi* (vegetable).

My parents raised my sister and me very "Indian" and sought to integrate their host-culture into their native cultural lifestyle. As a result, I grew up being proud of and interested in my heritage, no matter how frustrating it was trying to balance two cultures. As a child, I liked telling people that I came from India and spewing out random facts, such as, "Did you know the Taj Mahal is in India?" or "My aunt lives in India and she talks British!" and the eternally proud pronouncement, "I've *been* to India. I'm *from* there."

By grade school I had traveled to India quite a few times. The experiences I had of the heat, countless people, poverty, sounds of street merchants, itchy mosquito bites, spicy foods, and loving relatives only intensified my attachment to the culture. It also helped that one of my father's brothers lives near us with his family. My sister and I are close to these cousins, who are the same age as we are. As we grew older, we talked through a lot of cross-cultural issues we had with our parents, laughed at the family idiosyncrasies, and shared a rare mutual understanding that was not possible with our "American" friends.

Many Indian families in our area, including mine, used to go to a devout Hindu man's house every Sunday where his living room was transformed into a religious space. The floor was covered in white sheets, and we'd all sit cross-legged, shoes off, listening to his words. He would read aloud sacred texts and preach, and we would all sing *bhajans* (religious songs) while he played the harmonium. At the end of the service we would all stand and sing the traditional ending song, the *arthi*. During this song people would go to the front of the room one by one and hold up a plate with a lit *dhiya* (wick made of cotton dipped in butter) and edible and monetary offerings, moving their arms to make an *Om* shape with the flame. Afterward, we would all eat the *prasad,* the blessed food, which was usually *halwa,* a saccharine and oily sweet. I never questioned these religious customs, nor did I feel strange taking part in them. On the contrary, when remembering these times I feel a sense of safety and warmth. Everyone knew each other. I have grown up calling my parents' friends "Auntie" and "Uncle"; it is these sorts of traditions that have kept our Indian community close.

I was the quintessential "daddy's little girl." My father is wonderful with children; they love him as much as he loves playing with them. He spoiled me and we had very happy times together—he made me laugh harder than anyone I knew. I always wanted him to put me to bed because he invented the best stories, came up with fun games, and created the greatest songs. I was a smart kid, which made my parents proud; there are few things more important to Indian immigrants than their children's education. I have no complaints about my childhood; my home life was worry-free and secure, and as the cute and precociously bright baby of the family, I could get whatever I wanted. I was happy.

Things started changing when I was in middle school. I transferred the idolatry I had for my parents to my big sister, who was in high school. I became her confidante, her partner in crime. I lied to my parents when she had boys over, and went to the "library" with her when she was actually going out with friends. I felt a bit guilty for lying, but by age 12 I related to my sister better than to my parents and our solidarity was in some ways necessary. I was beginning to like boys, listen to rock music, question religion, and realize that I did not always agree with my parents' values. All of this made them unhappy and apprehensive. My father and I were not getting along, and it seemed his temper was becoming our fifth family member. My mother's worry that I was straying from my academic focus became overbearing and I suspected that things would get much harder when my sister left for college.

Once I was the only child in the house, my parents and I started arguing more and more. I began to note the differences between the way my family and the families of my American friends worked. With the new choices and decisions that came with my age, it grew harder for me to feel normal, given my parents' reaction to the changes I was experiencing. For instance, they expected me to remain obedient and unquestioning, ignoring the fact that I was getting older and forming my own value system, which often conflicted with theirs (seemingly unavoidable when raised in one culture under the guidelines of an entirely different one). When I disagreed with them, it was taken as a sign of disrespect. A typical response to my questioning was, "We are your parents. You do not question us. We know what is best." This upset me because I felt that I should be most comfortable expressing my views and standing up for my beliefs with my parents, which is, admittedly, a Western ideal.

I was different from my sister, who usually internalized her discontent in order to prevent a conflict. This led my parents to believe that she had been more obedient than she actually was, which made my "disrespect" even more unexpected to them. They thought the issues with my sister had prepared them to have better experiences raising me, but I usually ended up speaking my mind, knowing it would likely escalate into hours of screaming, crying, and slamming doors.

The fights with my parents continued through high school. During that time I never could keep my mouth shut—I *had* to speak my mind and do some things I knew they disapproved of. I knew this would lead to more fighting, but I had a real problem with not being allowed to say what I thought to my own family. It was so hard to deal with the pressure I felt from them and from myself to achieve the über-identity of the perfect mixture of a dutiful Indian and an independent American girl. I was to excel at school, obey my parents, maintain their traditional values, repress any sexual desire or questioning, be home by 10 at night on weekends, get into a good college, respect my heritage, participate in extracurricular activities, be a star in the school play, and so forth. It was confusing for me to maintain this identity and also experiment with things I felt were natural for my age, but which my parents most certainly did not. I did not want to fight with my parents, but I felt it was my right to express myself regardless of whether or not they agreed.

Despite the negative situation at home, I managed to accomplish a great deal in high school. I maintained high grades, participated in community service activities, was involved in drama, had good friends, and won awards. My parents and I agreed that these activities were important and expected. While I fulfilled these expectations, however, I never received the praise I wanted from them. I still wanted more than anything to please them, yet the only recognition I received was from other people. I just wanted my parents to tell me they were proud of me, without my having to ask, but they only told me what I was doing wrong and did not really understand why I needed to hear *from them* that they were proud of my accomplishments. This hurt and left me confused about what they wanted from me, and what I wanted from myself. How much did I have to fit into their mold for them to be happy with me? I could not be the perfect Indian daughter, having been raised in America. I had low self-esteem despite the positive qualities others thought I had and was struggling hard to maintain some sort of control over my identity. This confusion and need for control manifested itself through a mild eating disorder and an omnipresent sense of unhappiness.

It appeared to others that we were a happy family. I never talked with my friends in detail about my situation at home; I did not want to air our dirty laundry, and I did not think anyone but my sister could understand. I felt that I had no control, and although I stuck to my beliefs, the two people who mattered most to me never accepted them.

As easy as it is to paint my sister and me as victims, we both know, despite our own resentment, that our parents cannot be demonized. They had reasons for being so angry and disappointed with us. I believe much of it has to do with their upbringing—just as my sister and I are confused about our identity as American-born children of immigrants, so too do our parents struggle with assimilation while trying to preserve their heritage. Their own parents' ideas about raising children in 1940s and 1950s India were the models my parents followed in America, where blind respect and obedience are far less easy to come by.

My sister is the only other person who understands the dynamics of our family and we depend on each other for advice and sympathy. Our connection is unbreakable. I could not have handled many of the issues I've had to deal with without my sister's support. She is my blood, my kin; she is a part of me. Whatever happens in my future, I need to be close to my sister, my *didi*. I would not feel complete without her.

While my family has had a profound effect on my identity, I have also been influenced by the relationships I've had. I fell in love for the first time during my freshman year of college. We were an interesting match. He was a moderate conservative from a close family, loved heavy metal music and girls who looked like Southern belles, and was extremely logical. Then there was me, the die-hard liberal from a dysfunctional family. I hated heavy metal, dressed more like a hippie than a belle, and existed for emotion. But these differences were what made us interesting to each other. My boyfriend challenged me, and we made each other look at things from another perspective. Granted, we argued all the time, but we were learning so much and our love was new and exciting. We gave each other our virginity and our promises.

After some time, however, our differences got in the way of our happiness. I found myself becoming so dependent on him and feeling inadequate. He seemed to consider what I said unimportant and when we disagreed he would be condescending and arrogant—a definite change from when we first got together. I didn't like who I became around him; I was silencing myself trying to be the girl that he wanted me to be, and this was infuriating. He had no real interest in my family or my roots, and I drifted away from those things. I felt most fully "American" with him, because those were the ideals he held high. During our junior year, we spent six months apart while studying abroad (I was in India, then London) and we realized that we were no longer meant to be together. I knew that I needed to be with someone who could respect all parts of me, especially after I reconnected with my heritage in India.

In London, I got involved with a female student. It was my first experience with a woman I was truly interested in (this was more than typical experimentation), but I was quite relaxed about the situation. I have always thought it natural to be attracted to people of the same sex and I have many gay, bisexual, and queer friends, but I knew my parents and extended family would be horrified if they knew. I was in awe that this woman wanted to know things about me that my ex-boyfriend never seemed to care about, and I was inspired by her dynamic and radical personality. We continued to date for a short while after returning to school, and her influence on me made me more politically active and aware. We have since remained good friends. Our relationship made me more conscious of and comfortable with my attraction to women, though I am primarily attracted to men. I view my sexuality as a fluid and flexible thing and do not label myself as this would only serve to constrict my sexual identity.

I was happier with my last boyfriend than I had ever been with anyone. We were together for a year, ending the relationship when I graduated from college and he was still a student. We shared many interests and beliefs and were deeply in love. He loved me for who I am, not who he wanted me to be. We shared all of ourselves with each other. I felt whole with him and comfortable in my skin. He was so giving, loving, and accepting, which made me more conscious of how I could be a better person. He raised the bar as to what I expect from a partner, particularly that he or she will bring out all parts of me with reciprocal pride and comfort.

Though these represent my most recent relationships, my romantic life really began at age 15, when a high-school senior started paying attention to me. He was smart, funny, charming, and caused me much heartache and teenage trauma. Other romances include a hippie I met at the beach, a bisexual actor 10 years my senior, a heroin addict, a born-again Christian, an egomaniac with an Asian fetish, and a fun-loving goofball who had had a short stint in prison. These romantic partners and others I have experienced, though all very different, have one thing in common: They are all white.

I have never been involved with a person of color. Although I think this is merely a matter of circumstance, I know it is no accident that I have never been involved with an Indian man. I think this has to do with fear; the fear that an Indian man will want to impose on me the subservient role that Indian women have had for generations. Many Indian American men I know see how their fathers are treated by their mothers and view that sort of relationship—being pampered, treated as masters, and feared—as the ideal. These men often have dated white girls throughout adolescence, but when it comes to marriage, they want an Indian girl, often one from India. Of course, these are generalizations and I know not all Indian men are the same, but my fear, nevertheless, prohibits me from objectively entertaining the idea of being with an Indian man.

Most of the men I know are white, and they tend to be more compatible with my personality than the Indian men I know. It has crossed my mind that I may be rejecting the idea of being with an Indian man to spite my parents or to transcend tradition, but I do not believe this is the case. I keep my romantic life hidden from my parents for the most part, so it is not something we discuss. Furthermore, I want to please them. Although I do many things that go against their beliefs, I have often wished that my values were in line with theirs. I would rather reach a level of understanding with them instead of doing things that make them angry.

I have thought about ending up with an Indian and I do see the benefits of such a situation. We would have a sense of understanding that I could not have with a partner from another culture. If we were to have children, it would be easier to have a common history. It is true that I have not actively sought out an Indian man, but I don't feel any need to at this point in my life. I admit that I should work on my bias against Indian men, but I believe that will happen by meeting more Indian men to whom I can relate—not typical "good Indian boys."

I am not the typical "good Indian girl." Feminism, activism, sex, and drugs have played a part in my life. If my parents knew, they would be appalled. They could never imagine their Ivy League, highly motivated, work-driven daughter would even think about doing drugs. Neither of them has ever smoked or consumed alcohol—the result of an unbroken promise made to their parents and each other. They have reconciled to the fact that I do drink occasionally, but it makes them uncomfortable.

The codes of my culture even travel with me to the bedroom. Sometimes while being sexually physical, my mind wanders to thoughts of my ancestors and certain family members. I think about how appalled they would be if they could see what I was doing and feel what I was feeling. It is an obsession with making my family proud and honoring my culture that is at the crux of my struggles with identity. This worry extends to almost every aspect of my life, but I nevertheless cannot deny myself the things that bring me joy. I am not promiscuous; I am young, curious, and safe. I am not an addict; I experiment lightly. I am more an artist than a scientist. I am a good Indian girl...just not the one my parents have in mind.

I began to achieve a greater sense of security with this cultural duality in my last year of college. My trip to India gave me a renewed outlook on my identity and how to stay connected to my Indian side, so I decided to involve myself in South Asian cultural activities at school. I joined three groups in one term. When I expressed my objections to the Asian culture nights and the stereotypes I felt they perpetuated, people listened and many agreed. Changes were made and an activist mentality began to influence the way these Asian groups thought about their culture.

I also wrote about my experiences and talked about my trip to India. For a comparative literature course, I wrote a lengthy prose and poetry piece about immigrant mothers, their daughters, sexuality, exoticism, and the balance of cultures. The work came naturally, as these were all issues I had thought about a great deal. I was extremely proud of this piece, and part of it was published in a student literary magazine. I read some of the pieces at an Asian drama group's production (which I helped organize) centered on the deconstruction of stereotypes of Asian women. I spoke to a group of freshmen at the college president's house about my trip to India and also held a discussion about the trip and how it affected my life when I came back to campus.

All this action was driven by my new-found connection to my culture, my personal culture—what I had made of myself after serious thought and introspection, visiting the country of my ancestors, experiencing relationships with people who validated the whole of me, and really connecting to the different aspects of myself that make me who I am. I was able to relate to who I was through the work I was doing and sharing with others. I feel strong now and confident in my cultural ties to both America and India. My confidence has strengthened my relationship with my parents, and I think we are beginning to understand each other better. It is really all about sharing. As we learn more about each other's cultural contexts, the previously closed doors of communication open wider. And while it is still at times an uphill battle, I am eager to take on the challenge, and not just with my parents. I love expressing these issues and my thoughts rather than keeping them buried and unexplored. It is as though a well within me was tapped and a rush of different rivers flowed out together, shaping me, shaping others, creating a *sangam*, a meeting of bodies, identities, and cultures.

ASHA: TEN YEARS LATER

I write this follow-up to *In Search of a Sangam* from my home in New York City, shortly after my thirtieth birthday. Eight-plus years have passed since that initial exploration. Those years have held a variety of transitions: numerous people, places, and things that have shaped who I am today.

After I graduated college, I moved back to London to continue my work in international education, traveling within Europe quite a bit for my job. London itself is an incredible city for young adults, and I immersed myself in its culture as much as I possibly could. As I did not have many friends there, I spent a good deal of time on my own, visiting museums, taking in the theater, and learning about the city. All this was wonderful, but just as compelling was the fact that for the first time in a Western city, my "South Asian-ness" was unremarkable.

Due to postcolonial immigration, there is a large population of South Asians in London, and I had the new experience of seeing people who looked like me everywhere—on the street, in businesses, and in the media. This led me to feel that being South Asian was pretty much normalized in London; gone were the days of explaining why I had brown skin and having the role of spokesperson imposed upon me. I was now in a city where South Asian culture was everywhere, and its influence was obvious. London provided an East–West hybrid environment in which I was far more comfortable than in the States.

I even had to change my lexicon and what I called myself. "Asian" in the UK connotes not East Asian but South Asian, and "Oriental" is the acceptable term for East Asians. I had spent so many years in the U.S. arguing about identifying myself as Asian ("India is in Asia too!"), whereas in London my identity was seemingly a given. However, I never did feel comfortable thinking of or calling East Asians "Oriental"; I suppose that term will forever feel objectifying and antiquated to me. But it was nice, for that year and a half in Europe, to just be Asian. I'm sure this sense of belonging—along with London's general magnetism—contributed to my becoming a bit of an Anglophile, and the irony of this is not lost on me: It was postcolonial immigration that allowed for an influx of South Asians into the UK, which resulted in making my time there more comfortable. This contributed to my adoration of the very nation that had brutalized my parents' homeland within their lifetime! In some sense, it is my parents' immigration to America that instilled in me a need for a hyphenated existence and for locating myself within a binary—something that London supported much more than the other places I've called home.

Living in Europe definitely kicked me into a more adult stage of life. I had never felt so lonely and yet so capable, as I had to navigate the city without the comfort of old friends by my side. Being half a world away from all that was familiar required more of me than I knew I possessed, and more than a few times I had to deal with difficult situations without the support to which I had grown accustomed for 22 years. From having to manage the relatively benign bothers of moving a number of times to a couple of jarring incidents of assault (once on a London street, and once on a night train in Russia), the outcome was a tougher, more capable young adult arriving back in the States in 2004, ready for graduate school.

I received my master's in education from a prestigious university on the East Coast. The program lasted one academic year, and I have never worked so hard in my life—nor thought so critically and learned as much. My notions of theory and practice were seriously challenged, and the pull of identity and adolescence as an area of focus was reinforced. I became very involved with alternative learning options for public school students. As a result of my experiences writing *In Search of a Sangam*, I studied an intensive qualitative research methodology that allowed for a form of creative nonfiction writing that I value deeply as a teaching tool.

Throughout graduate school, I was struck by my relative lack of practical experience with young people, so when the program concluded and I moved back to my hometown on the West Coast, I started a job at a nonprofit organization working with adolescent girls in the public school system. I ran group programs that focused on critical examinations of girlhood, media literacy, and activism and mentored girls on an individual basis. The work and the girls were phenomenal, and I fully stood by the mission of the organization.

I like to think of my work with this organization as "guerrilla educating," as we were going into public schools and doing somewhat radical work with mostly disenfranchised youth, addressing issues that were considered taboo and were unsanctioned by the system. It was incredible to discuss ideas such as feminism, institutionalized racism, and sexism with adolescent girls, giving them the opportunity to speak and be heard and to turn what they had to say into some sort of action. I was lucky to have my sister provide these kinds of experiences for me when I was an adolescent, and I would have benefited even more had I participated in the types of programs that we were offering our girls. Since we were an independent agency, we were able to do much needed work while avoiding the bureaucracy that those employed by the school system encounter as soon as they walk in the door. The relationships I developed through this, with both my colleagues and the girls, hold strong today. Furthermore, I got the practical experiences I needed to complement the theory I had studied intensely in my schooling.

It was wonderful and challenging to live as an adult in the city in which I was raised. The city itself is gorgeous and invigorating, both socially and environmentally. I knew that living at home with my parents was out of the question; things had certainly gotten better since college and I had no desire to let the situation regress. My apartment, however, was a mere 12-minute drive from my parents' house. That, and our insistent investment in one another, presented new challenges.

Although I had been living on my own for a few years, my parents still had a tendency to impose certain values on me, and I still had a tendency to fight back with the ultimate goal of mutual understanding, which rarely occurred. Or, if it did, it was momentary, and both parties inevitably reverted to our original mind-sets. I use "inevitably" not with a sense of derision, but of acceptance that it is difficult to change one's belief system. More to the point, I cannot hold it against my parents for sticking to their guns, as I do the same. However, this did not make things terribly easy.

My parents are not familiar with my chosen field of Education, and their lack of knowledge tended to translate into disappointment instead of inquiry. I would invite them to events my organization held that presented the work we were doing with the girls—and the girls themselves—and although my parents certainly saw the value of the work, they did not quite understand why it was so compelling to me. I never told them the whole truth, which is that my interest in this field is partially due to my own girlhood and adolescence being fraught with deep confusion and questions about identity, while feeling undersupported. The intersections of gender, culture, race, and sexuality are things my parents may comprehend intellectually, but speaking with them about such matters on a personal level can be too close for comfort...or productive conversation.

Another point of contention during that period came in the form of a tall white musician raised in a fishing town in Alaska. He had never gone to college and came from an evangelical Christian family (he had defected). He was my boyfriend, and the above description is of course reductive and does not express how much we loved each other and how much fun we had together. My mother had a hard time with him more for reasons of class than race, although his white-ness certainly did not help. This was something she could admit to and chalked up to her worry that I was with someone who didn't share my experiences, although her way of communicating this was often hurtful. My father did not have much to say on the matter because I did not share details about my romantic life with him.

The disparity between my boyfriend's education level and mine was challenging. He had wanted to go to college but his family did not have the money nor did they emphasize that going to college was important. In their community, many people did not go to college and were successful and happy in life. He began to attend a community college a year into our relationship, partly due to my influence. He would come home and tell me all the things he was learning, and while I was happy for him, I slowly began to realize that the growth he was experiencing through school and our relationship did not match up to my own. He was very dependent on me and was uninformed and undereducated about many things, which made me feel like his teacher quite often. These issues led to resentment on both our parts but at that point we were two years in and too far gone, and there were other wonderful elements in our relationship that sustained us. We were living together and had become so enmeshed with one another that our issues—some of them unfixable due to things we had no control over—simply became a part of the fabric of our relationship.

I did not tell my parents that we shared an apartment, and they never found out. I felt bad about the dishonesty, yet it was necessary if I wanted to live the life that made the most sense for me at that time. Keeping things secret was shockingly easy, despite the fact that my parents lived so close by. They never came over unannounced, and they rarely asked questions about my boyfriend anyway, given their discomfort with both the idea of a boyfriend and this one specifically.

I spent a lot of time defending my boyfriend to my mother and trying desperately, angrily, and forcefully to get her to understand my experience, even while he and I were dealing with our own issues. These frustrations built up and led me to a decision that has served me well since. After a particularly frustrating and hurtful interaction with my mother, I came to the fairly obvious realization that my parents' values and my values for the most part would not change, but that how I dealt with the instances when our values did not agree could change. I essentially stopped trying to get them on my side and stopped inciting conversations that I knew would turn into arguments. Achieving harmony outweighed full understanding at times, and as such, there was no need to cause each other discomfort and pain. This was difficult at first, because in my family, our investment in and love for one another often translates into expecting each others' behavior to change. But in changing my own behavior and expectations, our overall dynamic has benefited.

In 2007, my boyfriend and I moved to New York City, where so many of my dearest friends have settled, he to complete his college degree and I to pursue acting and film. It was interesting to throw myself into a professional world about which I knew very little, beyond the theater I had participated in throughout my schooling. In the first year there, I took some great classes and acted in a few films and commercials. I learned so much from those experiences, including the disheartening truth that racism and sexism run rampant in show business, and that to make a living in that world, many actors must unfortunately endure those truths. It was a challenge to set aside my ideals for a time in order to immerse myself fully in that world. Eventually, though, my ideals won out.

Although I gained a great deal from my acting experiences, I felt I wasn't contributing much value to the world, and I wanted to be back in an environment where I felt confident and useful in my work…and had health insurance and a regular paycheck. So after a year in New York, I put acting on the back burner and took a job doing qualitative research for a nonprofit I had admired for years. I was now living in a vibrant city near many of my closest friends and, having gotten the New York actor experience relatively out of my system, was doing satisfying work. Socially and professionally, things were good. However, my relationship was falling apart; after four years together, my boyfriend and I went through a painful and damaging breakup. It took me a long time to heal from this, despite the fact that I knew it was for the best. One positive outcome from this was how it affected my relationship with my parents.

Because I was so distraught over the breakup, my parents finally seemed to slip into the mode I had wished would be a constant. I had remained quite neutral for some time and did not share much about my boyfriend, so when things got really bad my level of distress shocked them into being supportive listeners and being there for me in the most literal sense. My mother came out to New York and stayed with me for a week, because I asked her to. In all my years of living away from home, I had never once asked her to do anything like this, so she knew things were serious. Her presence and strength helped me a great deal, and since then, I have been able to be a bit more honest and open about my relationships and life choices.

My sister's life choices have also buttressed this freer way of being with my parents. In the years since *In Search of a Sangam,* my sister and I have remained as close as ever. She is married now and has a child, so the dynamics of our relationship have naturally changed, but I still consider her the person who knows me best and the one I credit for so many important choices I have made. Her husband is white, and in the years they were dating, this created an unfortunate struggle with my parents; my mother simply did not recognize that there was a level of care between my sister and her partner that perhaps was not evident in her own marriage. Nonetheless, once the ring was on my sister's finger, he was welcomed into the family like a son. It took him some time to adjust to this, as he rightfully had built up some resentment for the years of unfriendliness. This, too, has passed, and with the recent birth of my nephew—my parents' first grandchild—the family has been closer than ever and my parents seem happier. I would rather not analyze this or worry that the baby provides a distraction from dysfunction that has always been there—for the time being things are great and I'm at a place in life where I would rather enjoy the lovely things about my family instead of resting on my cynicism.

This sense has come into play with my personal life as well. I am currently involved with an Indian man who is a successful performer and activist. We have a great deal in common and are excited about the relationship. What is interesting is my parents' reaction. They were very happy as soon as I told them that we were involved. Even with his nontraditional and fairly unpredictable career, the fact that he is Indian and highly educated seems to have pushed criticism aside. My age most likely has something to do with this as well (my father recently sent me an article about single women approaching 40 being too "picky" and how they should just "settle"), but it is also clear to me that if this person were white, my parents would be none too pleased. But because he is Indian they are pleased, and within minutes of informing my parents of our involvement, they began asking questions that hinted at marriage. The same was true with his parents. Then the Googling began. Our parents not only Googled their children's partners, they Googled *each other.*

On the one hand, all this enthusiasm and support and questions and interest are wonderful, as I've never experienced this with my parents and it's something I've always wanted. But on the other hand, the glaring double standard is a bit hard to swallow. It is frustrating that the support was not always there; it is not as though I am with my current boyfriend because support was withheld in the past. In other words, I could not be with this man without my previous relationship experiences—experiences that my parents seemed to wish I did not have. But after all is said and done, I feel about this situation the way I feel about our family's current state of relative harmony: "Don't look a gift horse in the mouth." I recognize the unfairness of the situation, and I lament the fact that wonderful people I dated previously (and I!) did not benefit from this unconditional support from my parents, but at this point I am not interested in pushing the issue, given that we're all basically happy right now.

So yes, ta da! I am dating an Indian man. This is my first relationship with a person of color. Writing *In Search of a Sangam* forced me to think about my previous tendencies and to turn a critical eye on both myself and the people I had chosen to date in earlier years. I had found myself in situations where I was a "culture teacher" far too often. My experiences with discrimination, exoticism, and my own learning and inquiry into race and ethnicity led me to seriously consider pursuing a partner from a similar cultural background. Since breaking up with the man I was with for four years, I have been more intentional and aware of my nonnegotiables, which has helped me select more suitable people to date. I am also much more driven by logic than ever. Rereading the way I described myself with my first boyfriend in college was strange. I certainly do not "live for emotion"; in fact, the pendulum has swung in the other direction and I am sometimes logical and unerring to a fault, which has led to someone I dated calling the way I handle relationships "officious." While I don't feel great about that descriptor, I cannot really argue with it, and it has helped me weed out people I may well not have before.

This is the mental space I was in when I got together with my current partner. When we first got together, I was sure that our similar interests, professional goals, and cultural backgrounds meant for smooth sailing. In fact, it was because of these similarities that we made too many assumptions about each other, which invariably has led to some backpedaling. While he is politically progressive and a creative risk-taker, he is traditional in many ways I had eschewed in favor of social experimentation and blunt communication. In some ways, he is the sort of "good Indian boy" that I cannot fully relate to. This leads to a whole different set of issues, but I will say that I get as much out of this relationship as I put into it on all levels, which is something that had been missing before. I am therefore much more committed to this person and working toward better communication and understanding. We also do some performing and writing together that is in alignment with our values, and this shared creativity is quite fulfilling.

And as for him being Indian, when we first got together it did sometimes surprise me to see our reflections in a shop window or to see my hand in his, our different shades of brownness commingling in a way with which I was unfamiliar. While this was certainly not off-putting, it was something I had to get used to. It's almost a radical action—for me—to date an Indian person. Many of my friends expressed their surprise that I was committed to an Indian man. My boyfriend got a little annoyed with my acknowledgment of this, as it made him feel that he, and this relationship, were exotic to me. Irony is no stranger, that's for sure.

In my previous piece and now in this follow-up, my romantic relationships take up a good deal of space. I felt embarrassed when re-reading much of what I wrote about relationships in *In Search of a Sangam,* thinking to myself, "Wow, I sure had a lot to prove!" But then I pause and realize that I did have a lot to prove at that time. Relationships were one way for me to place myself outside an expected norm, and forming my sexual identity was important and, well, fun. But eight years later, things have evolved. I am much more settled and grounded and less concerned with identity formation. At this point, I feel as though my identifiers are more or less understood and now it is a matter of enhancing and maintaining them. I have settled many of the issues with which I was previously struggling, such as cultural identity and sexual identity. The self-exploration I was so engaged with in college and the few years after has served to form the basis of an adult life. When writing the previous piece, I was just getting exposed to the notion of dualities and becoming comfortable within binaries. At this point, these are ingrained in who I am and are manifested in my professional, creative, academic, relational, and social choices.

I cringe a bit when I read the *sangam* metaphor, as it seems a bit lofty to compare my identity struggles as a young adult with an ancient force of nature. Depending on the mood I'm in, however, I could argue that struggles with identity are just as strong a natural force—that they are both common and astonishing, particular and universal.

THE HATRED WITHIN

This writer wrestles with issues of family, ethnicity, and self-esteem. José, a twenty-year-old Latino junior, whose parents emigrated to the United States from Central America, explores his early experiences at school and his growing belief that his academic success made him not only "different" from other Latino/Latina students, but "better." Only when he reaches college does he come to understand this attitude and his disdain for his parents' relatively humble origins as a form of internalized racism. Drawn into the major Latino organization at his college and assuming a leadership role in student government, he comes painfully to name and eschew his self-hatred and embrace his developing Latino identity.

We were always horrible to the poor old man, Mr. Connors. He was the stereotypical high school substitute teacher—scolding us in a voice that echoed off the back wall and putting us to work with boring written exercises. We would respond by acting up, throwing papers, talking back, and pulling practical jokes—tormenting him in any way we could.

"Poor old guy," I thought. No more than five feet tall, he was bald except for the fringe of white hair that circled his bare dome. He wore rectangular eyeglasses and always came decked out in a full gray suit. I think it was the only suit he owned because he seemed to wear it whenever he substituted.

One morning, only a few minutes into the tormenting, the national anthem began over the P. A. system. As always, we stood up while the music played. Usually we did a good job of being quiet, but this time my friend Andrew and I kept joking and chatting as the music played.

When the song was over, Mr. Connors did exactly what I expected the typical "old-timer" would do. He began to yell at us for showing disrespect to the nation, but instead of focusing his obvious anger at both of us, he looked dead at me.

"Why don't you try that in your own country?" he barked.

Silence. I was in absolute shock. Did he really just say that? Without a second's pause I responded, "Why don't you try that in yours?" I took a step forward. There was no mirror there, so I have no sure idea what I looked like. But knowing how I get, I'm sure my face turned a bright red, my eyes became narrow and angry, my eyebrows crouched down. When I'm enraged, I make it very obvious. And it usually has the desired effect of intimidation because it's such a contrast to my usual jovial expression.

"This *is* my country," he answered back without a pause.

I took a few more steps forward. Not rushing to him, but with a slow threatening pace. "Well, this is *my* country, too."

"Well, how about your parents' country?" he asked, seeming not to realize that he was pushing me more and more and that with every comment he uttered, he was becoming more and more offensive.

"How about *your* parents' country?" I snapped back in the same mocking tone.

"My parents are indigenous," he said smugly.

The word at the time was unfamiliar to me. Although I was mad at myself for not knowing it (I wanted to step above this man as his intellectual and physical superior), I shot back, "What the fuck does that mean?" I didn't know what had come over me. I didn't swear at teachers, even substitute teachers. I joked, I kidded around, but I was always as respectful as my sense of humor allowed me to be.

He answered back by saying that the word meant his family had always lived here. Since he didn't look Native American, I had to assume he meant his ancestors came aboard the *Mayflower* or a similar absurdity. At that point I was at the foot of his desk, an arm's length away from his gleaming dome. I had no idea what I was doing. How can you ever be prepared for a confrontation like that? What did I hope to do when I reached him? Hit him? Spit in his face? I stood there barely a second before Andrew and my other pal Dave came from behind me and pulled me away, yelling, "Come on, José, back off! He's not worth it." And I knew he wasn't worth it. But what was it? What had happened to me? What did I think I was going to do? Why was I so enraged?

I wasn't the kind of student who turned violent so quickly, not with students and especially not with teachers. But something had come over me. My shock and disbelief at his words had drawn me magnetically toward him. Did he really say that? To this day, it remains the first situation that comes to mind whenever someone asks me if I have ever encountered outright racism. It was a slap in the face. But in hindsight, the incident reveals more about me than it does about Mr. Connors.

Why did he look at me and not see a student like any other, or even an annoying teenager who had little respect for his country? Why did he appear to view me as a brown-skinned foreigner who didn't belong and deserved to have his identity questioned by a high school substitute teacher? That day in my sophomore year I felt like a minority. I felt like a Latino student. I felt like I didn't belong. Every other day, however, I took pride when my friends told me, "José, you're so white."

I'm surprised that it isn't harder to admit. As I see it now, I was a sellout in high school. I was a box-checker. I was a coconut. Name the insult and I was the epitome of it. In college, a friend referred to Latino students who didn't recognize their background or culture as "those who didn't associate." That was me. I didn't associate.

My high school was pretty diverse. The students in the Honors and Advanced Placement courses I took, however, were almost entirely white. I was lost, along with a handful of other students of color, in a sea of white faces. Given the fact that my classes were full of white students, it's no surprise that my friends were all white as well. I occasionally hung out with the one other Latino student whom I had known since kindergarten, but he, too, didn't "associate." He dressed in khakis and corduroys, polo shirts and button-ups, clothes that most people considered "preppie." And in my high school, preppie was synonymous with smart, and smart was, with a few exceptions, white.

Daniel, my good friend from the fourth grade on, was white with blond hair and blue eyes. My two best friends at the time, Nelson and Sara, both had dirty blond hair and piercing blue eyes. The pack of a dozen or so girls I hung out with junior and senior year were, with few exceptions, white. All of them were upper middle class. Most of them owned cars when they turned 16. These were my friends, and I was proud of them.

But it was more than just the fact that they were white. I don't think there's a problem with having a lot of white friends, and I don't think I sought them out because of their skin color. They were just the people I saw every day. But what *did* matter was the attitude and thoughts that grew from this valuing of whiteness. Why did Mr. Connors's comments hit me so hard? Precisely because I was in denial of the fact that I was any different from my friends. I was like them. They were like me. It hurt me to be singled out as a Latino because, deep down, I really did believe that I was better than most Latinos. I was smart. I was hardworking. I was ambitious. I was successful. I was funny. These traits, I thought, were uncharacteristic of most Latinos. Mr. Connors brought me down, and I'm sad to say that that was the biggest reason he upset me so much all those years ago. He tore me away from my misconception that I was accepted and belonged in the white world, which I saw as the embodiment of the good, happy, and successful life. He forced me to confront my own racism.

I talked to my mom about this late in my senior year of high school. I actually complimented her on her parenting skills. I pondered how she had managed to raise us in a way that made us better than most Latinos. It never occurred to me how wrong this thinking was. I would never have dared to repeat my racist thoughts out loud. But at the time, I thought them. I saw other Latinos and would often assume the worst. It was easy to convince me that one was a drug dealer or a criminal, as I was already biased against them. And I always made that distinction clear: I, and for the most part my nuclear family, was not a part of *them*.

But these were all thoughts I kept buried deep down inside. I continued to check off "Hispanic" whenever forms asked for the optional race/ethnicity classification. I took pride in it then. With so few Latinos who aren't wastes, I figured I was helping myself. They would see me as an anomaly, I told myself. I was unique and that made me very happy.

So, besides the little box that I would check off from time to time, my culture and background meant nothing. In fact, I would treat it as a joke:

> "Quit stealing my money, spic."
> "Hey, don't look at me, I'm just a spic."
> "Ah, those spics just don't get it."
> "You're such a grubby, grubby spic."

These were words I spoke, phrases that sprung out of my mouth and the mouths of my closest friends. They were always said in jest and I always approved. I found it funny, because I thought being called a spic was pretty damned ironic. I recall a white friend telling me I was more white than he: I acted white, I dressed white, I talked white. In essence, to him I was normal, and normal was white. You're not part of a gang? You must be normal, you must be white. You don't shoot up every morning or carry a gun? You must be normal, you must be white. You don't speak Spanish in school, you don't know how to Latin dance? You must be normal, you must be white. And I laughed when he said I was a spic. How funny, I told myself, me…a spic? I thought I was anything and everything but that.

Besides these occasional insults, which I then thought were perfectly fine, my days at school had nothing to do with being Latino. I was normal, I told myself, therefore my ethnicity couldn't be my prime characteristic. I considered it a contradiction. This kind of thinking—this utter disdain for who I was—is something most people will never be able to understand. I think it's natural for adolescents to question their identity, but I did more than just question: I denied everything that was natural to me.

I would avoid the sun as much as possible late in high school. Why? Because I tan pretty easily and I didn't want to get too much darker than other students. A slight tan was okay, but I didn't want to get carried away. I didn't want to stick out. Sometimes I would actually fret over my darkening summer tan. How can I remain as white as possible? I would look in the mirror each morning and wish not just that my skin and features were different, but that my whole ethnicity could be washed away. My self-hatred lay at the core of my being. And that's where I kept it.

When I brought my friends home, I would be ashamed when my mom and dad, whose English was so bad, spoke to them. I would cringe when my dad tried to crack jokes because his thick accent made him sound like some teenager in a man's body. I would be embarrassed when my dad swore without pause and told them some anecdote. I would never bring my parents to school as other children did for events or programs. Worst of all, the superiority I felt over Latinos I also felt over my parents. They were older, and more experienced, but because they couldn't communicate on the phone with their mortgage bank as well as I could, or because I understood the seven o'clock news better than they did, I felt like I stood on a higher plane. I used to look at my best qualities as traits that were somehow incompatible with the language I spoke at home, the color of my skin, and the values my parents taught me.

My story, my struggle as a Latino student in a white community, is also the story of my parents. The two cannot be separated. I now realize that much of my journey is a continuation of what they began so many years ago. They emigrated illegally from Honduras to the United States several years before I was born. In Honduras, my father was on his way to becoming an engineer; my mother was a teacher in the school system. When they came here, they lost everything and were forced to take menial jobs in a country where the language confused them. Within months, they were caught and sent back by la migra. When they came to the United States the second time, they struggled constantly but they also thrived. My oldest brother Armando, who is nine years older than me, immigrated with my parents. My other brother Steve, five years older than I, was their first-born in America and therefore was given the most American name they could think of.

Until I was seven years old, we lived in the "poor" section of our city. Surrounded by black and Latino kids, the feeling I can most recall is fear. I was scared of riding the bus to school. I was scared of the other kids. I was much like the scared white boy in a black neighborhood. I was scared of the others because I saw myself as inherently different. Even in elementary school, I had begun to develop the self-hatred and racism I would carry with me throughout my adolescence. All I knew was that while I was home, I had to cover my head with my pillow to drown out the police sirens and gun shots. But when I went to school and sat with the "smart kids" in the reading and math courses, I was nestled in a peaceful, white community. When my parents were finally able to save enough money, we moved out of the poor section and into the white community I had held so dear.

My father was, and still is, a drunk. Drinking was more than just something he did; through the years it had become a part of the man. I cannot imagine him without a beer in his hand, just as I cannot separate the man from the violence he inflicted. I respected and looked up to my father when I was young, but perhaps most of that came from my fear of him; fear of what he would do if I misbehaved. He was a pretty intimidating man, with a big round beer belly and huge biceps and calves. Some of my earliest memories are of me hanging off his extended arms, like a skillful monkey swinging along the trees. He had a loud, booming voice. His Spanish was always rough and convoluted. It wasn't that he spoke poorly, it was just the slang or expressions he picked up and used like Standard English: "So I told him, 'Hey guy, fuck you, okay? Fuck you.' " He seemed always to be telling a story, always swearing, and, of course, always drinking. He was in his forties, but to me he sounded like a teenager trying to be cool. But as I grew up, I came to see him as a meaner, darker character. He wasn't just big anymore, he was scary. His resonant voice, which sounded like he was yelling even when he was in a good mood, often brought me to tears.

The last time my father hit me is still vivid in my mind. I was in seventh grade. I had a paper route all through middle school, and I usually delivered the papers right after school. One weekday after school I went to a friend's house instead of delivering my papers. We hung out the whole afternoon, playing cards and telling stories. I didn't get home until a little after five o'clock. I froze when I saw my dad standing on our front steps as I rode my bike into the driveway. He stared at me, clearly angry. My dad didn't even wait until I was inside the house to start yelling. "Que hora es esta para llegar?" He asked why I was late. Living in front of the high school, I was aware of the crowd of students staring at me as my father scolded me. I went inside, angry that my father would embarrass me like that. As soon as I was inside, he slammed the door and continued his abuse: "Donde estabas, babosada?" In Spanish he called me a little shit, irresponsible, no good for not calling and telling him where I was. His face was bright red as his words tore through me.

As he stormed upstairs, I knew where he was going and what he was getting. The door to my brother Steve's room, which is down the hall from the kitchen, opened up and I saw his face pop out. I clung to Steve as little brothers tend to do. "If he hits me, I'm running away." I whispered, "If he hits me, I swear, I don't care, I'm running away." Tears were already streaming down my face and I braced myself for what I knew was coming. I heard my father pound down the stairs. He swung a belt and I foolishly tried to block the blows with my hands as he screamed to me to put my hands down. Again and again he brought the belt down across my thighs. The pain spurted in quick stings. There's no pain worse to me, at least in my memory, than the feel of a belt against my skin. I just wanted him to stop. I screamed louder, begging him to stop.

Eventually he stopped, probably tired of my screaming and tears; he turned abruptly and went upstairs. I remained crying, curled up in a little ball on the kitchen floor. I wished that I had the guts to actually stand up, grab my things, and leave the house forever. I had imagined and planned it so many times before—what things I would take with me, where I would go. But it was never meant to be anything more than a product of my imagination. Instead of making my plan a reality, I cried, just as I had done so many times before.

I'm not sure if he had been drinking that day or if it was just a bad mood. I mean, why hit your son for being late? My father, and the way he made me feel that day, became the personification of Honduras and my cultural roots. He was exactly what I wanted to avoid becoming. When he drank, I saw him as a stupid, pitiful fool. And it didn't take long for me to project those feelings on to all minorities around me. Except my mother—whom I saw as different.

My mother is the sweetest woman in the world. She would do anything for me, including staying married to my father. She did it for me because she knew a divorce would hurt me. She did it for me because she didn't want us to have to move out of our nice home in front of my high school. She did it for me because she needed my father to help pay for college. I guess I take it for granted that it really was all for *me*. But there's no doubt in my mind that it was.

I was born with a heart murmur, which made me vulnerable as a child. My family took extra care of me, but more than anyone my mother was anxious for my safety. It was partially because of her personality but also due to the circumstances. The combination of my sickness at a very young age and the fact that I was her last child—forever her baby—meant I was bound to be treated differently. She poured the last of her motherly instincts and care into me. Well into high school, she would tuck me in at night and wake me up in the morning. Some nights I asked her to rub my back and, though she jokingly complained, she always did it. My closeness with my mother was a contrast to my father, whom I saw as the enemy.

As I grew up, my importance in the family and in her eyes grew. Armando never finished high school and failed my parents' dream of being the first son to graduate college in America. Steve failed similarly after only two terms away at the state university. I became their last chance. Out of 32 cousins on my father's side, I am the fourth youngest yet only the second to go to college. When Armando got into trouble, my dad unloaded on him in the only way he knew how. My father's mother had supposedly whipped my father into submission many years ago. A rope would have been a welcome change to some of the instruments he was beaten with as a boy in Honduras. Yet somehow he grew up loving and thanking his mother for every bit of punishment she handed to him. Similarly, my brother Armando has consistently defended my father for the pain he has inflicted on us. He, out of all of us, has stood by as my father's sole defender. For that reason, among others, my brother Armando and I did not often get along. Even though he knew my dad beat me, Armando felt he had gotten it much worse and viewed me as a spoiled brat.

My mother did not defend my father for most of their marriage, nor did she fight back. She quietly withstood his verbal abuse whenever he drank too much. Over time, however, whether it was the freedom she felt now that she was in the United States or her own personal growth, she began to speak up and assert herself. When he yelled, she would yell back. Usually, though, she was the voice of reason to his temper tantrums. Most of the time he didn't listen and kept on shouting, stalking off in anger and sleeping for the next few weeks in the basement, where he had a bed. Eventually, when I was in high school, my father moved most of his clothes down there and for months at a time would not sleep in his own bed with my mother. Through it all they stayed together...although *together* is a strange word to use for two people who never spoke, never stayed in the same room together for more than a moment, and were married, it seemed to me, in name only.

When they argued, my dad would say anything to interrupt her, to keep her quiet, to regain the peaceful life he remembered from Honduras. Her spirit took him by surprise. This wasn't the way it was in Honduras, he must have thought to himself. This wasn't the way it should be. The wife, he felt, was supposed to cook his food, serve him his drinks and meals, clean the house, stand by him always, and never talk back. But my mom, the wonderful woman that she is, would not stand for that. She knew that she was an American woman now and that things would have to change. Sometimes, crying to myself, I would hope that my mom would just give up and stop arguing back. I respect her now for being strong, but as a little boy I just wanted the shouting to stop. But no matter what, I always blamed my father. He was exactly what I didn't want to become and yet he was also the biggest male presence in my life. In my mind he represented Latino males, therefore I had no desire to grow up and become one.

As easy as it is to blame my father, another side of him, a gentler one, surfaces in my memory. He isn't always the man who beat me and yelled at my mother; sometimes he's the man who sacrificed so much for his family. During my sophomore year in college I was profiled in the college newspaper as a campus activist. The article described everything I'm involved in and all of my accomplishments. I referred to my mother as the "force in my life." A few days after it was published, I sent the clipping home. I was worried how my father would take it. When I finally spoke to my mom about it, she said they had read it together and they both had cried. He was not angry or jealous, as I would have expected him to be. She told me that my family had had a barbecue and invited all my family members. Sometime during the party, my father pulled out the article, which he had already taken to work to show his friends and translated the article into Spanish for my relatives. My mom told me that everyone was so proud of me, but my thoughts were with my father. This is the man I call my dad, this is the man who, along with my mother, I strive to prove myself to each day in spite of his harshness toward me. When I look back on my life, I won't see it as a success unless both of my parents see it that way as well. In the back of my mind is the knowledge that if things had gone differently 20-odd years ago—if my parents had made just a slightly different decision or if my father hadn't worked half as hard—my life would be completely different. I owe something to them, whether I like it or not, and that knowledge drives me to achieve, even when I feel that "I have too much to do."

That's why my narrative can't be separated from my parents' story. Their journey to the United States didn't end when they arrived for good or even when they finally became citizens. The two stories continue in tandem, and just as important is the extended family they left in Honduras and the extended family that traveled with them. Growing up, I was often surrounded by my many aunts and uncles, cousins and second cousins. Just as my father became the embodiment of the Latino man—everything I didn't want to grow to be—my extended family also represented my ethnicity, my culture, and the target of my racism.

I saw my nuclear family as different from their little clans, and as I grew up, *different* also meant *better*. We Garcias were somehow special. My aunts were either single, divorced, or remarried. My cousins were constantly being arrested, having children out of wedlock, causing their parents grief. My cousins were the only Latinos I had any close connection to, so, to me their behavior exemplified all Latinos. They got into trouble, broke the law, stole, cheated, lied, and were disobedient. Although my brothers and I occasionally exhibited some of these behaviors, I nevertheless saw us as above it all. My female cousins got pregnant, moved in with boyfriends, married and divorced early—all the kind of behavior that I considered "subwhite." To do the wrong thing, then, as I saw my cousins do the wrong things, was to be less than white, to be *not* succeeding in America.

It is true that my brothers and I were generally better behaved, and better educated, and better mannered than many of my cousins. But instead of leaving the comparison there, I took it a step further and said that this was because they were Latino and were acting it, while we were Latino but we had somehow overcome our heritage. Overcome our heritage! This idea disgusts me now, and yet there was a time I didn't even question it. I didn't think of my family as successful because we were Latino or in addition to being Latino, but *in spite* of that fact.

The notion of overcoming my heritage recalls a poignant incident that occurred during a family vacation to Honduras. On the road, a small child around my age came up to our van and asked for a ride. We told him we didn't have any room, but as we started to drive we noticed that he had climbed on the back of the van and was prepared to ride with us, at 50 or 60 miles per hour, holding onto a ladder. At the time I disliked the little brat; I couldn't believe he had the nerve to try and hitch a ride from us. A dozen years later I think of that kid and can't help but see myself. If circumstances had been different, I could have been him. That notion would occur to me again and again, but at the time, and even as I packed bags for college, I still looked at that boy—at so much of my identity—with disdain.

My parents didn't pressure me much to succeed; I put the pressure on myself: I was the one who had to bring respect to my family after Armando dropped out of high school and Steve dropped out of college. Armando and I constantly argued, and he refused to come to my high school graduation. I think my success only highlighted his failure. My parents' pride in me was a sharp stab at him. He had been expected to be the first one to do so many things that I was now doing. Steve was more complacent, always assuming he would return to school and catch up with me. And that's how I left for college—angry with most of my family, convinced that I was better than my family and my heritage, and bearing the burden of bringing home what my parents wanted to see: a good report card and a college diploma.

For the most part, college was everything it was supposed to be: I was having the time of my life and meeting so many amazing people. It wasn't until my first meeting of La Unidad, the Latino student organization, that I had my first confrontation with the hate inside me. I had gone to the meeting because I felt an obligation to go. Despite my belief that I was better than my background, I was also confronted by the feeling that my status as a so-called box-checking Latino was what got me into college. Why else would I have identified myself as such? *Associate, identify*—words like these meant the difference between being seen as an outsider to the Latino community or a link within it. If you identified, that basically meant you acknowledged your heritage, you went beyond your box-checking status.

I went to that first Unidad meeting because I felt an obligation, not because I felt I would gain anything from it. I didn't want to be seen as a Latino student by the mainstream but I also didn't want to be seen as a sellout by the Latino students. My self-hatred and hatred of my ethnicity was deeply buried, and I had no intention of making it known. I barely thought about it, and that's the way I liked it. But my first weeks at college were characterized by a sense of exclusion, a sense that I didn't fit in anymore. Dressed in Abercrombie and Fitch, attending their parents' alma mater, most students seemed so different from me. I was afraid someone would suddenly discover that I didn't really belong. I had an overwhelming feeling that I had to start my life over again, build myself back up, yet I didn't know who I was or how to go about it.

That first Unidad meeting we all sat in a stuffy room, the Latino students on display for one another. I was immediately hit by the feeling that I was very *unLatino*. The others somehow exuded more Latinoness. It was in their accents, the speed of their speech, the Spanish words they mixed into their English. They all talked about home cooking and dishes that they loved, and although I loved my mom's home cooking, I didn't know the correct names of the foods she prepared. But most important, they all seemed to know more about their individual cultures. They were more culturally, socially, and politically aware than I ever thought I could be. What did I know about Honduras? I couldn't even tell you what kind of government they have there, let alone how "my people" are doing. What did I know about Latino culture besides what I learned in school, which was nothing? My cultural ignorance had never even occurred to me as a problem; suddenly it became a very big one.

The worst moment was when we went around the room and introduced ourselves. One by one they spoke, pronouncing their names with a full Spanish accent. Some people I knew always did so, but a few caught me off guard. *Drew* became *Andres, John* became *Juan;* the speed at which people said their names increased, and as we quickly went around the circle, I didn't know what to do. Of course, I could easily have used an accent, but I never did and I didn't want to do so just to fit in. I even had a fear about doing that. What if it came out badly? What if I couldn't even say my own name right? I didn't want their eyes on me, them to snicker and know that I was only a fake. I just wanted to come to the meeting, sit back, and feel like I had made up for the fact that I checked *Hispanic/Latino* instead of *white*, which is what I wished I were, or *Other*, which is what I felt like.

When the introductions finally came around to me, I blurted out my name, *José García*, with a full accent. I felt like a sellout, not because I didn't want to be Latino, but because I was willing to hide my true self in order to be accepted as Latino. I was more confused than ever. Inside I knew that I thought poorly of Latinos and that my racism was deeply rooted, yet I was willing to act unlike myself in order to be accepted by my Latino peers. I didn't know who I was or what I wanted. I only knew that I wanted to be accepted. I wanted to please everyone, and was finding I couldn't please anyone.

My confusion got worse before it got better. I had gotten involved early freshman fall in my college's student government. Representing the student body, the organization constantly worried about whether or not they were truly being representative. So they would literally take a count based on gender and race/ethnicity. I wasn't just a normal involved student, I was the token Latino, or so it seemed to me.

The word *token* was one that I would get to know well as time went on. Token Latino, token minority, people of color versus minority, ignorance versus racism, the relationship of power in racism, prejudice, institutional racism…these were all terms and phrases that I had never been acquainted with before my first year at college. I had a crash course in being nonwhite. I'm convinced that if you asked a white person, half of those terms would draw a blank response. It's not simply because they're white, but because they have had no contact with these issues. I'm a great example. I had never considered any of these issues, yet I was that person of color, I was that token minority. I was *supposed* to know. That lesson came to me during a student government meeting when I was asked to give my opinion as a Latino. I wasn't asked to give it as a student who happens to be Latino, but to give the official Latino opinion, as if all we Latinos got together one day and took a straw poll on a number of issues, all of which came out unanimous. There is diversity among races, but there is also diversity within races. I wanted my friends to be color blind. I didn't want to be seen as Latino or ethnic or other. In a short time, I went from hating my ethnicity to not minding it but still being grateful when people could ignore it. The inner hatred I had grown up with was gone, but something rotten remained. I still had a way to go before I would embrace and actually be proud of my culture, rather than just tolerating it.

I continued going to Unidad meetings, continued struggling through my ignorance. I heard other students of color talk about the racial issues they had confronted growing up. I began to find more and more aspects of my childhood that related to their childhoods—similarities in being the children of immigrants. Most of all, I was surrounded for the first time by students who shared my skin color and also shared my academic success. I was no longer the exception in a sea of white faces. The wall I had built up between myself and my ethnicity began to break down. Despite being 70 percent white, my college introduced me to diversity. So before I realized it was happening, that lifelong correlation between *white* and *successful* stopped making sense to me.

I recall a late-night conversation with my friend Jake who is half Latino and half white. He casually mentioned that he was against affirmative action, that he saw it as reverse discrimination against white students, and felt that it only served to emphasize racial lines more. As he put it, "Why should white people today have to suffer for what white people in the past have done?" This comment led to a passionate debate. I argued that, despite what he believed, there was a racial divide in this country. It was social, as evidenced by my high school substitute's behavior years before. It was economic, as evidenced by the poor section of my hometown that bussed me in and out when I was younger. It was educational, as shown by all the white faces in my upper-level classes from elementary school through high school. It was cultural, as witnessed by the isolation I felt at my first Unidad meeting. "You're right," I argued. "Most white people of today have nothing to do with what happened years before. But that doesn't erase the problem. That doesn't change the fact that minorities are still suffering because of what happened years before. Furthermore, whether whites are directly at fault or not, it doesn't change the fact that whites have benefited. Because others have lost, whites have gained. It's not a question of right or wrong—it's just the way things are. But that doesn't mean we shouldn't try to change things." Jake kept arguing that minorities just needed to "stop feeling sorry for themselves."

That night I developed my own theory on this subject: "Look Jake, it's like life is this one big long-distance race. Ever since the race began, the minority runners have been oppressed, kept back, slowed by slavery, by conquest, and so on. And all this time, the white runners have been getting ahead. Suddenly, all restrictions are dropped. No more slavery. No more segregation. Everything is made equal. But is it really equal, Jake? All that equalization under the law doesn't change the fact that all these white runners have had centuries' long head start. How does that translate to real life? In economics, in education, in social attitudes? These are all big problems, and they call for big solutions. I don't think affirmative action is the best long-term solution, but it is a temporary one until people are willing to make the bigger commitment."

Jake said that he used his Latino background to get him into college, just as he used his running talent (he was recruited by the college for cross-country). That was all his identity as a Latino meant to him. With my mind entrenched in issues of race and ethnicity, I was outraged at him for saying something like that. And yet just a few months before, I could have said the same thing.

At college, once I began to deal with the long-suppressed issues of my ethnic identity, the floodgates opened. Sometimes I got in serious arguments and found myself saying things I couldn't believe I was saying. In those moments, I claimed all white people were racists or the United States border should be completely open all the time. But that was part of my learning process, of pushing forward. I was in the process of testing, trying things out, seeing where thoughts would go, and then evaluating whether I still believed them or not. I was trying to find myself under years of buried ignorance, self-hate, and prejudice toward my own culture.

In another late-night conversation with friends, I recalled that small boy who had wanted to hitch a ride with us in Honduras, whom I had disliked so much. "What's so different from me and so many of the naked kids I see running around in Honduras, begging on the streets? Sure, I think my drive and my work ethic have been important, but I think the key difference has been the opportunities I have had—attending schools that are leaps and bounds above anything in Honduras and pursuing so many things that my parents never had the chance to. And yet it might have been completely different. It could be another kid sitting here today and me in Honduras. That's why I don't think I'll be happy in life unless I'm helping them realize their own potential. I want to give others all the opportunities that I had." And the minute I said it, I knew I believed it with all my being—I knew I would never look at my role or purpose in life in the same light again. I was never religious, and yet I felt I had found my calling. I knew then I could never be an investment banker or businessman. My place was in service, in education, in any field where I could use my skills to improve the lives of others and help them open doors.

In spite of my new insights, the same demons remained inside of me. When you look at yourself in the mirror for years and see someone who is unattractive because of his skin color, hair color, speech, and other characteristics, those negative feelings don't go away easily. I felt I had a big nose, that it was too round and not slim enough. I hated the fact that I would always be a good four inches below average height. I even came to dislike my boring brown eyes and black hair. My own insecurities about how I looked and fit in remained. Even though I was growing intellectually and emotionally, I had not yet purged many of the old thoughts that haunted me.

My self-hatred was also hatred of my background and my relatives. My perception of myself and others had been altered by all the new people I met at college. Generalizations I had held to—that all Latinos are lazy, all students of color are inferior to whites—were shattered while I was at school. My relationships with members of my family and their relationships with each other had also been forced to change as a result of my absence. My leaving home was exactly what my family needed.

Just how far the healing had progressed is evident in a radiant photo taken at Armando's new apartment, which he shared with his fiancée, Molly. In the photo, we're embracing each other tightly. My father has one arm extending far to his right to reach my brother and the other hand is tightly grasping my mother's shoulder. My mother is smiling beautifully; it's a genuine smile. She seems truly happy—happy to have her family all around her. You can almost read her thoughts: She has her family together again, different than before, but together. Caught in that photo is me kissing my brother. For no other reason than because I was feeling happy and wanted a funny picture, I embraced Armando's face and kissed him on his right cheek. He remained smiling while looking at the camera, his arm tightly around me. After the photo was taken, Armando wrapped his arms around me and pulled me in for a full hug. Steve came over as well. And right there, in the kitchen of my brother's new house, with my parents and his fiancée watching, Armando began to apologize to me for mistreating me for years and years. As we embraced, Armando sobbed, "I'm so sorry, José, I'm so sorry for everything I put you through. But you know I did it because I loved you and wanted only the best from you. You're my little brother, there's nothing I wouldn't do for you." He then opened his arms to Steve, and with the three of us wrapped in each other's arms, forming a little circle, Armando continued, with tears in his eyes, "You guys are my brothers, my little men. I love you two so much. So fucking much! I'm always going to be there for you guys, whatever you might need. You fucking come to me, all right? There's nothing I won't do for my brothers." The tears were coming down my cheeks now, and Steve, usually calm and reserved, also began to cry. Our coming together in love and reconciliation was the climax to what I had slowly been developing the whole year—my acceptance by and of my brothers after years of alienation. While we hugged, I remember hearing my mother tell my father to look over at us. I sensed her deep inner happiness. She was so proud to see her sons finally come together.

Several months later, I took another step forward in my journey. I interned in Washington, DC, working as a research assistant for a nonprofit organization focused on strengthening the Latino community. I found myself surrounded by people who had centered their lives around making a difference in the Latino community. Two men in particular, leaders in the organization, further altered my views on Latinos. Both had gone to Ivy League schools, and their résumés were packed with incredible experiences. They could have done anything they wanted to in life, but they chose to give back to their respective communities. I met many prominent Latinos through them, and my perceptions of Latinos, which had expanded exponentially since high school, was further improved. Any significant prejudices I had were eliminated by the success of these two men. I admired them *and* they were Latino. In the past, I would have joined these two facts by thinking, *in spite of* their being Latino. It's such a small detail and yet reveals so much about how I thought.

I was still working in DC when I flew home for the weekend to see the production of a musical in my high school. I saw the show with Dan, my friend since the fourth grade. I told him about my involvement in student government, my increased activism, and life in general at my small liberal arts college. But since I was in DC at the time, I also mentioned my internship and the great time I was having. With pride, I pulled out my business card. "Empowering the Latino community?" He read off the card, smiling at me and waving the card to a mutual friend from high school. "Look Chris, José is Latino now. Look at the card. Our little brown friend's creating community!" His tone was mocking, and they both began to laugh as they gazed at the card. "This is the biggest load of PC bullshit. I can't believe you're a part of this crap!" He laughed louder, staring at the card in disbelief.

I felt crushed. This had been my childhood friend? This had been the life that I had enjoyed so much? I was ashamed of who I had been and what I had believed, but I didn't think the shame ran so deep. Was there anything I could turn back to? Was there anything that didn't stink of my racism? It had been a while since I felt so uncomfortable, fidgeting in place, wanting to be anywhere but there. And right then I was struck with a realization that came just before I would have begun feeling sorry for myself. "Hey Dan, fuck you," I said. His mouth opened in disbelief, his laugh stopped in midbreath. I continued, "Just because you haven't grown up in the last two years, doesn't mean that I haven't."

"Hey Mr. Latino, don't take it personally. I just think that doing this sort of thing is very unlike the José I knew in high school," Dan said, handing the card back to me.

"A lot about me is unlike the José you once knew. People change, Dan, and ya know what? I'm happy with the changes I've made." I gave both of them one last look in the eye and then returned to my seat in the theater. I don't think I was particularly articulate or eloquent, but I got across what I wanted. I didn't back off.

As the show continued, I recalled that late-night conversation with Jake and the passion with which I spoke of privilege and racism. An image of that boy from Honduras came to mind and I again imagined myself living his life. I then remembered Mr. Connors, the substitute teacher, and the anger he had made me feel. I reflected on the dozens of conversations in which I called myself a spic and spat on my culture. Finally, I thought of my mother and father and all they had given me and continue to give me. Dan, who silently took his seat next to me, had accused me of being "very unlike the José he knew in school." I smiled, happy that he was right, proud that I didn't joke along with him and deny what I had spent two years forming, what is still forming, what I hope never stops forming.

- - - - -

UNA MUCHACHA DECENTE

Jessie, born in Puerto Rico, emigrated to New York City with her family when she was a young child. She explores in this case how her strong family ties, others' belief in her, and her own commitment helped her avoid the possible dangers and complications of her urban community. She describes how she remains connected to her friends and family, despite her experiences with gang violence, indifferent teachers, and under-resourced schools. She watches friends drop out of school, deal drugs, and become involved in local gangs because they seem to lack the support systems she has. College provides a new set of challenges, as she faces the ignorance of others and the impersonal academic demands of the institution. Jessie's determination to succeed makes us believe that indeed she will.

I was 17 years old the first time I considered purchasing a gun. Many of my childhood friends were dealing by the time we entered high school and had already established contacts with gunrunners and black market dealers around the city. There was nothing to it, I thought. I would use what was left of my summer earnings to cop a gun from one of my boys and still have a little extra cash to thank them for their services. It would be as easy as going to the bodega to buy my mother a can of Goya beans. It was only a matter of stepping out of my house and speaking to Joey, Red, or Edwin and everything would be set. A gun guaranteed security, ensuring I would never have to prove my physical prowess to individuals who mistook my reticence for an inability to defend myself. I was tired of fighting. A flash of my gun would emphatically demonstrate my capabilities without necessitating the physical and emotional distress that every altercation induced in me.

One crisp Saturday morning when I was 16 years old, I was buying my mother a birthday present at a nearby mall when two female gang members attacked me. I can still hear my glasses crash against the floor as the first attacker struck my face with her fist. Disoriented at first, I quickly caught sight of my assailant's face and employed the most crucial defense strategy my older brother taught me during childhood: Never stop swinging. By the time the cops arrived on the scene, the officers had trouble distinguishing the perpetrators from the victim: One of my attackers fearfully stood over me while I threatened to take the life of her comrade whose neck was firmly locked underneath my arm. A female officer demanded that I loosen my grip but I would not budge. Two officers then restrained me while another officer helped the first attacker to her feet. After a few witnesses intervened to help explicate the situation, the officers arrested the gang members and advised me to press charges. I refused. Moments later the girls were released. The first attacker sauntered away, tears streaming down her cheeks, while her sidekick cupped her hand over her bloody nose. I sat listlessly on a bench watching their figures diminish as the distance between us increased. A part of me wanted to catch up to the dynamic duo and apologize for their injuries. Another part of me wanted to keep swinging. When the girls were no longer in sight, two officers accompanied me to my apartment. My heart sank as I realized this incident could potentially mark a succession of violent attacks. It was only a matter of time before I would confront gang members seeking revenge for their kin. Gang violence never ends.

When I was 17, my attention dramatically shifted from myself to my family's welfare. The day before Mother's Day, I was practicing how to parallel park a few blocks away from my neighborhood when I received a frantic phone call from my mother—she walked into our apartment moments after a band of robbers had burglarized our home. Minutes later, I arrived at the apartment. I embraced my mother as she stared blankly at the debris concealing much of the floor. I slowly inched my way to my bedroom remembering I had purchased my mother's present earlier that morning. I searched through the rubble hoping to find my mother's necklace. It was gone.

Perhaps the most troubling aspect of the entire incident was unveiling the robbers' entry and escape routes. We live on the first floor of our apartment building. The burglars climbed through our living-room window, adjacent to the courtyard of our building. Our courtyard is one of the busiest spots in our neighborhood. People constantly pass through this area, play handball, smoke, drink and have barbeques and birthday parties. Needless to say, there were countless witnesses who were either in cahoots with the suspects or unwilling to speak up. A few days after the robbery, my brother's friend informed us that the attack was a mere warning. Local gang members in our neighborhood were after my brother. My brother was spotted wearing a sweater with yellow lettering during his last visit from college. Yellow was a Latin King color. Luckily, my brother returned to school the night before the robbery. Nevertheless, it was only a matter of time until our apartment was robbed again or any one of my family members was attacked. I refused to sit back passively waiting for the cops to notify us once they apprehended any suspects. My family was in imminent danger. I had to take matters into my own hands.

Although I had never officially joined a gang, I knew plenty of individuals in my neighborhood who would fight for me in the event of an altercation. My brother's "boys" assured me they were more than willing to defend me when and if "anything went down." Nevertheless, I did not want to get anyone else involved. My family's welfare was my responsibility. On my way home from school, I found my friend, Red, at a pizzeria across the street from my building. Red had dropped out of high school two years earlier and started dealing when he was 16. He had heard about the robbery and asked if there was anything he could do to help. It was at that moment that I informed Red about my interest in purchasing a gun. Surprised at first, he asked what I planned to do with it. I did not know how to respond. I arranged to meet Red and his "affiliates" three weeks later in front of my former elementary school building. When the time came for the exchange to occur, I was nowhere to be found. As much as I rationalized my intentions for owning a gun, to the point of neglecting the potential consequences for purchasing an illegal weapon, something inside kept me from taking that final step. When the time came to protect my family, I was ready to put my life on the line. Nevertheless, I could not fight fire with fire.

Decisions, decisions. Verdicts like yes, no, maybe, sometimes, always, and never were shaped by the values and experiences that have influenced my upbringing. My life experience has taught me to value integrity, respect, and honor in any decision I make. My parents raised us in a pious home where these values were instilled in us from the moment we opened our eyes. Speaking respectfully and honoring our elders, believing in things unseen, caring for those in need, learning that love does not have a face, color, or creed shaped our perceptions and interactions with the world around us. While we did not have many material possessions, these principles were priceless as they carried us through difficult times and had even more significance when life was blissful. As I grew older, my love and respect for people and my faith enabled me to chase dreams I sometimes had trouble envisioning. Others' faith in my abilities was also a catalyst for my drive to succeed and make decisions that would not compromise my sense of responsibility and would bring me closer to my goals.

My friends, teachers, and loved ones believed I possessed the ability to change circumstances that threatened to undermine my quest to succeed. I had the potential, capacity, and intelligence to make it. There were "no ifs, ands, or buts about it," as my third-grade teacher would often say. However, it was up to me to use my God-given talents without having to resort to the same methods and philosophies that many of my peers and family members were utilizing to resolve immediate needs they felt their parents, teachers, government, or society routinely neglected. While I grew up in an area where violence and criminal activity tainted my childhood with the uncertainty of a brighter tomorrow, at the end of the day there was a home I returned to— a support system that was unlike anything I would encounter throughout my daily treks to school or my childhood masquerades with neighborhood peers. I learned the greatest lessons about life within my Brooklyn tenement, our second home since migrating from Puerto Rico. Mom and Dad lived a life of faith that taught me I could move mountains—and over the course of my life, I would.

I was born amid a flickering light dangling from the ceiling of maternity ward C12 in *Hospital de El Distrito De Aguadilla*, in Puerto Rico. To my left was the vast Atlantic—the waves slapping against the surf as gentle zephyrs pulled the tide further onto the shore. To my right sat my father, his rugged hands enveloping his face as he stared blankly into the eyes of his creation. Mom cradled me in her arms, her cheek pressed against my rosy forehead as she whispered a prayer. How could he possibly manage to support a family? There was no money. Nevertheless, in the midst of all the uncertainty, there was hope.

When I was living in Puerto Rico, my grandmother and I often sat outside right before the stars emerged. We would start counting *las estrellitas* one by one until the sky was flecked with a mosaic of radiant white flecks. By then there were too many stars to count. I remember wishing I could fit the sky into my pocket when I was a child. When we moved to New York City, the sky changed. At night, my Brooklyn sky did not reveal the sea of stars that poured out of my Puerto Rican sky. Nevertheless, sunny days were still as bright as my grandfather's sapphire eyes. Rays of sunlight glistened, reflecting from bottle caps and shards of glass strewn across broken sidewalks—remnants of street-corner brawls from the previous night. Although my surroundings were remarkably different, it was only a matter of time until I called my Brooklyn apartment home.

My first home in New York City was the maroon monolithic housing project at Mott Haven Avenue in Brooklyn. The streets were peppered with empty crack vials discarded from the binges of the previous night. Over the years, I became familiar with the colors of the caps: red, blue, green, and purple. The red caps were the most common. When my father had saved enough money from working as a custodian, we moved to another area.

Our situation moderately improved. The smell of urine in the halls of 2364 Decatur Avenue was slightly less pungent than in the Mott Haven projects. Unfortunately, the proportion of stabbings, shootings, and drug use in the area had not altered. Our apartment was broken into during my senior year of high school and my older brother got mugged three times before turning 18.

I still remember the challenge of writing with mittens on my hands. On cold days it was the only way to finish the multiplication tables in my CIMS book. The orange glow of the space heaters was our only source of heat besides our coats. My father had explained that the landlord sometimes forgot to send oil to the building. Nevertheless, we needed to complete our homework, not because my parents nagged us but because it was the thing to do. To my siblings and I, it was what every child did before watching TV or going to church for *Missioneritas* or Royal Rangers (religious equivalent to Girl/Boy Scouts). The way I understood it, everyone in my family served a different function. As a child, my function was to complete my homework and tidy up the house before my parents returned from work. My parents' responsibilities included working, cooking, reading bedtime bible stories, and singing hymns and reciting prayers in the morning before we were off to school. Nothing got in the way of our roles and duties because we each contributed a vital component to our family's upkeep.

When we faced hardships, Mom taught us to count our blessings because "as bad as things get, they could always be worse." Mom and Dad knew all about worse—before being orphaned at 13 my father suffered years of abuse from his father, and he did not own a pair of shoes until he was eight years old. Sometimes a cup of warm orange tea (made from orange leaves in his backyard) was the only meal he and his eight siblings would have for days at a time. One of 14 children, my mother grew up on a small farm in Puerto Rico. She was pulled out of school by the sixth grade to help my grandmother maintain her household. Mom has also experienced her share of hardships over the course of her life. My mother's advice continues to shape my perception of the world today. In light of my mother's counsel, I thought my apartment was just as good as any. I did not mind the nights I slept in the coat I received over Christmas with the matching scarf and hat Abuelita (grandma) gave me for my birthday. Home was home. I was happy to have a roof over my head, clothes on my back, and parents who loved me when life was good and loved me harder when life was not so good.

Growing up, I viewed my block as my playground. My friends and I played hopscotch and freeze tag in the courtyard of our apartment building and invented new games when old ones became boring. Sometimes we would sit on the front steps of my building describing the shapes, animals, and people hiding amidst the clouds. My younger brother, Manny, always saw puppies—most often Chihuahuas or baby pit bulls chewing on toy bones.

Before church service on Sundays, my friends and I waited for Mr. Frosty, the ice cream truck, to stop by. Sometimes the myriad of options overwhelmed us—there was the snow cone, the Mario Pop with a gumball nose in the center, strawberry shortcake, the choco-taco, the banana split, chocolate, strawberry or vanilla milk shakes, and so on. So many options, so little time before Sunday school started. Most of us chose the timeless classic, the Mr. Frosty special—a vanilla ice cream cone with multicolored sprinkles. One afternoon I discovered that twirling the cone fast enough created a "rainbow tornado." From that moment on, in remembrance of that momentous occasion, my friends and I would twirl our cones and admire our rainbow tornadoes before taking our first bite into Mr. Frosty.

When we walked home from school we were careful to tiptoe past Juanito's spot as he slept in front of the bodega, holding his plastic "change cup" imprinted with a faded Domino's Pizza logo—the red and blue ink was still vibrant, the green ink faded to a yellowish hue that reminded me of my elementary school's chicken noodle soup. When Juanito was awake, he shook his cup like a maraca, his coins ringing like church bells that awakened me in the early morning when it was time to say my prayers and get ready for school. He told us stories of the good life in Puerto Rico, when he still had his right leg and would climb up palm trees to knock down ripened coconuts. Although he never told the same *quento* twice, his stories always ended with the same moral: "Be good to the ones you love, finish school, and never join the military."

Summer vacation was the happiest time of our lives. When school was out, games of "hide-and seek," "steal the bacon," or "kick the can" filled our summer months. Only the kids whose parents *both* worked made trips back to Puerto Rico, Santo Domingo, or Florida for the summer. Nevertheless, when the sun beat down on our backs and plumes of steam began to rise from the scorching asphalt, nothing could beat dancing in front of open fire hydrants. When the sun hid its face, we spent most of our summer nights teasing the sky as we tried to outrun the moon. It did not matter how long or how fast we ran—it seemed as if the moon was sitting on our shoulders the entire time.

For years this was my childhood. I lived to be outside with my neighborhood friends, cousins, and brothers discovering new adventures. However, as I became older my mother began to restrict my outdoor privileges. By the time I turned 12, I was forbidden to hang outside with my friends as I was "becoming a young woman and the streets were no place for *una muchacha decente* (a respectable young girl)." To this day, while I understand my mother's intentions, I can still feel remnants of my resentment as I relive that brisk April afternoon when my friends stood in our courtyard patiently awaiting my arrival. I never showed up. In my eyes, this was probably one of the most abominable decisions my mother ever made. It was a source of contention between my mother and I for years thereafter. Why couldn't I go outside and play with my friends? *Muchacha decente?* At 12 years old, who wasn't a *muchacha decente?* I just wanted to play handball, basketball, stick ball, or freeze tag. What was so vile about playing hide-and-seek in our apartment building? I could not see how these recreational activities could threaten my status as a decent and respectable girl.

For months I would stare outside from our first-floor window watching my friends play in our courtyard and longing to once again be a part of their world. They were only about five feet away from where I sat, and yet they seemed so far away from me. Sometimes my buddies invented basketball games where they used my arms as a basketball hoop. I held out my arms in the form of an oval from our living-room window as Luis, Eddie, Tony, and Stephanie took turns shooting the basketball into my arms. They stopped playing when my friend Stevie accidentally missed my arms and busted our living-room window. Nevertheless, I could not give up. Sooner or later I knew I would once again be allowed to hang outside with my comrades. I convinced myself that this was probably just a phase Mom was going through—she would get over it in no time.

Days, weeks, and months passed, and there was still no sign of change. When I grew tired of waiting for my mom to come to her senses, I attempted to sneak outside on numerous occasions. Not surprisingly, there was always a neighbor or a *comadre* who would stop me dead in my tracks because my mother had already notified them about her decision to restrict my civil liberties. After a while I grew tired of fighting with my mother because I knew she would not relent. From that moment on, my block never looked the same. Over the years the friendships I had developed throughout my childhood subtly altered. I would often see my neighborhood friends in passing, but as we grew older, the glow of our childhood innocence dulled to a subtle glimmer as handball and kick the can evolved into the formidable behaviors and activities we were too afraid to talk about when we were children. I realized that the girls whose parents allowed them to chill outside with their friends adapted to lifestyles that often undermined their safety and well-being and severely limited their prospects for success.

Throughout the years, many of my friends became the people we spent much of our childhood trying to avoid—the men who promised to buy us candy if we delivered small packages in our backpacks; the feeble women with tracks of blood running up and down their arms who begged us for train fare or cigarettes; the gunrunners and gangsters we were too afraid to look at when we ran into the streets to retrieve our lost basketballs or handballs. Others died tragically before the age of 17. Some were killed during drive-by shootings, run-ins with rival gang members, or drug runs gone bad.

Unlike my friends who involved themselves in activities and behaviors that jeopardized their lives, my choir buddy, Anthony, was different. My sophomore year of high school, my chorus teacher invited me and three other students from our class to audition for the Brooklyn Academy of the Arts Program. Mikey, Anthony, Janelle, and I were told to arrive at the local community college one chilly Saturday morning to audition in front of six directors. When we arrived, there were approximately 75–80 students anxiously waiting to audition. We watched each student walk one by one out of the small auditorium, some with pink slips, some without. We soon learned that pink slips meant you made it. Luckily, for Mikey, Anthony, Janelle, and I, we all walked out of the audition with pink slips and bright smiles. Every Saturday thereafter we would arrive at 9:30 A.M. sharp (or risk being sent home) at the community college performing arts center for approximately four hours of vocal training and two hours of violin lessons. If we acquired more than two absences over the course of each semester, we were immediately removed from the program. There was no question—our Saturdays were grueling. Our directors were tough and oftentimes unforgiving. If any section was flat during a rehearsal, every individual in that section was required to sing the entire piece ALONE, until the culprit was discovered. Nevertheless, it was a small price to pay for making beautiful music. We learned about operas, symphonies, and other magnificent pieces of music created by composers we had never heard of before. We rehearsed classical pieces in foreign languages we didn't understand. And we loved every minute of it. Our chorus was well-known throughout the city, and we would often perform at various functions and assemblies. We were on television on numerous occasions and in newspapers. We felt important. Mikey, Anthony, Janelle, and I looked forward to every Saturday (albeit with some apprehension). We were so thankful to have the opportunity to engage with a different type of learning experience and ultimately create something at the end of each semester that would make our friends and family members proud. Our performances were worth every embarrassing moment or seemingly endless rehearsal. We understood that at the end of every semester, our hard work paid off in a way that we never expected. Unlike school, where the benefits of our hard work were often not so clear, creating music in the All-America choir enabled us to embrace the fruits of our labor and show others a side of us we never really knew existed.

Although Anthony was ridiculed by many of his friends for spending his Saturdays *singing* in a choir, he felt the program kept him busy, away from his block and out of trouble. Anthony was determined to make it without dealing or engaging in illegal activities, and he involved himself in programs he felt would keep him "focused on doing right, you know?" We had "bright futures in our hands," he would often say. By our sophomore year, Anthony dubbed himself the "best tenor," while I was only a "mediocre soprano." Our beautiful music ended the morning I received the call that Anthony had taken his life. That afternoon I turned in my uniform. I could not bear the thought of seeing Anthony's seat empty during rehearsals. Young people are not supposed to die—especially not like this, I thought to myself.

Over the years, as familiar figures in my life continued to fade, it took some time to accept that death meant coming to terms with the reality that I could search every corner of the earth and never find these people again. As difficult as it was to say good-bye to people and memories that I cherished so deeply, I accepted these losses as something that would only make me stronger in the long run. I came to the realization that this was life and I needed to accept it in order to move on. My family's support and my mother's guidance helped me to keep moving as she reminded me *"hay remedio para todo menos la muerte"* (there is a solution for everything except death). I decided that nothing except death itself would stop me. I prayed that my loved ones and their families would find the strength to keep moving. I understood that such tragedies have a tendency to eclipse hope with anger as unanswered questions and grief oftentimes evolve into a bitterness that compels many to seek revenge, thus perpetuating the cycle of hate that news reporters and journalists so easily publicize in newspapers and two-minute news segments that depict the ghetto as a lost world without hope—without real people who hurt, feel, speak, live, and breathe like everyone else.

As the years progressed, I witnessed many of my friends lose sight of their goals and aspirations amid trying circumstances that rendered their determination futile. As hard as I tried, I could not figure out where it all went wrong. Many of us believed we would grow up to be doctors, astronauts, scientists, lawyers—big-time people who worked downtown and donned fancy business suits. Others dreamed about becoming hip-hop singers, actors, and actresses—people we saw only on TV and on magazine covers. There was no doubt in our minds; we were going to make it big. However, there were others whose parents believed they would "turn out just like their fathers—no good, lazy, good-for-nothing, low-lives who will probably die young or spend the rest of their lives in jail." I can still hear Darren's mother yelling over his music: "that's right—you gonna meet yo father in jail—good fo' nothing, bastard." I believe many of my friends internalized these negative perceptions and were afraid to try because they were convinced they were going to fail. Darren wanted to be an artist, but he dropped out of high school and started dealing at age 15. He has been shot on numerous occasions and has been in and out of jail since the age of 16.

Unfortunately, our schooling experiences gave us the same impression; we were not expected to succeed. I attended a large, overcrowded public high school made up of about five thousand students. Gang violence haunted my freshman year. My high school was a hotbed for violence between rival gang members who often clashed during our lunch periods. We were often forced to hide behind parked cars as we waited and waited for police officers who never showed up to secure our surroundings. Metal detectors, security guards who unjustly criminalized us, and dilapidated facilities were part of our daily reality. From the outside, our school resembled a prison. All of the windows above the first floor were barred with aluminum gates. Our lab rooms were a joke. Half the time we did not have materials to carry out experiments and would have to "estimate" our results. Our schools lacked essential resources and suffered from teacher deficits that tainted our educational experiences with disappointment and strife. We were lucky if our teachers showed up to class regularly. My senior year of high school, my physics teacher often walked into class about half way through the period and after taking attendance would take an "extended lunch break"—he would not return until halfway through the period the following morning. Furthermore, we were blessed if our teachers were qualified to teach the subjects they taught. Given these conditions and the varying needs of the student population, our schools were ill-equipped to manage the obstacles affecting students' lives outside of the classroom. Many of my friends walked into their schools carrying a world on their shoulders that kept them from seeing any tangible benefits in schooling. Their motivation to adhere to school demands dissipated in light of difficult circumstances that skewed their perceptions of a brighter future. Broken homes, neglect, physical and sexual abuse, and drug and alcohol abuse were but a few of the challenges that marred students' life experiences.

School environments that are incapable of assessing students' needs and experiences cannot provide students with an effective educational experience. Many of my friends and family members could not engage with school culture because teacher expectations and academic standards were sometimes inconsistent with their needs or experiences. School, the one place where students could escape the negativity surrounding their lives, if only for six hours, was not prepared to deal with their needs. Our school conditions told us we were not worth the expenditure because we were destined to fill the ranks of our predecessors. While there were not enough math textbooks to go around for everyone, metal detectors greeted us at the entrance of our schools supervised by security guards who treated us like the gang bangers, drug dealers, and criminals we were destined to replace. Our schools helped reaffirm our place in society—and our place was the streets, jail, or death.

Despite these circumstances, I enjoyed participating in my school's social scene. During our lunch periods we were allowed to eat outside on the main avenue made up of numerous stores and restaurants that overflowed with students when school was in session. When Foot Locker and Footaction publicized the release of new Air Jordan sneakers, Timberland boots, or Nike classics, we were always the first ones to know. During my freshman year of high school, many of my friends and I found after-school jobs. I was employed at a pharmacy in Manhattan where I worked as an expert gift-wrapper and a stock clerk in the cosmetics department. At the age of 14, I was able to begin to assist my family financially. There was no greater feeling than being able to contribute to my parents' financial needs. My overtime also gave me the opportunity to purchase clothing my parents could never afford to buy me. I felt so independent and confident.

My best friend, Frankie, was my better half throughout my public school educational experience. We had known each other since the third grade and over the years had grown closer than sisters. We were involved in everything together. From hanging out, studying, attending club meetings and outings, tutoring each other in areas we struggled in, and attending church services and youth group meetings, we were one another's sidekicks—we were "joined at the hip," Mrs. Ruiz, Frankie's mother, would often say. Our temperaments also complemented each other. While we were both shy, somewhat quirky, I was a little more assertive and at times more impulsive than Frankie. She would always encourage me to step back and analyze situations and "slow down" before making any brash decisions. Throughout elementary and middle school, Frankie usually stepped in before altercations at recess erupted into fights. I was quick tempered when it came to defending myself, and Frankie often encouraged me to utilize positive strategies to resolve conflicts. Conversely, when I felt Frankie was being too much of a pushover, I encouraged her to stick up for herself and take risks. We were a dynamic duo who would one day become "famous physicians and discover the cure for AIDS and cancer." We were each other's support network. While many of our friends and family members were not as involved or engaged with school, Frankie and I kept each other grounded because our goals and aspirations were in the same place. We wanted to succeed to be able to help friends and family members who were unable to make it. We believed getting an education was the only way to make our goals come to fruition. A couple of days before going off to college, Frankie and I made a pact that we would "use whatever skills, talents, gifts, God has blessed us with to change the world and make it a better place—for everyone." We called this pact, the "No More Ghettos" contract.

Although many of us came from different ethnic backgrounds, we all came from the same kinds of neighborhoods and many experiences united us. There was no such thing as a social hierarchy. We were all working-class people of color going through many of the same struggles and challenges in our daily lives. Many of our parents were immigrants escaping a past of destitution and despair. Our parents pursued dreams and goals that might someday become manifest in the lives of their children. However, many students did not have a support system that helped them buffer much of the negativity surrounding their daily lives. It was all the more difficult for my friends who came from single-parent homes, who were foster children who experienced abuse and neglect, who were victims of domestic violence, or whose parents were substance abusers. Many of my peers who lacked a support system that would enable them to envision prospects for a more promising future just lost hope. Crystal Ruiz, one of my closest friends during middle and high school, dropped out and started dealing drugs because she did not believe that school would help her get anywhere. Crystal needed "money now to help my family, myself, and my mom—aint no one else gonna do it for me—I can't sit on my ass waiting for school to get me what I need...what my family needs." Crystal felt she did not have time to wait around for diplomas or college degrees because she felt she was neglecting the immediate needs in her family. She had four younger siblings to look after and a mother who was mentally ill. She never met her father. Her family's well-being was her responsibility.

Although many of the students in my class dropped out of high school before graduation, some of us still worked hard toward envisioning prospects for a brighter future. Something always told me there was more to life outside of my present reality. Although I did not know what that reality looked like, I hoped for a better tomorrow, dreamed of a brighter future just over the horizon, and always tried to change the circumstances I had control over. When I was a child, I imagined I had the world in my hands—I could change almost anything so long as I worked hard and prayed harder. I carried this blind determination with me throughout my life believing there was always something I could say or do to change situations that had the potential to undermine my goals or aspirations. Nothing would get in the way of my future. As I grew older, and the situations surrounding my life continued to change, I sometimes struggled to accept those things I could not change. When circumstances threatened my sense of responsibility, my determination to secure important aspects of my life would skew my rationality.

When it came to college, I had no idea what I was getting myself into. The fact that I was going to college was already a huge step for a young woman in my family. Not only was I going to college, I was going to one of the best liberal arts colleges in the country. I had no idea what that meant. It was not until I arrived that I felt the sting of isolation that accompanied my awareness of color and the implications of difference that separated me from the majority of my peers.

Move-in day at college was an experience I will carry with me the rest of my life. Just as I crammed the last box of my belongings into the trunk of my mother's Mitsubishi Galant, my brother drew my attention toward a fern growing in a tiny fissure between the sidewalk and the wall of my apartment building. "See Jessie, that's you right there. You gonna make it." I stared at the fern for a moment wondering how life could sprout in such a miniscule, virtually arid world. I admired the fern for its strength and determination—for its ability to thrive despite such unfavorable conditions. Nevertheless, I realized the fern stood alone. Questions began to flash through my mind: Where did everyone go? Where was my brother? My cousins? My childhood friends? Growing up, I was convinced we were all headed toward the same goals, destined for a chance at a better life. Enmeshed in my quest for success was the safety and well-being of my loved ones. When I arrived at college, I realized I was alone. All of the familiarity that surrounded my everyday existence at home was gone. I was dreadfully alone.

When I reached my dorm room, I remember standing amidst my belongings not knowing where to begin. My roommate's family all joined in to help Olivia get settled. Mom left the instant I transported all of my belongings into my dorm room. One terse good-bye and she was off. No surprise there. She was afraid I would see her cry. Out of the corner of my eye, I observed my roommate and her family as they unpacked and organized her belongings. My bedroom at home was nowhere near the size of my dorm room. Where would I begin? Making my bed seemed like the simplest feat to accomplish at the moment. As I unpacked my bed set, I stared off into the distance for a moment as I remembered my mother's final words: "Don't ever forget who loves you, who you are, and where you come from." At the time, my mother's counsel seemed more like an admonition than a word of advice. I awoke from my reverie when my roommate's sister tugged my shoulder and offered to help me arrange my belongings. I do not remember responding but sure enough Nicole began to help me set my bedsheets. A few moments later I began to converse with my roommate and her family. I learned that my roommate's father was an engineering professor at Dartmouth and her mother was a stay-at-home mother with a college degree. After asking me a couple of questions about my neighborhood and background, Mr. Hanneman immediately commented on my use of *slang* in my vocabulary: "so—what exactly do you mean by *mad* hot?" Silence. What didn't he understand?

"Well, umm, I mean that...umm—I mean it's like...its really warm."

"ohh...ha ha ha...Ok—well then," he replied as his wife interjected:

"And your parents...what do they do for a living?"

"Well, my dad works as an assistant cook at a hospital. And my mom, she's a cashier at a pharmacy downtown," I responded.

"Oh, ok. That must be nice...uh...to work in Manhattan."

I mean if you enjoy being treated like a second-class citizen, I suppose it would be nice to work on Madison Avenue. Customers often denigrate employees like my mother because they are perceived as dim-witted, incompetent, and altogether uneducated ghetto trash because of their accents. Yes, Ms. Hanneman, I can see how working downtown would be nice for individuals who enjoy that type of maltreatment on a daily basis. As much as I wanted to speak my mind, I held my tongue. I merely nodded my head after her response. I was beginning to get accustomed to the awkward silence that followed my responses to their questions. I did not understand why, but they seemed a lot more uncomfortable than I was. Mr. Hanneman and his wife left later on that afternoon. Mr. Hanneman's final words: "You might want to write down some of those slang words and definitions you commonly use—I have a feeling Olivia will return home sounding a little like you." I smiled and shook Mr. Hanneman's hand.

A couple of hours later, my hallmate's mother invited me into her daughter's room. "I saw your picture in the student directory—it says here that you are from Brooklyn...I am so happy my daughter lives right across from you. You are Latina, right? Maybe you can teach my daughter Spanish, I dunno—teach her about your culture...I'm so excited!" Once again, I responded in silence. I nodded my head, shook my hallmate's hand, and walked back to my dorm room. I never felt so confused in my life. That day set the precedent for the interactions and events that would shape my college experience thereafter.

My relationship with my roommate and hallmates started out fine. I treated and spoke to them just as I communicated with my friends from home. However, it was not long before I began to understand the implications of our difference. I could not relate to many of the subjects they discussed because I never encountered many of the authors they studied throughout their educational careers. They often made references to American classics that I had never heard of: *Anne of Green Gables* was among the most popular. They were astonished to hear that I had never read or watched such a "timeless classic."

I was told I had a Spanish accent, that I used "interesting street vernacular," that I spoke "urban." I was asked if I was ever shot at or stabbed, if I was "mixed or half-black," if I had any children. One student also asked me how it felt to be a product of affirmative action. I tried my best to ignore many of these comments. I needed patience because I realized I was also learning from their experiences and backgrounds. However, when I was called a fugitive, my relationship with my roommates and hallmates changed indelibly. That afternoon I had my headphones on as I worked on problem sets for my math class. My roommate and a couple of hallmates trotted into our dorm room. "There's my little fugitive," my roommate blurted out. One of my hallmates intervened and inquired why she called me a fugitive. "I mean, she's Puerto Rican. She understands." Everyone giggled and laughed, and I ripped off my headphones. For a moment I feared my temper would get the best of me. I did not understand what one thing had to do with the other, but something inside me burned. Nevertheless, as much as I wanted to say something, anything, I could not utter a word. I was perplexed. Why am I a fugitive? Because I am Puerto Rican? Or is it, I am Puerto Rican because I am a fugitive? Does being Puerto Rican somehow imply that I am a fugitive? And if so, HOW AND WHY?

I lost trust in my roommate and many of my hallmates after that day. While we all remained friends, I kept them at a safe distance, and our conversations did not deviate from normal everyday exchanges. As different as their experiences were, I never made generalizations or erroneous interpretations about them or their backgrounds. I resented the comments they made about me, my experience, my ethnicity, my speech patterns, my style of dress, etc. I hated every minute of it. The majority of the time I simply did not understand how anyone could have such perceptions about my people or me. I also could not believe how such intellectually gifted people could make such misguided generalizations and assumptions. What I found most frustrating was their attitude toward my annoyance at their ignorant statements. They often chastised me for being "way too sensitive" and assured me that they could make such comments because they were my friends and meant no harm.

Those initial interactions with my roommate and hallmates affected my interactions with my peers thereafter. As the semester progressed, I heard more and more comments that undermined my self-esteem. I was no longer as confident as I once was. I became much more reticent and reserved. I did not want to share my perspectives with anyone because I was afraid it would give people more reason to judge me. I just wanted to chill with my peers and not worry about difference. I did not want to be different any longer. My difference made me stick out like a sore thumb when all I desired to do was chill and fit in.

When it came to academic life, I quickly learned that my best was not good enough. Quite frankly, my best could not get me a D in chemistry. I came into school wanting to be a doctor. That was my lifelong dream. However, when our chemistry professor informed us he would start the semester operating on the assumption that we learned chapters one through five in high school, I knew I was in for trouble. I was lost from day one. However, I was determined to learn what I did not know and ultimately catch up to my professor's lectures. Lab work was another story. I had never seen half of the materials and gadgets we were using to conduct our experiments. When I asked my lab instructor how to use certain tools or equipment, she would not bother to answer my questions. She often shook her head and told me to "hit the books" and get a personal tutor. I dropped chemistry after failing the numerous quizzes and lab exercises that I tried so hard to pass. I had never tried so hard at something and still failed. I became angry at college for taking my dream away from me—for making me feel incompetent and lazy. I also struggled in my other classes because I did not have the writing skills that my professors expected.

After a while, I stopped caring about my education. I felt so guilty for leaving my family and friends only to enroll in an institution I did not fit into. After a while, I did not want to fit anywhere at this college. I wanted to leave and forget all about my disheartening experiences. If this was what college was really supposed to be like, I wanted nothing to do with it. After my freshman year, I decided I would drop out and get a job to continue to support my family. This decision seemed sensible at the time. I knew I was capable enough to work. I had worked since I was 14 years old. I was tired of putting my all into something that failed me time and time again. College showed me I could not measure up to my professor's expectations even when I gave it my best. It was not my fault that the schools I attended were under-funded and that the math, science, and English curricula were consistently watered down to help more failing students pass state exams. When I arrived at college, I could not think, speak, or write like my peers. Who was I kidding?

At the end of my freshman year, though, I got to know students like me, some of whom came from neighborhoods that were in close proximity to my home. It was refreshing to find people who had experienced many of the same hardships upon arriving at college. It felt good to know that I was not the only one. I was not making things up. By my sophomore year of college there was a group of about 10 of us who ate, studied, made *arroz con habichuelas* (rice and beans), watched movies, went bowling, and often vented about our experiences at Swarthmore and our struggles to balance our sense of responsibility back home with our academic obligations. This support network helped us to stay focused on the greater goals ahead of us and overcome the difficulties that often demoralized our efforts to succeed. We were destined to make it—no matter what the cost.

The second semester of my freshman year I also took my first education class, where I started learning about students like me who came from inner city areas and attended public schools that lacked essential resources and suffered teacher deficits and administrative support. I also came to know professors who were willing to help me learn how to write and think about concepts that were important to me. When I interacted with these professors, I did not feel dumb or incompetent. A precious handful of professors helped me to understand that my lack of preparation prior to college did not reflect my intellectual capacity and that it was only a matter of time before I would be able to compete confidently at the level of my peers. My professors' drive to help me write, think, and speak at college helped me to embrace the reality that I had the potential to achieve anything so long as I was determined to work hard and keep moving.

The morning I decided to meet Red for the exchange, I could hear my mother reciting the psalms and hymns she loved so much. As hard as I tried, I could not shake off one verse: "Even though I walk through the valley of the shadow of death, I will fear no evil...for thou art with me." When all was said and done, I realized I was far more afraid of the consequences of owning a gun than I was of anyone harming my family members. In the hood, violence never ends. I refused to feed the cycle of violence that claims the lives of thousands of children, young people, and adults living in hoods like mine across the United States. I had faith that my family members would be safe, and I prayed for their protection every morning and every night. Today, while we live on the same block, in the same apartment, my family is still safe. In one form or another, purchasing a gun would stand in the way of my future. I simply could not let this happen.

There is no question: I will succeed. My success is based in the hearts of myriad friends and family members who continue to live out their hopes and aspirations of a better tomorrow through me. While I do not think I am special, I am loved by many people who believe in me. I cannot fail. I will not fail. There is just too much at stake.

WHAT IF I DON'T WANT TO WHISTLE?

This is the story of a young black man who grew up living with his mother and half sister in modest circumstances in south central Los Angeles. In spite of economic hardships, his mother is determined that her children receive an excellent education. Orion attends a succession of mainly white private schools that prepare him well academically, even while they undermine his sense of racial pride. His struggle to achieve a sense of self, compounded by his battles with anxiety and his insecurities concerning relationships with women, makes for a very challenging adolescence. Only late in his college years does he open up in his relations with others, question his internalized racism, and align himself positively with the black community.

It was a bright California morning, but at 7:55 my classroom with its high ceilings was still cold, and I shuddered at the prospect of discussing race that day. In my senior English class at my boarding school outside of Los Angeles, I was the only black student in a class of eight. On most days the color of my skin was not an issue, but I dreaded the times when we talked about racial matters. Although no one voiced the thought, I knew that my comments on the subject would be assumed more valid than others'.

We had been assigned two essays to read the night before. The first was a paper explaining what the term *nigger* meant for black people, and the second was about the life experience of a black man in New York City. In the latter essay, the narrator had adopted a strategy of whistling classical music during his evening strolls in order to prevent whites from crossing to the other side of the street as he approached them. My muscles tightened as I anticipated the discussion, not wanting to hear ignorant remarks about race and then have to bear the weight of correcting them without appearing overly sensitive, angry, or condescending.

The class discussion began with the essay on the word *nigger*. Students searched desperately for a politically correct way to speak about the reading. "I thought it was interesting," said John tentatively and noncommittally. Brian added, "I guess it was good, but I just can't understand why black people would call themselves a name that is so insulting."

I remember the look Mr. Manson gave as he shrugged his shoulders in response to Brian's question. It was as if he were struggling to keep a straight face—like he had selected this particular reading as a practical joke. With his knowing smile, he seemed to be pointing out the stupidity of "those niggers" who don't even have enough sense not to insult each other.

I didn't know how to tell them any more eloquently than the essay had that the term *nigger* was not insulting coming from one black to another; especially when spelled with an "a" and not an "er," it was completely dissociated from the way racist whites used it, as far as my black friend Carter and I were concerned. I felt like a person of a religious faith trying to explain to nonbelievers why it was that I believed: Some things just can't be explained logically.

Not wanting to enter the conversation, I averted my eyes. My anger built; if the teacher had not understood the article and could not even regurgitate the arguments provided by the author, then why was he teaching it? Feeling powerless, I wondered what would have happened if I hadn't been present. Would the discussion have become an open forum for everyone to voice his or her condescension for blacks?

"Well, do you understand it?" Mr. Manson, as expected, asked me. I nodded in return. "Do you mind trying to explain it to us?" Even though it was a lost cause, I tried to make it clearer. Attempting to explicate the various connotations of the word *nigger*, I tripped over my words in anger and confusion for five minutes before I finally gave up all together and we moved on to the next essay regarding whistling classical music to put white people at ease. Everyone agreed that it was unfair to be black in New York and get treated as a thug. Then my friend Jay added, "Yeah, it's too bad, but at least he found a good way to get around it." There were nods all around, and I felt blood rush to my face. "That is not a viable solution to his problem," I blurted out. "The guy wasn't free! To be treated civilly you have to whistle? That means you are assumed guilty until you prove your innocence." I likened the situation to having to show someone a list of credentials, or having to shuck and jive, whenever you wanted to be treated with respect. "Can you imagine a nation of 'free men' who have to sing and dance in order to show that they aren't dangerous and be treated fairly? What would happen if you couldn't whistle? Or God forbid, didn't feel like whistling?" But I was the only person who saw how this was problematic. Reading the facial expressions around me, I could tell people thought that I was causing unnecessary trouble by being "too sensitive" about the issues, so I silenced myself.

In many ways, I fit the demographics for the stereotypical black male. I grew up in the inner city raised by a single mother without ever knowing my father. Yet, in other important ways, I do not fit the profile. My mother was an attorney, and as children my sister and I attended elite private schools on 90 percent scholarships.

My sister is three years younger than I am. We have different fathers, neither of whom ever married my mother; she tells us that at a certain age she wanted two children and then she got them—by two different men. My sister has had more contact with her father than I have had with mine. He lives in the same large West Coast city we do, and my mom and sister run into him once every couple of years, often to my sister's embarrassment.

I do not know my father at all. I am told I met him once when I was three. I'm not sure if I actually remember it or if I have constructed my memory of the incident: I just picture him lifting me up in the air in our front yard. The only photograph that survives of him is his driver's license. I know that he was 6′ 2″, weighed 201 pounds, and shares the same last name as me.

My mom used to drive me by an apartment building, pointing and saying, "That's where I met your father." That statement always left me uneasy, and I struggled to make sense of the motivations behind it. What exactly did it mean? Was it supposed to comfort me? Did it comfort her? From time to time, she would drop one-sentence descriptions of him into our conversations. "Your father was a salesman," she would say. Or, "Your father used to run track." But I never knew, for example, at what level he ran—was my father a champion? "Your father busted his leg open riding a motorcycle," she would tell me. But I didn't know if that meant he had a limp or any other physical, emotional, or psychological trauma because of the accident.

I don't think of my father too much, but as I write this I sometimes think that I might remind my mother of him, perhaps when she sees me from afar, walking toward her. At times, I reflect on which of my qualities, positive and negative, might resemble his. I wonder if my mom misses him, if she ever loved him, and how long they knew each other before they slept together. I wonder if my mother told my father and my sister's father about how she wanted children. If my father is anything like me, I can imagine him doing my mom a favor and supplying her with a child. But I can't imagine what was going through his head as he agreed. Did he even care that he was going to have a child?

In the end, all I could do was try to make the very little I did know about my father fill the great void where the images and memories of him should have been. When I was in third grade, people would constantly ask me, "Don't you miss not having a father?" And eventually, I was forced to liken it to not having a tail. "Do you miss not having a tail?" I would respond. How can you miss something that you never had?

My mom and I have always had a contentious relationship. I think now, at the age of 21, that a possible source of this friction was the dysfunctional relationships she had had with men—and her consequently negative attitudes toward them— which she projected onto me. My mom may not have properly dealt with her "issues" with the men in her life, including her children's fathers and her own father as well. Oftentimes when arguing with my mother, I felt like the topic at hand had the emotional baggage of wrongs done to her years before my conception. Growing up, I could not communicate with her without her seeming to take everything as a personal attack. I think this lack of communication may have led her to sense that I wasn't appreciative of all she was doing for me—which may have been true.

My mom valued education and insisted that I go to private schools. She saw how much energy I had and knew that public school would be too trying on my patience, so she sent me to the Jordan School, an overwhelmingly white campus of five hundred students from kindergarten to eighth grade. I went to school with the sons and daughters of doctors, lawyers, business people, and movie stars. My family, however, lived in a one bedroom house that was really a garage converted into a home. Above all, my mother was a single mother supporting her family on a single salary. Although she was an attorney, she was honest—and thus not rich. My mom, my sister, and I shared one bed, which I often wet as a child. Our home was a perpetual mess, and I hated not having my own room in which I could be neat and organized, like all of my wealthy, white academic peers. I didn't care how big or how nice our house was as long as it was clean and acceptable. I never wanted to show off; I just wanted to pass by unnoticed.

Our house was in south central Los Angeles—only three blocks away from where the Reginald Denny beatings took place—and I hated returning home to it. When we got out of the car and walked to our house, me carrying my sleeping sister over my shoulder, we would have to duck behind parked vehicles when cars drove by for fear of being shot. We were never the victims of such crimes, but I do remember going to sleep with the sounds of helicopters circling around the house as if we were in a war zone. Those helicopters, I thought, were undoubtedly hunting down a black man for some asinine crime. The noise of the propellers made me think of a plantation owner thundering on horseback through his fields just to instill fear in his slaves.

We drove one and a half hours each day to get to and from school. Our 1979 blue Toyota Corolla looked like a relic from World War II, recently hauled out of a junkyard and destined to spend the remaining years of its life as an embarrassment to two black children going to an affluent white school. It was the single most potent symbol of the divide between our peers and us. I didn't care where I lived because the kids at school didn't have to see that; but they did see our car, and it was like a huge propaganda machine announcing the arrival and departure of the two poorest kids at Jordan. At the traffic circle where everyone stood waiting for friends, we would get out of the car and bowls of cereal and other junk would fall out, creating an embarrassing mess.

All through my time at Jordan, I stole from my peers—things like electronic games and portable audio devices, not for the enjoyment of the goods themselves, but to wield some social clout. I wanted to walk around with an accessory like all the other kids who had Game Boys and Casio watches that functioned as calculators and stored phone numbers. After stealing though, I'd usually feel so guilty that I tried to throw the stolen items away.

I was constantly comparing myself to the students of my school. I remember in kindergarten asking my mom questions about myself as we drove into Jordan. I once wondered, "Why can't I be white?" Somehow, I already felt like my identity was unsatisfactory. In fact, until I was 12, my experiences were such that I had concluded that all white people were rich and all black people poor. When I revealed this to my mom, she was shocked.

From an early age, I was frustrated by our family's financial situation, which neither my mother nor I could change, and at school I felt isolated and cut off from any maternal protection. As a result, I felt as though my mom were the reason for all of the injustices in my life, and so I resented her. She in turn began to resent the situation she found herself in—a single mother working very hard to send two children to an elite private school, one of whom, a son, who would openly tell people that he disliked or hated her.

I remember being disappointed in kindergarten and first grade when at schoolwide recitals I would perform in front of an auditorium filled with nicely dressed parents and not see my mom. It became worse after the recital. "Perhaps I just missed her," I'd think to myself. "She'll come through in the end. She's my mother." I would rush out of the back doors of the auditorium and run toward the front with all of my peers expecting to see my mom walk out. But she didn't. I was introduced to a strange new world of being alone.

In third grade, we had a Thanksgiving potluck at school, where everyone brought in a dish and the children dressed up. I remember the children laughing at me and the way I ate, saying I was making a mess. I felt so bad and embarrassed that I began to cry and didn't finish the meal. When my mom came and asked why I looked so down, I told her that I hadn't gotten to eat any of the pumpkin pie that I had brought in; one of the teachers explained what had happened and how the kids had made fun of me. After hearing the story, my mom went out and bought me a pie, thinking it would solve the problem. But it didn't, and I had learned my lesson: When I needed my mom to be there she would not be. I knew that she cared, but I also felt that she knew nothing about and had no influence over the world I was living in at school.

In the mornings, I would occasionally arrive late, which I thought was a situation to be worked out with my mother. Yet the teacher still chose to call me out and humiliate me in front of my peers, telling me to be on time. In the afternoons, sometimes my mom had to come late to pick me up, and members of the faculty would have to stay after school and wait until she arrived before they could leave. I felt guilty when this happened; the teachers' body language and curt sentences were as loud and powerful as any insults they could have said. I knew they were mad at me and my mother, but what could *I* do?

In the new environment of school, my connections to my family and home life seemed to be severed and to serve no purpose; so I had to teach myself how to survive and adapt. My mom was like a god. She had created me and the situation I found myself in, but she was rarely present. To trust in her after experiencing the pain I felt in her absence would have required a faith so immense that I would have been crushed under its weight.

In light of the distance between my mother and myself, relationships with others became more and more relevant in my life. In south central Los Angeles, I had only a handful of black companions; the Hispanics were all friendly, and they were mainly who I hung out with. My most lasting impressions of black people were of the couple of black neighborhood bullies who had beaten me up and stolen my bikes multiple times. Meanwhile, the black kids at the Boys' and Girls' Club I belonged to made fun of me for the way I spoke, saying I sounded "white." I began to view young blacks as threatening and unaccepting of me. The problem wasn't that I myself did not feel I was black; a quick glance at my exposed arms and legs clarified that. It was more a question of how everyone else viewed me. In the black community, there is always a concern that successful black people are trying to deny their "blackness." Certainly, some blacks feel that once they are successful they have nothing to do with the black "struggle." But this was never how I felt.

In the sixth grade, my mom signed me up for the Big Brother, Little Brother program in the hopes of providing me with a long overdue source of male guidance. A long period of time elapsed before I was officially assigned a Big Brother, so in the interim my mother located a coworker who was willing to temporarily act as one. Sherwin was a very friendly older black male in his early fifties. We were both interested in computers, so we spent all of our time playing video games and building machines. He was probably the best black male role model I ever had: He was intelligent, patient, honest, and friendly. However, three years after we had applied, I was finally officially matched with a Big Brother; when this happened— and when he started coming on to my mother—Sherwin was phased out of my life.

My new Big Brother, Jim, was a 30-year-old, white, Jewish male. Over the 11 years that we have been paired together, Jim has provided me with a considerable amount of financial aid and has always been there for me emotionally as well. However, there has been a lot of tension and little communication between Jim and my mother. On my mother's part, the conflict lies in the fact that Jim is a male and wealthy, which has led her to believe that I would immediately assume that whatever he says is of more worth than what she says.

I went to high school at Blair, a mostly white, affluent boarding school of 250 students, and my first year there was marked by an increasing sense of anxiety. I was tired of being pigeonholed as black and seeing the contributions of my "race" over the pages of history being limited to slaves and uppity freedom fighters. There seemed to be only three blacks worthy of study: Martin Luther King, Malcolm X, and Rosa Parks—as though blacks had made no contributions or changes outside of the civil rights movement. I felt that these heroes lived in a social and political climate far different from my own, and I found it very difficult to incorporate their lessons into my daily life. I was also reluctant to accept any of the alternative black role models the teachers presented to me because they didn't speak to any of my personal interests; they were not meant for me specifically but for any black person, and they were not appreciated solely for their talents. Their first achievement was that they were black and whatever professional accomplishments they had made came second. I wanted the order of appreciation switched: I wished their professional talents to be appreciated first and foremost, with their race mentioned as a trivial afterthought.

Another source of the increasing sense of anxiety I felt upon entering Blair was the socially challenging environment. At boarding school, for the first time I spent protracted periods of time with my peers outside of an academic setting. During my freshman year, I was bothered by a group of kids who seemed rebellious and claimed to be thuggish in spite of the fact that they were attending an elite boarding school. As a result, my style of dress changed from the tough boy gangster image, with big, baggy pants and basketball jerseys, to one of well-fitting khakis and polo T-shirts. This decision was of some importance to me because I felt that in rejecting that thuggish style of dress I was rejecting my culture. But dressing in a way that seemed through association to glorify drugs, money, violence, ignorance, and the mistreatment of women wasn't a true reflection of what my life was about. Similarly, in seventh grade I had stopped listening to the rap and hip-hop radio stations because the deejays presented themselves as ignorant. I wasn't rejecting black culture or music in general, but I was rejecting rap's nihilistic messages and what the deejays were choosing to define as black culture. I was not a "sell-out" or someone filled with self-hatred. Viscerally, I just could not accept negative images that harmed my sense of self-worth.

During my time at Blair, my only black friend was Carter. He had a short temper and an aggressive personality. His outlets were poetry and basketball. Although we were the only black males in our class, I did not feel closer to him as a result. In fact, our sociocultural differences made me feel somewhat estranged from him. I did worry sometimes that I gave blacks like Carter the impression that I wasn't proud of my heritage because I spoke so differently.

During one spring break, my mom invited Carter to visit our house. This was the first time a friend of mine had ever come to stay at my home, and I did not know how he would react to our circumstances. Also, although we were of the same race and from similar economic backgrounds, it was difficult for to me decipher Carter's speech. With the language and cultural barrier between us, I began to lose faith in the belief that all blacks could understand one another due to skin color. My skin color did not help me decode the strange words that permeated his vocabulary, like "yo," "B," "tap," "chill," and "bitch" (which was used to refer to all women).

On the first day of spring break, we rented movies from the public library, and as we watched one around midnight, we began debating the movie's story line. Soon our debate escalated into a heated argument that moved beyond the movie's plot. Eventually Carter became enraged and screamed, "You don't even trust me!" He told me that earlier that day he had asked me what kind of music I listened to and I had told him rap, but when he looked through my CD collection, he found that I also listened to classical and alternative rock. He seemed hurt by this, which shocked me, as I didn't think I had the ability to upset anyone at all— let alone Carter, who seemed so tough on the exterior.

I hadn't told him what other music I listened to because I still wasn't secure enough in my identity, racially or otherwise, to openly share who I was and what my interests were. Some of the music I listened to was made by white people, and I didn't want him to consider me a "sell-out." I didn't know how to tell him that

I had been beaten up and made fun of as a kid for acting and talking "white." At the end of the conversation, he made me confident that he was not going to judge me based on the genre of music I enjoyed, and I felt comfortable opening up to him.

By the end of the vacation, I was using his lingo nonstop. Once he referred to my mom as a bitch but then immediately apologized. "That's alright, I know what you mean," I said. But averting his eyes, he said, "Naw, that's not cool. I really do like her." And I believed him.

Throughout our time at Blair, Carter and I continued to grow closer, especially after I spent a week at his apartment. I felt I understood him better after seeing where he was from, yet I still wondered what he thought about my blackness, as race rarely came up as a topic between us.

Because of our close relationship, I asked Carter to write me a peer recommendation for college. It was at this point that he finally allayed some of my insecurities by telling me that he did not feel that I was a "sell-out." Still somewhat unsure, I asked him about the way I spoke. He considered for a moment and replied, "That's just the way you speak. You change when you are around me and when you speak to a Mexican and when you are in French class. You just have a knack with languages and you change accordingly. It's just about learning how to adapt." These words were some of the most comforting I have ever heard.

Besides Carter, my two other best friends in high school were Phillip and Jay. Jay and I were extremely similar. We both enjoyed math and were rather serious. We used to exchange stories about how we would both wake up on Saturday mornings during junior high and spend the first couple of hours in bed just thinking. We had similar conceptions about society and the same insecurities about what qualified as intelligence. Both procrastinators, we bonded over our consequentially subpar performances on papers and final exams.

Regardless of grades, Jay was implicitly considered one of the smartest guys in our class and almost everyone respected him. He was extremely logical and did everything for a reason, whereas I would act on instinct and impulse. Jay understood me better than anyone else and taught me a lot of lessons about what it means to be a friend. I had misguided ideas about the nature of friendships: I thought that the minute you got into an argument or a fight that you should call it off. It was hard for me to entertain the idea that you could be mad at someone you still liked. Jay realized that if I did something that appeared to be done out of malice, it was probably because I didn't really know the source of my anger or that I was trying to get attention. He was a good listener, and I could tell him about very personal things.

Phillip joined us during our sophomore year. The grandson of a famous playwright, Phillip was bright and good humored and had impeccable taste in literature and music; and he would never lower his standards to suit the politics of skin color. When I stumbled upon a black hip-hop trio in his CD collection, my curiosity was piqued. I had not been impressed when I had heard one or two of their songs before, but seeing that Phillip owned their album led me to reconsider their merit.

When Phillip took a course on "Black Authors" while I opted for a class on "The Boarding School Experience," he approached me curious as to why I hadn't taken the course he was taking. I didn't know how to explain to him that I felt estranged from schools' representations of blacks. However, as the term progressed and he read books by Toni Morrison and Ralph Ellison and insisted on how good they were, I wished that I had taken the course. In these ways, Phillip helped me to find my way back into black culture, music, and literature.

One of Jay's most important contributions to our friendship was encouraging me when I decided to start seeing a counselor for my anxiety during my freshman year. In fact, to my surprise, all of my friends fully supported me in this. I saw the counselor once a week for half a year, and though she didn't cure me of my anxiety, she did help me cope with it. One of her best suggestions was that I keep a journal. I began writing almost daily to loosen the grip of emotional paralysis through self-expression.

I remember the first day I began writing. It was a free period and rain was falling outside the library window. I was feeling anxious but started writing in my spiral-bound notebook anyway; and before long the words just flowed out of me. I felt like I was in the throes of mania. There was something magical but at the same time sort of sickening to me about the whole process—as though it were an unhealthy happiness. My thoughts were definitely me, but they were frightening. Excuse this comparison, but I related my journal writing to the work of Goya: beautifully dark and complicated pieces that reflect an intelligent but tortured mind.

Writing became my outlet; I wrote about everything. I let my friends read my journal until junior year of high school—it felt good to get things off my chest and share them with someone else. I felt that I was being my true and honest self in my journal entries, and I wanted everyone to know the part of me that never got a chance to surface in daily conversations. At one point, Phillip had stumbled across a passage where I admitted to feeling somehow incapacitated by my skin color. After reading the entry, he approached me confused, wanting to talk about it more. He felt for me, not in a pitying way, but as a friend, and the way he approached me made a huge impact on the response he was given. Had I been approached in a condescending way, I would have been defensive about the inquiry. Although we never got around to fully addressing the issue, it was his concern that mattered most to me.

My close guy friends and my writings helped me to develop and further understand myself, but I still wasn't comfortable around girls. I never would have asked out Karen, my first girlfriend, left to my own devices. I hadn't much experience with girls, and I didn't quite know what would be required of me and what role I was supposed to play. When Karen told me after dinner one night in tears that she liked me, I wasn't sure what to do. I either didn't believe it or didn't know how to take it; I think a lot of this had to do with the lack of love I had for myself.

Karen and I dated only for a short while during the freshman year (although I never told my mom about her, because she had said that I couldn't date until

I was 30). Suffering from acute anxiety at the time, I ended up saying things such as "Let's just go out on weekends," thinking that over the weekends, without the pressures of school, I could be a better boyfriend to her. But this suggestion made me seem shallow—and even sleazy. My behavior was sometimes aggressive and cruel, and I realize that this was, in part, a result of my frustration for feeling forced into the relationship. It wasn't just Karen; I couldn't cope with the idea of going out with anyone. I felt that it was another part that I would have to play that I didn't have the lines for.

I do not feel that my relationship with Karen, or with any other girl, was complicated by my race. Sometimes I wondered if girls were attracted to me because of my skin color, but I am fairly positive that no one dated me to live out any sort of fantasy about black men.

Although I didn't understand this at the time, I feel that my *own* insecurities about my race did permeate my relationships and other aspects of my life. It took my Asian American advisor to point out to me the importance of being aware of your own race. Sophomore year, he wrote on my report card that he was concerned that I had not begun to address the importance of race in my life. My mom agreed with him and brought the issue to my attention, as race had always been a vital component of her life, and she wanted to make it important in my life as well. My mom made whites seem like the enemy, but in attending primarily white schools my whole life I did not see how being race conscious was going to help—especially when *I* was the one who would have to negotiate life amongst whites, without her there to support me as I treaded alone on enemy territory.

Instead of making enemies of whites, I tried to minimize my differences by ignoring the issues surrounding race. I was afraid that if I confronted them, I would suffocate under the pressure of a problem I had no means of resolving. So when my mother and my advisor brought the matter up, I didn't know how to react.

I didn't *know* what it means to be black. I didn't feel *black*. I felt like me. I didn't think that I had any contributions to make to any discussions about "blackness" that would aid in a white person's understanding of the concept. I had always attended white schools, and I had not thought that the people there were racist; I had white friends who seemed to like me. Looking back, I think the truth was that I thought we *were* somehow inferior; I hadn't yet learned what a black person had to be proud about. What I associated with black culture were dashikis and dreadlocks and other things that weren't a part of my daily life.

When I went back to school the day after my advisor had spoken to me, I ignored his suggestion. I didn't know what to do about my "problem," so I avoided confronting it. I did make advances on the relationship front, however. I began to realize that I didn't have to treat women the way I had treated Karen. The turnaround was mostly precipitated by my love for my sister, with whom I had an ideal relationship. I thought I should try to model a relationship with potential girlfriends after the one I had with her: one of mutual respect and understanding. My love for my sister became a mantra for the rest of my high school career. She earned my respect because she was always there for me, well-spoken, and able to get along well with my mother.

My next serious relationship occurred during my junior year in high school. Her name was Nicole, and she was a freshman and the youngest of three sisters, all of whom lived fairly troubled lives, dealing with the stigma of coming from a divorced household and the fact that their mother was dying of brain cancer. I probably would never have asked Nicole out, but she waited patiently and let me come around in my own way. Nicole was important to me, and I was determined to learn from the lessons of my relationship with Karen. I decided that no matter what I felt, I would not allow myself to take out any undue aggressions on her. Throughout our time together, I felt that I was able to accomplish this, but we broke up nonetheless due to extenuating circumstances.

Nicole's mother died the summer after we broke up. We tried to get back together my senior fall, but it didn't work. She kept referring to jokes that we made during our last year of dating. It felt like she was trying to return to the period of our past when her mother was still living; until I told her, she hadn't noticed this. I explained to her how much I cared for her and that I didn't think it would be healthy for us to see each other under the circumstances. She agreed that it would probably be for the best to break up.

Overall, I enjoyed our relationship; it taught me how to identify and channel my feelings and to treat people appropriately. Although sad, I left Nicole feeling good about my ability to maintain a healthy relationship with a woman. With that in place, I moved on once again to the issue of race that I had been putting off confronting.

One day after sports practice, my friends and I went to visit Benson, a sophomore, in his dormitory. He had all sorts of expensive digital audio-visual equipment and told us how he had caught his friend Tony on tape falling off a couch and hitting his mouth against the coffee table, and that we should watch it. He added that Tony had said some pretty offensive stuff in the video and that he didn't want us to take offense, eyeing me warily. We assured him that it couldn't be that bad, so he began the film. When we saw our friend hit his head against the coffee table, we were left so amused that we asked eagerly what came next. Benson said that the following part was offensive, and he didn't want to show us, but we pushed and he reluctantly played it.

In the video, Benson had asked Tony, who was white, to say something, and he chose to say, "The Negro should go back to Africa." Given that Tony's style— his dress, musical tastes, and parlance—was strongly influenced by black culture, it was shocking that he purported to hold these racist beliefs. Once we had seen the clip, everyone turned to me, expecting me to be vehemently upset; but I didn't know what to be. I was surprised and speechless and tried to shrug it off. Was this racism, I wondered? Did this often happen when I wasn't in the room? And if it did, what was to be done about it? I began to feel helpless. If this was racism, who was there that I could tell? And what would *they* do about it? This was one of the first experiences where I learned a harsh reality about the way others viewed my race.

I also learned a lesson about a condescending dimension of affirmative action during a school assembly my junior year for the highly selective National Merit Scholarships. The headmaster read the names of the winners, and to my surprise mine was called. I was wary; surely I had not done as well as the other people being called up. When I was handed my award, I immediately noticed that it was of a different size and color as the others: My award was for noteworthy achievement in the African American community. I was incensed and embarrassed. Why the special attention? No one else noticed this discrepancy, but I wanted to be treated fairly and not judged by a different measuring stick. It made me feel that society had decided that my race was inferior and that we should be rewarded for whatever work we could produce, regardless of its quality.

I graduated from high school without having resolved how I felt about race and what it meant to me to be black. When I arrived at college, I was still very unsure of my own identity. Conversely, my freshman-year roommate, who was a Native American, was very proud of his culture. He felt no shame about his heritage, and would tell me about going to the Native American Society and how he took part in a pow wow. I admired the way he spoke confidently and respectfully about his people. I had thought that any society that was not completely in sync with mainstream white culture would feel ashamed of their differences. I was surprised that he didn't feel this way. I wanted to ask where he got his pride, hoping that it would rub off on me.

Inspired by my roommate, I joined the African American Society (AAS) on campus. Although I had long felt distanced from the black community and feared that they might not accept me, I participated timidly in their events, and, in spite of the fact that I felt a little awkward, I never stopped. I had joined the AAS not in order to have fun, but out of a sense of responsibility. I felt like I owed it to the black community. Still, I didn't know how to "behave" with other members of the AAS. I was afraid that my awkwardness would once again evoke emotional abuse and that I would relive my childhood experiences at the Boys' and Girls' Club.

A turning point in the formation of my racial identity occurred my sophomore year during an off-campus program in Barcelona. There, I found out, much to my surprise, that I would be living with a black Spanish family with three brothers close to my age. I was shocked. Up until that point, the members of my biological family in the States had been the only black people that I knew of that spoke Spanish.

I do many things that most stereotypical black people would not—and every time I find others of my race doing the same thing I am shocked. It's as if doing something positive or unique makes me an outsider in the black community. It could be that there are lots of blacks who don't like violence, like to read, are fond of the idea of falling in love, and enjoy theological debates. I, however, have not met them. With the way mass media implies that the only way a black male can succeed is if he portrays himself as ignorant or violent, I don't think that many blacks believe that they can do otherwise: It wouldn't be black. Although aware of these messages, I was not impervious to them, and I felt that when I met my Spanish brothers, I had to act rough to show that I was worthy of their camaraderie.

At one point when I was on the verge of proving my toughness, my younger brother stepped back with a surprised look that seemed to say, "What is this guy doing?" The looks on his older brothers' faces betrayed similar sentiments. Although they did seem sort of impressed with my bravado, they did not make generalizations about my being just another rough black American. Instead they said, "*Pues mira que fuerte Orion es*—Look how strong Orion is." It was like being looked at as if I were an individual human being. It made me realize that blacks in the States, or at least me, tended to look at other blacks as if they are animals incapable of acting otherwise.

My journey to Spain was the first time since seventh grade that I attempted to formulate a different definition of "blackness." I decided that the concept of blackness was an illusion. I decided to free myself from any definitions of blackness and to simply live and be whomever I wanted. I decided to pursue whatever interests I had without fear of them not being the "black thing" to do. In Spain, I felt free to define myself, to learn to snowboard, to read, to write, to learn French, to skateboard, and to play guitar. When I returned from Spain, I told my family and friends how blessed I felt for having had the educational opportunity to travel to Europe.

Yet, while I had come much further in comprehending myself, I was still having trouble understanding the opposite sex. By senior year, I had not yet had a steady girlfriend my entire time at college and I was still a virgin. I called Jim, my Big Brother, who insisted that finding a girlfriend was not as hard as I was making it out to be. He suggested that perhaps I should start considering that there might be a more serious issue at work. I started thinking seriously about all of my sexual and romantic experiences. I then told him how many of my babysitters and I had abusive sexual relationships when I was younger and that I was concerned that this might affect how I related to women. Although I had written about being sexualized by my 20-something-year-old baby-sitters in my journal, I had never mentioned it to any adult. After a short silence, Jim replied that he felt this new information was beyond his training as an amateur psychologist and that I should seek professional help.

So in the fall of my senior year I went to see a counselor at school about my love life—because I was 21, in college, and a virgin. I was prepared to open up and talk about my babysitters, my mom, my sister, Nicole, and Karen. I wanted to be as candid as possible so that the counselor could see the situation as clearly as possible.

As it turned out the psychiatrist was a black man, which was helpful to a certain extent because I felt I could tell him openly about my recent concerns about dating someone black. He asked me if I thought it mattered or if I had any preference about dating one race or another, and I told him no. If I liked a girl, then I liked a girl; it just so happened that most of the girls I had an interest in were white. I did, however, think Hispanic, Indian, and from time to time black women were attractive, too. I thought that the relatively limited number of instances in which I had dated or had had interests in black women was due to the scarcity of blacks in my educational environments. For the greater part of my life, I have been surrounded by whites. And the blacks I did see tended to have different social backgrounds from me and so I didn't always get along with them.

I told my counselor how I felt an uncomfortable pressure to date and marry a black woman. I had overheard my mother in an argument with one of my older cousins about interracial marriages. She was yelling in the kitchen that she would not even speak with my wife if she were nonblack. My cousin was asking her, "But what if your son met a nice Asian lady in college and wanted to marry her? Would you still disapprove?" My mother responded that she would not allow her to come over to the house. She began referring to my wife-to-be as my "decision." She said, "Well, he and his 'decision' can stay and live on one side of the city, but if he wants to come visit me, he'll just have to leave his 'decision' at home."

Although my counselor didn't really help me solve my insecurities about feeling pressure to date a black woman, a good Hispanic friend of mine, Ivan, told me not to worry about what others thought, because a relationship involves just two people. I asked him if he felt pressure from his parents to marry someone Hispanic, and he said no. He said that his mom would probably prefer it if he did, but she wanted him to be happy more than anything. He encouraged me to understand that my mom might be acting out of love because she thinks it would be easier for me to marry within my race.

I feel certain that, in general, the representation of my race in my school experience has had negative effects on my self-esteem. I hated discussions that singled me out as different, and perhaps inferior, to my peers. I have mingled in educational communities that are predominantly white, and this racial isolation led me to endure long periods of insecurity about my blackness. I eventually formed a sense of colorblindness, believing that race is irrelevant in human relations. The merits of blacks are so rarely praised by the dominant social group in America that it is often hard to be convinced of our self-worth. Up until my senior year at college, my education took me away from a culture where my ethnicity is seen as a source of pride.

Still, my private education was in many ways helpful in providing me with opportunities. I am currently a week away from graduating from an elite college that I may never have attended had it not been for the unbending will of my mother, who insisted that I attend a secondary institution of rigorous academic standards. I feel indebted for the many experiences my education has given me: running in the country, camping, rock climbing, horseback riding, deejaying for a radio station, and teaching and living abroad. I am grateful that I can read, write, and express myself eloquently; but most of all I appreciate the confidence my education has granted me in terms of my academic ability.

Now, one week before my college graduation, I look back and reflect on my journey from being a black child who wanted to live without race to becoming a person who is beginning to formulate a valid racial identity. I have come to realize that in the United States a black person cannot grow up healthily without reconciling himself with his race. Although my own reconciliation with my race is not yet complete, I want to share the conclusions I have reached so far on what it means to be black with the community around me; I believe I can do that by teaching elementary school students in public school in Atlanta, which I plan to do after I graduate.

My choice in going to Atlanta is partly based on my wish to finally connect with and be surrounded and affirmed by people of my race. A Hispanic friend of mine told me that it is silly to choose where I live according to skin color, but it makes sense to me. I feel that with my personal experiences and interests I would have a lot to offer no matter where I went, but I feel that it is particularly important to provide a positive role model for other black youth perhaps in the midst of negotiating their own racial identities. I wish to counterbalance the negative portrayals of blacks with positive, truthful ones—ones that aren't created and selected by someone for financial gain. I would like the children I teach to come to whatever conclusions they want, but I want them to have more than just one definition for being "black," one that is broader than the media's portrayal. After all these years, I believe black is not incompatible with peace and happiness. Blackness is what I want it to be.

ORION: SEVEN YEARS LATER

Seven years have passed since I wrote my essay during the last term of my senior year at college. In that time I've taught for five years with the School District of Philadelphia, acquired a master's degree in special education, and become a landlord who owns 11 rental units. This fall I began business school in Chicago. I recognize that in my original essay, black identity, affirmative action, romantic relationships, and family were some of the major themes. In this follow-up, I hope to return to these topics and to address others that are now more pressing for me to explore, such as spirituality, which I want to touch on first.

Spirituality and mysticism are important paths that I've been exploring since completing college. For a long time, I tried to view the world through the lenses my education had given me, but I have since come to realize that there are ways of seeing the world that simply were not encompassed in Western thought. Delving into Eastern philosophies validated this for me. For some time now, my heart's desire has been to be at peace with myself and to view things with perfect understanding. I think the secret to this is cultivating compassion and patience for everyone—especially oneself. To that end, I now meditate daily and keep a keen eye on my thoughts and feelings. I believe that if I am upset by a situation it is because I am viewing it incorrectly, and I enjoy taking time to reflect on my thoughts. Until I am able to remove my ego, and thus my nonpeaceful and non-compassionate feelings, from a situation, nothing can be seen clearly. While I may not be able to change all of my surroundings and circumstances, I do believe I can choose how I react to and interpret them.

BLACK IDENTITY

In my earlier biography, I discussed race as a black student who had attended a private high school where I was part of a tiny minority and as a student at an elite college, where I again was part of a small minority. Seven years later, I'm now able to discuss race as an adult teacher in Philadelphia, where most of the people I inter-act with are the same color I am. I began the first essay by describing my discomfort discussing race and racism in an all-white educational setting. To be honest, I'm not sure that I would feel any more comfortable now having to "defend" my race in a similar circumstance. Part of the reason now, as it was then, is that it would catch me off guard, as I'm not often in situations where pointed questions about race arise. While attending a historically black college to obtain my master's, most of my professors and peers were black. At work I've had black bosses and black mentors. I've hired black contractors and have worked with black real estate agents. As a result, I have not felt like a minority in quite a while. In these settings, I did not feel undermined by my skin color or the need to defend myself against racial prejudice. Race was a non-issue.

Nonetheless, the question of race still affects me in negative ways in an academic setting. When I was accepted into business school, I wondered what role race played in my being accepted and whether I was truly qualified. I was surprised to learn that my feelings were not unique. In a recent discussion with a fellow graduate from my college, I was surprised to learn that we both feel, even in 2010, that being black is like having to navigate the world wearing a heavy wet blanket. We shared this perspective, despite the fact that we had not known each other in college and have since traveled in very different circles. He became a musician holding managerial positions at health clinics, whereas I became a teacher and invested in real estate.

When I first moved to Philadelphia, I spent a couple of years befriending a young man named Jean-Jacques. We met in front of a public library where he was feeding the homeless and where I had been studying for certification exams. I think we were impressed with each other's accomplishments as well as our differences. He was a talented art student from Haiti, and having attended art school in Philadelphia, he was my guide to the city. He was also a conduit to exploring my spiritual nature. Jean-Jacques introduced me to *Remember, Be Here Now*, a book from the 1960s that provided me an introduction to Eastern spirituality.

Part of the reason I moved to Philly was to prove to myself that I felt comfortable with my race and with assuming a place within the black community. In my essay, I wrote that "the problem wasn't that I myself did not feel I was black" but that the opportunities to expose myself to and embrace people of color were limited. When I graduated, I was ready to put action behind my rhetoric. I thought that surrounding myself with people who looked like me would be good for my self-concept. When I attempted to explain this to my nonblack friends, I was met with perplexed looks. "What does *that* mean?" their faces seemed to say. At the time, I felt self-conscious. It was hard to explain what I intuitively knew: Living amongst blacks was the right thing to do. It was also an experiment, as I had never lived among blacks before. Now when I think about the looks my friends gave me, I wonder if I was not misreading them. Were they really belittling my choice, or were they dismayed by the implication that they were somehow less important or inadequate because they weren't black? In their minds I might have been sending mixed messages about race. It's hard to say.

Once I came to Philly and met Jean-Jacques, it all began to make sense. My new life in Philly was at once challenging and familiar. I felt affirmed living amongst blacks. In high school, the idea of surrounding myself with black people was odd. As I neared the end of high school, my mom wanted me to attend a historically black college or university (HBCU)—unless, of course, I could attend an Ivy League school. She felt there was something I was not getting at the institutions I had attended and that it would be affirming to be in a majority black school environment. At first I was appalled by the thought. I didn't know many black people outside of my family, and I wondered what was so special about blacks that I needed to be around them exclusively for four years. However, when I thought about it, there was something a bit unsettling, even to myself, about my visceral opposition to the idea of attending an HBCU. It made me uncomfortable to realize just how distant I had become in regards to "my own people." But now I wonder if this was just a normal teenage response to a parental suggestion.

Perhaps as a result of my education or because I'm hypersensitive to the situation, I still feel undermined by affirmative action. It's hard to know the extent to which race played in my acceptances into business school. Were my life story and achievements striking enough to make up for the discrepancies between my test scores and GPA compared to those of my peers? It's difficult to reconcile this without concluding that something is unfair, even if historically justified.

Trying to parse out what made me attractive in the eyes of admission committees is probably a fool's errand. There are so many ways you can perceive the world. I think viewing it solely from the perspective of race is very limiting and ultimately detrimental. It imprisons me and takes away my agency. Part of me believes that race is irrelevant, but in the back of my mind I'm constantly questioning whether or not this is true. Self-doubt becomes a self-fulfilling prophecy. Being black isn't limiting. What is limiting is self-doubt and self-imposed limitations. These seem to disappear when in a majority black environment, which brings up the question: Am I really more comfortable with my race when in an all-black environment, or is it simply the fact that I can ignore its significance in this setting?

I don't think being black has any real significance; I think people assign significance to it. Among blacks I would argue that race doesn't have any more significance than the fact that everyone has a nose or two ears. Because everyone has them, they aren't worth discussing. Among Americans, especially white Americans, race is perceived as a difference and therefore has significance. I've never been insecure about my ears, but then no one ever brings them up. If people made ears the main factor for being successful, intelligent, or attracting a suitable mate, then yes, I think I would be insecure about my ears too.

At the end of my original essay, I said I looked forward to serving as a role model for black youth by teaching in an inner city. Although I am uncertain about the legacy I will leave with the students I have taught in the School District of Philadelphia, I consider my time with them a success. My primary goal was to give my students alternative examples of what it meant to be black. In that essay, however, I never described how I planned to provide these alternative examples.

Growing up, I appreciated people who listened and treated me respectfully, so I sought to meet my students' needs by treating them with dignity. I downplayed the importance of race and treated everyone compassionately. I sought to help my students realize that their best selves were independent of race and gender.

When deciding on how to interact with my students, I thought back to a conversation I had with a friend in high school who once told me off-handedly, "I bet you'd be good at getting straight A's." His suggestion opened up a new possibility for me—it opened the door to success. My GPA began to improve because I found out that it was okay for me to succeed. Therefore, I wanted to teach in public schools to plant the idea that it's okay to succeed. Rather than teaching them what it meant to be black, or male, or focusing on being a positive black male role model, I attempted to exemplify being a good *person*. After all, I had to think about the rest of my students, who were at least 50 percent female and 75 percent non-black. Furthermore, I found myself asking, what does it mean to be black? To be male? These ideas seem so arbitrary. Being a good person is clearer.

So, was I successful? Was I able to fill this role, despite having been brought up in a very different environment from the kids that I was teaching? Yes and no. The first year of teaching is hard. I think it's that way for many teachers no matter the school. Was it any more difficult for me because my students were black, Hispanic, poor, unprepared for school, and attending a poorly managed school, whereas I came from a privileged, white learning environment? Probably. But these differences were also the source of my inspiration. They reminded me how much I had to offer my students. Having grown up in the inner city and having a natural affinity for children, I felt I had insights into my students' behavior. I was able to translate that understanding into terms they understood. Once I improved my classroom environment, relating to my students came naturally.

And yet, there were setbacks. I was assaulted several times by students, mostly "emotional support" students who weren't getting the services they needed. My sexuality was sometimes questioned during class, which interrupted lessons. However, these interruptions were not wholly unwelcome. I viewed them as opportunities. The students were exhibiting honest opinions and concerns. I believed that if I could treat these interruptions delicately, they could become teachable moments that would enable me to foster care and compassion. Nonetheless, after five years of teaching, I left the school district. My efforts seemed to be swallowed up by a system that was too immense and bureaucratic. I often describe the Philadelphia school district as an outsized, sinking ship.

RELATIONSHIPS

Since graduating from college, I've had two long-term relationships; the first lasted a year and the second was off and on for about two years. I don't have any preference in terms of race for the women I date. However, it so happens that both women were white teachers. Although I maintain that race is not a factor when I date, I fear that when dating white women I'm reinforcing the stereotype that black men, especially successful black men, prefer white women. Race never really comes up with the women I am dating. There's an attraction. I like them. They like me. And that's it. I try to keep it simple.

With my first girlfriend, Christina, I don't think I grew very much. She was unwilling to commit to being in a relationship so it felt like a yearlong fling. With my second relationship, it was somewhat the same, but we were willing to work a lot on communication and therefore grew a lot as people. Some might think that I've only been seriously involved with white women because I find them more attractive, but I don't think that's the case. I'm attracted to women who stand out because of their unique style and personality. I am interested in women who will make good mothers, who are emotionally healthy, optimistic, and strong.

In my biography, I said I did not know much about my father while growing up and that I didn't think about him very often. This didn't upset me then and it doesn't now. I've already come to terms with his absence. This wasn't the case with my family on my father's side, who I met one summer when I biked to Texas. I met two of my father's siblings, who took his loss very hard, and my own half-brother who took his absence very personally. In one conversation, my uncle told me of my father's passing. He died due to complications related to dialysis. I've been told that drug users are among those most in need of this treatment, and there was a suggestion that drug use may have been the cause of my dad's health problems. My uncle spoke hesitantly and sadly. I wanted to comfort him and share in his grief, but I couldn't—it's hard to grieve for someone with whom you never had a relationship.

I have occasionally wondered if my dad's genes were responsible for the differences in my temperament and my mom's. Her side of the family seems pretty relaxed and somewhat reserved, whereas a part of me has always been wild. If you didn't know me better or if I didn't keep such a watchful eye on myself, you might even think I did drugs!

I didn't think that my temperament was a familial trait until I met my father's side of the family. My gregariousness, my love of the new and different fit in seamlessly with the ribaldry of my dad's family in Louisiana. I found out that some characteristics that have always defined me and set me apart are directly traceable to my father and his side of the family. According to my aunt, my father had dreadlocks, as do I, and he too would have been into riding a bicycle across country. Visiting my father's side of the family made me feel complete. It was nice to know that a whole set of behaviors and feelings that I had tried to contain had a place. It felt like my soul, my truest self, now had a home.

My half-brother was now about 30. Unlike me, he had taken the absence of our father quite hard and quite personally. Whereas I had written off my dad's absence as a sort of social malfunction and sympathized with the man, my brother had felt abandoned. I found that unfortunate and odd. I tend to have an irrational fear of social situations, and I attributed my dad's absence to a similar idiosyncrasy. I could understand how fatherhood could be overwhelming, especially if you have little or no self-esteem or if you never had a father yourself. In any case, I never took it personally. But then again, I lived with my mother, who is a phenomenal lady, so when people spoke of parents while I was growing up, I felt my mom covered that term. I imagine it must have been harder for my half-brother, who lived with his grandmother, as a grandparent is simply not a parent. I also don't know if he had a peer group or siblings who were as supportive as mine.

I can easily describe my mom as phenomenal now. Since college, our relationship has improved considerably. We communicate several times a week, and I often turn to her for advice. I think she's changed a lot, but my sister insists that I've changed too, which may be true. However, when I think of the lifestyle my mom now leads, I can't help but think that a major change occurred in her.

Looking back, I would not complain about anything my mother has done for me. She has done so much with so little that speaking about her with anything but affection would be ungracious. Don't get me wrong—having a warmer, more emotional, and more nurturing parental figure would have been an amazing emotional and psychological benefit to me. However, now that I understand a little bit more about the nature of people and relationships, I can understand how being caring and nurturing might have been difficult when added to everything else she had to be and do.

My mom's disapproval of women I dated because of their race has melted away since she's started dating again. Maybe she understands now how difficult love can be, or that anybody who makes me happy should make her happy. Who can say? On a recent visit, I noticed that she was able to be more emotionally honest, so I asked her during a family meeting if she's noticed the change in herself. I also asked whether she was under a lot of stress while raising us. She answered both questions with a resounding "Yes!" And we all laughed.

I'm grateful to have a functioning relationship with my mom. Our relationship began to improve when I started investing in real estate. After graduating from college, I told my mom about my interest in real estate. To my surprise, she was very enthusiastic at the news. It was if she had been waiting for me to say those words my entire life. Soon, we became investment partners. On the first property I purchased, I provided the cash and desire, she supplied the temerity and documentation. (It would be a couple of years before I would qualify for my own loan.) During our partnership, we got into the habit of talking frequently. Our collaboration gave us a forum to converse constructively and marked a true turning point in the dynamics of our relationship. I had chosen to be her partner in business, which maybe assured her for the first time that I respected her wisdom as a person and as a mother. Surely this improved how we related to one another.

FUTURE PLANS

And now I am heading off to business school—but why business school? Why now? There are several reasons I want to pursue a business degree. First, I've decided to donate $10 million in my lifetime to help end disparities in education and support sustainable living. I figure that kind of money can only be made with intention, and business school, I'm told, is all about that intention. Second, having worked in the nonprofit sector for over five years, I feel like there is simultaneously not enough discussion and a lot of misunderstanding between those with money and those with good intentions but little money. I believe the people with good intentions could use an insider and advocate to help them raise capital and run more efficient organizations. Third, I have wondered why people who want to protect endangered resources don't pool their assets and purchase said resources. In short, I want to attend business school because I intend to do good and I want to do it on a large scale.

It's rather funny. Upon graduating from college, I thought that receiving my degree meant I was an adult. I thought I was officially grown up, and that I had everything worked out. I thought I'd never need to ask for help again, and I'd never have to go to school again. One master's degree later and about to get another, clearly I still haven't gotten everything worked out!

■ ■ ■ ■ ■

A LATINIDAD, I CANNOT, WILL NOT HIDE

Viana grew up in challenging circumstances in an impoverished New Jersey city, where she was raised by a passionate single mother who had journeyed from Honduras to the United States in search of a better life. Viana escapes the underresourced educational system by receiving a full scholarship to an elite private high school, but is faced continually with the stigma of being an affirmative action student and is haunted by the fear that she is "not supposed to be there." At her Ivy League college, Viana becomes more confident in her abilities as a student, asserts her pride in her Latina identity, and finds a place within the school's tight-knit Hispanic community. As she gets involved with her six-year-old brother's struggles at her old elementary school, Viana makes plans for a future in education and child psychology while recommitting herself to her heritage and family ties.

"Yeah, the thing that I like about SEEDS (Scholars Educators Excellence Dedication Success) is that it's based on economic status instead of on racial status," I say as Lisa and I walk to lunch. "They have cut-off points. Your family has to make no more than a set amount according to the number of people in your family. So we have white kids in the program too. I think colleges should do something more like that rather than just look at race."

"See, I still have problems with that," she replies. "If I were to have applied to SEEDS, I wouldn't have been accepted. See, my thing is—what about those like me who are in the middle class and can't get help because we make too much money, but aren't rich enough to go to boarding schools and stuff?...It's not fair that we don't get any help just because we have more money than you."

Frustrated, I say good-bye and walk away, pretending I am in a rush to get somewhere. I cannot help but feel that Lisa was upset that I was able to get into a program like SEEDS and somewhat envious that I went to Phillips Exeter Academy. She thought it was unfair for people like me who "don't make as much money" to get help. Sometimes I feel like yelling, *"I'm poor!* It's not that we make slightly less money than your family, who owns a house in the suburbs and can afford to take family vacations and buy all brand-name clothing and go tanning and get their hair done all the time. *I am poor!"*

Too often, I see the white middle and upper classes argue against affirmative action. I, too, disagree with the proposed action that is based on race; but I support programs that base aid on economic status. Many white people are poor as well and could use the kind of help I have received. I feel Lisa thinks that only a few people of color deserve to attend selective schools and the rest who go are granted free rides. Does she think I deserve to be there?

"You went to Exeter?" That is the shocked response of almost everyone, no matter whether white, black, or brown, once I reveal that I attended Phillips Exeter Academy. Yes, it is a prestigious, elite, majority-white school, but it, too, had to join the trend of diversifying its student population. Therefore, a little poor brown girl from a little poor city was the perfect answer for Exeter. I was the exact opposite of the stereotypical rich white male Exonian. However, I was not accepted into that school or into my Ivy League college just because I am "brown" or Latina, and this is something I have had to prove to myself and to many around me over the past seven years.

Growing up in poverty, survival was a challenge. The oldest daughter of a single mother, I helped her raise the three younger children since the two fathers did not. I worked hard in school because I knew what was expected of me. I was the typical overachiever who worries and stresses, which I do to this day. Somehow I have succeeded academically, but no matter where I am in the world, I am always reminded of the money troubles that my family faces.

What has gotten me here? Why have I made it all the way to college when so many others from similar backgrounds have not? Maybe it is my mother's strength or high expectations. Perhaps it is because I am the stereotypical overachieving oldest child. Could it be because of my teachers and their support? Could it be my determination and resiliency? Maybe it is the poverty that I am fighting to get away from. Perhaps it is because I can project myself into the future and plan accordingly. Could it just be fate or luck? This is what I am trying to understand.

My first memory takes me back to when I was almost four years old. By that time my mother and father had split up. My mom, my younger sister, Isis, and I relocated from New York City to Paterson, New Jersey. My father had court-ordered visits and was allowed to take Isis and me to his apartment on weekends. One weekend, instead of returning us to my mother, my father abducted us to Honduras, my parents' native country. He moved us from concrete hut to concrete hut in the countryside of Honduras every two weeks. I am told we were in constant motion for six months during which two-year-old Isis and I ate white rice every day with Honduran black beans in a bowl full of black bean water. While Isis always remained at home with our father, I was allowed to walk down to the *pulperia,* or market, across the street by myself, but Isis and I were never together without our father around.

My memory of my rescue is that I am four years old when a woman with sunglasses and two men in suits walk into our dark, concrete hut. Running through the darkness with me in his arms, my father and I reach the backyard, and he propels me over the concrete wall, in an attempt to hide me in another yard. The woman shrieks, "Danilo, what are you doing? Don't let her go!" My shirt lifts up and my belly and chest rub against the rough concrete wall. My toes desperately search for a solid surface to rest on but all I feel is cold water in the deep laundry sink full of water beneath me. A man runs to me, wraps his big hands around my tiny waist, and thrusts me back over the wall into my father's hands. "What the hell are you doing? Are you crazy? She would've drowned! Take her back!" he remonstrates. I am now back in my father's arms and we are in the living room. Isis is hiding, crouched behind the sofa chair my father and I are sitting in. I am perched on his lap, head buried into his chest and arms wrapped tightly around his waist. "Danilo, let her come to me! Let her go!" the woman demands. "I'm not holding her back!" My father lifts his arms to demonstrate my freedom.

The strange woman with sunglasses speaks directly to me, "Mamita [Sweetie], don't you see who it is? Don't you recognize me?" She pulls her sunglasses off. "Mami? Mami!" I scream. "Isis, it's Mami! It's ok!" Jumping off my father's lap, I dive into my mother's arms. A huge smile stretches across my face as I squeeze my mom with my skinny arms. Isis deserts her hiding spot and dashes to my mother to join the reunion. We go to a hotel room where we shower and put pretty dresses on. My mother has told me Isis and I ate with such hunger it seemed we had not eaten in months. The next time I saw my father was through court-ordered, supervised visits in the United States when I was eight years old.

My father has been a big part of my life, although he has not been around for most of it. He never held a steady job because he would hardly ever go to work; when he did, he was usually late. Because of him, the man I marry will need to be ambitious and motivated, not just *seem* educated like my charming father. He must be a man who seems likely to be with me forever. I will not be rushing into any weddings! And I know that I, too, will be ambitious, motivated, and making my own living in case things do not work out as planned. I cannot be dependent on him because I will not allow myself to need welfare like my mother did when she left my father.

I have spent much time wondering why I am so resentful and unforgiving toward "that guy," as Isis and I have termed him. Is it because I blame him for our poverty? Is it because I feel I grew up fatherless? I think it is because he had nothing to complain about and yet he could not handle being a father. I am mad because of all the lies he told us. He had three beautiful, smart, good, loving daughters; spent four years gaining Isis's and my trust and love back; had a second chance when Jasmine, his third daughter, was born; and yet he chose to throw it away, chose not to fight for it, to give it all up. When I was 12, he took another trip to Honduras and never returned, losing his U.S. residency. Luckily for him, this means he does not have to worry about the fifty-thousand-plus dollars in child support that he owes my mother.

I just thank God for giving my mother the strength to leave my father when she did, because I cannot even imagine what my life would have been like if we had stayed with him any longer. Although my mother has been human and thus not perfect, she has been my fuel, my inspiration to accomplish all my goals. I have never met a woman with my mother's relentlessness and strength, and I hope to emulate even half of it. At age 17, my mother left Honduras for Paterson, where she had family. She and an aunt, Concha, hired a *coyote,* a man who helps people get across the border for a living. They trekked through northern Mexico and swam across the Rio Grande at the U.S. border. When I was 17, my challenge was to finish my fourth year at one of the world's wealthiest schools. Deportation and death were not real concerns.

My mother has four children and has raised all four alone. Although she is still with the father of the two youngest children, we do not all live together, not because we do not want to, but because of circumstances. Mario has his own business, a Laundromat, in Brooklyn. He has provided financially for all of us, especially his own children, but my mother has raised all four without him living with us. "Mario, you need to sell the laundry and just move in with us," my mother asserts. "The day you want your children's love and affection, they're going to give you a kick in the ass, and they're not going to want to deal with you. They haven't had their father around like they should have." His living arrangement has been one of the few sources of arguments between my mother and stepfather.

Maybe if Mario had lived with us, I would not still be resentful toward my father because I would have had a replacement father. Mario has been involved with my mother since she left my father, but I did not truly feel that I loved him until the end of high school. In order to survive, my mother went on welfare and was able to go to school to learn English while welfare paid for Isis's and my private preschool and day care. My mother never had a steady job but always had odd jobs that ended quickly. For a while she cleaned apartments and worked in a department store. She then sewed in a clothing factory with her sister Lydia and many other immigrants, most of whom were illegal.

My mother continued to apply her knowledge of sewing by making dresses for her girls and sewing beautiful stuffed bunnies, which she sold for $60 each. Sewing is my mother's education. She became a seamstress at the age of 15 because her parents could only afford to send one child to school. My mother dropped out so that her older brother could graduate from the military academy, Escuela de las Americas (the School of the Americas), an academy based in Central America but headquartered in Georgia. He was supposed to become a great general and be successful. Fortunately, he dropped out of the school, which produced heartless killing machines for Latin America. Although he did live as a wealthy businessman in Honduras, he is now an illegal immigrant in the United States, earning less than my mother. Unfortunately, my mother was never fully educated. She took adult classes to learn English, she cannot write grammatically correctly in either Spanish, her native language, or English, and she cannot get her General Education Development (GED) test because she does not remember algebra or geometry.

However, sewing and all her odd jobs were not enough for her to support the family. Mario did give my mother money, but he also did not make enough to support himself and all five of us. The real problem was that there was a six-year difference between the youngest of the first pair of children, Isis and me, and the second pair of children, Laura and Anthony (Tony). Isis was finally going to school when Tony, the youngest child, was born. That meant my mother had to stay at home until Laura and Tony could attend school because she could not afford a babysitter or day care. Therefore, my mother stayed on welfare, a system with security that also assured her $300 a month in food stamps; WIC (Women, Infants & Children) vouchers, which gave us free food such as dairy products and baby formula; Medicaid, which covered medical expenses; and Section 8, which subsidized our housing.

Many people believe that those on such public assistance wish to live that way and enjoy the free money. I hated it. It still brings such pain and tears to think about being on this assistance for 10 years. My mother did not find a job and get off assistance until I was 14 and on my way to Exeter. Welfare had a program that sent people to a vocational program for a few hours during the day and then into a part-time job in the afternoon. The proudest I had ever been of my mother was when she was placed in "Food and Nutrition" at a nearby hospital and was no longer in the welfare system. While preparing trays of food, taking them to patients, and then picking them up, she plodded throughout the hospital for hours each day. My mother's joy and relief at getting off welfare compensated for her tired feet and achy back. Tears filled my eyes at the thought of my mother having a job and us getting off welfare. I did not have to go to Exeter as a child on welfare. People asked me, "What does your mom do?" I could proudly reply, "She works in a hospital." I did not care what she did; I told them honestly that she brought people food and worked in the cafeteria. What I cared about was that my mother had a job, finally.

In order for my mom to work, and since I was leaving for boarding school, Isis had to help around the house. Isis and I—well, mostly I—had been babysitting the younger kids for seven years. I was definitely nervous about my daydreamer sister watching over them, but it all worked out. My mom regularly worked 12-hour shifts. A few times she did not get home until two in the morning, but it all paid off because she was given a full-time position with benefits. After five years of working at the hospital, my mom and a manager got into an argument, which resulted in her simultaneous quitting and firing. While she got her license for commercial driving, my mother collected unemployment checks. For a few months she drove a school bus but was then hired by New Jersey Transit, the state's public transportation company. She is once again starting at the bottom, working part time and fighting her way to a full-time position with benefits. This job seems to be the one she is going to keep because the hourly wage is in the teens, and once benefits kick in, everyone in the family, including Isis and me, will be covered.

Honestly, what keeps me going is knowing how much my mother was able to handle. With all the pressure she had to support us and keep us fed, clothed, and healthy, my mother never turned to inappropriate behaviors such as prostitution or drugs. She taught by example, and she taught me to work hard and keep a positive attitude.

As much as I love my mother and as much as I consider us to be friends, there is one thing that we will never see eye to eye on: her racism. Although she says she is not racist, my mother holds racist views. Ironically, her family is dark-skinned. I am one of the lighter members of the family because of my father's fair complexion. I am the color of creamy peanut butter, and my mother, like many of her siblings, is the color of cinnamon. My aunt Lydia has pleaded with my mother to understand and accept that we do have black ancestry, but it is always to no avail. "No, Lydia, our grandmother was not black. She was a bit dark but we aren't black. That's it!" responds my mother firmly.

Two of the biggest arguments I have ever had with my mother centered on the clash of our views on race. The first happened the summer before my first year of high school. Isis and I had been contemplating how to raise the topic for weeks. That weekend we were in Brooklyn visiting Mario at his apartment. Knowing what I was about to say, I took a deep breath and we walked into the small, dimly lit kitchen. Mario, with his back resting against the wall, sat on one of the little chairs around the square table. My mother sat next to him at the round corner of the table. "Mario, we wanted to talk to you and Mami about something. Now, I know that sometimes you guys might just be joking and stuff, but Isis and I...well, we were just feeling that sometimes you guys sound racist. I just don't like how you guys say some stuff sometimes." I stood in front of my mother darting my eyes between their faces and the floor as I passed this judgment on them. "What?!? No, we're not racist! I mean, I understand what you're thinking, but we don't hate black people or anyone. Whatever, if you don't bother me I'm fine, ya know," Mario defended himself. My mother's response, which was in itself racist, was: "I tell you all the time how I played with the black kids in Honduras. We would jump rope and go to school together. We don't have anything against black people."

My mother and Mario sent us away, as we held our tongues and remained unconvinced by their replies. On the way back home to New Jersey at the end of the weekend, my mom secretly admitted, "You know, Mario might be a little racist because his uncle had a restaurant in Honduras and his uncle hated the blacks that went to the restaurant. So I think that attitude rubbed off on him a bit. But I did play with the black kids."

Three years later, after finishing my junior year of high school, I am watching some talk show like Ricki Lake, when my mom comes in and sees a black woman and a white man kissing and says, "Ugh, what a sight." My mother looks down at my brother, who is about eight years old at the time, and says, "Papito [Sweetie], you know you can't marry a black girl, right? It wouldn't be good." She continues speaking, laughing deeply from her belly as she makes an inappropriate joke I cannot remember now. She added, "People should just stick to their own races." My brother looks up at me from his spot on the carpet. With furrowed brows, he asks me, "That's not right, right Viana? What Mami said isn't right, right?" I looked at

Tony as I shook my head and rolled my eyes in disapproval of my mother. "No Tony, Mami isn't right. You can marry a black girl if you want to. As long as you love a person, it doesn't matter what color they are."

Hearing my comment to Anthony, my mother yells from the kitchen, "And don't think I don't know about the boy you went out with. I know that black friend of yours was your boyfriend, don't deny it!" "Yeah and...so?" I defiantly reply. I knew what her issue was but I had had enough. "So? So!" my mother echoes in astonishment as she returns to the bedroom and begins screaming angrily at me. "Everyone should be with their own race; blacks with blacks and whites with whites!" I get off the bed and scream back: "Yeah, except that you'd prefer I be with a homeless, dirty white guy! Just as long as he's not black, right Ma? Whatever, I'm never gonna think like you. Just accept that! We should all stick to our races except that all of us should be with white people."

As I beat the mattress with a plastic soda bottle, Isis runs into the room and pushes me away from our mother. Having been screaming so close to each other, we had one another's spit on our faces. Anthony crouched on the floor in a corner, wide eyed, not believing what he was seeing. "But being with a white guy is different!" my mother asserts. Isis, tired of being caught in the middle, yells, "*Yah!* That's enough! Stop it, both of you! Look, poor Tony. You okay, Tony?"

If we were cartoons, my mother and I probably would have been bright red with steam coming out of our heads. She left the room, and I wiped my face of the tears that had spilled out with my anger. I still had one last thought, and I was not going to hold my tongue because she was already mad, and I wanted to piss her off even more: "And what you don't know is that I have had white boyfriends, and Hispanic boyfriends, and mixed boyfriends! I don't care whether they're brown, black, white, green, yellow, red, purple! As long as he treats me well and we like each other, I'm happy!" I proclaim myself the winner of this argument since I had the last word. After hearing about the ordeal, my aunt Lydia confessed that the thought of me being with a black guy kept my mother from eating for two days. Since that day, my mom and I have not spoken about race and race relations.

In Paterson, I went to school with other Latino children, but also with blacks, East Indians, whites, and a few Asians. Paterson is a racially mixed city with a mixed public school system. In high school, I was surrounded by people from places like Saudi Arabia, Japan, China, France, Mexico, Colombia, as well as most of the United States. I was also exposed to students in homosexual and bisexual relationships. This diversity has continued in college and has shaped my open-mindedness.

In the seventh grade, I and eight other Paterson students were accepted into the program that led to my argument with Lisa—New Jersey SEEDS, which was for disadvantaged children with academic talent. It involved intensive summer sessions and Saturday classes during my eighth-grade year. I recall my excitement in telling the news to my seventh grade homeroom teacher one Monday morning. "Mrs. Mitchell, I got in!" We were in the hallway, getting ready to go into class and start the day. When she heard my news, her eyebrows, cheeks, and lips all moved upward, as she let out an excited squeal. Mrs. Mitchell was a strong-looking woman with broad shoulders and must have been almost six feet tall. She grabbed me by the wrists and began flinging me up into the air while she jumped around in circles, forcing me to jump with her. She laughed, and all the students looked confused about all the excitement. At the time, Mrs. Mitchell was the only one who really understood the implications of my acceptance into the SEEDS program.

That summer the nine of us, along with another fifty or so students from West New York, Jersey City, Passaic, and a few other cities in New Jersey, were bused to a private day school in Englewood, New Jersey. After a tough but fun summer, the group was reduced in size by half based on the quality of our work, each student's effort, and how well each student got along with others. Phase II, the worst of the three phases of SEEDS, was dark, cold, and way too early. Every Saturday morning I caught the bus at 6:30 for classes that began at eight and ended at three. I had my SEEDS homework, which I did every Friday night, along with my daily eighth-grade work. During this phase, we learned algebra and prepared for high school English and the Secondary School Achievement Test (SSAT). We also applied to and interviewed with private secondary schools.

When I asked two classmates in Phase II why they stopped coming to the program, the male said he had to get a part-time job and help around the house, and the female said her parents did not want her to go away to school. They were both Latinos. Of the nine Paterson students that had started out, six were Latinos. I was the only Paterson Latino to make it through the whole program. Two boys did not accept the offers they were given by private schools because not enough financial aid was awarded and because of long bus trips. That means that out of nine students, only two of us attended a private high school. I was honestly just lucky with Exeter.

I showed up to my Phillips Exeter interview in blue jeans and a T-shirt because I was so unexcited about interviewing that I did not bother to change my clothes after school. Worried that her broken English would not be good enough for the interview, my mom seemed more nervous than I did. I went into the interview and honestly do not remember doing anything other than just relaxing and talking to the woman as if we were hanging out eating ice cream. I have no recollection because I truly did not care, and for once I was not worried. After the admissions officer spoke with my mother privately, both women reappeared, laughing so hard and being so moved by their talk that my mom was wiping tears off her cheeks. "What the heck just happened?" I thought. We said our farewells and went home.

After a few months, the admissions officer who had interviewed us called our house. She left me in shock when she told me I had been accepted to Exeter, and she left my mother crying tears of joy. She also informed us that we were getting a free train trip to visit the school. My mother called Mario and all my family members to tell them that I was going away to New Hampshire to attend private school. As soon as I arrived on campus, I fell in love with the school. I was lucky: I later learned that my grades and SSAT scores were not necessarily Exeter level, but they were great for a student from Paterson. I also learned that the SEEDS staff had only asked me to interview to fill empty time slots because the Exeter admissions officer had been nice enough to make the long trip to New Jersey.

My acceptance into SEEDS was very different from the acceptance into Exeter, but both had similar goals. Each wanted to help out underprivileged, bright, hard-working students. However, SEEDS accepts students based on economic status. Basically, if you are a promising student and your family is near or below the poverty line, you are accepted into SEEDS. At Exeter, grades were definitely a factor; my SEEDS advisors had to vouch for me because of my C in algebra. But instead of taking only economic status into account, Exeter considers race.

Every April, when college acceptance letters were coming in, affirmative action became the most controversial topic on campus. "You don't have to worry, you're Latina. Everyone's looking for Latinos. It's easier for you to get into college. But I'm Asian so it's gonna be really hard for me because I have to be so much better than all the other Asians," commented a friend nonchalantly. During high school I heard this regularly. The problem with affirmative action is that, too often, those who do need that extra help do not get it. Instead of poor blacks and Latinos, those who get into these elite schools are usually well off.

People who claim a Latino background often come from wealthy families that do not even acknowledge this heritage until it is time to "check the box" on an application. This fuels the idea that "you are only here because you're Latina." I have been very involved with clubs and extracurricular activities at school since my elementary years. However, in high school I did it in part because I enjoyed them but also because I thought they were my main ticket into a good college. I also thought they would give me some value, importance, and credibility at such a fancy school that I "wasn't supposed to be at."

I was accepted at an Ivy League college, but during my freshman fall trimester I thought that I was not capable of surviving and would have been better off at a non–Ivy League school. That term I earned a high C average. I did not believe in myself and started believing what people had said: that I was only accepted because I added color to my class, not because I am capable and smart. That winter I worked hard to see what some effort would get me. My average that term was 1.22 points higher than my fall average. I started believing.

My involvement with nonacademic activities is how I demonstrate my value to myself and others. I have not only mentored and done research but also volunteered at the local public schools and been a teacher's assistant for a college course. I recently won a national scholarship, was granted a prestigious summer internship, and was tapped into a senior society. This is how I show others and remind myself that I am capable of being at such a great institution. It is not just because I am Latina but because I can bring a different experience, intelligence, and drive to the table. I *am* worthy. I must never forget that.

At college, I am very aware that I am Latina. Although I am light skinned, I am still darker than most of the students all-year-round, despite their artificial tanning. My hair is long, wavy, dark, and very thick: I "look Latina." My *Latinidad* is so apparent that I cannot hide it, nor do I wish to. When I walk down the paths here, I hold my head high and look straight ahead. I have to show that I am proud to be who I am, even though I am different from most.

During my first year I was more involved with the Latino community than I am today, in my junior year. I attended meetings of the student Latino organization and enjoyed going to the dinners and dances put on by the Latino fraternity and other groups. Although I am still friends with a few who are involved and am still friendly with most in the Latino community, I have drifted away from it. Nevertheless, I am still known by most of the community members and as a Latina on campus. A few weekends ago, when newly accepted high school seniors visited the campus, I stopped by the reception at the Latin American, Latino, and Caribbean Studies house. I did not recognize the female giving advice to the visiting Latino high school seniors in the living room, but I thought it was my own fault because I never hang out with the community.

I whispered into a male Dartmouth student's ear, "Yo, Mark, do you know who she is?"

"Not a clue!" he immediately whispered back. Then he added, "I've seen her around, but all of a sudden she wants to show up at something and hang out with the Latinos. You know after this weekend she'll disappear and we won't see her ever again."

The Latino community at my college is somewhat unforgiving if you do not make your Latinidad always known. What is funniest about Mark's comment is that he never hung out with the Latinos his freshman year. The statement he made about the female in question is how I felt about him when he all of a sudden decided to join the Latino fraternity, even though he had never made himself a part of the community. Knowing how hard it could sometimes be to accept the group and have the group accept you in return, Mark was still as unforgiving of the woman as I, who had accepted the group and was accepted from day one. Logically, ethically, I know it is not good to reject people like this woman, because it can be a hard community to break into. People have their personal reasons for not being involved, and sometimes it is just because they do not like the others or because they are afraid of being rejected. Instead of helping these people make a smooth transition into the community to make it stronger, we talk about them behind their backs and fulfill their suspicions. We might act like this because we are bitter toward those who "checked the box" just for admissions purposes. Claiming Latinoness to better their chances of admission, they deny it once they are on campus. It is frustrating because my college boasts that 7 percent of its student body is Latino, when in reality only about a third to half of that percentage self-identify as Latino. The college believes we have made great strides and that diversity is at its peak, but in fact it is not.

My strong Latina identity is interesting to me because I have not always felt I embodied the culture. At home I have always been the skinny one in the family. My aunts and uncles called me *flacucha* or *flaca*, skinny girl, while growing up. They called Isis *gordita*, little fat girl. After years of this, we accepted our roles— Isis has accepted that she is the chunky one and I have always tried to be the skinny one. Thinness is the thing that all admire and try to achieve in my family. Therefore, Isis has been harassed by family members like our aunt Lydia, who would tell her to stop eating because she was too fat and would warn me whenever I looked like I was gaining weight.

Isis's chunkiness, though, provides a body that many Latinos admire, with curves that our culture has accepted and that are typically beautiful features. Many give Jennifer Lopez credit for showing off her body and making a curvy body acceptable, but they fail to realize that her shape is newly acceptable only in the white community. A voluptuous, curvaceous body is what Latinas have always desired and what Latinos have always been attracted to. On Spanish-language television, thin women show off their hips, round bottoms, and breasts that add to the curves.

Perhaps more significant to my family than Isis' body type is the challenge confronting Tony. My brother has been diagnosed with a learning disability in reading and as having both attention deficit/hyperactivity disorder (ADHD) and oppositional defiant disorder (ODD). Having been told that he learned differently, he felt that it meant he had a "mental problem," as he puts it. He believed that he was innately dumber and less capable of succeeding in school. Therefore, he struggled to learn how to read, and when it was too hard, he became frustrated, yelled at whomever was helping him, and walked away from the reading session. He eventually stopped trying because he was afraid of failing.

Having read Tony's individualized education plan (IEP), which informed teachers and parents of what the school was doing to attend to Tony's learning difficulties, I noticed that a few things stated in the doctor's report were not addressed in the IEP. Fortunately, I had taken a great course on special education in my freshman year of college. Taking the course to better understand my brother, I learned the laws and practices and the steps a parent could take if their child was not being adequately served. Sophomore year, in early September, I was at home when Tony's fifth-grade teacher called on three of the five days of his first week of school. I talked to the guidance counselor, school psychologist, and Tony's teacher on my mother's behalf. They were convinced that the school was not enough for him and that he needed to attend a special education school with kids at his intelligence level. Although Tony has many difficulties, he is a very bright boy, but because he has very little self-control, he is unable to put his intelligence to good use.

After hating his school at first, he has just finished his second year there, completing sixth grade. Now he is only a few months behind his reading level rather than two years behind, and he has become more confident that he is smart and capable of succeeding. Striving to do well, he has started stepping in the right direction to overcome some of his insecurities. Anthony has been my inspiration for my career choices.

Seeing the struggles that both my mom and brother have gone through with school makes me really angry and passionate about helping those who may be in similar situations. Although my first language, Spanish, is not as good as I would like it to be, I can still communicate effectively with Spanish-speaking parents.

I hope to advocate for people who struggle with the laws or with the language and who are impeded from understanding their situation because of them. In my teacher certification courses, I am learning techniques that would include all children and even make a child who believed he was dumb feel adequate and capable. Much of my brother's low self-esteem comes from school, and I hope to boost children's self-perceptions while they are my students.

Although education is a great passion of mine, becoming a child psychologist is my goal. I believe that education and psychology are intermingled and that my passion for both is due to that belief. Speaking about his thoughts and feelings, Tony and I do not come to definite decisions and conclusions that "fix" the problem, but he always seems to feel better and at least listened to by the end of our conversations. I understand that it is easier for him to talk to me because I am his sister and he knows and trusts me, but I hope I can bring such comfort and relief to other children who just want someone to listen to them.

When I started my teacher education courses, I wondered how my mom felt about my becoming a teacher. People of color often choose professions such as business and engineering, fields other than education, that will bring them more money. I fully understand their choices and that sometimes they are influenced by parents, and although I do sometimes think I should just study business, it is not where my heart is. I decided to talk to my mother about my decision, in part to seek her approval but also just to inform her.

"Ma, now I don't know if I've talked to you about this but...how would you feel about me becoming a teacher? I mean, I still want to become a child psychologist but before that I'd like to teach. What do you think?" I asked apprehensively. "You know that I have always told you that I don't care what you become as long as you're somebody in life," she replied. "Graduate and be somebody; that's all I ask! You don't want to continue living this life. When you're a professional, you're not gonna have to worry about money anymore. That's what I want for all my children."

The most I can do to repay my mother for her sacrifices and all she has provided for us is to work hard to achieve my goal of becoming a professional. It will not only be a gift to her, but to me as well, for all of my hard work and strife. I understand more than most how important an education is to make your life happy and successful. As a rising senior at Dartmouth College, my family is still in Section 8 housing. No matter how much money we receive through assistance and from Mario, we are still just as broke and penniless as ever. My 40-year-old uneducated mother is currently earning close to $15 an hour. My 23-year-old boyfriend who has a master's degree is earning about $33 an hour. Mami has a job; he has a career.

I am also proof of how important a supportive network is. I have had family and friends encouraging me and believing that I will succeed. In my senior year of high school, I met a freshman girl who is half black, half Dominican. She was a foster child with many blood and foster siblings. At the age of 12 she was raped, and at the trial her biological mother went against her, stating her daughter was never raped. The girl's boyfriend was in jail for selling drugs. This life is unimaginable to me, with hardships I wish on no one. Yet, she was accepted at a great boarding school. I promised her that I would return for her graduation. A few weeks ago, I kept my promise and returned to Exeter's 2004 graduation. My boyfriend thought I was crazy to return because of some silly promise I made. When I found Maria in line for the procession, she screamed out, "You came!" The people there to see her graduate consisted of three black female graduates, three teachers from her junior high school, her principal from junior high, and myself. We were her family, her friends, her support. She is off to Spelman College, a historically black female college, in the fall. She has thus far succeeded, and I know she will continue to do so.

I appreciate my life with all the ups, downs, and obstacles handed to me. I love all the people who are a part of it and am actually grateful for having had a humble upbringing. It has given me drive and has made me truly appreciate the little things. Many say this, but I get excited when a friend brings me a chocolate bar or when my mother makes my favorite meal, or when I see a chipmunk while I am walking around campus. However, I am exhausted. I am tired of struggling to survive at the elite schools I have been fortunate to attend. Seeing so many people in Gucci, Ralph Lauren, and Prada apparel does bother me and make me jealous. Yes, I wish I had Prada bags and Gucci shoes. But it also bothers me because it reminds me, makes me aware that even though my family is no longer on welfare, we are still at the poverty line. We still have to struggle every day and do not even come close to having the kind of wealth many of the people who surround me daily enjoy.

Because of my ethnicity, I have had to prove myself. On campuses where my Latino features have made me very visible, I felt that I had to step up and do as well or better than those around me. Luckily, I had many experiences in my younger years that made me strong enough for this challenge. I have family support and a reputation to uphold. I also have self-motivation and self-pressure that come from striving to be an exemplary oldest child. I know who I am and where I want to go. I will continue fighting to get there.

VIANA: FIVE YEARS LATER

When I first read "A Latinidad, I Cannot, Will Not Hide" in its published version, I was uncomfortable at how exposed my life had become. In that essay, I changed peoples' names to protect their identity and wrote about my supposed hometown of Paterson, even though I grew up in Passaic, a neighboring city. Although rereading my chapter five years later made me think there was nothing too outrageous, I was still not comfortable with sharing the story with all of my friends and family. There were many events and information of others' that I shared that they would not want to see in such public material. Therefore, by not letting them know about the story, they do not have to deal with that reality I lived and wrote about.

I think this feeling of wanting some cover or protection comes from my new work this past year. In the fall of last year, I began a doctoral program in clinical psychology at the University of Connecticut. One of the major aspects of clinical psychology that has become engrained in me is keeping confidentiality when others trust you with their personal information. This confidentiality feels broken in some of the stories written in my previous chapter. Nevertheless, I have another opportunity to add to current literature about young people of color and will do so, hopefully this time without breaking this sense of confidentiality of others.

My first chapter concluded at the end of my junior year of college. I am now gearing up for my fifth-year college reunion. Much has happened in the past six years, but economic status and race have continued to be important issues in my life. During my senior year at Dartmouth College, I woke up after a nap one evening with a terrible toothache. I tried to ignore it as the pain would lessen at times. Finally, I decided to make an appointment with a local dentist thinking that perhaps it was just a cavity. Since I did not have dental insurance, I knew all the costs would come out of my pocket as dental visits for the previous five years had. I ate all of my food on the left side of my mouth for two weeks as I waited for the appointment. Finally, the day had come only to find out that I needed a root canal as soon as possible. The dentist explained that it would cost about $2,000 for the entire procedure or he could pull out the molar for $100. Sitting in my car in the parking lot, I called my mother bursting into a rage of tears and heaving breath. There was nothing she could do to help me.

After talking to some friends, I decided to go to an advisor. We all figured that being a student on financial aid at such a wealthy school I would be able to get some help from some place. I explained my situation, crying again about the fear of losing my tooth, hoping that this man of color who also grew out of poverty would understand my plight. His response was, "Some of us just have bad teeth. My mother lost her first tooth in her early twenties, too. Sometimes, you know, it just happens." He offered to give me the $100 to pull the tooth. This was not a response I ever expected. It befuddled me that he could not understand the impact that losing a tooth would have on one's self-esteem, emotional health, and overall self-image. My middle-class friend Lisa felt I was overexaggerating, but as I told her, "You would never let someone pull your tooth and be ok with it if a root-canal could save your tooth."

This is not a decision that most people at institutions like Dartmouth ever have to make because most have dental insurance or the cash to pay for such emergencies. I have family members with missing teeth because they could not afford dental care and they have expressed their embarrassment about this many times. My mother always made sure to bring us to the dentist as kids, using Medicaid to pay for our routine care and even the braces I wore for two years. When my mother began working at the hospital, she no longer received Medicaid, but also did not have dental insurance. I was an adolescent with a job and therefore paid for my own dental care out-of-pocket. My teeth were a sign of pride and still are. I often get compliments about how beautiful and white they look. They are one of the reasons I can smile proudly and speak confidently with others. Teeth are a symbol of one's status in society.

I decided to meet with another person, this time a female dean who was also of color. She could not believe the response I had received from the previous advisor stating, "If it ain't broke...I mean if the tooth is ok and it can be saved then there's no reason to pull it. I'm really sorry someone told you that." I never told her who I had spoken to previously, but felt validated by her statement. With emergency funds, this dean was able to find the money to pay for my root canal. In order to keep costs to a minimum, I went to the Tufts University School of Dental Medicine, driving down to Boston from New Hampshire two or three times within a month. I did the same with a dentist in Massachusetts for the crown. Surprising as it may sound to the previous advisor, I have not had problems with any of my teeth since.

During the year of earning my master's at the Harvard Graduate School of Education, I worked various jobs, sometimes three at once, to stay afloat. That July I moved into a small but wonderful apartment with Robert, my partner, in Hartford. Although my mother was not terribly thrilled, as shown by the expression on her face, she agreed that it made sense. Robert, who is a Puerto Rican and Peruvian man, and I had been together for almost four years at that point, with three of them being long distance. Moreover, legally I would not be allowed to live with my mother while she received subsidized housing, but I knew I would not be able to afford a place of my own. Therefore, moving in with Robert was accepted as a smart financial decision. My summer job only lasted for the month of July and I did not receive my first paycheck as a full-time elementary school teacher until the middle of September. Needless to say, I was strapped for money during August, especially when it came time to buy many of the necessary school supplies such as bulletin board materials. This period would have been virtually impossible to survive without Robert's help.

During orientation days and faculty meetings that first month, my principal always reminded us that we were privileged to be middle-class teachers while many of our students did not have the same fortune. I had to fight the urge to raise my hand and say, "Excuse me, I'm not middle class. I have a middle class salary, technically, but I'm not quite there yet." Finally, in about November I started feeling less overwhelmed and more in control over my money situation. Since September, I had been saving money in a retirement fund as well as a savings account. I had also paid Robert back and started paying many credit cards down. Growing up, my mother taught me that a smart woman never told the man in her life how much money she really had. Although I disagreed with this thought, I did believe that a smart woman always had enough backing to live on her own if need be. The feeling and fear of having to depend on my significant other for survival was waning.

Robert and I are solidly middle class now, yet many members of our families struggle daily. Financially we are able to support ourselves so that we may live comfortable, stable lives. However, we do not have the means to provide for our other family members. Although it is not my job to do so, I still often feel guilty that I cannot give to my mother on a regular basis. She has told me that many of her acquaintances assume that my sister and I send her money consistently. This is expected, as it is the tradition that many Latin American families carry out, sending money back to their parents in their country of origin. I would love to be able to carry on this tradition and sometimes feel pressure to do so. But thousands of dollars in school loans and every day expenses do not allow it, especially now that I am a graduate student again. It is still my hope that one day I will be able to help more financially.

Although money matters have always been a very salient aspect in my life, racial issues have not been far behind, especially since high school. As an adult, it has been interesting to see how often I am utterly shocked at what people still think and say. My time as an elementary school teacher consisted of three highly trans-formative years. The school at which I taught second and third grade was in the poorest neighborhood of its town in Connecticut. My first class was comprised of roughly equal numbers of white, black, and Latino students with about 75 percent of the students being on free or reduced lunch. By my third year, there were two white students in my class of 18 with about 85 percent on free or reduced lunch. Yet, I was one of only three teachers of color at the school, with a Puerto-Rican man being hired at the same time that I was.

In order to improve teacher effectiveness, our faculty meetings centered around "Courageous Conversations." This was a book and curriculum of race-based topics meant to educate adults about the importance and difficulties of being a racial minority. The hope was that teachers would begin to understand the challenges faced by many members of the families in our school, whether it was the children or the parents. In turn, it was expected that teachers would be more understanding of certain situations and interact more sensitively and appropriately with parents and children. Perhaps this idea was too bold or the principal was too new and progressive, having been hired just months before me, but many of the teachers did not buy into this plan. They believed it was a waste of time and that they already treated everyone fairly. Albeit, all the teachers worked extraordinarily hard in the school, putting in more time, energy, and effort than one could ever ask. Nevertheless, they were still oblivious to the implications of certain conversations and interactions, using phrases such as, "I don't see race." After some time in educating oneself about race relations, one knows that not seeing race is (a) impossible and (b) dangerous. Seeing race does not mean you are racist, it means you are a human product of our human society. It is also necessary to see race in order to know that one's perspective and daily life might be very different because of their own race.

I quickly became an outspoken colleague at these faculty meetings, as it is in my nature and, again, I was one of three teachers of color. At the start of my second year, I joined the brand new "Equity Team," which consisted of the teachers of color and white teachers from each grade level, as well as the principal. This team was responsible for furthering ourselves in our journey of racial awareness and developing the faculty meetings for the year. We spent hours every month or so working on these ideas. Yet, teachers would share with me their dislike of "Courageous Conversations" with sighs and oh brothers, knowing I was of color, knowing I was on the committee.

During the first year of being a part of the team, several poignant events occurred in my personal life. One weekend at the beginning of the academic year, Robert and I went shopping for school supplies at Staples in the neighboring white, middle-class town of West Hartford. As we walked around with a cart full of notebooks, pencils, crayons, and such, a white woman approached us asking Robert for help with some supplies. He looked around and finally understood what was happening. He explained to the woman that he did not work there and was shopping too. She apologized and walked away. Although we were taken aback, we brushed it off blaming Robert's red-collared shirt, which is the Staples' uniform, and his youthful face for the mistake. A week later, we returned to the same Staples for more supplies. Again, a white woman approached Robert, interrupted our conversation, and asked for help with an item. Robert let her know he was not an employee. She walked away without apologizing. This time he was wearing a grey t-shirt with huge, red, block letters that read "PHILLIPS EXETER." We were unable to explain this interaction away.

Several months later, we went to Macy's to buy new luggage for a trip Robert was taking to England. He had been chosen by the National Education Association, the national teachers' union, to join a group of teachers in Grantham, England, to learn more about the Magna Carta and its connections to the Declaration of Independence. Because of our frugal upbringing, we are both very careful shoppers. We looked at the different luggage and their prices for about 30 minutes. Finally, we went to the counter with the luggage we wanted. Before ringing us up, the older white man behind the register snidely remarked, "Oh, you're actually going to buy something." At that moment, I wanted to respond by leaving the piece of luggage there and saying, "We just changed our mind." Instead, I took a few steps away and let Robert take care of the transaction. The man might have made that statement because of how long we took to choose the bag or because most people just browse and do not actually buy much luggage. He might have also been bored or having a bad day. Maybe we looked too young to afford or to need the luggage. These are all thoughts that any young couple might have in response to such a comment. However, we also wondered if it was because of our race, something a young white couple would not have to think about.

I shared all of these events only with my principal, who is white, because I was afraid of the justifications and denial that would be proposed by the white teachers on the team. My principal anticipated my thoughts and feelings when she heard these stories, validating my reactions. Finally, one day at an Equity Team meeting I decided to share the Macy's luggage story with the other teachers there. The oldest teacher in the room responded with her own story about the day that she went car shopping with her teenage son who was dressed sloppily. To their dismay, they were unable to promptly get helped. She equated this experience with my own claiming, "Oh please, nowadays sales people are just rude to everyone. It's unbelievable how rude they can be. No one would help us." My original worry of justification and denial had realized itself but taught me that my intuitions and instincts are often feelings I should trust. I nodded my head in agreement with her but added that in my case we also wondered if race played a part in the event. My principal supported my point by explaining that the white teacher and her son did not have to factor race into their equation when thinking about their incident.

In these events, no one used derogatory terms or highly inappropriate behavior and therefore were not conspicuously racist. However, one cannot be naïve enough to believe that we are now living in a postracial society. Many use the election of President Barack Obama as the prime example of the end of racism. While canvassing for the Clinton/Obama primary in February of 2008, several voters, both Latino and white, clearly stated that they would not vote for Obama simply because he was black. After Obama's victory, the backlash and reactions demonstrated by so many Republicans and white Americans were incomparable to any previous elections. Moreover, those small, everyday events previously described can easily be seen as racial microaggressions, slowly chipping away at one's self-worth through acts of disregard toward others' feelings due to unconscious white superiority. Although perhaps everyone encounters rude people, one's own race as the reason behind that rudeness often only comes into question if the person experiencing that rudeness is of color. Most whites do not have to wonder if another white person mistook them for a Staple's employee because they themselves were white; or if they were spoken to rudely at Macy's by another white person because they themselves were white. However, for a person of color, racism, no matter how subtle, can always be a true explanation for the inconsiderate actions they have endured.

As a graduate student now, I continue to work on matters that impact people of color from urban areas. Psychology became an interest of mine in high school after an introductory course with an amazing teacher. Through several research and internship experiences in college and graduate school, I was able to meld the worlds of psychology and education together. These experiences, along with personal interactions as a teacher, helped me understand how children's and their family's mental health can hugely affect the family's ability to strive for educational attainment and financial stability.

Consistently, I dealt with many students who needed more mental health support than I was able to provide in my classroom. These students' difficulties often impacted the entire class because so much time would be spent on managing those students, rather than actually teaching the class. Moreover, because I taught at what was considered a "failing school" under the No Child Left Behind Act, any instructional time we did have was focused on test preparation. As time went on, it seemed that if I wanted to affect change in any community, teaching would be a slow-going method. Therefore, I decided to turn to a different career in which I was already interested. With a doctorate in Clinical Psychology, influencing policy decisions and creating greater changes for a larger group of people seemed more possible.

My hope is that my research will positively impact the lives of urban people by informing others about the cultural context of physical, emotional, and mental health, as well as educational experience. Moreover, through clinical practice I hope to be a pivotal component in supporting family systems by guiding families in ways to adjust their functioning. Potentially, this may have a much more far-reaching effect than I might have as an elementary classroom teacher.

I have also joined the Working Families Party, a liberal political party in Connecticut originally founded in New York City. This party fights for economic and racial justice through political means. With campaigns and hard work promoting living wages, paid sick days, and higher taxes on the wealthy, they have slowly been making big changes in the state. After many door-knocking and phone-banking events for friends running for city council and then Senator Barack Obama, this fall Robert ran for a seat on the Board of Education. Officially, I was his treasurer but, naturally, I was his "right-hand woman." After months of what seemed to be never-ending work, many friends, family members, and the political team gathered at a local restaurant/bar to await the results of the election. Fourteen hours of poll-standing in the November cold were not enough to contain our excitement and celebration when we learned that Robert had been elected to one of the four seats. The most touching moment that night was when a member of the political team came to me and said, "Viana, it would be very easy to dismiss all of the work *you* put into this. You did an awesome job. Congratulations." So far, this experience has taught me that politicians' wives are some of the strongest people around. Too often they are not given the credit they deserve and instead are thought of as trophy wives. Fortunately, Robert comes to me for advice and my opinion. He often shares his thoughts and the events of board meetings. Although it drives me crazy at times, I appreciate him involving me in his political adventure.

At the moment, I am completely wrapped up in planning an affordable yet elegant event for our August wedding. It is a constant battle between my frugal brain and emotional brain, although frugality is winning this one as usual. It has been a group effort as many of my successes in life have been. With the help of our families, Robert and I should be able to start our lives as a married couple with little to no debt from the wedding. Having met a 21-year-old Robert when I was only 19 years old, we have been very fortunate that our development into adulthood brought us along the same path. Even though we have our disagreements, overall we strive for similar futures. As the years have continued to add up and time has rolled on, I have become happier and more confident. I greatly enjoy my life and hope for more of the same in the years to come.

THE GIRL IN ME

Emily is a twin, and determined to avoid her sister's tomboy image. She works hard at being a girl, from using nail polish to having crushes on boyfriends. She finds, though, that she silences herself everywhere except in the journal she keeps throughout adolescence. As she gradually comes out as a lesbian, to herself, her friends, and her family, her internal, written self emerges as a public person, someone who can engage fully with others through humor, conversation, and physical relationships.

I tried—God knows I tried. No one can accuse me of going down without a fight. I began shaving my legs at the appropriate age (around 13), I applied lip gloss every few minutes, and I composed long, prosaic diary entries about the depth and color of various boys' eyes. I giggled and went to sleepovers and wondered when I would get my period. My hair, though plain and often unkempt, was long. Also, I had low self-esteem and worried a lot. No one ever had to ask me whether I was a boy or a girl. I was, like so many adolescent girls, clearly working my way toward Alpha Female status.

I never made it.

Oh, sure, I had the normal feminine accoutrements: Besides the diary, the makeup, and the hairless (if not shapely) legs, I indulged perpetually in crushing on boys, and I even managed to snag a boyfriend when I was 14. James was quite a catch by eighth-grade standards, in that he was only a little greasy and occasionally even punctuated his grunts with complete sentences. Our relationship began one balmy April night in that breeding ground of all great romances, the middle school gym. He asked me to slow dance; I acquiesced; and, midway through the song, he confessed his months-long crush on me. When he asked me if I would go out with him, I knew what to do—I said yes. And when the song ended, I knew what to do—I ran and told all of my friends about it and didn't stop talking about it for about three weeks. James was great and all, and I couldn't wait to spend time with him, but right now I had the very important duty of sharing this amazing news with every single one of my acquaintances. They provided the appropriate shrieks.

James and I dated for five months—eternity for eighth graders—but things didn't go very well. Though we often held hands, and though I placidly accepted his occasional peck on the cheek and quietly listened to his analyses of the merits of various television programs, he wasn't satisfied. I didn't understand. I sat around waiting for his phone call, and when he did finally call, he insisted I turn on the same TV show he was watching, so I would understand and appreciate his witty commentary. I watched TV for him—on a *school* night. I'd never done that before. What more could he want?

And yet he wanted more. He told me he loved me, and I said, "Um. Thanks." He told me he wanted to French-kiss me, and I said, "Um. No." I wasn't a complete slut, after all. But then he called me a prude, and I didn't say anything; instead I French-kissed him. It was disgusting. Adolescents should be made to sign a contract saying they will not stick their tongues in anyone's mouth until they are at least 16 or 17 years of age. But we had no contract; we had a terrible slobbery make-out session on his mother's couch, instead.

Soon after that, he dumped me. I went to high school single and ready to meet boys. I had contact lenses. I had confidence. I practically had *breasts* by now (I was a late bloomer). I was going to find a new boy, a cute boy, a nice prude boy.

This turned out to be problematic. And the problem was not the quality of the male population at my high school—there were plenty of new boys, cute boys, even nice prude boys. The problem was me. Something inside me wasn't working right. The girl in me—the girl who wore lip gloss, shaved her legs, and loved boys—was broken.

*   *   *

From an early age, maybe four or five, I knew what a girl was. "Girl" was the nail polish my babysitter carried in her purse, the bras my mother wore, the splash of shiny curls on TV. I was girl. My twin sister was girl, but she was bad at it.

We were fraternal twins, and I knew instinctively this was a good thing. It wouldn't behoove me to look like her. Tina refused skirts and threw tantrums over dresses. She tagged after our brother—our elder by three years—and played cowboys with him and followed him to the tops of trees. She could beat me up; often she *did* beat me up and not without good reason. When I learned the word "tomboy," I decided to adjust the phrase to better suit my boyish twin. Hence, the nickname "Tina-boy" was born.

"Tina-boy," like all good insults, stuck hard and stuck fast. Even her own friends used it against her (and when they did, she would turn around and hit me, returning, I suppose, to the source of the word). Like many twins, I struggled to create an identity clearly separate from that of my sister. And perhaps one easy way to do this was to verbally demonstrate my disgust with her masculine tendencies. Not that I was ever really "girly-girl" in my own behavior—I climbed the same trees Tina did, and I caught the baseballs she threw at me. Nevertheless, the taunt persisted: "Tina-boy!" upstairs after dinner, when our parents wouldn't hear. "Tina-boy" during recess at school, where her friends could hear. "Tina-boy!" in the backyard, as I ran and my sister barreled after me in a mix of rage and tears. I couldn't have said why I called her that name; she couldn't have said why it made her cry. We were six years old.

But we both knew gender. Gender was everywhere.

Our parents did not pressure us to be "normal" girls—nor did they insist my somewhat solitary brother give up his reading and hiking for sports like baseball or football. My sister almost never had to wear a dress, and we both joined the local softball team. Mom and Dad were liberal for a reason: Mom had been a tomboy herself, as a child, and she remained uninterested in fashion, cooking, and other stereotypically feminine trimmings. Dad was happy, after realizing his son wasn't interested in baseball, to discover two little girls more than willing to run after his fly balls.

Our parents also encouraged all of us kids to think independently and do what made us happy. For instance, my parents didn't watch television. My mother read mysteries because mysteries made her happy, and my father listened to opera because opera made him happy. If these examples of my parents' independence do not seem noteworthy, that is because my parents were not exceptionally weird. We were not an aggressively eccentric family. Our parents taught us to be respectfully nonconformist, docile in our differences. Like them, we were not to be different for the sake of being different; we were to be different if and when being true to ourselves meant being different from what the majority did or believed.

My parents certainly didn't have to worry about me being different for the sake of being different. As a child, I spent much of my time striving to minimize the discrepancies between myself and my peers. It wasn't difficult to figure out who I was "supposed" to be. We lived in a very homogenous town; most residents were middle class, white, and politely but deeply conservative. The public schools were superb, but many parents chose to send their children to private institutions. The farmlands between neighborhoods were gradually overtaken by more neighborhoods and bigger houses. I grew up with the implicit belief that most people in America lived in a town exactly like mine.

Because everyone looked and acted roughly the same, I became obsessed by differences between my family and everyone else that felt huge—insurmountable—but were in fact quite small. My parents were middle class, white, and, interestingly, in spite of their own forays into nonconformity, politely but deeply conservative, just like everyone else. But as an insecure child, I did not see these similarities—these were the elements of my existence that were so ingrained as to be invisible. I saw the differences.

My family didn't go to church or visit friends or watch hours of television—instead, we read books. I became addicted to books long before I realized that compulsive reading was not a universal obsession. But I quickly became aware that my family read much more than other families and that there was a word for this. We were "nerds." And so I found a way of articulating the difference between myself and the rest of the world. I was nerdy.

I assumed it was this nerdiness that made me unable to live like a normal girl, to French-braid my hair and find a skirt that felt natural on my body. It did not occur to me that these could be separable issues, this love of reading and this inability to do gender properly. I was eight years old; I was not exactly in the habit of analyzing the social fabric of my identity.

I knew that I couldn't give up reading; reading was without a doubt the best thing I had going for me. Books were a welcome respite from the stress of trying to live in a world so rife with stressful situations. When you read, you don't have to make decisions about anything, about what pants to wear or who to sit next to. You just let yourself go—you didn't exist—you just get pulled along by the current of words.

At this particular point in my life, not existing was often as close as I got to happiness.

So I read, and reading was my real life—the *Baby-Sitters Club*, then *Sweet Valley High*, then *A Tree Grows in Brooklyn*, then Steinbeck, Willa Cather, and Harper Lee. When I wasn't reading, I went mutely through the motions of having an existence. I did not talk. I understood the power of words, and I wasn't ready to commit to have words of my own—not out loud, anyway.

On paper was a different matter. From fourth grade on, I kept a diary, a jumble of complaints, gossip, and secret thrills. By middle school, I was obsessed with—and doing absolutely nothing about—the disparity between the "real me" who appeared in my stories, poems, and journals and the pale shadow of a person who stalked the edges of other peoples' lives.

*   *   *

There are multiple strands to this story, multiple strands that became braided into the singular problem of who I was. It is hard now to express how unified everything felt to me during childhood, how naturally and unconsciously I connected reading and silence and gender. It's hard to express now, with my adult (and decidedly collegiate) habit of analyzing, breaking things down, examining the miniscule. But people forget: Childhood is not like that. When the boys rode past my house on their bikes and called me "Mute Girl"—a clever tribute to my unresponsiveness—it was not merely my silence they mocked. They mocked my books, my journals, my plain hair, my athleticism, everything.

In a way, though, I was lucky. They did me the privilege of affirming my femininity, of calling me "girl." My sister was not faring so well in that department.

If the bulk of insults hurled my way reflected on my silence—if that had become my defining feature, my biggest weakness—my sister was far more likely to hear remarks about her gender. Kids called her a boy, and later, when they learned the words, a lesbian, a dyke. Sometimes they said it to me: "Is your sister a lesbian?" I was ashamed of her.

My shame only increased with age, and by middle school, I was ashamed of most things; I could have made a list. I was ashamed of my brother (he was too nerdy); my sister (*was* she a lesbian?); my parents (everything about them, just *everything*, was embarrassing); and myself: my grades, my silence, my lack of friends, my flat chest, my hair, my glasses, my voice, my eyebrows, my handwriting, my fingernails, my everything.

I was unable to look people in the eye. I was unable to speak. I was too ashamed.

And so I wrote. I wrote obsessively, fumbling through the questions I couldn't bear to take to another living person: Why didn't this boy like me? Why had that girl stopped speaking to me? Why hadn't I been invited to this party?

I wrote bitterly about an incident in sixth grade, when my best friend at the time did grave insult to me. We were sitting in English class, done with our work early (we had been thrown together by our status as the smartest kids in the class, and, in fact, we would graduate from our large public high school as valedictorian and salutatorian), and Shereen was complaining about her lack of friends in class. "I wish I had more friends," she said.

"Why?" I asked. "You have *me*, after all." I was half joking, implying that I spoke in jest but actually meaning it very seriously: Was I not enough?

"Yeah," she said, unconvinced. "But, no offense, you're kind of boring."

Later, I wrote furiously: *I am boring. She's right. Of course she wants more friends, better friends. I have no personality. I don't talk. I just sit there like a lump.* This was true. Even among my few close friends, I spent the majority of my time acting as if I was trying to achieve status as an inanimate object. There was some part of me that did not feel as if I had friends at all. In eighth grade, I bitterly announced during French class that I had no friends. I personally offended at least five different girls, girls I sat with in class and giggled with at lunch; it was a callous thing to say (I was not yet aware that anyone besides myself could suffer or feel insecure). But in a way it was true: Some part of me, the part with which I most closely identified, was not connecting with other human beings. In a sense that felt very real to me, I *didn't* have any friends.

This was the part of myself that came out on paper. In fact, it wasn't the fault of my classmates that I didn't consider them my friends; it wasn't because they weren't smart enough, kind enough, or good enough. It was my own fault for hoarding this self, for keeping it limited to pen and paper, for not having the courage to share it. I recognized this fact, but I didn't know how to translate this "real me" off the page and into the world.

And there were other parts of me, deeper, more frightening parts that I could not even bring myself to write about on paper. I never wrote that I was ashamed of my sister, ashamed of my association with her. And I certainly never wrote that I thought I might be gay.

But it was there, a shadow of a notion lurking inside me: *I might be gay.* It surfaced once in a while, but I chose to bury it again. I couldn't face it; it was unbearable. The idea started when I was very young; then, it was inarticulate, because I didn't know what gay was. My sister and I played with our troll dolls, taking on the identities of our favorite trolls, and our characters were always male. Our trolls drove around in fancy sports cars, lived in mansions, and seduced and won countless women. It was always more fun to play at being boy trolls, because they got to do the things Tina and I wanted to do. And if they had girlfriends, well, that was only because we both wanted romance, and if our characters were male, it only made sense that they would fall in love with women. It was a game.

Still, we never played trolls with our other friends.

I remember the first time I really *looked* at a girl. It was seventh grade. My friend Anne and I were standing at our lockers, chatting, when I suddenly looked at her lips and wondered what it might be like to kiss her. I had never thought about kissing in quite that way before; certainly I dreamed of my first kiss, but that was with a boy, and it was hard to imagine. I always assumed that was just because I didn't know anything about kissing—how could I imagine what I didn't know anything about? But here I was staring at Anne's lips and feeling like I could imagine it. They were soft and full, not at all like a boy's lips. They were *kissable*.

Then the moment ended, and I decided never to think about it again. I went back to daydreaming about various boys, and in fact, I really did believe, if a bit too resolutely, that I was in love with whatever boy I happened to be thinking about. I thought constantly about dating different boys—so how could I be anything but perfectly normal? I would never have thought to identify my feelings about certain females as crushes. That idea didn't occur to me when I looked at a girl in my gym class and admired the ease with which she played dodge ball, or when I couldn't stop staring at an older girl on my volleyball team, the one whose face was so beautiful.

I never wrote about these instances. Instead I described in detail the face and habits of my crush and future boyfriend James. When he finally asked me out on the night of that fateful dance, I turned, after shrieking to my friends, to my journal: *Is this real?* I wrote. *Can this be real?* Dating was something that happened to other girls. For the several months of our relationship, in fact, my life felt unreal, no longer my own. This was a clue. Dating James didn't quite fit with the rest of me. I assumed this was because I had never dated before, and perhaps this was partly true. But I did not consider that I might be dating the wrong person—or, worse, the wrong gender.

I did write about my misery when one of my close friends got a boyfriend—somehow, although I was dating James by then, it seemed as if she had betrayed me. I had never lost sight of my priorities even after I started going out with James. I still stuck with my friends first. But Michelle was actually spending more time with her boyfriend than with me. In other words, she actually *liked* her boyfriend. This was baffling; it made me feel vaguely insecure. Was I supposed to like James as much as she seemed to like Chris?

It was mostly a relief when James dumped me, though I sobbed after I got off the phone with him. I no longer had to force myself to enjoy his presence in my life or his tongue in my mouth. And anyway, what did it matter? I was starting high school.

I hoped to achieve the following modest accomplishments during high school (as articulated in my journal the summer before): I would acquire a close-knit group of male and female friends who would enjoy books and the arts; I would acquire a boyfriend who would enjoy books and the arts and also pass for moderately attractive; I would get good grades.

My efforts were not a total failure. I did get good grades.

The main problem with high school, besides my general inability to relate socially to my peers, was the utter lack of crush-worthy boys. It was rather astounding. Were my standards so high? Was it normal for a high school with a population of some twenty-five hundred students to house within its walls not a single attractive, intelligent boy? Did the census know about this? Did the other girls know about this? But that was part of the problem. All around me, girls were routinely developing crushes on and entering into relationships with these very same boys. They did not seem at all dissatisfied with the quality of the males in their lives. Even my sister asked a boy out (he said no). Something wasn't right. Mustering all of my willpower, I developed a half-hearted crush on Jason, who was in my science class. He didn't talk much, and he had nice eyes. In my journal I attributed to Jason all sorts of positive attributes: He was sensitive and passionate; he read books; and, most importantly, he secretly adored me.

Meanwhile, in math class, there was Katie. Katie was the most beautiful girl I had ever seen. Her eyes were so *big*. I would look at her in class and wish fervently that I could be like her. That was what I repeated to myself like a mantra: I wanted to be like her. I wanted to be like her. It wasn't that I liked her—it wasn't that. She was just so smart and pretty and nice. Everyone probably wanted to be like her. I tried to gauge whether other people admired Katie as much as I did, but as usual, the general population did not seem to share my sentiments. So I kept my thoughts to myself and watched Katie from afar. I *really* wanted to be like her.

One day in math class, we were assigned to work in the same group. I was terrified. I was wearing the wrong sweater. Katie pulled her desk over and began talking to me—talking to me!—and writing things down. I nodded mutely. I had no idea why my stomach was making this moment into such a big deal. It wasn't a big deal, it was just a class assignment, it was just some girl.

At random moments during the day, or at night, when I was falling asleep, Katie's face would materialize in my mind. I pushed the thought away.

Meanwhile, Tina and I were trying hard to establish ourselves as separate entities. We now shared the same group of friends, although she was more established within the group than I was. I felt, as I always had, vaguely ashamed of my sister, even when no one else was the least bit troubled by her behavior. But it was more problematic now, because I knew this shame was wrong; I knew it made me a bad person. I couldn't help it, though. I wanted her to stop being so...so *much*. Why did she have to keep her hair so short? Why couldn't she dress like a normal girl? Why did she laugh so loudly? Why did she talk so much? I tried to emphasize the differences between us by keeping my hair long, keeping quiet, and keeping my clothes as normal as possible. I couldn't quite meet her eyes in public.

One of our friends once told me, in strict confidence, that she had over-heard boys in her gym class discussing which one of "the twins" was the hottest. Every boy had cast his vote for me. My friend waited for me to squeal; they had picked me! But I could only stare dully at her, the storm inside me made inarticulate by its intensity. How dare they insult my sister? *How dare they?* At the same time, I felt a prick of pride in my chest—they had picked me! And then, I was nearly bowled over by my shame; I was taking pride in beating my own sister, in something superficial and cruel. I didn't know what to say to my friend.

Maybe that was why I didn't talk, all those years. I sensed that my feel-ings—about my sister, about myself, about the pretty girl in math class, about anything—were not quite right. I wasn't sure I deserved to speak.

It wasn't all bad, though. I was often miserable, but I wasn't *always* miser-able. I made some friends with whom I could talk; they were sarcastic, smart—bookish, even. I began to notice that I could be funny, that my friends laughed when I played up absurdities. Here at last was a method by which I could consis-tently relate to people. Never mind that my parents were concerned that I didn't take anything seriously. Never mind that my father called me a wiseass anytime I made a joke. I had discovered a way to break this silence that had gagged me mute for years: I was funny. Mine was not exactly a humor born of happiness, or even good-natured silliness, but it was something.

Now, of course, after years of using jokes to get through social situations, I understand that jokes can be another kind of silence: They are another way of keeping myself one step removed from people. Sometimes I make jokes and I don't even want to; I want to say something genuine, something about how I feel. But the joke rises most naturally to my lips. I don't mean to denigrate humor, though: It got me through much of high school.

The summer after my sophomore year, I went to an academic camp. I was terrified and certain that I wouldn't make any friends, but luck was with me. One girl, Amanda, singled me out from the beginning. Amanda and I were inseparable for those three weeks; we wept at the camp's end. Every night she would sneak into my room, and we would sit on my bed and giggle and whisper for hours after lights out. Everything was funny with Amanda, and for once, my jokes didn't feel dry or bitter—they came from a sincere happiness.

Amanda and I stayed in touch, and during my junior year, I went to visit her. I had been at her house for about 20 minutes and was looking through her bookshelves when she said, "So, I've been thinking. I'm not really interested in boys anymore."

"What, you?" I joked. Boys were her favorite conversation topic. "What are you going to do with yourself if you don't talk about boys?"

"Well," she hedged, "I'm just not that interested in boys."

I remember the moment I began to understand. I was holding her copy of *A Tree Grows in Brooklyn*—I had been paging through it, only half-attending to her words—and my throat felt suddenly thick.

"I just don't think I'm feeling very heterosexual right now," she said. She actually *said* it. Out loud.

I stared down at the book. "Oh," I said.

"Is that okay with you?" she asked.

"Oh, yeah," I said quickly. "Yeah. Sure."

I couldn't even joke. It was that familiar feeling—there was too much going on in me, I couldn't even begin to address it out loud, so I shut down. I nodded vaguely as she explained that she had come to this realization a few weeks ago and was still trying to decide whether she was *gay*-gay, or just bisexual. She hadn't determined whether she actually hated men or just didn't find them particularly attractive.

"Well, that's good," I said when she paused. "I'm straight," I added, somewhat irrelevantly.

"Of course," she said. "Peter and all." Peter was my latest crush. He was a boring, chubby boy with a bowl cut, and I was obsessed with him.

"Yeah," I said. Right about then her parents called us down to dinner, so we obediently trudged downstairs, though not before she informed me that neither her parents nor her sister knew she was gay, so I should probably not mention it during dinner.

She really didn't have to worry. I wouldn't have ever mentioned it again, if she hadn't kept bringing it up.

It wasn't that I was homophobic. I believed very strongly in gay rights, a vague term whose meaning I did not fully grasp, but whose importance I would quickly defend. Theoretically, gay people were perfectly fine. There were some gay gym teachers at my high school—or so it was rumored—and that was fine. I heard that gay people lived in cities, and that was fine. Gay was just fine by me. But Amanda was not just any gay person—she was my *friend*. She was my very, very close friend, with whom I had giggled and shared a bed. I decided that Amanda was mistaken about being gay. I tried to explain this fact to her, but she seemed convinced. Somehow, during the course of my visit, she determined that she was, in fact, very gay, and not bisexual. I rallied hard on behalf of heterosexuality.

"Maybe you're just *afraid* of boys," I suggested.

She raised her eyebrow. "Oh, really," she said.

I looked away. Amanda was, if anything, the least fearful person I knew. It was unlikely that she was afraid of boys.

I left Amanda's house feeling shaken, but it was easy to stop thinking about the whole thing once I was home again. I could sink back into the usual routine: jokes, boys, homework, boys, and, of course, Melissa.

Melissa was my newest friend, and, I decided, a much better friend than Amanda. Melissa and I just related on more levels. We both worked on the newspaper, for instance, and we both shared a similarly absurd sense of humor, and, oh, yes, we both liked boys. We really had quite a bit in common.

Our friendship was incredibly exclusive; my acquaintances dribbled away as I realized I didn't need them anymore, because now I knew what true friendship was. Melissa and I giggled constantly at private jokes and raged together against the loneliness and frustration of being a dork in a middle-class jock high school. I sought her out in the hallways and went to her house every weekend. In math class, I didn't pay attention: I wrote her notes and drew her little pictures.

For the first time since I could remember, I was genuinely happy. Days were bearable because I had class with Melissa, because I would pass Melissa at her locker, because Melissa existed with me in the same building at the same time. I could get through history class, and bus rides, and lunch, by thinking of her. This did not seem particularly strange to me; this was what friendship was. If there was a small part of me that wondered about the intensity of my feelings, it was a very quiet, submissive part. It kept quiet if I wanted it to. And I wanted it to.

Melissa was funny; she was intelligent; she understood me. When my sister understood me, it felt suffocating, like she was pinning me down, like my genes were giving me away, like I would never escape from her knowledge or her shadow. When Melissa understood me, it felt liberating. Like I was in love.

When a thought like that slipped past my careful censors, I rationalized: Well, sure. I do love Melissa. She's my friend. Friends love each other.

I don't know exactly when I began to face it. There was no special moment when I had a revelation—there was no instance when it became suddenly and irrevocably clear to me. But it became harder and harder to ignore the fact that I would pass up a date with any boy on Earth, even if he were perfect in every way, to spend time with Melissa. But I didn't just want to spend time with her. I wanted to look at her. I wanted to kiss her.

Part of the reason I was able to acknowledge my feelings was because I was fairly confident Melissa felt the same way. She gossiped about boys, sure, but so did I. She liked me better than anyone else, that was obvious. She wrote me notes during school, she e-mailed me obsessively, and she invited me over all the time. "I'm crazy about you, Emily," she wrote once. We were clearly in love. It would be hard, of course, but it was bearable because we would do it together. I didn't particularly think of myself as gay at this time—I thought of myself as in love with Melissa. We were beyond labels. Eventually we would admit our feelings to each other, and we would be even happier than we already were. I settled back to enjoy the ride.

When I told Amanda about my feelings, it was because I wanted her to confirm that yes, it sounded like Melissa was crazy about me. She seemed more interested in the fact that I was attracted to a woman, which confused me: This wasn't about women, or even a woman. This was about Melissa. I just wanted to know, did she think Melissa liked me? Didn't it sound like Melissa liked me?

Amanda couldn't say whether Melissa liked me. She had never seen us together.

Yes, but didn't it *sound* like it?

Well, maybe. It could be.

For weeks, months, I bombarded Amanda with e-mails, relating another incident that I felt demonstrated Melissa's obvious affection for me. Amanda bore my obsession well; she wrote back, she counseled, she consoled.

And consoling was in order. One day in January, Melissa informed me that she had a date with a college boy. I was stunned. I tried to take it lightly; I tried to brush it off, she was curious, she was experimenting. But the date turned into another date, and another, and dates turned into late-night phone conversations and visits to his campus for the weekend. They made out; she told me about it.

Suddenly I was very much alone with this *thing* that I had assumed we shared. I didn't know what to do. For the first time, I began to realize my feelings had implications: *I might be gay.* I might have to live that life. And I might have to do it without Melissa.

*   *   *

Even now, describing a part of my life that is over five years old, describing a fear I have long since shed, I tremble. I had no idea how to be gay. I didn't know any gay people, except the gym teachers, and who knew if they were really gay? And who wanted to be like them, ugly, mean, mocked? I knew Amanda, of course, but she wasn't an adult; she didn't know anything more about living a gay life than I did. She hadn't yet told her family about her orientation, and she had never had a girlfriend. We were equally clueless. Now, of course, I know how much it helped to struggle with her, but at the time, her presence in my life seemed singularly unhelpful.

I became obsessed with renting gay movies, sidling over to the gay section of the bookstore, looking at gay websites online, and then deleting the Internet's history so my family wouldn't find out what I'd been looking at. I wanted to understand how gay people existed, how they got through the day. How they stopped hating themselves. I began to try out the word, repeating it silently to myself: *Gay.* I still couldn't quite handle *lesbian.* It sounded so ugly. It was tinged with the brutality of an insult, the word hurled at my sister for so many years. I wasn't ready to identify myself with that word. I was ashamed to think of those boys laughing at her, at me, at us. I was furious to think that I had the very flaw they had pinpointed in my sister.

I was somewhat consoled by the fact that Tina was not gay. In a way, it even made me happy: I was *different* from her now. We were distinguishable.

I applied to and was accepted by a college known, among other things, for its student population's liberal attitude toward homosexuality. I read stories by and about gay college students; I began to understand that I might be able to be gay at college. Not now, not in high school, but soon. Meanwhile, I tried coming out. I told Melissa about my orientation, half-hoping she might be jolted by my confession into one of her own. No dice. She was very comfortable with my sexuality, far too comfortable to be hiding behind her calm façade some struggle of her own. It was her total inability to relate to my feelings that made her so supportive. I understood this. I remembered how I'd reacted when Amanda had come out to me. When I tried to tell Amanda she wasn't gay, I had something at stake—my own sexuality. Melissa had nothing to lose, nothing to fear, and she meant it when she told me she believed me, supported me, and remained my best friend.

For the remaining months of high school, I tried my hand at girlhood one last time. I might be gay, I reasoned, but I could still be pretty. I didn't have to be ugly, or—I practiced my new vocabulary—"butch." I attended the prom with a male friend and did the whole thing, makeup, dress, and hair. I was extremely pleased with my appearance. People noticed. "Oh, Emily," someone said, "you look so *nice*. I didn't even recognize you!" I had stopped plucking my eyebrows, but I kept my legs smooth and my shorts well above my knees. My hair hung to my shoulders.

College changed me, of course. Most of my friends now would never believe I wore a dress to my prom; they are dumbfounded when I mention that I once plucked my eyebrows, shaved my legs. They try—and fail—to imagine my hair anything but short and neatly combed. I have become, in other words, butch. I am a lesbian, a dyke, I am every word those boys could think of. I am ugly, by their standards—standards that were once my own. I wear baggy pants. I think I own a skirt, but it is buried in the back of my closet, irrelevant.

I came out to my friends in college, as soon as I could muster the courage to do so, and I have not had to pretend here. I got a girlfriend. We broke up; a few months later, I got another one. It was absolutely amazing to me that I could have relationships, and we could walk around on campus holding hands without hearing slurs. We could have dinner with straight people. I could be friends with straight people—and gay people. I could cut off all my hair and dress how I wanted and feel, for the first time in my life, as if I had a body. Not just that I was attractive, although I did feel attractive. I literally finally felt like I had a body, like I *was* a body. I had never realized it: I had been invisible to myself for years. I had been afraid to look like what I was. I had been ashamed of what my body wanted.

I began to talk, too. I made friends far more easily than I had anticipated, and people liked me. I could talk seriously with my friends; I didn't always have to make everything into a joke. I began to turn my writing into poems, and I took classes, submitted my work to publications, and participated in readings. The yawning gulf between my public and private selves began to diminish.

The summer after my freshman year, my sister came out to me. I was the first person she told; she knew about my sexuality, and she turned to me because she expected me to understand and support her. I failed her. Instead of listening to her, I was angry with her. Instead of talking to her, I scoffed at her and condescendingly assured her that once she gained the wisdom and experience I had gained from a year of being "out," all of her questions would dissolve. I was secretly fuming at Tina. I didn't want her to be gay. Didn't she understand? Now we would be the Gay Twins. Now our parents would have two gay children (though at this particular point, I had not yet informed them that they had even one). Now the one thing that made me different from her, the one thing I owned for myself, I had to share with her.

I stayed angry for a long time, though I tried hard to squash my feelings, and I never told her what I felt. Instead, I scrambled to come out to my parents first; I'd be damned if I was going to wait until coming out was cliché.

My parents took it admirably. I have many gay friends, and I know coming out to one's parents is often rocky. But my mother, whom I told first (on the phone) tried hard to hide the fact that she was crying, and my father called later to tell me they would always love me, no matter what. It was uncomfortable, but it wasn't unbearable: I was lucky. My parents are nothing if not consistent: They love their children quietly but deeply. They think for themselves. They are not the kind to be lured into hysteria over their daughter's sexual orientation.

I was having a good time at school, especially with the burden of coming out to my parents lifted from my shoulders. I had stopped shaving my legs and wearing makeup. I cursed; I spit. I just didn't feel very girly. I felt more like myself and more attractive than I ever had before, but I didn't know what I was anymore. The word "transsexual" was tossed around a lot at school, and I wondered if perhaps my breasts were a mistake; maybe there was a boy inside me just waiting to come out. But I checked, and I didn't find one. I still identified with the emotional inner life most of my female friends described. The few male friends I had were gay.

I was often uncomfortable when I found myself in a group of heterosexual men and women. I was openly gay, so males didn't flirt with me, and I had no interest in flirting with them. I wanted to flirt with my female friends. But they were less interested in "playing along" with my flirtation once men came into the picture. I resented their attention to the opposite sex. Worse, I didn't know how to act. Even in a group of friends, there are sexual undertones based on potential attraction, and when I was surrounded by heterosexuals, there was no potential attraction. I felt like I had no allies. Hyper-attuned to these undertones, I sometimes submitted to silence rather than fight to create a space for myself. These moments were among the few when I still felt the familiar gag rise to my mouth and muffle me.

* * *

I am going to graduate in a few weeks. My college years have already taken on a distant quality; I think constantly about the future. But I see the logic of my future, and I see how squarely it rests on the experience of my past.

I will be certified to teach English to middle-school and high-school students soon, and as part of my certification, I completed a semester of student teaching. I think reading and writing have an incredible power to shape our idea of what is possible for ourselves and for the world; I can't forget the comfort I found, as a lonely teenager, in books about gay adolescents. *They existed.* I want to share this experience of finding myself in books and on the page, of discovering the power of my own voice. I want to help kids who close themselves to possibility because the possibilities are unacceptable or unthinkable; I want to show them books where people do the unacceptable and the unthinkable—and then prosper.

I never came out to the students I taught this past semester. Sometimes I wanted to. Sometimes, when a student asked if I was married or if I had a boyfriend, or when a student called something "gay," I wanted to stop everything and tell them. I didn't; I couldn't. They liked me, and I was scared to risk losing their affection and respect. And I don't know whether I will find the courage to take this risk with future classes.

I did tell one girl, the first person under 18 to whom I have come out. This was not a girl from school but a girl I tutored through a program at college. April was 12 years old. We worked together all year, and she talked to me constantly about her struggle with her sexuality. I listened but said nothing about myself, believing she was too young to handle this truth about me. Finally, a few weeks before our sessions ended, she asked me whether I was gay, and I decided to be honest. Maybe it would help her; maybe she could handle it. I introduced her to my girlfriend, and I told her how happy I was, how my parents knew, and my friends. She asked question after question: How did I know I was gay? When did I tell my parents? Who was my first girlfriend? Why did I try to look like a boy? What was wrong with boys, anyway? Did I hold hands with my girlfriend in public? Did people harass us on the street?

People called her a lesbian sometimes, April said. Did people ever call me a lesbian?

I told her the truth: I explained that when I was growing up, people often called my sister a lesbian, and I said I thought that was the worst possible insult. I said I had become the very thing I feared, but I had discovered it was not an insult and not something to be afraid of. Or ashamed of.

For the last few weeks of tutoring, April was not the same. She seemed a little afraid of me. But she continued to ask questions, and she continued to insist that she did not want our sessions to end before the semester ended. Sometimes she asked me about my male friends and then suggested I dump my girlfriend and go out with them. Each time she made this suggestion, I calmly explained to her that this was not who I was. I'm happy this way, I told her.

I don't know what April's eventual preference will be—she's still young, much younger than I was when I first began to consider the possibility that I might be gay. But I wanted her to know that gay people existed and could find happiness. I wanted her to see what I had not seen as an adolescent.

* * *

My sister and I attended the Philadelphia Dyke March last summer. We tried to "out-dyke" each other as we prepared our outfits; her hair was shorter and spikier, but my pants were baggier. She got points for her baseball cap; I got points for my necklace, designed for men.

"Let's go, lesbo," I called when I was ready.

Our parents looked us over and raised their eyebrows; they knew about both of us now. They had tried giving us razors for Christmas, a subtle encouragement to shave our legs. The packages remained unopened.

"Be careful driving," my father said as we breezed past.

We will.

"Have a good time," my mother added.

We will, we will.

We walked out. We got in the car.

"Let's play gay music," I said.

We did.

PART II

RELATIONSHIPS

THEORETICAL OVERVIEW

This section of the book focuses on relationships, specifically family and peer relationships. Until the 1970s, psychoanalytic and neopsychoanalytic theories yielded the most prominent and influential explanations of the processes by which adolescents' relationships with their parents and peers change from childhood to adulthood. Anna Freud and Peter Blos described the process of adolescents' individuation from their parents (Blos, 1962; Freud, 1946, 1958), and Harry Stack Sullivan wrote about the development of intimacy through best-friend relationships (1953). Since that time, social science research has often contradicted these theories, leading scholars of adolescent development to evolve new ways of thinking about adolescent relationships. Psychoanalytic views on adolescence have evolved (Blos, 1979), with some new perspectives, such as attachment theory (Allen & Ladd, 1999), drawing on aspects of earlier psychoanalytic theory. Other theoretical models of adolescent development center on aspects of adolescent relationships that were not the focus of the psychoanalytic perspective. For example, cognitive developmental theory (Kohlberg, 1968; Selman, 1980; Smetana, 1988, 1989) focuses on how children's understanding of their social world becomes more organized and complex as they proceed through adolescence and clarifies how more sophisticated cognitive skills may change parent–adolescent, sibling, and peer relationships. Evolutionary theories discuss how both cognitive growth and pubertal development propel the child from dependence on parents to connection with sexual partners outside the family (Belsky, Steinber, & Draper, 1991; Gray & Steinberg, 1999). Most current theoretical models of adolescents' development now recognize the effects of changing environments on adolescents' social relationships. Critically important social contexts include school and work sites as well as changing social expectations of adults regarding teenagers (Collins, 1995). This introduction briefly notes some of the most important issues in the study of adolescent relationships that are raised by these theories and related research studies and mentions some ways in which the cases in this portion of the book may be used to foster discussions of these topics. Students who are interested in more in-depth study could read a number of excellent overviews of current research and theory on parent–adolescent relationships (Collins & Laursen, 2004; Collins & Repinski, 2001; Grotevant, 1998; Steinberg, 2001; Steinberg & Silk, 2002) and peer relationships (Brown, 2004).

FAMILY RELATIONSHIPS

The psychoanalytic understanding of adolescent–family relationships has traditionally viewed adolescence as a time of profound inner turmoil and outward conflict—a time of "storm and stress." Explosive conflict with family, friends, and authorities was thought of as commonplace. This view was based, to a great extent, on the theoretical work of the psychiatric community in the 1950s and early 1960s (Blos, 1962; Erikson, 1959, 1966, 1968; A. Freud, 1946, 1958). Largely on the basis of their experience with adolescent psychiatric patients, these clinicians and theorists described adolescence as a time of extreme psychic and interpersonal stress. Emotional crises and upheaval were viewed as appropriate responses by the adolescent to major psychological and societal tasks required during this phase of life: dramatically reducing psychological dependency on parents, separating from the family, and forming an adult identity. Adolescent turmoil was not only inevitable but also necessary for subsequent normal personality development.

This storm-and-stress perspective of adolescent family relationships is still perpetuated by the media and is often assumed by the public. Scholars of adolescent psychology, however, are in the midst of developing new ways of describing, explaining, and understanding adolescent–family relationships. These new approaches differ from the long-reigning classic psychoanalytic perspective in several ways. One way these new perspectives differ is in the assertion that adolescents and their families are more likely to negotiate changes in power, responsibilities, and modes of intimacy through a continuous series of minor, although significant, daily "hassles," rather than through tumultuous, warlike conflicts. The majority of conflicts in adolescence arise over mundane issues such as family chores, curfews, eating practices, dating, and personal appearance. Data from empirical studies with nonclinical populations of adolescents and their families from the past forty years have led to a radical revision in our understanding of how adolescents separate from and remain connected to their families. The majority of research now clearly refutes the notion that most adolescents undergo severe emotional stress and family conflict during this period of life (Collins & Laursen, 2004; Adams & Laursen, 2001). A variety of studies using such diverse methods as epidemiological surveys (Rutter, Graham, Chadwick, & Yule, 1976), phone interviews (Montemayor, 1983), and time sampling with electronic beepers (Csikszentmihalyi & Larson, 1984) have shown that for most families with adolescent members, serious conflict and disorganization are not characteristic states (Hill, 1987). Evidence drawn from various kinds of self-reports offered by nonpatient adolescents and their parents provides no support for an inevitable dramatic increase in family conflict from childhood to adolescence.

In fact, the frequency of conflict with parents declines from early adolescence to midadolescence and again from midadolescence to late adolescence (Laursen, Coy, & Collins, 1998).

In general, the family is not at risk for great turmoil or disorganization during the adolescent years; the search for greater independence from the family is not usually played out in major battles between adolescents and their parents. Instead, current studies look for smaller, although still highly significant and lasting transformations in sharing of power and responsibility and in the nature of family intimacy through daily renegotiations. Adolescents usually value their relationships with their parents, and these relationships change and adapt as the adolescent becomes an adult member of the family (Adams & Laursen, 2001).

It would be a mistake to conclude that conflicts between adolescents and their parents or siblings are insignificant or rare and that their presence indicates family or individual psychopathology. Any valued human relationship undergoes stress at times, particularly when the relationship must adapt to change within an individual. However, the majority of parent–adolescent conflict situations are not associated with lasting problems, although chronic and unresolved hostility between parents and adolescents does predict adolescent maladjustment (Hauser, Powers, & Noam, 1991; Smetana, 1996). Given this understanding of the experiences of most adolescents in the United States, how do the cases presented in this book help you to understand conflict and transformation between these adolescents and their parents? Cases 9 and 10 may be used to clarify your ideas concerning what characteristics are important for an optimal parent–adolescent relationship. In what ways do these families hinder or foster their teenagers' independence, achievement, identity, or intimacy goals? Are there any problems that could be associated with a pattern of family interaction that exhibits no conflict? How can "normal" developmental tasks of adolescence, like identity development, occur in the context of troubled family relationships, as seen in Cases 9 and 10?

In cases with severe family conflict, you might ask which adolescent issues trigger aspects of the tumult in these families and when is conflict a product of a long-standing family system. Case 10 provides a powerful description of a family under severe stress and an adolescent's extreme strategies for coping with that stress. Clearly, some of these strategies strengthen resilience (e.g., Chhaya's perfectionism reinforces her ability to succeed at many demanding tasks, including school), while other strategies (e.g., Chhaya's anorexia) eventually cause more pain than relief. Chhaya's case is a reminder of the variety of patterns that lead eventually to successful young adult adaptation and functioning. Cases in other sections of the book may also serve as examples of atypical family situations leading to severe stress in adolescence (see, e.g., Case 1, "Someday My Elders Will Be Proud").

Contemporary approaches to describing adolescent–family relationships now also emphasize adolescents' continuing need for maintaining intimacy and connection with parents and siblings (Collins & Russell, 1991). In "The Family I Have" (Case 9), Myra realizes that she has a strong desire for a closer relationship with her brother. Earlier psychoanalytic theories focused primarily on the process of separation from the family. Results from studies that have observed adolescents' interactions with their parents have indicated the importance of family interaction styles that permit conflict between members in a context of support (Baumrind, 1987, 1989; Powers, 1988; Powers, Hausser, Schwartz, Noam, & Jacobson, 1983), acceptance, active understanding from parents (Allen, Hauser, Bell, & O'Connor, 1994; Hauser, et al., 1984, 1987), and parental expressions of individuality and connectedness (Grotevant & Cooper, 1986). Closeness is maintained through different behaviors and activities in adolescence than during childhood: Close physical contact and joint activities with parents decrease during adolescence, but conversations that convey information and feelings increase (Hartup & Laursen, 1991). These conversations are more likely to occur with mothers than with fathers, most likely because adolescents spend considerably more time with their mothers (Steinberg & Silk, 2002). Most of the cases in this book are strong illustrations of adolescents' heartfelt need to be affectively connected to their families.

Another important difference in newer approaches to understanding adolescent–family relationships is the strong effort to encompass descriptions of a *wide variety of patterns* of family relationships, rather than focusing on explaining one primary picture of how "normal" adolescents interact with their families. Instead, a wide range of adolescent family behaviors is considered relevant to understanding adolescent adaptive responses to growth in relationships. This new perspective seeks to include more diversity in the adolescents and families studied. For example, regarding this, it is crucial to understand the varieties of adaptive family functioning in African American, Latino, Native American, Asian American, and other groups of adolescents in U.S. culture (Cooper 1994). It may be helpful to contrast the family pictures described by adolescents of European American descent in this section with pictures of family life described by adolescents from different ethnic backgrounds (see the thematic index and Cases 3, 4, 5, and 6 among others) and by other students in your class. Cases 5 and 6 illustrate the importance of adolescents learning skills from their parents for dealing with racism and discrimination. Scholars of adolescent psychology have also begun to examine adolescent–parent relationships within families with diverse structures, such as single parent, stepparent, and noncustodial parent families. Research findings show that the majority of children and adolescents that experience the divorce of their parents are more resilient than was once expected. An important factor for facilitating a healthy adjustment to the transitions that accompany divorce is the adolescent's relationship with at least one involved, caring, and authoritative adult (Hetherinton & Stanley-Hagan, 2002).

PEER RELATIONSHIPS

Many cases throughout the book discuss peer relationships, and the reader is encouraged to look in the thematic index following the table of contents for cases that can be found in other sections but include material on peer relationships.

For example, "Someday My Elders Will Be Proud" (Case 1) and "Seeking the Best of Both Worlds" (Case 18) describe the power of peer pressure when an adolescent's ethnic culture is different from that of the dominant culture. The sections on sexual identity are also useful for examining romantic relationships.

Peer relationships include close friendships, cliques, peer groups and crowds, and romantic relationships. In an excellent review of peer relationships during adolescence, Brown (2004) notes five major themes in research findings regarding adolescent peer relationships. First, adolescent relationships are characterized by instability (Connolly, Furman, & Konarski, 2000; Elder, 1985; Feiring, 1999; Strouse, 1999). Second, research has increasingly focused on describing the behaviors and processes by which adolescents manage conflicts in friendships and romantic relationships (Galliher, Rostosky, Welsh, & Kawaguchi, 1999; Welsh, Galliher, Kawaguchi, & Rostosky, 1999) and pressure and influence one another (e.g., Dishion, Spracklen, Andrews, & Patterson, 1996). Third, conflict is common in adolescent peer relations and can both support healthy growth in coping strategies and, under some circumstances, lead to maladaptive outcomes (Welsh, Grello, & Harper, 2003). Fourth, there are important links between adolescents functioning in different types of peer relationships e.g., functioning in close friendships predicts functioning in romantic relationships (Connolly et. al, 2000; Furman, 1999; Furman, Simon, Shaffer, & Bouchey, 2002). Fifth, peer relationships change throughout adolescence in accordance with developmental growth in the domains of cognition, puberty, and identity.

Cases in this and other sections of the book may be used to explore and illustrate each of these major themes. For example, cases may be analyzed to illustrate and understand some of the reasons underlying instability in peer relationships. Jack's case (Case 11) provides a window through which to view the importance of the existence or lack of close friendships in high school, while José, Jack, and Andy's cases (Cases 4, 11, and 12, respectively) illustrate the crucial nature of close friendships in the transition to college—and how those friendships shift as individuals continue to change. The case of José (Case 4) and his struggle to "fit in" can be used to examine how peers are used as a means of social comparison and how peers can be an important source of information outside the family. The role of popularity—fitting in with desired cliques, being rejected or neglected by peers—is acutely felt by all adolescents included within this section on peer relationships.

Current theory and research also underscores the importance of connections between the quality of family relationships and the quality of close peer relationships (Gold & Yanof, 1985; Parker & Gottman, 1989). The case of Chhaya provides excellent material for a discussion of the impact of family relationships on the development of peer relationships. Chhaya's ways of relating to her high school friends mirror the way she relates to her family; she is afraid to show anything other than her "perfect" self. In Case 13, Is This My Life, Dorothy experiences shifting family relationships as a result of her choice to have a baby. What are the aspects of close friendships and romantic relationships that the adolescents in this book value, and how do these values change as these adolescents mature?

THE FAMILY I HAVE

As a child, Myra loves her somewhat eccentric family. As she enters adolescence, however, she begins to distance herself from them because their eccentricity begins to seem "strange." She engages instead with friends, academics, and activist causes, in both high school and college. Her adopted brother's difficulties in and out of school lead her to reflect more directly on her relationships with members of her family and the family's general process of interaction. In college, she begins to renegotiate these relationships, holding onto her independent and separate self while exploring what it means to be part of her family.

The red-lit number on the face of our answering machine announced that the machine stored twenty-eight messages. I began to play them and quickly skipped through the first fifteen or so as I searched for a message from a friend relaying details on an activist event we were planning. As I slowed my advance through the messages, I noticed that many of them had been left by the same automated voice. "This message is to inform you that your ninth-grade son has been reported absent from one or more classes. This absence has yet to be explained. Please call your son's grade-level office—BEEP... This message is to inform you that your ninth-grade son—BEEP... This message is to inform you that your—BEEP... this message—BEEP... this message is—BEEP... "

I sighed with exasperation at the fact that no one but me had bothered to delete the messages and clean the tape. Yet, I paused to reflect on my brother's attitude to school, which was significantly more badass than mine had been. "Michael sure figured out that it doesn't matter if you skip study hall faster than I did," I mused. By my junior year of high school, I'd loosened up enough to occasionally cut a gym class to go grab lunch or finish my math homework, but I was significantly more uptight than my younger sibling, who had recently blossomed from a shy kid who liked watching nature channel specials on the emu and collecting Star Wars cards into a suave socialite, much cooler than me.

Michael's social prowess, far more conventional than the silly humor and activistic passion that I had used to build my own social circle, was just one of the characteristics on an unending list of the differences between me and my brother. Despite our polar characters, Michael and I had a friendly albeit distant relationship. The close bonds of our early childhood had ended abruptly with my entry into kindergarten, where I succumbed to the peer pressure of my classmates who informed me that little brothers were *not* friends. They were annoying. Before that Michael and I had been comrades in fun: cutting eyeholes in paper bags to create torso-sized masks and setting up tents in front of the TV where we could cuddle with each other and blankets while we watched "The Sea Gypsies." There had been none of the typical jealousy that comes with new siblings.

I attribute this initial lack of sibling rivalry largely to the ownership I felt over the decision to have another child in the family. Because giving birth is an unpleasant process, my mother claims, my parents chose to adopt their second child. While at two years old I clearly had no veto power in this decision, my parents gave me a sense of agency in the adoption process. "I want to adopt a girl from Brazil!" I proclaimed.

"Okay, we'll look into that," my parents responded seriously, "but we're not sure if it will work out. How would you feel about having a brother from Vietnam?"

"I want a brother from Vietnam!" I ordered. In addition to feeling that I had picked out the new person who would soon enter my life—unlike my unfortunate playmates who would be saddled with whatever sister or brother happened to pop out of their mothers—I relished the adoption process that must have been painful and painstaking for my parents. The meetings with social workers, the creation of books of photographs, and the purchase of stuffed animals mailed to Vietnam, each of these events was an adventure for me.

After Michael finally arrived, a warm April after his second birthday when I was 4, I quickly forgot that he was adopted. Having an Asian brother complemented our family's Judaism nicely in allowing me to share stories during the diversity lessons of my liberal education, but other than that, it didn't really factor into my daily life.

In fact, many of the factors that seem like they should have been of paramount importance at that time didn't seem to impact the experiences of my childhood. Maybe it's that childhood is this time when your family is still your first and sometimes only reference point. You haven't yet been exposed to all these outside influences that tell you which of your experiences are normal and which experiences distinctly aren't. The fact that my parents slept in different bedrooms didn't phase me—they both snored and would wake each other up all night long if they didn't! My brother's night terrors were just a problem that had to be dealt with, like an earache. My father worked until seven or sometimes nine at night, and my mother was a graduate student working through her courseload at a snail's pace. What other way could a family be? What was important were the raucous lab parties that took place on our porch; the globe game that Michael and I played identifying countries to win red-hots from my mom; the sound of

A Jar of Dreams or *Fried Green Tomatoes* read by my mother before bed; and the trips to the gas station with my Dad when we got to pick out *whichever* candy bar we wanted. When I was a young child, I made a remark that later became famous in my family: "I have the best parents. I love Mama so much because she spends time with us and reads us stories and loves us. And I love Papa so much because he gives us candy and toys." As a child, I loved my family unconditionally, not picking up on the fact that some of the things that I regarded as wonderful or normal might be perceived by outsiders as problematic.

The proud love I'd felt for my family as a young child and in my elementary school years swiftly dissolved as I entered my secondary education. I began to notice more and more "strange" things about my family. I cringed when my mother insisted that I continue to call her and my father "Mama and Papa" rather than the more adult "Mom and Dad" because she didn't like the way "Mom" sounded. I couldn't understand why it was so difficult for my mother to pack me PB and J on white bread with a juice box and chips for lunch (I instead found myself with pickles, matzo, rye bread with nutella, and seltzer water). I could no longer explain to my peers why my house was atrociously messy, why my parents slept in separate bedrooms, or why my brother had more Pokemon cards than he had friends or As on his report cards. The fact that my mother was proud of her obesity—"no one wanted to get to know me for who I really was when I looked like Barbie"—suddenly became a huge issue in the appearance-oriented world of adolescent girls. My intellectual, eccentric parents were suddenly at a disconnect with the normalized teenage world that I had stumbled upon. In seventh grade, when I asked my mother for last-minute help on a report on an artist and she *insisted* that I write about Rubens instead of suggesting a more standard Van Gogh or Monet, I made a decision. I don't know if that decision was conscious or not, but from that point on I became as independent from my family as I could be.

That was the last time I ever asked for help on a homework assignment (with the exception of ninth-grade biology, during which my cancer-researching father was a valuable asset). I completely ceased asking my friends over to our house, always going to their homes or meeting them downtown instead. I rushed through family dinners in order to meet my waiting homework. I struggled to stop asking for favors; I packed my own lunch and walked places or got rides from friends rather than from my parents. I had chalked up my family as dysfunctional and weird. By high school I had clear-cut goals: good grades, activist causes, and strong friendships. In my grand scheme of things, I felt that my family was only a liability when it came to tackling the challenges I placed before myself. More and more, my family dropped into the background.

The recession of my family's importance in my daily life was mostly simple, gradual, and unnoticed. Most teenagers assert independence from their parents; it's part of growing up. My father never commented on the fact that my withdrawal was perhaps more significant than that of his colleagues' children. Perhaps he expected me to skip family dinners for homework and to prefer spending my summers at camp over family vacations. Maybe the intermittent contact during help with biology homework or when we watched TV together and the relative lack of conflict were satisfactory to him.

At the time, I'm not even sure that I realized that I was withdrawing more than my other friends. It was the girl who stayed home from weekend get-togethers for family dinners who seemed lame and odd, not me. Spending time or thoughts on my family simply was no longer a priority; these had been usurped by worlds my parents seemed to know nothing about: friends and clothes, extracurricular commitments, and SAT prep.

While my father didn't seem fazed by the changes in my time schedule and attitude, my mother was deeply affected. She sometimes articulated her unhappiness in the face of my abandonment of our family and my obligations to our shared household. Perhaps because she was upset about the changes in my behavior, our relationship became more and more antagonistic, which in turn caused me to distance myself further. Frequently, we would have long and intense verbal battles. They would start over something that seemed small, maybe tension had already been building, I don't know. I'd be sitting at the table doing my math homework, sleeping in bed, or for the first time in weeks relaxing in front of the television. My mother would interrupt me, to tell me about some dishes I had to wash or a pile of stuff I had to move. "Look," I would say, struggling to assert that I *knew* what I had to do and I had my priorities in place, "I have an Algebra test *tomorrow*" or "I haven't sat down to rest in *weeks*. I'll take care of it after this." My mother would respond by asserting my selfishness or lack of responsibility and the disagreement would erupt into a volley of screams and cruel quips aimed to hurt the other party. Eventually, my mother would say something that I found so horrible—you're a creep, a horrible daughter, you only care about yourself—that I would begin to sob and exit the room, slamming the door behind me. Sometimes the shouts would continue from separate rooms, but eventually, almost always after I lay crying alone, my mother would enter the room and hold me and comfort me until I stopped crying.

I wondered why our fights always followed this pattern, why my mother would provoke me when she knew what the end outcome would be. I think sometimes there would be a reason behind our fights and some temporary consensus would be reached. Sometimes, whatever was really troubling me about our family would come out during the climax of the argument, or while my mother comforted me afterwards: "You and Papa don't really love each other." "You're *never* going to finish graduate school. Michael and I stopped you from getting a job." "You spend too much time taking care of me, Michael isn't going to do well in school." And then my mother would soothe me and inform me that this wasn't the case, that if I had just spoken to her earlier, this misperception could have been cleared up. There would be momentary calm, and the volcano would not erupt for another few weeks.

Occasionally, however, the fights wouldn't resolve in that manner. My mother would just go on being antagonistic and occasionally cruel and never come to rescue me. I remember one fight erupting during a five-minute car ride to a friend's house and her casting me out of the car in tears to ashamedly greet my friend with a red and salty-wet face. When my mother abandoned me in my misery at home, I would go find my father. "Don't you think she's being unreasonable?" I would ask. "Don't you think if she let me have some *input* into the way we organized the house I would clean it more?" And my dad would assure me that I was indeed the reasonable one and that my mother was indeed irrational. But he would also tell me that I just had to placate her and move on.

I was not a violent or angry teenager. I have never fought with anyone the way I fought with my mother. The angry words and outrage that flew were a release of energy, but they were not behaviors I liked displaying—so I distanced myself from my mother further. But maybe this strategy amplified the problem.

While my parents in general and my mother specifically provoked me to retreat from my family, the physical and emotional distance between us expanded to my brother as well. During these years, categorical observations all too often formed the bulk of my thoughts of Michael. I didn't think about him as a person I knew, but rather about him as an abstract unit of the family. I had a brother: He liked soccer. He was good at art. He was bad at school. He was adopted. These observations complicated my relationship to abstract concepts like race, talent, and academic success but didn't really texture my day-to-day interactions with the boy I shared a house with. Our relationship didn't go very deep—I didn't particularly feel like I *knew* him that well, despite the fact that I felt a strong sense of love for the brother I'd watched grow from afar. At this point, my relationship with Michael was similar to my relationship with my parents, although I didn't feel the same strong, protective sense of love for my mother and father that I did for Michael, and in the case of my parents, our distance seemed purposed rather than coincidental.

The space in my life and emotional consciousness that opened up when I distanced myself from my family filled so quickly that it seemed like I hadn't pushed away my family and childhood pursuits but that new activities and relationships had crowded them out. I clearly and consciously defined a personal path to success for myself that consisted of a mélange of typical teenage perfections: popularity, appearance, academic success, and more personal goals: political involvement, intimate friendship, having a unique character. My days suddenly filled themselves with school, hours upon hours of homework, the synagogue youth group, dance class, activist clubs, and other activities. I also began to fill my life with new people. The importance of friendship in my life grew tenfold. With the independence of adolescence came the ability to meet friends for dinner at downtown restaurants, to bike over to their homes unaided, and later to go for long drives to nowhere. I quickly developed a steady and nurturing group of friends who were similar to myself.

Together we embarked on adventures and projects. In middle school, two of my friends and I always walked home to one of their houses. There we completed our pre-algebra and French homework, ate dried cranberries, and watched movies. We made a project of folding one-thousand paper cranes for my friend Emily's bedroom. Everyday after school we would listen to music and fold and fold and fold while we chatted about things that I don't even remember but that seemed incredibly important at the time. My friends were fun, and the things they liked and did seemed *so cool* especially in contrast to the bizarre tastes of my family.

In high school, these types of friendships continued and intensified. My small group of a few girls who played stringed instruments and worked hard at school expanded to include about ten other kids who liked music and art, were intellectually engaged, and liked to have silly and spontaneous fun. We had calculus study groups (renamed Algebra 4 to seem less intimidating) that degenerated into giggle sessions, and we ate every lunch together in the band room. I remember having incredible amounts of fun with my friends in high school: cooking dinners together on the weekends, going paddleboating, filling buckets with water and bobbing for apples during lunchtime, taking easels to coffee shops and drawing the patrons, swing dancing and going to jazz concerts, playing ultimate Frisbee in the park, taking county highways to drive-in movies, and embarking on photo-scavenger hunts that we designed ourselves.

This core group of friends—as well as other friendships that I built with other politically involved kids in the later years of high school—also shared my values (values that all of our parents also shared) and pushed me to think and develop those views. We'd bring the *New York Times* to school in the mornings and talk politics over lunch. We got angry when we saw discrimination in our school; we thought critically about our role in the world. In middle school, my friends and I did every fund-raising walk we could find, and by the end of high school, we'd graduated to a 450-mile AIDS bike ride. My friends challenged me, and together we explored our role in the larger political world. We formed clubs, and through those clubs, I made new friends who were intrigued by political issues and power structures. Together we figured out what it took to learn outside of school, to implement recycling programs, and to pass city council resolutions. We learned about how, even as teenagers, our power in the world could be so profound, but also so limited.

I formed another important group of relationships at summer camp. Each summer I'd pack my bags and head to the wilds of upstate New York. There I had space to grow and develop on my own. My role models were college-aged camp counselors; there were no real grown-ups in sight. In a social world composed completely of my peers, I stretched my wings and really felt like I grew. There were boys at summer camp with whom I flirted and felt normal. There were girls at summer camp with whom I could candidly discuss issues of body image, feminism, and superficiality. Isolated from the real world, we critiqued the messages the media, our schools, and our parents sent us about what it meant to be successful and what it meant to be good. I felt independent and loved in that environment.

I held on to my summer camp friendships during the year, too. I exchanged e-mails and paper and pen letters covered in collages and doodles. Every night my best friend and I would have long conversations via instant messenger. We'd exchange notes on the opposite sex, on the banality of high school, on whatever current event was big news, and on what Bob Dylan was like when he was our age. Every so often I'd take the bus down to the city for a New Year's party or a long weekend with my summer camp buddies. When we were old enough to drive, these visits took on an independent and wildly fun flavor as we drove around the suburbs making surprise visits to friends and leaving poetry in the mailboxes of crabby neighbors.

In addition to being fun and challenging, many of my friends were also steady and reliable. I listened to their problems and they would listen to mine. We discussed the typical troubles of adolescents: eating disorders, drug use, romantic relationships, friendship difficulties, the pressure to succeed academically, as well as simply recounting the events of bad days. When my family seemed weird or crazy or impossible, I had people to go to. I never really talked to them about any serious issues with my family—fights were mentioned with flippancy and the oddities that bothered me were reduced to humorous incidents. But when life at home seemed impossible and strange, I could usually count on a study date or evening of SCRABBLE with my steady and levelheaded friends.

This isn't to say that my friends were perfect—they were annoying or petty at times—and this also isn't to say that my family truly was completely dysfunctional and awful, or even that as a teenager I felt that way all the time. My adolescence was characterized by a disdain for my "weird" family and a quest for independence. But, I was also a fairly culturally critical kid. I knew from the social science books that I read in my free time that cookie-cutter normalcy wasn't all it was cracked up to be. I loved some of my family's idiosyncrasies. Who else did I know that had been brought to gay pride marches and counter-protests at abortion clinics since infancy? Who else's parents had lived together since college (despite the fact that they hadn't married until they were past thirty) resulting in the repetitive story of when it was Papa's week to cook and they ate borscht soup all week long? I was proud of my father's research—who else knew that cayenne pepper could cure cancer?—and the myriad of talents that my brother had, but didn't pursue: "Yeah, he was the best kid on the soccer team, but he didn't like running so he quit. You should see this flip book he made, though!" The feminist example that my mother set for me provided me with armor for many of the challenges that my female peers faced in adolescence, and my feminist identity stayed with me throughout all my years of schooling. I used the resources that my parents had to offer: A dinner with them and some family friends gave me advice on how to plan a rally—how long it should be and where tables should be set up. My father's job of accepting graduate students to the university yielded advice (which I sometimes later discarded) about college applications.

I managed to deal with what I perceived as dysfunction and inefficiency in the family unit by distancing myself from it through high school and the beginning of college, yet I had a basketful of funny stories about my "weird family" that I'd whip out at a moment's notice. I had a penchant for the quirky and eccentric and during lulls in conversation wouldn't hesitate to mention that my parents lived together for twenty years before they got married—and when they did, it was at the spur of the moment in Taiwan. By the time I entered college, my mother finally had a job and my brother finally had friends. The house was sometimes clean! Things seemed to be stabilizing: My family didn't really consume much of my time, but they were a helpful conversation piece that I could use when I needed them and even appreciate in real-life interactions. I'd even started to be comfortable enough with my family that by winter break of my first year of college (following my brother's example), I was cool with bringing a few high school friends home to hear stories from my inebriated father about the kangaroo he was planning to meet on his next business trip to Australia.

But of course, as always happens, things changed that following spring. I thought that my brother's life was going well, judging from the crew of kind friends that seemed permanently glued to the TV in our basement and the sweet girlfriend he'd recently acquired. I chased any worries about his grades or school attendance from my mind by reminding myself that Michael couldn't and shouldn't grow up to be like me, that academic performance was only one measure of success. But that April, my mother called me on my dorm room phone to check in and let me know that even though Passover was over, she still wanted to send me the Passover package she'd been planning as soon as she figured out how to ship pickled lemons. When I inquired about how my brother was doing, though, the tone of our conversation changed.

"We've been having some trouble with Michael lately," she said. She then went on to list a litany of issues that had recently come to her attention. Michael had completely stopped going to school, was failing all his classes, was hanging out with different kids, and was smoking pot every day, maybe even more than once a day. All this came as a shock to me. For some reason, I had assumed that my brother, like me in high school, didn't touch substances. I thought he skipped gym class—not every class, every day. I thought that because his friends seemed so clean cut and nice, since they did fine in school, that they'd take care of him. But none of this was true. I felt bad and helpless because my brother was apparently in such a spot of trouble in his life. But I also felt guilty because we were so distant that I hadn't even realized it.

During childhood and early adolescence, it had been the norm to have distant or even antagonistic relationships with siblings. After all, I'd ditched my lame-o little brother because of kindergarten peer pressure. In elementary school, I went so far as to be mean to Michael, calling him stupid and blaming him for my misdeeds. ("I don't know where the candy on top of the refrigerator went. You should ask Michael.") By high school we were friendly but distant. It all seemed correct. But now, in college, I looked around, and it seemed like everybody was best friends with his or her sibling. I was surprised by the long phone conversations my roommate had with her sister, by the fact that my best friend openly admired her older sister, who was clearly her role model. And it was hard to listen as my friends discussed how funny it was to watch their younger brothers and sisters undergo the same college search process that they had and whether they thought their siblings should go to Brown or Pomona. Not only did I wonder if the suddenly abnormal lack of friendship between me and Michael was a shortcoming on my part, I also wondered what role I had played in causing his current difficulties.

At this point in my life, my everyday activities were colored by a sense of logical efficiency. The first thing I did was to tackle the problems in Michael's life the same way that I would tackle any other problem that surfaced in my life: by analyzing them. Who was to blame for these new problems? Was it my parents who had not been involved enough in my brother's upbringing? Was it me for abandoning my brother in favor of other pursuits? Was it me for encouraging my parents to do their parenting job from a distance and showing them that everything would turn out all right if they did that? Was it our large public high school which catered its attention and energies to highly motivated students like me, allowing students like my brother to fall through the cracks? Was it my father for the hands-off approach he took to parenting, leaving the important decisions about Michael's life to my mother's—perhaps unsound—discretion? Was it the attention deficit disorder with which Michael had only been recently diagnosed? Was it low self-esteem influenced partially by the way I called him "stupid" at the drop of the hat as a youngster? Was it the traumatic experiences he'd had in day care as a toddler?

As I moved back further and further in Michael's life searching for the root causes of his present difficulties, I stumbled on a series of factors that I'd only recently begun to consider when thinking about my brother. It wasn't until I was 13 that I looked across the dinner table and fully realized that my brother looked different from me. It was much later in high school when I first thought about the fact my brother's children would not inherit any of my genetic material— no one would ever say that my niece had inherited my eyes or love of dance. And it wasn't until college that I realized that my family fit the definition of a "multiracial family"—because up until now I had assumed that my brother's ancestors were the same French and Hungarian and Russian Jews who passed on their genes to me. All these startlingly obvious, yet belated and intellectualized, observations began to shape my conception of my relationship with Michael toward the end of my high school years and the beginning of college.

Now that Michael's life seemed to be spinning out of control, I wondered what role these factors played in his life. My school classes on race and ethnicity reminded me that my brother's growing-up experience, as a child with brown skin and Asian eyes, must have been significantly different from mine. I remembered the elementary school kids who'd asked Michael if he ate dogs, the kid at summer camp who had called Michael "chink" during a physical fight, and the distant cousin from small-town Wisconsin who had told me that Michael must be very, very smart since he was Asian. I then allowed my mind to wander in a far less politically correct direction. Could some of Michael's problems stem from genetic factors? Had my work ethic and intellectual prowess been inherited rather than learned from my parents? And then, the worst question of all was raised in my mind: What if we hadn't adopted Michael and my parents had just chosen to have another biological child? Would that child be succeeding? Would that child be my friend?

These thoughts were difficult and felt like a betrayal of the younger brother that I loved so intensely, albeit distantly. I couldn't imagine my life without Michael, with some paler, less athletic boy in his stead. I pushed the adoption questions out of my head and focused on the present.

As problem after problem unfolded in my brother's life, I watched from a distance and kept the issues secret from my friends. I was never home for more than a month at a time, and in that time I tried to be kind to Michael, observing the tension between him and my parents. Most of my information about the drama of Michael's late adolescence was relayed to me via phone conversations with my parents, not through phone conversations with Michael. Each time I called, it seemed like a new horrible thing had happened. In my memory their chronology is blurred, as if the events of those years are an avalanche of horribleness, and it didn't matter the precise order of when each chunk of snow and ice hit the ground, it just mattered that they were falling fast and that they were dangerous. And the chunks were scary. Over the course of the next year, Michael got violent when he got drunk, ran away from home and was not heard from for months at a time, was arrested, lost friends, stole money, was beaten up, and broke up with his girlfriend—the only steady and positive thing in his life.

Like I said, I don't really remember when each event took place, and perhaps that's because I didn't talk with anyone about these incidents. My mother lost her job because of the time and energy she was spending dealing with and fighting with Michael. This was a huge blow to me; I'd been waiting since I could remember for my mother to finish graduate school, to get a job, to become a normal mother. To have this wonderful, normalizing thing taken away hurt me and thrust the gravity of the situation in my face. And my brother was missing. And I had homework to do.

I also had friends to see, friends who didn't know what was going on. I chose not to confide in my friends for a variety of reasons, I suppose. Because I'd never told my friends about the previous problems I'd had with my family. Because it would be awkward to say to them, "So, how was your bio test?" "It was fine." "Did I mention that my brother is dependent on marijuana and has run away from home? Oh yeah, my mom lost her job, too." Because I didn't want to dramatize the situation and make it about me and not my brother: "Yeah, did you hear about how tragic and dysfunctional my life is? Yeah, it's pretty bad..." Because I was embarrassed and ashamed of the way my family acted. Because I didn't want my friends to constantly check in on me, as if I were a fragile thing that needed helping. This was my brother's issue, and I wasn't quite sure where I fit into everything.

That October, I took a day off of class to attend synagogue for the Jewish New Year. I reflected over the previous year, the goals that I had set and accomplished, where I had fallen short. I once again wondered where I fit into my family in general and my brother's problems in particular. I thought about the hundreds and hundreds of hours and all the energy I'd poured into activist causes over the previous year: The Sweat-Free Campaign on my campus. My school's Committee on Equal Opportunity. Voter Registration. The AIDS Ride. How could I devote so much of myself to helping strangers raise their wages or pay for HIV drugs when my brother, who should be one of the closest people to me, floundered while I did nothing? I'd spent the last five years of my life ignoring my family, I decided. For whatever reason, I felt that this distance was wrong, incorrect. This year, I resolved, they would be a priority, though I wasn't really sure what that meant.

It meant calling home rather than waiting for my parents to call me. It meant calling my brother's cell phone to leave friendly messages on his voice mail. It meant coming home for breaks to find that my brother had returned from whatever friend's house he was crashing at in order to sit on the couch with me while I watched him play video games. Like I said earlier, just because my brother and I didn't have much in common, just because we weren't "close" the way some siblings were, didn't mean that we didn't profoundly love each other. He came home to see me.

By making small efforts, I placated my conscience. The family box could be checked off on my to-do list, and I felt slightly better about the whole thing. But that didn't mean that Michael did. When he had run away, I couldn't even contact him to make an effort to be there for him. So I just waited and waited. At times, the waiting hurt. But day to day, it wasn't really *that* painful of a waiting. Despite the fact that I'd pledged to make my family a priority in my life, my life was filled to the brim with other things. We'd won the Sweat-Free Campaign, but I'd barely taken time to claim any victory before thrusting myself into the anti-Taco Bell movement. I was applying to study abroad. There was plenty of drama with my friends, who also were constantly urging me to "play more." School, as always, demanded much time and energy. My boyfriend and I—or was he my boyfriend?—were going in circles trying to figure out if it made sense to be dating. I had babysitting jobs to attend to and tours of the campus to give. I was organizing a large service-learning program for the kids at summer camp. So worrying about my family was an intermittent thought that surfaced occasionally when I called home or when I read an article in the *New York Times Magazine* about the author's meth-addicted son that caused me to cry uncontrollably alone in my dorm room.

The thoughts of family surfaced again when I received yet another phone call. Michael had come home. He'd run out of other options, none of his friends would have him any more. I was glad. I bought a ticket to go home for spring break.

Despite the fact that it seemed like Michael had hit rock bottom and could now only bob to the surface, things were still difficult. True, it did seem that Michael could only move up from where he was—but he didn't follow a linear path upward—things were (and still are) like a roller coaster with him, and I constantly worried that he wouldn't get back on track enough. Especially since he had shattered some of the old mechanisms he'd used to deal with problems in the past.

Michael had always had a special, close relationship with Mama. He turned to her for advice and unconditional love. But upon his trauma and homecoming, his relationship with her degenerated to resemble the fights I'd had with her when

I was in high school. But in this case, the fights were drawn out, never ending, and sometimes physical. I sided with my brother, both because I felt that that was my role and my duty as sister, and because I remembered how our mother could suck you into a fight you didn't want to have, let it escalate and escalate, and then blame you for each action you took. I wanted her to put down what she was doing and fix my brother. Instead she engaged him in verbal battles. And when those battles turned physical, she took the drastic step of calling the police and getting my brother enmeshed in the legal system, an over-18-year-old charged with domestic violence. Michael retorted, for the first time, by insisting that my mother was not his *real* mother, and removing the photo of his biological mother from its place on the piano in the living room to bring it closer to his lair, the TV room where he slept, played video games, and entertained friends.

Despite the overtures I made to my brother, and the fact that family now had a higher-up spot on the to-do list that was my life, my efforts did not always bear fruit. There were moments: good conversations on the cell phone, a carefully drawn out birthday card thanking me for being a good sister, and a steady stream of "I love yous" and "I love you toos." But more often than not, my trips home to see him ended up being the two of us sitting in separate rooms, him turning down my invitations to accompany me out to dinner or to the grocery store, me watching him play Rainbow Six, and a couple intermittent conversations about how weird our parents are. Was it enough? What should I have done?

When my overtures didn't pay off, I found myself wondering if it takes two to tango. I never stopped assigning blame for the situation. I blamed my mother. I blamed my father. I wasn't sure if I should blame myself. What's a sister supposed to do? My parents told me that my job was just to love him and be his friend and be his ally. But how was I supposed to do that, and what was that really doing? I knew that there was not that much that I could do and gradually began to doubt how much my parents themselves could affect the situation without a willing partner. But assigning blame to Michael seemed fruitless and incorrect. I knew that with a few alterations in action (going to class, for example) he could have easily turned his life around and harnessed the reservoirs of potential harbored in his person. But those few alterations seemed impossible, given Michael's anger, fear, low-self esteem, and depression. Who could I blame?

When Michael left, in some ways I became closer to both of my parents. There was finally something to talk about that we were all interested in, that I could only discuss with them: Michael. My parents negotiated a tenuous line: how much to tell me, how much to involve me. They knew I was Michael's sister and not his parent and didn't want to overworry or overinvolve me. At the same time, they knew that I was very concerned and no longer a child. My parents negotiated the line with skill, and I came out of the situation drawn closer to them by the information they shared and the responsibility they assumed.

After my mother lost her job and became embroiled in the battle with Michael, however, the oddities in her personality that I'd chalked up as (sometimes lovable) eccentricity seemed symptomatic of mental illness or at least out of touch with reality. The changes in her behavior—or maybe her behavior didn't change and I just noticed it for the first time—led me to remember the oddest symptoms of strangeness she exhibited when I was growing up: She loved being fat despite the health problems it could cause and refused conventional diets and exercise in favor of "sleeping more" or "eating the foods I love so I am satisfied and will eat less." She seemed to be sick all the time and would lie in bed all day. She was always starting some new educational program, never finishing and getting a degree. She would start projects around the house that she would never finish—cleaning the bathroom door or the drier duct or maybe varnishing the floor. She changed her name legally because she never liked the way "Jeanne" sounded. She wrote her own version of "happy birthday" and banned the traditional version because it was annoying. These idiosyncratic projects consumed time she could be spending working toward a concrete goal. Instead, the little details of life swept her away in their seemingly paramount importance.

I remember these problems and projects receding into the background when my mother got a job running therapy groups for children who had been sexually assaulted. Aside from the strange office politics in which she embroiled herself, the way she occupied her time seemed worthwhile: It helped others and brought home a paycheck. When she lost her job and became entangled in my brother's problems, though, my attention again swerved to focus on her strange ineptitudes. In the absence of work, she devoted time and energy and apprehension and nervousness to our local Yiddish choir, composed of almost-senior citizens from the various synagogues in my hometown who liked to get together once a week and sing old Yiddish songs about potatoes and the like. This laid-back, peripheral activity suddenly became the focus of her life: Photocopies needed to be made, songs needed to be practiced, and rehearsals needed to be held in our home. We needed to host the after-performance potlucks. Anything that got in the way of Yiddish choir was bad. Her spending habits also troubled me. She spent her money (which she didn't have in the first place) on a foam memory pillow or a pair of earrings for me that I didn't want. She insisted on practicing Spanish for three hours a day and got horribly upset when she was unable to. While the Spanish practice was intended to help her get a job doing therapy in Spanish, I wondered when she'd be proficient enough. She was fluent, but the job search never began.

With my mother strangely out of commission and my brother flailing, my Dad really came home from work for what seemed like the first time ever. Suddenly it was Papa who arranged the meetings with the school social worker, who hired a lawyer to get Michael out of the legal trouble my mother had put him in, who drove him to school each morning, who cooked dinner with him, and slipped in wise, fatherly talks about what it would take to get Michael graduated from high school and into culinary school.

I'd always admired my Dad's efficiency and logic. Sometimes these traits would be displayed to me—but only after my mother came up short. I'd come to my dad, complaining about some complicated way my mother wanted to purchase my plane tickets or get me from extracurricular A to extracurricular B.

My Dad would smile and tell me to calm down and, with the same logical precision and imagination that allowed him to run a lab, get large grants from the federal government and discover cool new things about "junk" DNA- he would make a plan to solve the problem that my mother could only complicate. I loved having my father step in and clear things up, but this only ever happened after all possibilities with my mother had been exhausted. My mother was the chief-in-command when it came to dealing with the children, and when I came to my father first, I was redirected back to Mama.

So, when my Dad finally stepped up to deal with Michael, I was relieved to have someone so levelheaded tackling the problem. On the other hand, old resentments were dredged up. "What would have happened," I'd wonder, "if Papa had been this involved *before* things had gone so wrong? Would Michael have been placed in a better school for him? Would he have better friends? Would the problem have been caught and dealt with earlier?"

At the same time as my parents's lives were realigning in terms of their relationship to Michael, their lives were changing in other ways. I often tease my father about becoming "bourgie" after I left high school. When a doctor told him that his weight could pose serious health problems, my dad started going to the gym for two hours a day, switched his diet from pork and steak to fish and salad, and subsequently melted from a Santa look-alike into a physically fit little elf. He cut down on the beer and joined a wine tasting class, where I'm sure he regaled his delighted peers with tales of his attempts to get flexible with the new spine ball class at the gym.

My mother, despite her apparent craziness and lack of a job, developed a new social circle—women from the synagogue who also happened to have sons undergoing problems similar to Michael's. These women also happened to be Weight-Watchers fiends, so my dad fit right into the crowd. Their lives, which used to be dominated by children and work, suddenly took the empty-nester turn, and they organized a social life filled with kayak trips and dinner parties. But the nest was not empty. Michael, at 19 with 20 looming in the distance, had still not graduated high school, still lived at home playing video games in solitude or with the occasional sketchy friend dropping by.

In high school, I had one of those great, touchy-feely English teachers who related every book we read to the pubescent teenagers in his classroom. *Catcher in the Rye* was about casual sex, *All the King's Men* was about how the past affects your daily life, and *One Flew Over the Cuckoo's Nest* was about the walls society puts around us, forcing teenagers to conform. One day when we were sitting in class relating some aspect of our mundane lives to some great work of literature, Ms. Scott turned to me and asked, "Do you like your parents? Are you close to them? Will you be close to them in the future?" I thought a little and responded, "I think I will like my parents a lot more and be closer to them when I get out of the house. The more independent I get, the more I think I'll be able to like and appreciate them. You know, when they don't control my life and are just people." I resented the control my parents had over my life; I truly felt that I was more capable of making decisions and running my life than they were. Perhaps this was true. I struggled to retain control.

I still struggle with the financial dependence I have on my parents. But other than that, I *am* in control of my own life. And now the struggle in our relationship is knowing where I am obligated to connect to them, and where I want to connect to them, now that our relationship isn't regulated by the control a parent has over a child.

With Michael, on the other hand, I struggle with my lack of control. Not only does it seem like if I knew the right words to say and the right actions to perform, I could repair my distant relationship with my brother, it also seems like I could solve his problems. Even though I know, as the daughter of a perennial psychology master's student, that Michael must be the one to exert his agency and decide to fix his own problems, this is difficult information to process.

Every trip home seems like it uncovers some old piece of confusion or pain that I am unable to resolve. So what keeps me coming home and calling home? I have this picture in my head of a family I'd like to be a part of some day, when I'm grown up and have a job and am the mother. In that family, the parents display an unending love and admiration for each other. The children are the focus of the home, and they are carefully tended to as they grow older and stronger. In this family, the love is apparent and when time is spent together, fun is had.

This is the ideal family that American culture projects. But that family also extends to the uncle and grandparents my brother and parents will be to my children. How can I yearn for an ideal family for myself in the future, while abandoning the one that I have currently? And then the question becomes, what do I owe my family? This family who has never been perfect and is not nearly always a joy for me to be a part of. When I was growing up, maybe because Michael was adopted, I remember talking a lot about "what makes a family." I learned that in some families there are two moms, and in some families there are no moms at all. In some families, there are just grandparents, or an auntie or an uncle. There are stepfamilies too. In Kenya, there are many families with no grown-ups at all. So what makes all these groups of people families? The answer that I learned so long ago, and the answer that remains true today is: It is the strong love that they have for one another that makes these groups families.

Not everyone is lucky enough to have a home filled with people who love them. I have had the incredible fortune of feeling a strong and profound love for my distant brother, my crazy mother, and my father whom I sometimes think did not do enough. The way they show their love for me can be unconventional and can make me unhappy or uncomfortable. But I think that I owe them love in return.

The question that remains, though, is what it means to be a part of a loving family and what my obligations to this group of people are. I don't know what my role was in Michael's downfall, but I'm pretty sure that I don't have the tools necessary to get him back on his feet. I think I can't mend the problems of my family members, and I know I'm not sure how to deal with them from day to day. This is a challenge that I'm sure will stay with me as I outgrow adolescence and move through adulthood. How are you supposed to be a daughter and a sister, but not a child? What is my role? All I know is that it has something to do with making my love available to my family. But I'm not sure how to do that. The only model I have, the model I dream of, is a sister and daughter in a very different, much more perfect family. I am learning to struggle to cast my notions of perfection aside in order to concentrate on loving the family I have, weirdness, dysfunction, and all.

FALLING FROM MY PEDESTAL

*Living in a family characterized by disharmony and constant threat of
divorce, this author traces her serious eating disorder to her attempts to
compensate for her parents' unhappiness by being a perfect child. But no
matter how hard she works or how perfect her grades, Chhaya's parents
remain unhappy and even criticize her efforts. The emergence of adolescent
sexuality creates a crisis in her sense of perfect self-control that is followed
by the devastating news that despite her obsessive hard work, she will not be
valedictorian. Drastically restricting her intake of food becomes a compensating
obsession and means of asserting self-control and achieving perfection. Her
health deteriorates and she is hospitalized. She learns that she must discover
her own realistic goals and give up her "insane drive for perfection." Her
recovery proves to be arduous and long, but by the end of her story she feels
she has turned the corner.*

So many people have asked me, "How did you become anorexic?" that I'm about
ready to tape-record my life story and play it back the next time the question comes
up. I try to explain using the analogy of a rainbow. The entire spectrum of colors
comprises the rainbow, but no single color can be extracted—they all blend together
to form a continuum. The same can be said of the illness. Anorexia wasn't something
that just "happened" to me—I didn't one day suddenly decide to stop eating. My
problems ran much deeper than simply "not eating." The disorder was my desperate
attempt to maintain some semblance of control in my life. It was a cry to establish who
I was, to pick up the pieces of my shattered identity. To make sense of this insidious
disease, and ultimately of myself, I must confront and examine the issues that led to
my using the eating disorder as a coping mechanism to deal with the turmoil that surrounded and threatened to suffocate me.

I am convinced that my childhood represents the beginning of much of what
led to the anorexia. My identity problem goes back as far as the elementary school

years and starts with my ethnic heritage. I come from what you might call a mixed background. My parents could not be more opposite in their histories if they tried—my father is East Indian and my mother is a typical WASP. As for me, I've gone through my entire life not knowing exactly what I was. I've always despised filling out standardized forms that ask for personal information, because I never know what box to check under "ethnic origin." The categories are neatly defined, literally black and white, and people who are "melting pots" like me present problems for this efficient form of classification. Technically, I'm more Indian than anything else, but I always feel deceptive saying I'm Indian when I'm really only a half-breed. Thus, I end up the perpetual "Other," an unclassifiable anomaly.

No one would guess merely by looking at me that I'm part Indian—my hair and eyes may be dark, but I'm quite fair skinned. The one thing that gives me away is my name—my horrible, terrible Sanskrit name which I'm convinced no one on this planet can pronounce correctly without help. I have lambasted my parents endlessly for sentencing me to a lifetime with this albatross around my neck. I can't even count how many times people have completely massacred my name, either in pronunciation, spelling, or both—the number is utterly unfathomable. I'm forever giving what I call my "name spiel," explaining the origin and meaning of my name. Since such an understanding requires knowledge of my background, the subject inevitably leads into a discussion of my family, one of my least favorite conversational topics.

Even though my parents' relationship was tenuous (to say the least), they never fought in public. No one would have guessed they were anything other than normal as far as married couples go. At home, though, the masks came off, the farce ended, and the boxing gloves were donned. The match would usually begin at the dinner table. Supper was the only time we all came together as a "family," if you can call it that. It typically started with something insignificant like, "Why didn't you fix mashed potatoes with the steak?" and escalated inevitably into the divorce fight. You could always tell when one was coming on. First, they'd bicker for a few minutes, then the voices would rise. The remark, "Why don't you just leave?" by either of them was the cue for my exit, for I could recite practically verbatim the arguments that would follow. Mom would snap, "You should go back to India. You haven't been happy since you left." Dad's bark ran along the lines of, "Why don't you move in with your parents?" In spite of all the fighting and all the threats of divorce that were made, though, it was always just words. Neither of the two ever acted upon their vow to end the marriage.

I think the instability and uncertainty of their relationship bothered me the most. The dark, intense fear always loomed in my mind—would this be the fight that leads to divorce? Is this fight going to be the straw that's going to break the camel's back? What if they're really serious this time? I'd be fraught with anxiety after every one of their quarrels. Within a few days, things usually returned to normal, meaning the usual strained relations in the absence of verbal brawls. Once I knew things were "safe," that divorce was not imminent and that we would remain a foursome, I could breathe a small sigh of relief, at least until the next argument.

When you're young, you think the world revolves around you. Given my egocentrism, I blamed myself as the cause of my parents' marital strife. I felt it was up to me to salvage their marriage, which I tried desperately to do. After each fight, I would ask myself what I had done wrong and how I could rectify the situation. Harboring intense feelings of guilt, I lambasted myself for not pleasing them and not living up to their expectations. Maybe if I'd cleaned my room like they'd asked ... I wondered. If I could just be good enough, I thought, they'd love each other and, in turn, love me. I erroneously believed I could bring my parents together by the sheer force of my will. Frustration over my inability to positively influence their relationship caused me to feel completely ineffective and inadequate. My solution was to be more perfect than anyone could expect a child to be, to hide all signs of anger and rebellion, in order to deserve and gain their love.

Being achievement oriented in school was my answer to many of the problems I faced. By making the grades, I was sure (or so I thought) to gain the love and attention I so desperately craved, not only from my parents but from my teachers as well. Because my family life was like an emotional roller-coaster ride over which I had no influence, I turned to school for comfort and security. I knew that by working hard, I could do well—in the classroom, I could exert complete control. As the perfect student, people would respect and admire me. Only if others saw worth in me could I be truly assured of my substance and value.

Unfortunately, my plan backfired on me. The more A's I received, the more my parents and classmates began to expect I would continue to do well. I strove endlessly (and fruitlessly) to impress my parents with my good grades. At the end of the marking period, I would rush home, report card clutched in hand, hoping to have glowing praise lavished upon me. Words can't begin to describe the crushing disappointment I felt when they merely remarked pointedly, "We knew that's what you'd get." Part of me was angry at having my hard work and accomplishment minimized. Whenever I mentioned my grades, all they did was preach about how "Grades aren't everything in life." Another common point they made was that "Common sense [which they felt I lacked] will get you farther in this world than will good grades." I felt I could never win with them. It seemed as though no matter what I did, no matter how hard I tried, there was always something lacking, something else I could and should have done better. I yearned for reassurance and affirmation of my worth, but because I felt that I could never be perfect in their eyes, I could never be truly convinced of gaining their love.

These traits I have described were present throughout my childhood, but no one ever recognized them as potential problems. On the contrary, my drive to be good, to achieve, to live by the rules, and to avoid disappointing or arousing the criticism of others was what made me a model child, even though I never felt like one. The severe misconceptions I held became dramatically apparent, however, with the onset of adolescence, for I was pitifully unprepared to meet the issues of this period.

As I entered high school, I became even more rigid in my interpretations. My self-doubt intensified, and my self-esteem plunged even lower. I was convinced everyone else was more capable, both socially and intellectually, than I. Never comfortable with myself, I constantly devalued my abilities, thinking I wasn't good enough for anything. Striving for perfection, for being the best (and then some), became my all-consuming goal, my purpose in life, to the point where I sacrificed all else. I studied all the time, believing that if I let up in the slightest bit, I would inevitably slip up and fail. All of my flaws would then be revealed, and I would be exposed for the imperfect person and the fraud that I was. To me, failure represented the loss of control, and once that happened, I feared I would never be able to regain it.

I became petrified of showing any signs that could possibly be interpreted as imperfection. I felt compelled to live up to and surpass the expectations of my parents, teachers, and peers in order to avoid arousing criticism, which I took as a personal attack. While others may have expected 100 percent from me, I pushed for 110 percent. So driven was I to succeed—or rather, to be seen as a success—that I imposed the strictest of standards on myself. Rather than creating a sense of pride, worth, and accomplishment, however, my role as the good, obedient, successful student—the girl who had it all together (at least on the outside)—caused me to feel increasingly empty inside. Paradoxically, the more "successful" I became, the more inadequate I felt. I began to lose control of my identity more and more as I fell victim to the Perfect Girl image in all areas of my life. I had no idea of who I *was*, only who I was *supposed* to be.

I denied myself pleasure throughout high school, never allowing myself to simply have fun. To do something for the sake of enjoyment brought forth incredible feelings of guilt and self-indulgence. I think part of this conflict arose from my parents' disagreement over issues regarding my (non)social life. My mother always had a tendency to be overprotective. She tells me that when I was an infant, she used to peek in on me, sleeping soundly in my crib, and pinch me ever so slightly, just to make sure I was still breathing. I think her reluctance to let me out of the house had to do with her overriding concern with shielding my brother and me from the dangerous outside world. At the time, though, I felt she was trying to suffocate me. I would vehemently protest against her fears; what reason had I ever given her not to trust me? "It's not you or your friends I don't trust," she would respond, "it's the rest of the world." My father, on the other hand, pushed to get me more involved with my peers. "Why don't you invite your friends over here?" he'd prod. I always found that suggestion rather amusing, given the nature of our household. If I asked to do something with friends, I was always bounced from one parent to the other to obtain permission, and usually they ended up arguing over the incident. As a result, I ended up feeling guilty for being the cause of their marital strife, a position that tore me up inside. Rather than jeopardize the family harmony (or rather, lack of discord), I often didn't even bother to ask to go out. I tried to avoid the conflict by removing myself from the situation.

I had friends throughout high school, but I always kept them at a distance, scared that if I let them get too close, they would see that I wasn't perfect and reject me. Relating to my peers was extremely difficult for me as a result, because rarely could I talk about my inner feelings. I equated the expression of emotion with weakness and vulnerability, so I always remained deadly serious and kept things on a strictly superficial level. To others, I must have seemed frigid, removed, and detached. I myself felt lonely and isolated. I desperately wanted to reveal the true me, but my intense fear of exposure silenced me.

Two specific events, both of which occurred during the spring of my junior year in high school, catalyzed the emergence of the eating disorder. One of these two major happenings involved my very first romantic encounter with a member of the opposite sex. Prior to meeting Kevin, I had had no experience whatsoever with guys. My self-confidence being what it was (practically nil), I thought no one could ever possibly be interested in me. An extensive "screening" process, with stringent standards that few guys could measure up to, was a way of protecting myself from unnecessary pain and hurt. If in every guy I met I found some fault that immediately made him undesirable as a mate, then I'd never have to worry about him rejecting me. I could remain in control and would therefore be safe.

My encounter with Kevin changed things dramatically. I met him in March at a two-day science symposium held at our state university. I had mixed emotions about Kevin—on the one hand, I found myself incredibly attracted to him and excited at the prospect of what might lie ahead, but at the same time, I didn't want to open myself up for fear of getting hurt. I wanted badly to be "swept away," to experience all the wonderful emotions described in romance novels, but reminded myself I should remain calm and levelheaded. After all, I was treading on completely foreign territory. My intelligence was of absolutely no use here, and since I couldn't rely on previous experience, I had to make sure I protected myself. Despite all of my hesitance, I was able to let my guard down long enough to experience my first kiss. Kevin and I, along with another couple, parked in his car in a secluded area of the campus. As the two in the back seat started going at it immediately, I sat uncomfortably in the front, eyes focused straight ahead. I was afraid to even look at Kevin, sure I'd flush with embarrassment. He would see right through me and realize how inexperienced with guys I really was. He was definitely the one in control here, as I had absolutely no idea how to behave.

We talked for a while (with his friends in the back continuing their dalliance), and then it happened. By "it," I am referring to one of the most monumental moments in a person's life—the first kiss. I had wanted mine to be as passionate and romantic as they come. After practicing on pillows for so long, I thought for sure I'd be ready when the time came. All of my rehearsing turned out to be in vain, though, for in no way did it prepare me for the intense emotions I felt. I remember the mixture of thrill and nervousness that jumped around in my stomach more than I do the actual physical interaction of our lips (which I simply recall as being warm and wet). Thinking back on the event, I have to laugh at how it came about. I had undone my seat belt while we were parked, and when we were getting ready to leave, I couldn't rebuckle it. As I fumbled with the strap, Kevin leaned over to lend a helping hand, but instead ended up giving me much more than just a hand.

I was exhilarated by the thought that this tall, intelligent, incredibly gorgeous guy actually saw something good in me, something more than just my grades.

He validated my sense of worth, and I began to think that perhaps I wasn't such a horrible person after all. Maybe there was something inside me other than the empty space that all the As in the world couldn't fill. Whereas my academic accomplishments gave me only a transient sense of self-satisfaction, the knowledge that Kevin liked me provided a warm feeling inside me that didn't fade away. For the first time in my life, I felt truly happy just to be alive.

In addition to the positive aspects of the relationship, there was, of course, a down side. I feared losing control of myself, a worry that was intensified by the fact that I was in completely new and unfamiliar territory. The incredible power of my feelings scared me immensely. In my family, I had learned the importance of always being rational and logical, of keeping my emotions in check and exhibiting self-discipline. Now here I was being "swept away," throwing all caution to the wind and acting purely on impulse and desire. The guilt I felt was extreme.

When I related the incident to my mother (the fear of telling my father loomed so large that I never talked about the relationship with him), I was thrown totally off guard by her reaction. I had pictured her throwing a fit and saying I shouldn't be getting involved with members of the opposite sex at my age. But just the opposite happened—she was glad I had met a "nice boy." Perhaps if he had lived in our town, she might have reacted differently. Given how far apart we lived, dating was never feasible, so she didn't have to worry about my going out late at night doing God knows what.

Kevin and I had been writing and calling each other on a fairly regular basis, and I began to entertain the thought of asking him to the junior prom. Though absolutely terrified at the prospect of rejection, the encouragement of my friends and mother (who actually offered to have him spend the night at our house!) finally convinced me to take the risk via the mail. At the post office, my hands shook and my stomach quivered as I took a deep breath, opened the mailbox, and dropped the letter down the chute. As soon as the deed was done, though, I thought, God, what the hell have I done?! I'm setting myself up for the biggest fall of my life! How stupid could I be to think Kevin would want to go with ME?!

I awaited his reply with nervous anticipation, checking the mail every day as soon as I got home to see if it was there. When the letter finally arrived, I was so nervous I could barely open it. My stomach was literally doing flip-flops as I began scanning the note for signs of his reply. When I read about how he would love to be my date, how he thought we'd have a great time together, and how he looked forward to seeing me again, I was euphoric. I was practically bouncing off the walls, so full of exuberance and utter joy that I thought I'd burst with energy.

Within a week's time, I found an outfit (gown, shoes, and a clutch purse—the whole set works), made dinner reservations and a hair appointment, and bought the tickets. Everything was in place when the big night finally arrived. After I finished getting ready, I decided to risk taking a look in the mirror. I was worried that I would find a brainy nerd who was trying hard to fit in where she didn't belong. The image that reflected back at me, though, caught me by surprise. With my hair pulled up and with flowers in it, my mother's pearl choker around my neck, the teal-colored gown flaring out around my waist, and the rosy glow of my cheeks (due more to my excitement, I think, than to the makeup I had applied), I was actually not half bad to look at. I felt as though I was looking at a stranger, for I knew the elegant young woman in the mirror couldn't possibly be me, the same person who always felt awkward and ugly. I truly felt like Cinderella, transformed if only for one night.

I was anxiety-ridden about seeing Kevin again—it would be the first time we had seen each other in some months. Everyone, both family and friends, loved him as soon as they met him. They all thought he was attractive, intelligent, and an all-around great guy. I floored everyone as I made my entry with him—not only had I myself been transformed, but here I was with a gorgeous date at my side. Finally, my feelings of inferiority melted away. I had always been recognized as smart, but now on top of that, people saw me as attractive. The culminating event that evening was my election to the junior prom court. Normally a popularity contest, I never dreamed of standing among the four couples who flocked the king and queen. When my name was announced, I arose from my seat, mouth agape, as everyone around me applauded. Again I had stunned everyone, especially myself—smart people simply did not make the court. Proving them all wrong gave me a sense of uniqueness that I cherished. I reveled in my now complete blossoming from a former ugly duckling into a beautiful swan.

In spite of all its magic, the prom experience stirred up the same mixed bag of emotions I had felt when I first met Kevin, only to a much greater degree than before. At the dance, Kevin's open display of affection bothered me tremendously. I felt uncomfortable expressing my emotions in public, especially since I wasn't even sure exactly what I was feeling. I had no idea how to behave, and so I distanced myself from Kevin. If he moved his chair closer to where I was sitting, I moved in the opposite direction. If he tried to hold my hand, I would fold my arms across my chest. I wouldn't even let him kiss me in front of everyone. He was probably totally baffled by my behavior—I know I myself was, but I couldn't help it. Since I felt out of control and didn't know what to do, I turned to the only defense mechanism that I knew from previous experience had worked—isolation.

After the weekend of the prom, Kevin and I stopped writing and calling each other. To add to my confusion, my mother and friends expressed their disdain for my handling of the situation. They reminded me that I had had the chance at a relationship with a wonderful person and had blown it, big time. My mother, who had thought Kevin was one of the nicest, most polite, handsome young men she'd ever met, laid the worst guilt trip of all on me. She made it seem as though he had done me this enormous favor, for which I should feel some sense of undying gratitude and obligation. "Here this nice boy drove all the way over here just to escort you to your dance, and how do you treat him? Like dirt." As a result of others' reactions to my behavior, I became even more miserable and disgusted with myself. This relationship represented the first time in my life that I had tested the wings of independence and trusted my own feelings, and I had failed. The incident reinforced my belief that I was worthless and incapable of making decisions on my own.

I mentioned before that the prom was one of two important events that helped catalyze the emergence of my eating disorder. The second event, which occurred within a month after the prom, was my guidance counselor informing me that I was not ranked as first in my class. My very first reaction was that some terrible mistake had been made. There was absolutely no way I could be anything but number one. I was the only person I knew who had maintained a 4.0 GPA, with nothing less than A's on all of my report cards. Becoming valedictorian had become my life; every aspect of my identity was in some way wrapped up in it.

When I expressed my disbelief to my guidance counselor, he assured me that no mistake had been made—I simply was not first. That's when the shock set in. I sat in his office thinking, "I have to get out of here NOW." The walls were closing in on me, and I felt as though I was suffocating. I quickly mumbled something about having to get back to class and practically ran out of his office and into the nearest bathroom, where I let the intense pain that had been welling inside me burst forth. My heavy sobs shook my entire body, and I was hyperventilating so badly I could barely breathe. I leaned up against the wall and slid slowly to the ground, clutching my knees to my chest and pressing my hot face against the cool wall tiles. "How could this be happening to me?" I screamed in my head. Why? What had I done wrong? Hadn't I sacrificed everything for the sake of the almighty grade? Wasn't I the perfect student? How could I pretend everything was normal when inside I was falling completely apart? Afterward I fought desperately to keep up my false image of control and stability, stuffing my pain down further and further inside me in the hopes it would somehow magically disappear. Everyone expected me to be number one—what would they think when they found out I wasn't? If only they knew.... I felt duplicitous and deceitful, as though I was projecting a false image that was just waiting to be debunked. I was falling from my pedestal, and I knew the fall would be a long and hard one from which I might never recover.

The fall was even more profound than I could have ever anticipated. It devastated my life to such an extent that now, five years later, I am still trying to put back the pieces and recover. An eating disorder, however, was the last thing I expected. In my mind, I had imagined people losing respect for me, devaluing my abilities, and seeing me for the incapable fool I felt I was. That didn't happen. The only person to turn her back on me was me. I was truly my own worst enemy, endlessly berating and cursing myself for being so stupid. Gone was the radiant, smiling teenager from prom night, so full of life and exuberance. In her place was an ugly, sullen person who could barely drag herself out of bed in the morning because she saw no purpose to her life. The change was dramatic, but no one ever commented on it, perhaps because I was so good at putting on a happy face, and perhaps because they felt (or maybe hoped) I was just going through one of the low points that characterize the average adolescent's life. What others didn't realize was that this was not simply a phase that would pass in time—it was to become a deadly disease that would grab me by the throat and nearly choke the life out of me.

I don't really know when the anorexia actually hit me. Thinking back, it seems to have been more a progression than an event whose full impact hits all at once. Why I turned to food as a means of establishing control in my life, I honestly have no idea. I had never been concerned with my weight prior to this time. I was always thin, but ate whatever I wanted—in fact, I was the ultimate junk food addict. Chocolate, candy, cookies, chips—if it was bad for you, I loved it. These items were, of course, the first to go when I started my downward spiral, and as time went on, the list of "forbidden" foods grew while my food intake gradually but steadily diminished.

The earliest recollection I have of anorectic behavior involves its isolation more than the self-starvation. During the spring of my junior year, I began skipping lunch. My friends and I usually sat together during the lunch period, eating and chatting. Instead of going to the cafeteria with them, I started holing myself up in the library, where I could be alone with my pain, as I felt I deserved to be. My friends immediately noticed my absence and commented on it. I told them I was simply doing my own research into the different colleges that interested me. I wasn't completely starving myself at this time, but what I now know were the early signs of my eating disorder went unnoticed at the time.

It wasn't until that summer that the disease began to intensify. With the school year over, I no longer had to deal with my teachers and peers on a daily basis. Thus, it became easier to isolate and confine myself to my own internal world, a jail cell out of which there was no escape. I felt I was divided into two separate personalities—one jailer and one prisoner, simultaneously beating myself up while begging for mercy. I would lie on my bed, behind the safety of my locked bedroom door, crying endlessly. One part of me was saying, "I hate you—you're stupid and worthless," while another part was pleading, "Please don't hate me— I'll work harder to make you like me." It was a no-win situation, though. There was no pleasing the jailer, no matter how hard the prisoner inside me tried.

As the prison walls began closing in on me, I fought desperately to hang on. I got a job waitressing at a nearby restaurant and tried to keep busy by working as much as I could. My work schedule made it easy to hide my eating patterns from others. Since Mom and Dad worked full-time, I was safe for most of the day. "I ate something before going to work and then had dinner on my break," I'd lie. If anyone at work asked about my eating habits, I'd say my mother was saving dinner for me when I got home. I was really clever about deceiving others, as most anorectics are, and delighted in the thought that I was able to pull the wool over everyone's eyes. No one would be able to figure me out, I vowed. By keeping to myself, I'd be safe and protected and could get back some of the security that I felt had been brutally snatched from me.

I started cutting back on my intake with the initial goal of becoming "healthier." I'll look and feel better if I get toned up and shed a few pounds, I told myself. After a period of restriction combined with exercise, I lost between 5 and 10 pounds, and did in fact feel better about myself. The source of my improved self-image wasn't so much being thinner as being able to accomplish something with tangible results as reinforcement. I could step on the scale and watch the number drop from day to day, just as I could feel my clothes getting baggier around my waist. Here was something I could do successfully! Maybe I wasn't good enough to be first in school, but I certainly seemed able to lose weight, a task that presents enormous difficulty for many American women.

I read every article on health, nutrition, and weight loss I could find. I sought the diets that offered the quickest route to losing weight, pulling together bits and pieces from each to develop an elaborately detailed plan of my own. I learned what foods were "good" and what foods were "bad," and became a careful label reader, comparing caloric and fat content for a wide variety of foods. Going to the grocery store was a big production—I would spend ages in each aisle, trying to hunt out the products that would give me the most food for the fewest calories. Almost paradoxically, food became my obsession, the center of my world. Pouring myself into losing weight became a substitute for pouring myself into my schoolwork.

As with all other areas of my life, I gave 110 percent to the illness (when I commit to something, I do a thorough job). My insane drive for perfection, however, once again turned on me, in the same way it had done with my schoolwork. Losing that first bit of weight left me feeling good about myself for a little while, but then I began to question the greatness of my accomplishment. After all, I told myself, 5 pounds really wasn't that much—anyone could lose that amount of weight in no time with minimal effort. Now, if I could lose 10 pounds, *that* would be something—shedding that much weight requires more commitment and dedication. If I could do that, I'd really feel capable of doing something important. Thus, longing desperately for that feeling of self-worth, I readjusted my target and continued in pursuit of my new goal.

Of course, once I reached this new weight, the same thing happened, and a vicious cycle developed. No sooner would I finish patting myself on the back than a little voice in the back of my head would squelch my pride, saying okay, maybe you achieved that goal, but I bet you can't meet this one…. I found myself getting caught in a cycle of self-destruction. Even though I craved success, I would go out of my way to ensure it eluded my grasp. As soon as I reached one goal, I'd set a new, higher standard. I was doing to myself the very thing I hated my parents for doing to me. Whereas I could detach myself from my parents, however, I couldn't escape myself. I internalized the frustration of not knowing how to please them, to the point that I was unable to recognize and meet my own needs and desires. Because I didn't even know how to satisfy myself, I was forced as a consequence to look to outside indicators of my value. My life became dominated by the numbers of the scale, which governed all of my feelings and emotions. If the number fell, I was secure and happy (for at least a little while). If it moved in the opposite direction or not at all, I panicked and tried frantically to think of a way to regain control of my body. I based my every mood on my weight, not realizing that in doing so I was setting myself up for failure—though I didn't realize it at the time, self-worth comes from within, and can't be found outside oneself.

As I continued my quest for a "wholeness," an identity I thought thinness would provide, I failed to recognize the self-destructive path I was following. My body became more emaciated, but all I saw in the mirror was excess flab that I had to be rid of. I rejoiced when the skirt of my waitressing uniform became so big I had to use safety pins to keep it up. One day while going through my clothes (which were becoming baggier with each passing day), my eye caught a glimpse of my prom gown, sheathed in plastic and hanging at the very back of the closet. I decided to try the dress on, just to see how it fit. As I removed it from the plastic, I thought about how far away the dance seemed—almost like another era, even though in actuality only a few months had passed. I pulled the dress on and zipped it up, only to have it fall past my bare and bony hips to the ground. Gone was the elegant gown that had transformed me into Cinderella. All that remained now was a mass of teal-colored satin lying in a pile around my feet. Though somewhat wistful over my inability to recapture the magical quality of prom night, I comforted myself with the thought that at least I wasn't fat like I had been then. Thinness was the one measure I could grasp hold of to convince myself I was better now than I had ever been.

I deluded myself into believing I really was doing fine. Though I experienced all the telltale symptoms of the eating disorder—constantly feeling cold (especially my hands and feet), hair falling out, problematic bowel movements, insomnia, amenorrhea, dizzy spells, skin discoloration, and the gnawing hunger that penetrated to the bottom of my stomach—I brushed them off in denial. I can recall only one instance that summer when I was forced to face the gravity of my illness. I remember getting out of bed and heading for the bathroom to take a shower. As I reached my bedroom door, I got a swift, overpowering head rush that nearly bowled me over. The room started spinning, and I had to clutch the door frame just to keep from collapsing. My heart started palpitating, and I felt as though my chest was going to explode. For the first time in my life, I truly thought I was facing death. I leaned against the door frame and let my body go limp as I slid to the ground. Stabbing pains pierced my heart so sharply that they blinded me. Oh my God, I thought, what have I done to myself? I prayed to God to please let me live. I'll eat, I promise I'll eat…. I won't try to lose any more weight…. I'll go back to eating normally…. Just please make the pain stop and don't let me die!

Being faced with the all-too-real prospect of death shook me up enough that I did fix myself something to eat. The frightening impact of the incident faded rapidly, however, and within a few days I was once again back to restricting. I passed off this danger signal, reassuring myself that since I survived the episode, I must be fine. When I tightened my grip over the food, I was in control—I was invincible, and no one could touch me. The eating disorder gave me an incredible feeling of power and superiority, a sense of independence. I could prove that I had control, that I could accomplish something on my own.

You may wonder where my family was in all of this mess. Didn't they see me slowly wasting away into nothing? I vaguely recall them nagging me from time to time to eat. I don't feel any resentment toward them for "letting" me become anorexic, for not catching me before I got as bad as I did. They were, I'm sure, in as much denial as I was. Acknowledging my disease would (and eventually did) open a Pandora's box full of problems, ones that went far beyond my not eating to include the entire family. My mother did get worried enough toward the end of the summer to call my pediatrician. When she explained my situation, his advice was to get me to take vitamins (just the solution to an anorectic's problems!). His failure to recognize the severity of my illness made it easier, I think, for my parents to gloss over the situation. Having a doctor's reassurance probably put their minds at ease. The family problems could stay safely locked away, at least for the time being.

I somehow managed to make it through that summer, and the beginning of my senior year in high school soon arrived. My mother tried to warn me of the reactions people at school would have to my emaciated appearance, but I could see no difference in how I looked now as opposed to how I looked at the end of junior year, when I was at least 20 pounds heavier. She was right on target in her assessment of the situation. I'll never forget the looks I received from my classmates and teachers that first day of school. Their eyes bulged and their mouths dropped in horror as they stared at the withered, drawn figure before them. Three months earlier, I had been a healthy teenager, and now all that remained was a skeleton covered with skin. I was incredibly self-conscious walking through the halls, certain all eyes were on me and that the topic on everyone's mind was my dramatic weight loss. Feeling like a queer anomaly, I tried desperately to cover my twig-like arms and hide my body under baggy clothes. My answer to the stunned looks was that I had been sick and was run-down as a result. Though I found it perfectly plausible, my explanation was met with skepticism. No one pushed the issue, though, probably due to my unwillingness to discuss the subject, evident by my curt responses to their questions.

Within the next few days, the nurse called me down to her office. Apparently, nearly all of my teachers had voiced their concerns regarding my health. I offered the same excuse to her as I had to everyone else—yes, I had lost some weight, but would be fine once I had a chance to recoup from being sick. She was skeptical at my insistence that everything was okay, but I promised to work hard to get back my health. I was, of course, lying through my teeth. I had absolutely no intention whatsoever of returning to what I considered my grossly fat previous weight. Did people think I was going to abandon my quest for thinness just like that, simply because that's what they wanted me to do? No way was I going to let all the hard work I had poured into this project over the past three months go to pot! I was annoyed with others meddling in my life. Rather than seeing their concern for its genuineness, I was convinced they were trying to undermine me. They just wanted to see me fail at something else so they could laugh in my face. Well, I wouldn't let that happen! I'd show them that I could achieve! They would marvel at how well I could shed those pounds and admire me at least for that, if nothing else. I thought that perhaps by being successful at losing weight, I could somehow make up for my intellectual flaw of not being valedictorian.

I was knocking myself out to impress others for no reason, though. The only one who cared that I wasn't first was me, but ironically, that was the one person I was unable to satisfy no matter how hard I tried.

I remember one key experience that clued me in to the severity of my problem. While going through candid photographs for the yearbook, I discovered two of myself. I picked them up to examine more closely and gasped in horror as I looked at the ghastly image captured on film. Her face was as white as a sheet, her eyes sunken, and her cheeks severely drawn. The blue veins bulged out of her stick-like arms, and her clothes hung limply on her fragile frame. She looked morbidly depressed, a pathetic creature who seemed ready to snap at any moment. Surely that person couldn't be me! Tears started welling in my eyes as I looked at that picture. What had happened to the smiling, vivacious teenager of the previous spring? She was like a rose that had bloomed and then withered away. I bawled uncontrollably as I realized I was falling apart. The life was being slowly sucked from me, and I was growing increasingly weak and helpless. Please God, help me get my life back together, I prayed. I don't want to die!

You may think that, having recognized myself as having this disorder, I would be well on my way to recovery. I know that's how I felt—now that I really *wanted* to get better, to get back to a normal life, I would. I tried to convince myself and everyone else that I could tackle and overcome this problem on my own. The solution was simple, I thought—all I have to do is eat and gain back the weight I had lost, and I would be fine. Unfortunately, it wasn't quite that easy. Anorexia nervosa had come to symbolize 17 years of emotional instability, psychological turmoil, shattered dreams, and bits and pieces of my fragmented identity. There was a lot more that needed fixing than simply my diet—all of the issues that permeated my entire life needed to be confronted and dealt with before recovery would be possible. It took everyone—my family, friends, teachers, and even myself—a long time to realize this and to recognize the full, devastating extent of the disease.

Though I really did want to get better, I was unable to regain the weight my body required. Having gone beyond the point of no return, so to speak, I continued to lose poundage. The nurse finally suggested my mother take me to a specialist, someone who might offer the assistance I needed to get better. I became absolutely irate at the very mention of the subject. "I am NOT crazy, and have no intention whatsoever of seeing a shrink!" I hollered at my mother. But she was adamant. The psychologist I went to see was unable to help me, though. My disease had progressed much too far by the time she intervened. About a month later, she told my parents there was nothing more she could do for me and recommended I be evaluated for admission into the Eating Disorders Service at a nearby children's hospital. Though I strenuously resisted the idea of hospitalization, my mother calmly but forcefully put her foot down: "We can commit you without your having any say in the matter." My parents were finally taking charge.

In terms of my treatment in the hospital, Mom and Dad focused more on the outer me—my body and its weight—than the evolution of my inner self.

Whenever I spoke with them on the phone or whenever they visited, the very first question was always, "How's the weight doing?" My recovery became framed in terms of numbers, the very thing I was trying so hard to get away from. I had based my entire identity on tangible indicators of my worth—grades, class rank, and weight—at the expense of my true inner being. As a result, I never established a self-directed identity. My work in therapy to evoke an awareness and understanding of the impulses, needs, and feelings that arose within myself was incredibly difficult and emotionally draining.

Before my admission, I had been closer to my mother. She was always the more reliable one. If I had a problem or needed something, I always went to her first. My father, on the other hand, was a lazy bum. I couldn't count on him for anything except for material objects. When I was in the hospital, this changed dramatically. Mom was like an ice woman. All the other parents felt guilty, thinking they were in some way responsible for their child's eating disorder. Not my mother. She staunchly and promptly informed me that she was not going to take the blame for my problem. At the time, I saw her as cold and heartless. I *wanted* her to feel sorry for everything she had ever said or done that caused me to be the way I was. She *deserved* to feel guilty for creating the sham of a family life I had to endure. My father, on the other hand, was easier to deal with when I was heavily dependent on him, as I was when in the hospital. I think he needed to feel needed by me, to feel in control of my life. He called me every night, just to find out how my day had gone. On his frequent visits, he would always bring fresh flowers, and we would sit and talk, watch TV, or take a walk. I remember on one occasion, we even made the bed together. It was times like these when I felt closest to him. I wanted to be taken care of, and he seemed willing to do the job. The combination of my not wanting to grow up and his wanting me to stay daddy's little girl helped to sustain this dependence. Though at the time I saw his behavior as a form of care and affection, I now recognize it for the power game it was.

Paradoxically, our weekly family therapy sessions failed to reflect these newly developed interactions. During that one hour, the family roles reverted to their usual prehospital form. At first, I actually looked forward to family therapy, thinking it would expose some of the important and volatile issues that had always been buried underground. Finally, we would be able to resolve our problems and, I hoped, become a loving, cohesive unit, the perfect family I longed to be a part of. Unfortunately, this miracle transformation didn't occur. Our problems ran much too deep for even a therapist to tackle. The sessions became as much of a sham as our family itself was. Every week it was the same thing. Everyone, with the exception of myself, shied away from the real issues, the potent problems we faced as a group of four individuals collectively termed a "family." My parents always wanted to discuss specific aspects of the Eating Disorders program, details that were "safe" for them—for example, "Why isn't she eating any red meat?" or "When is she going to get back to eating normal foods?" Getting them to recognize that food was not the main issue, that the eating disorder cut far deeper, to the very core of my identity (or lack thereof), was the most difficult task I faced. I would try to bring up a particular aspect of our home life—for example, my parents' marriage or my brother's attempt to shut himself off from the rest of the world. Before I could even finish my account, though, my father interjected, shaking his head and protesting, "She's making too much of this and blowing things way out of proportion."

The dismissal of my emotions as trivial wasn't nearly as bad as what came next. "Our family life may not have been wonderful," Dad admitted, "but it was relatively normal until she began this whole mess and disrupted all of our lives. She's the one with the problem, not us." I sat dumbfounded, not believing my ears. How could he possibly lay the entire blame on me? Did he honestly believe I had planned on becoming anorectic, that I set out on some mission to destroy our family? I refused to just sit back and let him heap any more blame on me. I had meekly taken all the denouncing for so long that I had internalized and turned it back on myself, resulting in incredible feelings of guilt and self-doubt. I couldn't stand the torture any longer. "You're wrong if you think I'm the cause of everyone's problems," I told my father point-blank. "We had problems long before I got sick." To my surprise, my mother then spoke on my behalf, saying to him, "You can't blame her for everything. We're part of the problem, too." Finally, someone was taking my side! I looked over to my mother with gratitude in my eyes, silently thanking her for saving me from drowning in a sea of guilt and self-worthlessness. At least she was beginning to recognize my problem encompassed much more than a simple decision to stop eating. Throughout this entire scene, my brother remained isolated and detached from the rest of us. When confronted, he would usually just shrug his shoulders. He had a grand total of two standard responses to the therapist's questions—"I don't know" or "I try not to think about it."

After six weeks in the Eating Disorders Service, I returned to the real world—back to my home and family and to my teachers and friends at school. Everything was pretty much the same, though. My parents still fought, and my brother still shut himself off in his room. I was still obsessed with food. Though I had gained weight and was now eating more, I still kept a meticulous log of every (measured) bit of food that entered my mouth. I refused to touch red meat, junk food, or any kind of fat whatsoever.

Eventually, I had to resign myself to the fact that I alone cannot repair the immense damage that exists within our family. Without the cooperation of others, my endeavor is doomed to failure. I have relinquished my role as the family savior, realizing I am unable to control the behavior of my parents and my brother. I can, however, change my own actions and reactions within the family structure. An important, and difficult, part of the recovery process has been extricating myself from the dynamics of the family in order to develop and accept my own independent sense of self.

I can't believe I'm almost through with my college career. So many things have changed since I was a clueless, teary-eyed freshman. Now I'm half through my senior year. Within the past year alone I have undergone a complete metamorphosis, beginning with my revealing my anorexia to the world. I had wondered for so long whether I would ever be able to overcome this wretched disorder, and finally, I have reached the point where I can eat when I'm hungry and stop when I'm full. My recovery has been due in large part to the drug Prozac, which has also made me less obsessive and less high strung. My recovery, however, has had its ups and downs. This past summer I fell into a deep depression. I felt like my life was spiraling out of my control, that everything I had worked so hard for was falling apart. I spent most of my days crying and mulling over things. I didn't even want to go back to school in September to finish my senior year, but everyone convinced me to do so. I got treated for the depression and finally decided to take medication for it. I had adamantly refused to do so in the past, though an antidepressant was recommended by two of my previous psychiatrists. When I think back to how bad I was this past summer, I'm so thankful that I got help in time and was able to turn things around before they got completely out of control. I'm finally starting to feel good about myself, comfortable with who I am, and actually happy!

A big part of the change in me is due to LOVE. Yes, I finally met someone who was as attracted to me as I was to him. He has stood by me through some of the worst times of my life, through fighting the eating disorder as well as depression. I started seeing him nearly a year ago. Things were rough at first, mainly because of my inexperience and the issues I was having to deal with about myself. I was freaked out about sex and mostly about opening myself up to someone. I had been so egocentric for so long that it's been hard to give some of that self-centeredness up. I also had my first sexual encounter with him. That was another issue I had a hard time dealing with at first, but now, after having lived with him for the summer, it seems pretty silly.

I thought for sure that we would spend the rest of our lives together, deliriously happy and in love. But this past summer really put our relationship through the wringer. We've been fighting a lot, but more than that, I think we've been starting to pull back from each other. We pretty much both know that June will bring with it not only graduation but the end of our relationship. It's been really hard for me to accept that what I thought was an infallible, perfect romance is actually not immune to problems. I really wish things had worked out the way we planned them, but I guess I should have learned by now that life doesn't always follow the plans you make for it.

So, you might ask, what happens next? Well, I have moved ahead, and after four long years, I have finally beaten this disease. I feel as though an enormous weight has been lifted off my shoulders (no pun intended), and that I am finally ready to move ahead with the rest of my life—to "live, laugh, and love," as they say. I'm optimistic about the future, for if there's one thing I've learned, it's that I'm a fighter…. And, more importantly, I'm a survivor.

LOOKING INTO THE SUN

*In Jack's childhood, he and his friend fight, play, and explore. By middle
school, these friendships fall away, and Jack sees himself (and is seen by others)
as a nerd, someone who has difficulty understanding how friendships work
and what is expected of him. He develops a few close friends in high school
with whom he could laugh and have adventures, but in college, again, the
few friends he makes drift away, and he does little to keep them. A period of
depression, during which he cuts his wrists, is followed by the reemergence
of both male and female friendships and work toward a more conscious
connection to others.*

My first memory—my best memory—is of Jason and me charging down my
front yard under a bright summer sun, armed with neon plastic baseball bats and
wildly clipping the heads off of dandelions.

"Defend Dandelion City!" Jason yelled.
"Defend Dandelion City!" I called back, swinging wildly.

We ran across the open field, driven by a frenzy of energy. We slowly tired
out, sat down on the ground, and figured out what to play next. And that's how it
went, day after day, during summer vacation: just my best friend and me running
through life as one big adventure.

With about 15 other kids in the neighborhood and my brother Tony, who
is a year and a half older than me, I was never at a loss for something to do. We
roamed freely from yard to yard, into the woods, along the river, to the fields
behind Mr. Davidson's house, and back home again. Time was measured by when
we all had to be home for dinner. Neither I nor any of my friends had a particular
identity: At any given hour I was a king, a spy, a police officer, a Ninja turtle, or

a ghost. I didn't even realize that there was or should be anything different about the two girls on our street—they joined in naturally with our large group of boys.

We filled the yards around Driver Lane with noise and running and games every evening during the school year and all day during vacations. As soon as we finished our morning cereal, my brother Tony and I rushed outside to knock on doors and find out who was around. When my brother wasn't around to fight, play, and explore, Jason and I were inseparable. Being kids together was great: Anyone could be anything, and at the start of each new game, there was a sense of freshness, a feeling that anything could happen.

As I moved into middle school and high school, I dwelled on those memories in a way that I knew meant that stage of life was gone. What happened to those days? Everything seemed so open and free, so warm and happy. I have such good memories of being a little kid. I have mostly bad memories from then on.

When I was in fourth grade, my parents took me to the optometrist. I was supposed to be picking out a pair of glasses, but no one had glasses in fourth grade except Erica, and everyone thought she was a complete nerd. And now I was getting glasses. I knew what this meant for me.

"But Jack," the optometrist cooed, "you'll get to pick out your own pair of glasses. And there are lots of people who think glasses look really handsome."

"And," I sniffed, "and that's supposed to make me feel better?" I knew the optometrist was just trying to make me feel better, but I vaguely hated her for treating me like this. The world could be cruel, I knew, and I didn't want or need anyone to help me blind myself to that fact.

By the end of elementary school, my adult teeth started coming in with visible patches of orange on them. The dentists didn't really know why, they guessed it had something to do with having too much fluoride or being sick when I was a baby. I felt like the ground was sliding out from beneath my feet, that I was still a kid but the kids around me weren't. There was a way they looked at me, as if from a distance, and I learned that it meant they were judging me. I wasn't the same as everyone any more, I was becoming somehow different. Around girls I began to be nervous and couldn't think or talk straight. I still had a couple of friends to play cards and games with, but it didn't feel like being back with the kids on Driver Lane. There, everyone did everything together; here in school, some kids would play with you and some kids wouldn't. Before long, I realized that the number of kids who would play with me was getting smaller.

By sixth grade I didn't have many friends—really just one, another kid also named Jack, who also had glasses and liked reading. Most other kids either made fun of me or humored me, both of which were painful. Jack and I used to talk about time travel and outer space—his dad was an astronomer, so Jack knew about all kinds of interesting things. Jason and I saw each other less and less in school. We weren't in the same class anymore, and the teachers started putting me out in the hallway to do math problems on my own. Doing math became a minor addiction with undeniable social consequences that I tried to ignore.

Besides, Jason had grown—a lot. He looked good, and I felt a sense of awe when looking at him. One of the girls on Driver Lane had a crush on him now, and she was so nervous around him that she didn't spend time with us anymore. More and more, I looked at Jason like an older brother. He was bigger than me, he got along with other kids better, and I knew that he'd protect me from the other kids at school. Meanwhile, my actual older brother was having a much harder time fitting in—it began when he took an interest in music and the arts. But despite all the help I got from Jason and all the time we spent together, I started getting the sense that Jason and I were just friends out of habit.

The problem with me keeping friends was that I liked school. No one liked the kids who were good at school. I figured this out about three years too late. Before I realized it was happening, I was already labeled a nerd, a fact one of the neighborhood girls shared with me one day on our hour-long bus ride home:

> Yes, Jack, duh, everyone thinks you're a nerd. You have glasses and you read books and do math all the time. I still think you're okay—I mean, you are a nerd, but I don't think it's that bad.

What? A nerd? What does that even mean? By the end of middle school, I knew very painfully what it meant. No one wanted to talk to me at school, and the other kids didn't even bother waiting for me to leave the room before making jokes about me. What had happened? I was so lost, things were hitting me too quickly. I had no friends. Even the other Jack stopped talking to me—he still looked kind of dorky, but people accepted him. And I had nowhere to go; my grade at school had only about 80 students, and everyone knew everyone's business and where everyone stood in some invisible hierarchy that remained elusive to me.

In middle school, new things kept happening that I didn't understand. On a bus ride home in seventh grade, Jason asked me if I wanted to go to a sleepover. He was inviting Jake and Mitch, too. Jake was in one of my classes, and I didn't know much about Mitch except that his parents were divorced. Jason and I used to do sleepovers back in second or third grade, but we hadn't done one in a while. The thought of being welcomed back into their circle was exhilarating.

During the whole sleepover, I felt like electricity was running through my veins. I got to eat potato chips and stay up late, but that was nothing—during a game of truth or dare, I made the very difficult decision to actually tell the truth about liking Stacy Pilamar.

"You like Stacy Pilamar!?!?"
"Yeeeahhh," I confirmed, tentatively, waiting for their response.
"EVERYONE likes Stacy Pilamar."
"I don't," said Jake. They started talking like a noisy crowd.
"Yeah, right, I bet you do. Everyone does, she's so hot," said Jason.
"Yeah, well, she's not as hot as Jessica."

"You think Jessica is hot?"

"Hot boobs at least."

"Jessica Barone, not Jessica Smith."

"Well, duh, not Jessica Smith. She looks like a cow."

"Yeah, I know."

What was going on? I had never heard anyone talk like this before. I'd never even told anyone that I liked Stacy Pilamar.

"Stacy Pilamar. Good choice," said Jake.

Mitch interrupted, "Still not as hot as Jessica."

"Do you think I have a chance with her?" I asked, figuring they'd probably know better.

Mitch laughed and then stifled it. Jason didn't say anything and looked at Jake.

"Well..." Jason started, "maybe. I mean, I don't know. I don't talk to Stacy Pilamar much."

"I bet she totally likes you," said Mitch.

"Really!?" I asked.

"No," Jake said, shoving Mitch. "He's kidding."

"Wait, really?" I asked again.

Jason said, "Um...well, why don't you ask her to dance or something?" Mitch laughed.

"What?!" I demanded.

"Nothing," said Jason. "Hey...come on, let's play Super Mario."

Later that night, Jake went to his backpack and pulled out a videotape.

"Check this out," he grinned.

"Aww, you brought it! Sweet!" laughed Mitch.

"What is it?" I asked.

"Porn, duh," said Jake.

I watched in absolute silence as I saw body parts and things being done that I had never even imagined. I was intrigued but also embarrassed and felt like the other guys were violating some private moment by cheering at the screen and commenting on what was going on.

"You guys, Jason's parents are going to hear us and we're going to get in trouble," I warned nervously.

"No way, we're all the way down in the basement and they're asleep. Besides, watching porn without the sound on is lame."

Afterwards, Mitch and Jake made fun of me for being silent during the porn and for not wanting to go with them to set off Black Viper firecrackers behind the Davidsons' house.

That sleepover left me feeling completely stunned. On the one hand, I felt closer to these guys, and closer to Jason, than I had felt toward anyone in years. But I also felt like I was getting in over my head: I didn't understand why they said most of the things they said, and although the gossip and swearing and dirty talking was exciting, it also seemed strange and wrong. But these guys were cool and I needed them to like me.

I had the same problem at school. The guys made fun of me a lot, and most of the time I had no idea what I had done. Even the guys who felt vaguely like friends acted as if they would turn on me if I did the slightest thing wrong. Things were even worse with girls. At a school dance, I finally did ask Stacy to dance. She said yes, but in her awkwardness and lack of eye contact, I knew she was just dancing with me out of pity. Sad and angry, I told myself I was going to change.

I figured if I wore clothes that were more like everyone else's I could pass for cool, or at least not be made fun of. I pushed my parents to let me get contact lenses, and the dentist was finally able to put shiny white caps on my teeth. It was my first year of high school, and I had been doing 300 sit-ups per day since the end of seventh grade. Jason told me I'd get stronger if I drank more milk, so I stopped drinking soda and started drinking about eight cups of milk every day. Bit by bit, I figured out how to get by, although I still didn't like or trust almost anyone around me. I needed a friend, someone who wouldn't hate me, and I needed a girl—at least one, decent, respectable girl—to like me.

Meanwhile, the Driver Lane kids didn't hang out together anymore. One girl became popular—and later, a heroin addict. Tony spent all of his time practicing for band concerts and going to an Air Force training club. He'd show up at home only to grab a bite to eat and then dash out the door again. Jason was in different classes and could benchpress more than my body weight. His older brother spent all his time in the band room, and kids started joking that he was gay. The kid who lived behind me started hanging out with the "dirties" who smoked in the school bathroom. As for me, I started to read philosophy: *Zen and the Art of Motorcycle Maintenance* and *Siddhartha,* Alan Watts and Krishnamurti. I became obsessed with how to get past what I considered the shallowness of cool kids, ditsy girls, showing off, pointless assignments…everywhere I looked in the world I thought people were shallow and simple, and I hated it. Every once in a while, I'd look out across the fields where we all used to play, and they'd be silent. It was eerie.

Tony and I still had each other. We had always been close, and over time we grew out of our petty brotherly squabbling and developed a kind of pilot–copilot relationship in everything we did. He built things and I programmed the electronics for them; he was the driver and I was the gunner; he learned to juggle and I learned to hold him up on my shoulders while he juggled. We gave each other code names, and with a touch of pride and mischievousness we referred to ourselves as The Brothers. Yes, we were still close, but he just wasn't around much anymore.

Around this time, I was lucky to make a couple of friends. The first was Andy. I was invited to a sleepover for a bunch of kids who liked a card game that I was into, and Andy accidentally broke a door latch at the host's house. I noticed that he was upset and scared that he would be sued and would be unable to pay for the door. I didn't know him, but he seemed really upset, so I found a few tools and put the door latch back together. When I was done, he asked if I wanted to play Super Smash Brothers, a video game, and he began teaching me the game that we would go on to play together for years. We also played cards and cracked jokes—what we called our Regulars. So started a friendship that lasts to this day.

The second boy was Scott. We had played on the same junior soccer team for a few years, we were both fullbacks. We'd talked a bit, but we started hanging out together when we found that we both liked playing some of the same trading card and video games. Finding these two friends had come at a good time, as my brother had an increasing interest in the Air Force training camps, and I wasn't his copilot anymore. Whenever I asked him to do something with me, he was suddenly too busy chatting online with girls or off to do something related to the Air Force.

Like me, my father finds interpersonal stuff stressful. His job often involves dealing with unpleasant issues in human resources. He once said his favorite job before he got promoted had been writing bus schedules because it was like solving logic puzzles all day. His tendencies became more apparent to me as I got older. One time during high school I slept over at my girlfriend's house for New Year's; my parents and I had a miscommunication and they didn't know that I was planning to do that. The next day, as my dad and I were running errands, he kind of stared out the windshield and began a torturously drawn out speech that went something like, "You know, the things that you do...can have consequences... and if something should come of actions that you take, it can affect your life in the future, so you have to be careful about things that could jeopardize..." I cut him off there. "Are you talking about me and Kristen? We're not having sex, Dad, it's fine." He seemed relieved, and the conversation was dropped. By that point, I didn't blame him as much for his behavior. He had told my brother and me more about how stressful his own childhood was and had even told us that he had seen a social worker to talk about his difficulty interacting with people.

When I think about my life, I realize that my parents didn't have a clear or decisive impact on my life. I don't think they've ever cared if I were a scientist or a teacher or an investment banker. Instead they provided some kind of silent guidance. Looking through my old toys later on, I realized that the majority of them were educational—like chemistry kits, a microscope, and puzzles. I liked that lack of direction from my parents, as I felt like I could do whatever I wanted. I think it contributed to my disdain for following directions (I lasted two weeks in the Boy Scouts and a month in the Civil Air Patrol) and gave me a chance to develop an independent mind. So, in their way, my parents had a big influence on me. I picked up a lot from them—patience and evenhandedness from my mom, being hardworking (sometimes to a fault) and not complaining from my dad, and a desire to live simply from both of them. These are character traits that they slowly transmitted to me over time and by example, so while my parents are important to the person I have become, there aren't many clear moments for me to mention.

It is my friends who have had the most noticeable, moment-to-moment influence on my life, and on that front, things were starting to clear up somewhat by high school. My new friends picked on me a little, but it was usually harmless one-upmanship and joking. I had trouble getting used to that. Finally, one of my friends told me bluntly, "When someone makes fun of you, just chill out and go with it. It's just joking around, you shouldn't take it seriously." And we laughed. When I think back to high school, that's about all I remember: laughing so hard that my sides hurt. That's not because our jokes were clever—they probably wouldn't make sense to anyone else—but because we learned to make fun of the world around us, to laugh at the ridiculousness of other people, the profoundness of stupidity, and the arbitrariness of teachers and parents.

And, bit by bit, I found myself in serious conversations with my close friends. Scott and I would talk about our frustrations with girls, and Andy and I began forays into "what does it all mean?" Discussing how I felt about things was tough: Most of the time I had no idea whether I was sad or jealous or angry—even happiness was tricky. I didn't always trust myself to be too happy, fearing that if I thought I was happy, something very bad would likely happen to me.

I was strongly drawn to these new conversations. Andy and I would go for hours-long walks around the school or the park and talk about girls, philosophy, track and field, and frustrations about school. We spent hours outside school practicing discus throws while talking about our throwing form and about life. I was impressed at how down-to-earth Andy was. In matters of girls, friendships, and relationships, he offered sound advice and gave me some much needed help understanding other people. He predicted, for example, that my first girlfriend would want to marry me ("Some girls are just like that with their first boyfriend, they think they've found The One"), and he was right on. This was weird, because Andy wasn't even in honors classes.

I felt better, more relaxed about life. Scott, Andy, and I spent all of our free time together doing something: playing ping-pong, video games, cards, Frisbee, or pool. Even as we talked about our hopes, our fears, and girls, we were always doing something. I didn't think about that until one of my teachers mentioned the differences between how guys and girls talked, how guys would sit looking at something else, whereas girls would face each other. I thought this over a bit. The idea of looking Scott or Andy in the eyes as I told them about myself...it would be overwhelmingly awkward. I didn't try it. I could talk to girls that way, but I couldn't talk to another guy that way.

But it turned out that I couldn't always avoid having to face my friends and talk. Bored one Saturday night with nowhere to go, I lounged around a dusty TV room with a few track teammates who I didn't hang out with much. We were looking for an adventure. Adventure, adventure, always looking for an adventure. Our collective desire to Do Something became more and more heightened with each break in the meager conversation, and each time we looked at our limited options. We lived in Millhaven, where there are three stores that all close before eight.

Someone suggested getting in the car and driving around: "Let's just go out and see what we find." Maybe we hoped that if we went out, something crazy and exciting would happen. By this point, however, I was 16 and more skeptical of that possibility; the older I got, the smaller the town seemed.

As we were about to drive past Scott's house, one of the guys suggested we pull a prank on him. No one had any good ideas, and besides, Scott's parents were not the sort to take a prank lightly—their house was furnished with the neatness of a museum gift shop. One of the guys bought a pack of cupcakes, so we settled for sticking two cupcakes to the windshield of Scott's van and drove away giggling. When Scott found out, he didn't talk to me for a week. I found this ridiculous, since we were in all of the same classes, did track together, and had about a 95 percent overlap in our group of friends.

After a week, Scott approached me after track practice.

"I expected more from you," he said, staring at me with a disappointed look.

"It was a joke! Just some stupid prank," I protested.

"I thought, here's a guy who's got my back, no matter what. And then he does something like this," Scott said, more upset than I expected.

"Dude, it didn't mean anything, it was just a joke."

Our conversation continued like this, reasonably, but on two completely different planes. Eventually, I got the sense this wasn't working.

"Look," I said, searching for a way to get through to him, "I don't consider this important. I see that you do, and for that I'm sorry. But you know that if anything really big happened, you know, like something serious, I'd have your back."

I really didn't know what I meant. I knew he wanted to hear this and that I did like having him as a friend, but I couldn't imagine what something "serious" would be. A breakup with a girlfriend, I guess, or maybe if someone tried to beat him up.

Scott seemed relieved, "Thanks man."

I thought to myself, "That was strange." Our friendship went back to normal.

Although we saw each other every day, I didn't understand Scott. We both ran track, did well in math, played the same video games, even liked the same girl a few times; and yet, I didn't understand so much of what he did. We spent a lot of our free time together, but he seemed to alternate between being very demanding and not caring about me. He didn't congratulate me when I got my SAT scores back. When I told him that I was voted track captain, he just stared straight ahead and was silent. And when I found out I was accepted early into Dartmouth College, he darted out of the classroom without saying a word. I thought he was a pretty weird guy sometimes. I mean, wasn't he the one always talking about the importance of friendship?

There wasn't much time left to figure it out. As college acceptance letters came in, I knew that soon we'd all be going our different ways. I would be going up north to study government, while Scott was going to be hours away studying engineering and Andy was headed to a local state school to study art. After all the hours we spent getting to know each other, I guess I should have been upset about leaving, about having to start over. But I wasn't upset, because even as our last summer vacation came to a close, I just couldn't imagine it happening. It just didn't seem real.

On the day of my high school graduation, I didn't ask anyone to sign my yearbook, and I left early so that no one could take pictures with me. Being there felt awful.

* * *

College was interesting. Once we all got past the first few months of telling stories about the pranks we pulled in high school and the places we'd gone on vacation, I found out that the people there were interested in discussion, interested in thinking. This was a nice change of pace: I could bring up a book I read without being called a nerd. I could share my musings about how society worked without getting blank stares.

On the second day of school I had found the Ultimate Frisbee team, a mysteriously open-minded group of astounding athletes and good-natured partiers. By the second half of my first year, my large roving pack of freshmen, high on possibility, had been narrowed down to a small group of teammates sobered by familiarity. I split my free time between Jack and Kate. Jack was another young man who looked much like me, struggled endlessly over ideas of morality and relationships, and shared my name. Kate was a cute girl who seemed fun. Besides, ever since I started dating in high school, I hadn't gone more than a couple of weeks without a girlfriend, and I really wanted one again.

I dated Kate for a year, even though after the first month I knew we had nothing in common and couldn't stand being around her. Most of the time I didn't even want to get intimate with her. But whenever she wanted to break up—about twice a week—I would adamantly defend the idea that we could make our relationship work.

"We just don't have the 'spark' that it takes to have a good relationship," she'd say.

"There's no such thing as spark. A relationship is just about getting along," I said, thinking her naïve.

Then one day, like so many other days, she called and said she wanted to break up. Something must have suddenly changed in me, because I just said "okay" and was glad it was over.

Shortly after breaking up with Kate, I started flirting with Aldina. Aldina was like a drug for me. She was everything I wanted and kept me in enough delicious pain to keep me coming back for more. She read constantly, despised the fakeness she saw everywhere in the world, and swore viciously in unprovoked fits of rage. One hour we'd be lying on the college green, looking up at the night stars and asking ourselves about the point of living, the next hour she would hit me and scream, "Get away from me, I'm no good, I'm just going to end up hurting you more!" Once I took her chicken soup when she was sick, and I couldn't read her expression—it was somewhere between thankful and sad. She was a challenge and a mystery, and I wanted to learn more, to share her pain.

I stopped trying to meet new people and held on tightly to a small, familiar circle of casual friends, all Ultimate Frisbee teammates. I indulged in the familiar, feeling warm and satisfied while lying down with five or six other girls and guys, having hot cocoa, and watching movies or playing Super Smash Brothers for hours and hours.

But something was wrong. I began intentionally misleading the people around me about my life. I rarely mentioned Aldina. I implied mysterious involvements, rarely looked people in the eye, and avoided giving straightforward answers to even the simplest questions.

"Where are you going?" Jack asked, catching me as I was leaving our room.

"I don't know. Nowhere, just doing stuff," I said.

"Are you going to see her again?" he asked, disapprovingly.

"I don't know, maybe," I said, flashing a grin. And maybe I was. And maybe I was just going to the dining hall.

I still managed to have some conversations with teammates, since I was often asked for advice. I shared with them the painfully idealistic thoughts in my head; looking back, I think people told me their problems because I was calm and listened, not because of the advice I gave. Jack and I were starting to grow apart, as he had begun seeing a new girlfriend and was becoming disenchanted with Ultimate Frisbee. I wonder if Jack knew that he was my only friend. As he drifted out of my life, I didn't fight to hold on to him.

I had a few confidants left—all girls. But they weren't quite friends. I couldn't hang out with them like I could with guys, getting comfortably lost in games. And there was always the chance that one of you would start liking the other. But they had such a powerfully attentive way of listening, and I was constantly amazed that I could get such sympathy and thoughtfulness from them, no matter what I said.

Around this time I started cutting my wrists. I don't know why. I didn't particularly want to die, although I always figured that it wouldn't matter if I did—after all, I'd be dead so I wouldn't care. That thought was oddly comforting and I indulged in it. I hid the cutting and didn't tell anyone about it, but on some level I was hoping someone would notice. I sometimes wore an armband, both as a way to cover it and as a way to draw attention to it.

Cutting myself was an exciting secret. I could feel the imminent possibility of death, a liberating thrill. It was the final ace up my sleeve, and I liked the idea of always having an escape route. Besides—and I felt this without any sense of drama, emotion, or exaggeration—I just didn't see the point of staying alive.

Aldina had once asked me, in the midst of trying to sort out some Big Questions for herself, "Aren't you afraid that your life might just amount to nothing, that you'll just, I don't know…die and fade away into nothing, and no one will remember you?" Looking up at the crumbling ceiling, I considered the question briefly. "Actually, I think that's inevitable, and kind of a nice thought," I replied.

Telling my friends about the cutting was unimaginable. Eventually I did tell a couple of people, girls I was close to. Come to think of it, I've never told another guy about it. I wouldn't want them to try to help—that would be way too uncomfortable. If they ever found out, I would say to them, "Never mind, whatever, that was a long time ago," and try to end the conversation as quickly as possible.

I never sought help, either from a professional or from friends; in fact, I didn't even think I had a problem. My world felt lonely and crazy, like a noisy bazaar where nothing really got done and most people were just looking to get what they could from you and leave. This feeling was sometimes relieved by moments of stunning natural beauty—like the time I hiked across a snow-covered farm near my house. As I stared blankly at the white expanse, I felt gripped by a force I can't quite explain. It felt like The World, the big world, was calling me back to its peaceful stream, and when I held a knife in my hands, I felt like maybe I could go join that peace. But those were the rare moments.

Returning home wasn't much relief. The pace of life in Millhaven now seemed painfully slow, and I didn't talk to my parents about my personal life. Andy was still around town; something about him seemed like he would never leave. My fingers danced over the familiar pattern of his phone number, and I wondered what it would be like to see him again. Finally I drove up to his front door, just like always, and with big smiles we drove right into a rush of inside jokes and "remember when" moments. We sat in the car, blasted ska music—just like always—and I drove us off into the night.

It was like time in our friendship had never moved.

We drove through memories: by Turner's house on the corner, past the fields where we threw discus, through the little town, same as always. We settled into our Regulars: absurd humor, Super Smash Brothers, cards, tea. But half my mind was outside the room wondering, shouldn't things be different now? The inside jokes started to make me feel uncomfortable.

"And then Mr. Roberts would probably come by with just a grilled cheese sandwich!" Andy quipped.

I chuckled distractedly.

"It's just like that time when Donnie was like, 'Hey guys, we gonna throw discus today?' "

The situation was starting to wear on me. Shouldn't we have changed? Grown? So much had happened to me. Having the Regulars as a backdrop to all of this was at least some comfort.

As I drove Andy home, we decided to take a walk somewhere, just like we always did. I picked a hill near the orchard; we'd gone up there in the past to meditate. We silently made our way up the hill in a combination of reverence for the night and avoiding being caught. We got to the top and looked out at the night scenery below us. There was a silence between us, periodically broken when one of us felt compelled to say something profound or funny. Mostly we just looked out and thought our thoughts.

I dropped Andy off without much more talk and drove home wondering what would become of us. The familiarity was comfortable, but it had started to seem shallow to me. Was that all we had? I looked back on all the time we spent throwing discus. What had it amounted to? And was I someday going to look back on my current life and friends the same way? I was leaving again, and I had no idea what things would be like next time I came back.

Little did I know I was headed off to the most miserable month of my life. Midway through my junior year, I took a trimester off from school to work in Shanghai with a friend, Kim. However, Kim hadn't actually been looking for a job, and the trip turned into a mere journey abroad. I felt obliged to stay with her to look after her. I was miserable. Shanghai was much colder than expected, but since I considered the unproductive trip a waste of time and money, I refused to spend money on a winter jacket. Or on adequate food. Or on new shoes when mine became worn and uncomfortable. Or on museum tickets, tours, or activities of any other kind. Kim found me insufferable and depressing. "It's like you just can't let go of things," she said. When she told me this, I broke down and cried for several hours. It was true, and I knew it. I cried guiltily for all of my misery and all of the unhappiness I had brought her.

Those few hours of crying were a beautiful catharsis, and afterwards I felt resigned to letting go of my numerous philosophical disagreements with the trip. I smiled more and tried to make sure that Kim had a good time. That became very important to me. But underneath it all, I still couldn't let go of something. I saw how I had ruined our trip and felt pressed to change my life and my attitude in some way that I didn't quite understand.

In the spring after getting back from Shanghai, it was once again Ultimate Frisbee season. Things were looking better. I had a few more friends on the team and didn't feel quite so isolated when the team traveled to tournaments. I stopped hooking up with random girls at frat parties, which always left me feeling empty. I also started to get to know one of my teammates better, Mason.

Mason is tough to explain. He's the most brilliant person I've ever met and probably the most empathetic guy. He almost never slept and would do crazy things, like showing up at my apartment at random hours of the day wearing a pirate costume and carrying a boom box, a board game, and a bottle of vodka and suggest that we start a game of drinking Candy Land.

We started talking on and off, but I didn't think much of it. He was one of those guys everyone on campus recognized, and I figured that to him, I was just another face. But I found myself sitting on a couch with him more and more, talking about my Big Questions. We both stared out from the couch, as if peering into an abyss. I felt a kind of comfort in talking to him—he was good at listening attentively and then offering his thoughts softly, usually not by telling me something directly but by asking questions to get me to say more about my thoughts.

There was once, just once, when I shared my feelings about sex to him. I almost didn't say anything, and when I did, I felt a naked discomfort. I continued awkwardly working my way through how to talk to him. When I finished telling him, Mason was smiling.

"What?" I said.

"No, nothing Socksy," he replied, calling me by my Frisbee team nickname.

I looked him over for a bit. "You've been grinning this whole time," I said. "What's up?"

"It's just... I'm so excited for you," he said.

After he left, I tried to figure out why he was so happy. I think it was this: I was starting to open up, and he noticed.

While on the Frisbee team, I had long been critical of taking the game seriously. I tried hard and wanted to improve and become very good, but I felt that caring too much about it would mean more attachment and eventually more pain. I was silently critical of teammates who seemed too invested in winning.

That spring our team found itself making a fierce comeback in a game that would put us on track for nationals. I was on the defensive line with Mason, who was playing even better than usual. In the end, we did it—we came from behind and won. After the game, we were exhausted but happy and out of our minds cheering. At that moment we really came together as a team. Mason was crying, I think because he found it all so beautiful. When I saw him, I felt like I'd been hit on the back of the head. What had I been doing? I felt like a little kid who'd been pouting, while Mason lived to put a smile on other peoples' faces—including mine, no matter how hard I resisted. I had to wake up.

In my senior year, I started going out of my way to welcome and mentor the new freshmen. And I really enjoyed it. I was also dating Summer, a thoughtful and quirky girl from another college whom I met playing Frisbee. We had so much in common and quickly became close. We'd go for long walks, sharing and laughing and getting to know each other. I think she's the first girl I've dated whom I really cared about, not as a girlfriend but as a person.

In the past, whenever I had a disagreement with a girlfriend, I'd think she was just crazy or needy and not thinking straight. I wasn't much interested in taking an open and honest look at her or at myself—I just thought I was right and wanted to prove it. Maybe I had been maturing without noticing it, and of course it helped that I actually liked Summer, so when she was upset I really felt bad too. That was new to me.

At any rate, things were looking up. I had fewer bouts of depression, although there were still some. I cut myself only rarely, and it felt less intense when I did. I started having conversations with friends about ourselves, which was tough. It was still so much easier to talk about some shared interest like Frisbee or Super Smash Brothers or to talk about our personal problems as abstract things, like, "I think there's too much pressure these days to be successful."

One conversation that sticks out was with one of my roommates. He was talking about what his plans were for after college, and I had the sense that he was upset. I instinctively wanted to pull back from the conversation, but at the time I was sitting in the passenger seat of his car and couldn't leave—at least he was driving and couldn't look me in the eyes. So he talked, staring straight ahead, and there was pain in what he said: pressure from his parents, feeling lost about his life, and a loss of control in his relationship. It hurt me to listen to it, and I sat there squirming. In the end, though, we did talk. I asked him questions, threw in some assurance and advice, and in the end felt a lot closer to him. We had been room-mates for three years but hadn't had an open conversation until then—just a few months before graduation.

Getting closer to my guy friends was a funny feeling. On the one hand, they were fun, interesting people I wanted to talk to and get to know better. On the other hand, talking to them about their pain and fears was for me like getting a shiatsu massage: I knew it'd probably feel good afterwards, but while it was going on, I felt a pain deep in my core. I couldn't figure it out—despite all my introspection and meditation, this habit of avoiding closeness didn't make any sense to me. These were, after all, my best friends.

Everything seemed to come to a climax at the end of college. It was about a week before we all departed, and the seniors were lazing around in the indolent days between the end of finals and the start of the graduation ceremonies. Mason came bursting into my apartment ranting excitedly about "the coolest trail he'd ever seen" and how we "had to go." By that time, mainly through Mason's influence, I had learned to ease up a bit, to leave my comfort zone and try things even if I didn't immediately see the point. We talked about things on and off as we made our way to the trail, which led down to a small outlook over the river. We found a broken-down couch there, where we sat and continued talking, with the conversation drift-ing toward more personal territory. We looked at each other on and off; I was getting better at making eye contact with other guys when talking about serious things.

I don't remember exactly how he told me, but he ended up saying something about how he really liked me. He might have even used the word "love"—he was the kind of guy who could say that about other people. I don't know if I've met any other guy who could pull it off. I was blown away; it was the first time another guy had said something like this to me.

"Mason," I told him, "I have no idea what you see in me."

"I know, Socks," he said.

It's been two years since that conversation and I still don't get it.

That day Mason also talked about some things he was worried about in his life. Like everyone else, I respected Mason for being so outgoing and determined to help everyone feel welcome and have a good time. I thought he was invincible. But he told me then that he felt compelled to be like that because he was insecure about whether people liked him. I didn't know what to make of that, but I was at least somewhat comfortable hearing him out, and I opened up about some things in my life too. I told him how I was crippled by a lack of meaning in my life, that sometimes I didn't feel any reason to live, and that I felt like a man living after the world had ended. I felt better after having said these things to him. It is a happy memory for me.

College graduation day was sad and awkward. I stuck around for pictures and to say a few goodbyes, but it hurt to hear everyone tell each other that they'd keep in touch, since I knew that a lot of them wouldn't. Sure, we were all friends while on the Frisbee field together or while playing Super Smash Brothers, but would any of it stick? Mason and Jack and everyone else—would I ever talk to them again?

I knew Summer would be staying in my life. The more we got to know each other, the more we found that we liked to do things together—cook, run, read, travel. I could talk to her about anything and be bluntly honest about parts of me that I was afraid of.

Feelings of depression were much rarer for me now. I was starting work as a teacher, a job that kept me on my toes and thinking more about my students than about myself. I had always heard that helping others was supposed to feel good, but I didn't grasp how true that was until I had the chance to experience it for myself as a teacher. I stopped cutting myself, not by making an active decision but by letting go and forgetting about it. Cutting had drifted into my life on some unremembered day with little conscious thought; years later, it similarly faded away.

There was, however, one clear moment along the path to stopping: the suicide of my cousin. He was very young, just barely a teenager. The reasons aren't completely clear, but he seemed easily frustrated, often unhappy, and had recently gotten into fights with kids at school. What affected me about his death was that I saw myself in it—I kept telling myself that it could have been me. Seeing that, I realized that being alive was a kind of gift. Seeing him die and realizing that I could have died too made me feel like I had been brought back to life, that I had both the dead man's gift of putting down his burdens and the living man's gift of life. I somehow felt as if I had died too, but that since I was in fact still alive, I could live peacefully on borrowed time.

In retrospect, I am not sure how to understand my cutting. Part of my uncertainty is that I never had anyone to talk it over with, to help me anchor this confusing situation with experience and an outside perspective. I also wasn't in tune with my feelings at that time. Maybe I was alone and sad. Maybe there was something therapeutic about the way cutting made me feel—like I had my own life in my hands. Sometimes I didn't feel like living, and sometimes I just felt like trying to make others notice me. How serious had I been about what I was doing and how much was I playing? There's no easy answer, and I don't worry about it anymore. I told very few people about it at the time, so no one asks me about it now. I still don't quite see it as a problem, but as some harsh terrain I had to cross and have no desire to tread back over.

The summer after graduation I moved back home. The next day, Andy joined me in my living room, where we played Super Smash Brothers, drank tea, and played cards. We talked about how weird it felt to graduate. He asked me about Frisbee. We got lost in another hour-long game of cards. I realized I'd never asked him about his art before. I made a mental note to do that sometime.

A little bit later I got an e-mail from Andy: "If you want to hang out, I've been working on this theory that we DON'T have to do for 8 hours. We can just watch a documentary or go to the park or something so the entire day isn't sacked."

I was sort of shocked when I received this. Did he feel like the day was "sacked" if he spent it hanging out with me? Or did he think that I didn't want to hang out with him and was trying to be polite? I realized then that I had no idea how he felt about our friendship—was he just seeing me out of habit or out of boredom, or did he actually enjoy doing things together?

*   *   *   *

I don't know what to do next. Andy and I joke around a lot, so it's hard to tell what he is really thinking sometimes. But in recent e-mails, things don't seem like jokes. For example, he casually dropped in a line about having panic attacks at three in the morning. I know that his parents are stressful for him, that he went to college to become an artist, and that he was laid off soon after getting his first job and can't find a new one. I want to help Andy, I want to say something, but I have no idea how to do it. I guess that's the way it's always been for me. I could never quite face my feelings around friends, couldn't quite share something about me that was real and raw. And although I'd like to open up with Andy, I'm afraid it'll be too painful to see how he's feeling all at once, to look at his feelings face first. It would be like looking into the sun. Did I ever mention that? That's what I think friendship between guys is like: the sun. You know it's there, and if you pay attention, you'll feel its warmth, but you can't look at it directly.

HOLDING MY BREATH

As a senior in college, Andy looks back on significant relationships with his friends and finds that they have helped him learn to be more comfortable with who he is. When he gives up his childhood love of theater and turns to sports in middle school, he assumes a masculine identity that remains important to him, even as he becomes more convinced of his homosexuality. In college, through friendships and romantic relationships, Andy learns to accept all aspects of who he is. He also finds that by being himself, he can contribute to change and the growth of others.

When I woke up that Tuesday morning and jumped down from the top bunk, my legs felt especially sore. The postseason lifting schedule is considerably more grueling than inseason. Lacrosse had gone on for four months. Once the season ended, we started lifting at full blast: front squats, back squats, single leg squats, off-bench squats, cleans, pulls, jerks. As I landed on the ground, six feet down from my bed, my quadriceps felt the impact.

I showered, shaved, brushed my teeth, and put my contacts in like any normal morning, except that I went over the conversation I was about to have so many times in the shower that my fingers turned prune-like after half an hour and that made it more difficult to hold my contacts. My fingers were almost insensitive to the touch of the small plastic objects, and it took me a few extra minutes before I finally got them in my eyes and the fuzzy world became visible. Back in my room, I paced back and forth, repeating words and phrases in my head. None of them sounded right. So I cleaned up the common room as one of my roommates remained sleeping in the bedroom. I straightened up all of the papers on the desk. I put all of the clothes from the chair away in the closet. I put my books on the shelf. None of these mindless actions could take my brain away from the task at hand.

I had worried for the last five years of my life how I would ever tell my parents that I was gay. But when I finally got the words out of my mouth with my mother sitting three feet away from me, my breathing finally slowed down. It didn't matter what came of it—whether she came over and kissed me or got right back in her car and drove home. She did neither. In my imagination, she was supposed to break into tears and tremble and hold my hand and say, "I love you." In my mind we were going to sit together and cry out our feelings and emotions. My mother seemed to have neither at the moment. She simply sat on that couch and told me that she and my father would always love me no matter what.

I showed her a picture of my boyfriend, Adam, and she smiled. She told me that she was just glad I would not have to do this alone, and then she strayed from the topic of homosexuality. I was ready to talk. This was the morning I had chosen to open up to my mother, to tell her the secret burden I had been carrying for too long, and here she was, essentially telling me that it was silly for me to have kept the secret. Why did I think it would be so upsetting to her? Why did I choose to let this eat me up inside when there was nothing to fear on the outside? She acted as if this was any other day of my life.

We went out to lunch, and then I took her to meet Adam. In my mother's attempt to avoid any awkwardness, she gave him a big hug (a welcome to the family kind of thing) and blabbered on for a while about nothing of any importance. When she left, I felt changed. I tried to remember my last family phone call, so I could remember it as the last time I would ever have to lie about who I was dating. Adam hugged me and told me how proud of me he was for coming out to my mother. He felt relieved. I didn't. The worst is yet to come, I thought, when my father hears the news.

The next morning, I awoke to read this e-mail in my inbox:

Hi:

I have one million questions for you—and when you are ready to talk, I am ready to listen. Every night, after going to sleep, we wake up in the morning. As a father, husband, parent, educator, and health care professional, I can honestly say that it is my life-long experience that one's sexual preference is not the issue—the central issue is that when you wake up you are excited with what you will be accomplishing during the upcoming day. Your dreams, goals, and enthusiasm for life are what really count. What we want to do with our precious and precarious lives and how we want to share the joy of living with others is really what this is all about. I am writing this note to tell you that I love you, am very proud of you, and look forward to some frank discussion with you when you come home soon.

—Dad

I started to cry. I needed to read the note again to make sure that my brain was not playing tricks on me. There was no way that I had just received that note from my father. For 10 years, I had thought about members of the same sex. For five years, I had actually thought about the reality of being gay. For the last three,

I had wrestled with my life, staying up all night unable to fall asleep because I was worried about how my parents would react. Adam handed me a tissue. Part of me was shaking, and the other part of me was completely at rest.

When I was younger, I used to wish for bad parents. I used to wish that my parents fought, or that they would get divorced, so that when I turned out to be really screwed up, everyone would know whom to blame. I hoped that they would stop loving me, so that I could pretend I was doing this to get back at them. But as I walked up toward class that morning, I knew how glad I was that my wish had not come true. My father had just told me that he loved me and was very proud of me. In class that morning, my friends asked me what was wrong, since my eyes looked red. I told them that I was just tired. It was true. I was tired of hiding my life from the ones who gave me life. I was tired of feeling guilty for something I never had control over, not a single day in my 20 years of existence. I was tired of worrying that nobody would accept me.

A week and a half later, my father took me out for a lobster dinner—my favorite meal—to open me up. As we drove out to the restaurant, I didn't worry about the things I used to worry about. Instead, I worried that my father would not be able to handle all the answers to his questions. How would he reconcile being blind to my sexuality for so long?

He grilled me about everything during our dinner. As we buttered our rolls, he asked me when I first knew that I was gay. "When I was 19 years old," I told him, "because I knew I would never love my current girlfriend. But really, it was when I was 13 years old, because I started to fantasize about the same sex. And I can trace it back to being aroused when I was 6 or 7. But actually, I remember when I was 4 years old, my friend Rod and I would lie on top of each other naked." My father gasped at this last remark. How could I claim to have known that I was gay at four years old?

By the time the clam chowders were served, we were well into my high-school experience. He asked what it was like to hide this from everyone, and I told him how awful it really was. He sympathized with me, but he found it difficult to match my emotions. His life works scientifically. There is always an explanation and something that we can learn from everything. We talked about the importance of trust and communication. I saw something new in his eyes. Was this man, in his mid-fifties, trying to tear down all the walls I had built and find out who his son really was? Every once in a while, he would pause and look down, unable to understand how he had let me feel so badly about myself, or how he had not been there when his son needed him. I tried to console him, saying, "Dad, I spent my entire adolescence trying to hide this from you. I became a pretty good liar, even to myself. How could you have seen this coming when I did everything I could to paint a different picture for you?"

I was full after that meal. My father was still full of questions. He would never see the world in the same way again. He had to turn his world upside-down in order to understand me and fit my life into it. The whole stigma of homo-sexuality was now part of his life, whether he liked it or not. In time, he could make adjustments to his world, to allow the current situation to make sense, but he could never go back to the way it was. That world no longer existed. He could never again look at a gay couple and wonder who made them turn out like that. When he heard a fellow doctor make an off-color joke about homosexuality, he had to speak up now, because it was my father's world that the doctor was making fun of.

Growing up I had every advantage that a Jewish kid from the suburbs would want, from private schools to youth sports to sleepaway camps. At the age of five, I entered kindergarten in a private school where my sister and brother were in the fourth and sixth grades, respectively. In second grade, I started attending Hebrew school three times a week, and that didn't stop until seventh grade when I had my Bar Mitzvah.

My early love was theater. By age six, I was creating my own musicals, writing the scripts and the music, and recruiting friends to perform my plays. In third grade, I joined a theater troupe with my friend Evan; we were the two youngest members of the group made up of mostly fourth, fifth, and sixth graders. When some scouts from the Boston theater district came to watch us rehearse, I was asked to audition for the role of Tiny Tim in *A Christmas Carol*. I was chosen as an understudy for the character and later received roles as a child in two other professional plays. It seemed that my life was set; my goal was to grow up to be a Hollywood or Broadway actor.

Throughout my acting days, my sister and brother often tormented me for being too artistic. I learned to associate arts with something bad, something nobody wanted to be connected with. My sister and brother would throw around the term "gay" without really thinking about sexual orientation. To them it was just an insult, something that little boys are supposed to avoid. They knew that it was more "gay" to write plays than to play sports, so I was surrounded by these ideas at an early age. One afternoon, before an evening performance at a professional play in Boston, my father handed me the new issue of *Time*. The cover read "AIDS and the Arts." The discussion that followed left me horrified. He asked me repeatedly if the men with whom I performed had tried to touch me in strange places. If his intention was to turn me away from the stage, he succeeded— that was the final professional play of my life. I never believed that my father was insinuating anything about me, or that he meant to do me any harm. As a doctor, he spends his life trying to improve health, and as a father, he wants the best for his children. But in trying to protect me, he alienated me. I knew I could no longer feel proud of my accomplishments around him.

Starting the summer after third grade, I traveled up to East Falls, New Hampshire—a town too small for its own post office—for overnight camp: eight weeks of sports, campfires, and cabin fights, culminating in an event called "color war," which I had the misfortune to lose for four straight years. It was at camp where I first developed strong friendships with boys of completely different backgrounds. Each year, we would come back to see each other, one year older, and we would hope to be placed in the same cabin as our buddies.

The first time I can remember being sexually aroused was during the second summer at camp, when I was 10 years old, watching one of my bunkmates change out of his bathing suit. It was my first real erection, and I didn't know what it meant. A few weeks later, another bunkmate was given a *Playboy* from his older brother, and we all sat around a bed and flipped through the pages, noting how hairy some of the girls were and rating their breasts. When a buddy asked if I was getting hard looking at the girls, I told him I didn't know. I asked him if he was hard, and he said of course, that he always got hard looking at naked girls. I noted this and also thought about my first erection earlier that summer. How funny that mine came from an undressing buddy while his came from a silly magazine.

My camp had a big teepee right in front of the main lodge, and the director said that on special occasions a few campers could have the privilege of sleeping in the teepee for a night. So during my third year at camp, five of us decided to drag our sleeping bags down to the lodge and spend a night under the stars. We didn't anticipate the rain soaking us nor did we plan the events of that night. I can't remember how it started, but I do remember another boy and I coupling off into one sleeping bag. Two others boys followed along, both in the same bag. The fifth boy put his head inside his sleeping bag and pulled the string tight so that he could not see what was going on.

We decided to pretend that we were boy and girl, acting like lovers, since we were 11 and did not know exactly how everything worked. We had our pants on during the entire scene, but our shirts were off and our hands were exploring each other's bodies. It felt so great to me, but I didn't know if I was supposed to enjoy it or not. My hand went up and down his back and I felt every bone and every bump from his shoulder blades down to his buttocks. One of the boys in the other two-man sleeping bag said that he was getting hard and asked if that made him gay. The other boy in his bag proclaimed that it meant nothing, that obviously we were all imitating having sex with women and that getting hard was just a consequence of this role-playing. We were just perfectly regular guys using each other to feel what older guys get to feel all the time.

When we woke up the next morning, we vowed not to mention what had happened the night before. We said we'd forget what happened, but I couldn't. I developed feelings for the other boy who shared my sleeping bag with me, and I think he felt the same way. We spent a lot of time together, but we never repeated what we had done in the teepee. Maybe we were in denial, or maybe we didn't understand our desires, but we were able to maintain a unique friendship without speaking directly about that night. You could argue that this was the first "homosexual" relationship of my life, but at that age we did what we enjoyed doing and didn't think much of it.

The summer after sixth grade my father again took me aside and told me that I was going to play football. He told me that I wanted to be tough, not a sissy, and that playing football would not only teach me to be tough, but it would show people exactly what type of person I was. "If you want to be cool," he told me, "you should play football and quit all of the acting business. You don't want to be a sissy, do you?"

When he told me not to be a sissy, we both knew what he was trying to say: Acting would make me gay while football would be the answer to everyone's prayers. My older siblings had been calling me gay for years for all of the singing and acting I did, and here my dad was telling me that I could forget all of that and start a new identity in middle school as a football player. There was a part of me that hated my dad for telling me to give up something that I loved so much. To assume that he could change me by changing my after-school interests was naïve of him, but, at the same time, I understood that he loved me and wanted what was best for me. In his eyes, I would benefit from my peers approving of me.

My athletic career took off from there. We had been a sports family for as long as I could remember. I loved sports, and they came naturally to me. I guess sports were just overshadowed by what seemed like my more natural talent: acting. I left the stage behind almost cold turkey and dove right into the athletic world.

I became best friends with Austin in eighth grade, my second year in middle school and my second year of football. Austin had a thin build, brown hair, and a boyish face and was almost a foot taller than me. We bonded during the seventh-grade football season. That first year I was clueless on the field and almost never got into the game. I didn't even know all of the rules. But during the summer after seventh grade, Austin and I went to football camp, and I learned how to be a receiver and a running back. By eighth grade, I led the middle school team in touchdowns. Austin and I became inseparable for the next few years. For a 13-year-old who recognizes his interests in other boys, the ideal relationship is with your best friend. I figured we could be best friends, and in private we could be boyfriends. Nobody would question us since we spent so much time together anyway. What I didn't know was that he never shared this fantasy with me.

While on a vacation to the Caribbean with my family, Austin and I were playing tackle football in the pool. As the contact increased, so did my arousal level. As I pulled him down in the water, I made sure to brush by his waist and let him know of my interest. Later, when we were back in our room watching television, I decided to continue our little game. Without saying a word to each other, I brought Austin to climax. He could argue that he was imagining a female with him and that I was the only thing he had to get him off. But the truth is that we had taken part in homosexual activity without speaking. Incidents like this occurred on more than one occasion, but he never initiated any of them. Perhaps to him it was just messing around with a friend. We never once talked about the few incidents, but I thought it was all understood. I, the initiator, wanted to continue that part of our relationship; he didn't want to talk about it.

By early junior year in high school, Austin and his girlfriend started sleeping together, and I knew that I had lost him for good. He pressured me to find a girl of my own and sleep with her, but I wasn't interested. The guy I fell for let me down; he switched over to the straight side and tried to drag me over with him. I couldn't change though. I was gay. While I may have been unable to say it out loud, I knew it then for sure.

I came to college with the intention of fitting in, being like everyone else, and graduating without attracting too much attention. I didn't envision life beyond college because, for me, there was no imaginable life. What gay role models did I have? My uncle and his boyfriend of 20 years? My family had made fun of them and their lifestyle since I was a baby. My understanding of grown-up gay men was that they were unhappy and disliked. This was hardly how I wanted to spend my life, so I blocked adulthood out of my mind. I imagined life until graduation, and after that I figured I would disappear. I would go and live the life I wanted without worrying about how I would be judged. Thinking back, it's funny to even consider disappearing into obscurity. I have never been one to sit in the background and let others steal the show. That is not me.

As soon as I got to college, I met three of my future lacrosse teammates. We spent the first few weeks of school together while the rest of the class ran through orientation meetings and scavenger hunts and carnivals. I always knew that my teammates respected me for my abilities on the field, but I was worried about portraying the part of a heterosexual college athlete off the field. One night, early in our first term, a few of my teammates and I ended up in the dining hall on our way from one fraternity to another. When the first cute blonde girl walked by our table, each of my teammates followed her closely with their eyes. Did they notice that I forgot to pay particular attention to the blonde girl? Perhaps they were too distracted to see.

Driving to the fields one afternoon during fall practices, a senior turned right to me and said, "Hey, what's your story? I never hear about you with the ladies. Do you get around?" I hesitated. A few seconds later, I managed a laugh. As I was about to respond with something like, "I'm not quite the player that you are," my roommate and best friend Chris jumped in and saved me. "He holds his own." And just like that, it was done. All it took was one sentence, one claim from a reliable source, and my manhood was restored. I didn't have to provide evidence, names, and descriptions of each girl I had been with. I didn't even have to say a word. Chris saved me that time. I didn't know how much longer I could keep up the act.

When I later ended up telling Chris the truth, he shrugged his shoulders, smiled, and gave me a high-five. That was Chris in a nutshell. He had a way of simplifying everything. Maybe he had really known all along and didn't need to make a big deal of it. Maybe it just didn't matter to him. He confirmed his confidence in me as a friend with a simple high-five. Why did something like this stress me out so much when I had friends who responded by giving me a high-five and a pat on the back?

During my sophomore year, as I was coming out, I roomed with Chris and Shane. Shane, my roommate for most of freshman year, was a fairly good-looking guy with brown hair who came from San Francisco. He was laid back, he liked to party, and we spent a lot of time together. I think Shane trusted me, and he appreciated my ability to make friends. We joked together, listened to music together, and most importantly we enjoyed each other's company. I felt that I had accomplished something important my freshman year, finding a quality friend at college.

While I didn't see Shane as the ideal mate, I certainly saw more than just a good friend. Many times, we would be up late at night studying, and we would end up getting into a wrestling match. If he ever sensed that I had become aroused by the physical contact, he never pulled back. I don't think that Shane was aroused in the same way that I was, but I am sure that he also saw me as more than just a close friend.

During my first three terms at college, I had experienced kissing and other intimate activities with girls on a few occasions, but I always came away from these nights feeling guilt from being unable to enjoy these "normal" activities, fear that the girl would see my lack of desire and tell on me, and a strange pleasure from participating in something that is supposed to bring me joy. At a dance party one night, Shane, seeing me turn down girls who might have been potential hookups, told two female friends that he thought I must be gay. The girls soon told me that my roommate and supposed best friend had been spreading a rumor about me. Completely uncomfortable with this situation, I laughed it off, thinking that my relaxed attitude would show these girls that I was clearly straight.

For three months, Shane and I continued to hang out and eat meals together, and we pledged the same fraternity at the beginning of the winter term. But there was no longer any depth to our relationship. It was clear what had driven us apart; he assumed I was gay and not telling him, while I was offended that he had spread rumors about me. I wrestled with the thought of coming out every day that fall term.

For years, I had considered myself gay, and I hadn't really questioned it in recent memory. But believing something and saying it out loud are two totally different things. When my friend Caitlin was over at my room one afternoon, I leaned toward her and whispered to her through cupped hands, "I'm gay." In saying these two words, it was like I truly became a homosexual. Up until that point, I only thought my homosexuality was something that could come true. But once those words were out of my mouth, I could never take them back. Caitlin shook her head in disbelief and repeated to me numerous times, "That's not a funny joke. I know you are kidding and it isn't funny." I put her hand up against my chest and she felt how fast my heart was beating. It took her 20 minutes of head shaking before she apologized for making this so difficult and not believing me in the first place. Caitlin was the only one I told for quite some time, but eventually I was able to say the words out loud and not feel bad about what I was saying.

My relationship with Shane was still fairly weak, and I felt partially responsible. So one night, instead of going to bed early as was my custom, I decided I would make the effort and appeal to him by staying up and making something of our broken friendship.

"Uhh ... this is pretty hard to say. I feel like you know what I'm going to say but here goes. All that stuff you said about me, what you thought about me, well, you were right."

"Yeah I know, dude. No worries."

"Ha. Well, it has been pretty difficult for me trying to deal with everything, and it didn't help much that you were spreading shit around. I don't know why you would have done that to me." He seemed to understand where I was coming from, and he apologized for the way he had handled it. That night we reestablished a closeness that we hadn't felt since our freshman year and maybe formed a deeper friendship than ever.

Adam, an older brother in the fraternity I had just joined, e-mailed me one night after a frat event and asked me if I wanted to get something to eat with him. Adam was about five-foot-ten, with a muscular build and gorgeous blue-green eyes. He was one of the better-looking seniors in school, and he was openly gay. After a crazy night of drinking that next weekend, I awoke to read this e-mail in my inbox the next morning:

> Hey, here's the bottom line. I have a bit of a crush on you. I am really drunk tonight, and I'm letting it all out. Sorry if this is not what you asked for by joining a fraternity. You seem like such a great guy, and I don't want you to be unhappy...

Despite some of the drunken rambling, it appeared that he had made the first move. I wrote him back and explained to him that I understood his actions and that I am indeed gay. He asked me to meet up with him that night so we could talk.

I told my roommates that I was going to the library to meet a friend to go over some organic chemistry problems. I met Adam at his car; he suggested that I might feel more relaxed getting away from campus. Something about the comfort in his voice made me forget all about any sexual attraction I had for him. I thought, "Here is this guy who came out to his entire fraternity and even took a guy to his formal. He knows what it is like and he can show me the ropes and help me along." When I looked over at this handsome guy, I saw a big brother, a mentor. He told me about coming out to his family, how difficult that had been for him but how easy they had made it for him. Adam kept trying to get me to speak, to open up, but I preferred to listen.

We drove through back roads on a lightly snowing night, and the car went in and out of lighted areas, in and out of the shadows. I thought, "If my roommates knew I was driving around the dark areas of town with a homosexual, what would they think of me?" We drove by a familiar road that I remembered running once with my teammates in daylight. I thought about my teammates, seeing me now in this car. When other cars drove by, I turned to the side so they couldn't make out my identity.

Just before returning to my dorm, Adam pulled the car over in a shaded area. He started to breathe heavily, and he started to babble something like, "Should I do it?" I asked him what was going on, and he just looked over and smiled. He reached his hand across my face. With this soft grip, he pulled my head toward his and we kissed. His heart was beating fast. I could feel his nervousness, but I did not share it. Perhaps I would have been more nervous if I had thought about it. But instead, I was thinking about the past, and how many kisses I had taken part in without feeling anything. The only kisses that I could remember were for show. In this car, I wanted to kiss him more. His lips, slightly chapped from the cold weather, met mine. His beard against my face was a new feeling. It was almost like I could feel his manliness rubbing against my face. My heart didn't start beating fast until he returned me to my dorm, when I thought of two things: how incredible that moment, my first kiss, was, and what I was going to tell my roommates.

After another evening in his car, I told Adam that we would have to choose a warmer spot. Those big winter jackets were ruining the moment. Adam and I agreed to meet in the library up in the stacks, an obscure area only inhabited during exams. Just being here with him was cause for concern, since he was openly gay. Someone who happened to go looking for an East Asian book at this time of night might stumble upon the two of us and piece things together. Sometimes I would close my eyes, clench my fists, and pray that I would not get caught. Other times I wished that somebody would just find me so I could end the whole charade and just bring Adam to my room like everyone else did with their girlfriends.

On Valentine's Day I told Adam that I wanted to spend the night with him more than anything. This was Valentine's Day, the day people spend with their special someone. I put on my khaki pants, a nice collared shirt, and I met Adam for dinner. On my way out the door, a few friends asked if I was going on a date, and I gave them a crazy look as if to say, "Me? Of course not. You guys know that I don't go on dates."

At dinner I told Adam that I wanted to get away from school with him so that we could share this special night together. Each time I expressed this interest, he countered by reminding me that his room was only a five-minute walk down the path. I knew that. I also knew that he had three apartment mates who were all in my fraternity. I couldn't bear to think that someone might see me walking into a room and immediately think "gay." Most of the older brothers in my fraternity thought of me first as the lacrosse player. I wanted them to get to know me before making judgments, but I didn't particularly mind the stereotype of the lacrosse player as it associated me with traditional masculine stereotypes. Being thought of as gay, however, evoked just the opposite stereotypes.

Eventually I gave in, willingly, but also feeling as though I was holding my breath under water and praying not to drown. I stood in the doorway at Adam's apartment unsure if I wanted to show my face. I took a deep breath and stepped around the corner. Bob, Adam's roommate and our fraternity brother, smiled and held out his hand to give me a high-five; Bob's girlfriend, Jennifer, said that it was good to see me again. Adam's eyes closed up just a bit as he smiled, one of those "I'm so proud of you and I don't want to forget this moment" type of smiles. Adam and I sat down next to each other on the couch, and I was sure that Bob and Jennifer would be completely conscious of every move that we made. I was wrong though. Holding hands, we watched television like any normal couple on Valentine's Day, and Bob and Jennifer couldn't have cared less about us. Bob was entranced by the show, laughing at every mildly funny joke. Jennifer, as self-conscious as anyone, was probably too worried about how she came off to notice me. As the evening went on, I began to undergo a transformation. I knew I wouldn't be instantly comfortable with this new self, but it was starting to grow on me.

After walking into his room Adam locked the door behind us, and I felt like we were alone, somewhere far off, like nobody could get to us now. He gave me a huge hug, as was his ritual, but this time our shirts were off and our chests met for the first time. He had a little bit of hair, but his chest was muscular, and you could feel the divisions of his abdominals. When we got into bed, everything felt so natural. It was one of those small college beds, wide enough for only one, so he slept on his back, and I slept on his chest. I turned my head to the side so that his shoulder became my pillow, and I lay down to sleep with my boyfriend, like lovers do on Valentine's Day.

We fell in love over the long, dark, cold winter at school. It happened on nights like our joy ride in the fogged up car, or when we waltzed across the frozen pond at two in the morning one night in February, or as we sat inside with hot chocolate as the wind howled down the street toward the river. I looked at him and saw a beautiful human being. Beyond his looks, he was an incredible person who thought of others before himself. He spent his afternoons with underprivileged children in the area and wanted to teach in the Bronx public schools after graduation. Besides all of this, he always showed a great deal of faith in me. I saw him as a role model as well as a boyfriend, and I saw no reason to break up in June. We said "I love you" to each other after we got back from a two-week spring break period without each other, and we never stopped saying it. Soon we would say the words so often that it began to feel like a greeting. Adam was my first love, and for this reason, I will always vividly remember moments spent with him.

We decided that as long as we cared about each other this much and weren't hurting anybody, we should stay together after his graduation. I was off from school in the fall term, and being away from school was a much different experience than being a student. I went to work each morning, came home each afternoon, went to the gym, ate dinner, watched a little television, and went to bed to get some rest for work the next day. Every night before bed, Adam and I would talk on the phone and tell each other about how our days had gone. On weekends we would visit each other, and this became our motivation to get through the week.

All of this changed when I was back at school for winter term and Adam was still away. I no longer had a set schedule, and I wasn't always free at any point in the evening to call Adam. He got upset because he was used to stability, part of which was hearing my voice before he went to sleep. When he told me that he thought about me all day and couldn't wait to talk to me, I would have to be honest and tell him that he hadn't crossed my mind all day and that I couldn't really talk more than a few minutes.

Winter term was pledge term and one of the new pledges happened to be a boy on whom I had had my eye for over a year. Keith lived on my hall that year, and something about him—maybe it was the way he looked at me—made me think that he could be gay as well. We had developed a friendship, and when he pledged my fraternity we got even closer. Many nights we drank together, and

I always had a good time. Sometimes I would go home and start fantasizing about Keith, and I wouldn't stop to catch myself just because I was with Adam. I let the fantasies go because in my mind, they were just fantasies—there was no chance that they would come true. I was with Adam.

By March, Adam and I both knew it wasn't working. He had emotional needs: someone to talk to on the phone, someone to visit him on weekends, and someone to listen to him and care for him. I had little space for someone else in my life, and I resented Adam for making me feel guilty. While we both felt our relationship had deteriorated, we had separate solutions. He wanted us to find a way to make it work, while I found no need to do so. Something in my mind had changed, some critical connection, some brain synapse completely reversed. I felt like he was a lost soul, someone who had fallen into a mild depression with his job and life in a big city and that I could not be the savior that he wanted or needed. I needed to take care of myself.

I had cut off emotionally from the relationship long before, and by Friday, less than a week after the breakup, I again saw Adam as a friend, a role model. I made a point to go drinking with Keith at the fraternity that night, and when the night was over, I took him back to my room. I had assumed that it would take some convincing, but it didn't. As we walked home from the fraternity, we were in constant physical contact. We elbowed and pushed each other as we walked past the library and up a slight hill to get to the other side of campus where we both lived, and it seemed like our hands were touching so closely that we could have been holding hands. When we reached the point where the paths diverged to his room or mine, I continued on the path to my dorm.

"Where are you going?" he asked.

"To my room. Come." He nodded with a slight smile and followed me to my room. As I unlocked the door and we sat down on my futon a few inches from each other, I realized that I had no prior evidence to suggest that Keith was in fact a homosexual. I had gone on gut instinct up until this point, choosing, unlike Adam, not to e-mail him with my feelings. When I leaned over to kiss him, making the first move as the older, more experienced guy, I recognized a somewhat confused but overjoyed look in his eyes. He had never before kissed a guy, and he had never even imagined this scenario happening in college. His blue hat sat atop his head at a slight angle, and I positioned myself in front of him. He closed his eyes, perhaps not wanting to see what was really happening, and I could feel his breath. It was heavy, and his heart was beating fast, just as Adam's had when he had tried to kiss me the first time. I was not nervous, though, just elated. I had this boy in my room, this boy on whom I had had a crush since I first saw him more than a year and a half before.

Keith has a youthful, boyish look. He swims competitively, and his upper body is strong. Hair covers his upper chest. When one of us lies down on top of the other, Keith is a few inches shorter than me. That night, when I took his lacrosse cap off of his head, I took comfort in the fact that I was in my room alone with the kind of guy who wears a lacrosse cap, the type of guy who nobody would ever imagine to be in my room. Keith doesn't fulfill any of the gay stereotypes. He is the type to take me to a sports bar where people would wonder if we are just buddies or if we are on a date, an aspect of mystery or ambiguity that I enjoy. He has an air of masculinity about him, and this is part of what attracts me to him. We can sit around and push each other and watch sports together. We are best friends, and yet we are so much more than that. This is what I had idealized since I was in seventh grade.

I have learned so much about myself, about the world, and about relationships from my two boyfriends in college. Adam was gay, everyone knew, and he wasn't ashamed. He told me that being gay was a blessing because he had the chance to change people's minds, and that he joined a fraternity because he wanted to teach tolerance to the Greek system. Keith, on the other hand, joined a fraternity because he wanted to meet new people, get closer with the members of his pledge class, and have a good time while at college. His reasons were much more like mine. We both like the party scene, the brother-bonding activities, and the tight friendships that we have made.

I have always been a fairly public and social member of my fraternity, and when I came out, nothing changed. My brothers respected me for who I was, and we never had any problems. I never meant to change anyone's mind, as Adam did, but just my presence and my confidence as one of the guys changed the way people acted in a positive way. For instance, when our social chair tells us about our parties, he tells us to "feel free to invite all significant others to the preparty," a subtle change from saying, "bring a girlfriend," something he said he did for me. Dating one of my fraternity brothers has been a touchy subject for some, but they were never vocal about it. Most of the guys were fine with it.

Being gay is a reality for me, something that was probably determined by the time I came out of my mother's womb. I haven't openly questioned why it happened to me in many years. At certain times, being gay has made me privileged. I have had the chance to affect many more people as an openly gay athlete or member of a fraternity than I would have otherwise. Being an athlete has always given me some sort of crutch in order to feel comfortable and secure with myself. Athletics are often associated with masculinity, and I have always used this conception to forge my identity. Perhaps I am a homosexual, but nobody perceives me as weak or feminine.

Coming into my senior year, I knew the younger members of the gay community at school would look up to me, and I thought that I should take a more active role in that community. I am now an officer in the Gay Straight Alliance, where we meet once a week and discuss important gay issues on the campus and beyond. It is a great chance to get to know guys a few years below me who are going through a lot of the same experiences I did. Now I see freshmen who have already come out to their friends and who contemplate joining a fraternity as an openly gay pledge, something I never imagined. At our weekly meetings, we often look at the state of gay rights in the country today. I have never been extremely interested in politics, but the Massachusetts Supreme Court ruling in

2003 inspired me, and I am not about to give up the right to equal marriage. Half a century ago, people said that interracial marriages were wrong and unnatural. Even though the courts saw this as discriminatory, it took another 10 years for the country to recognize legal interracial marriages. Now that the courts have found discrimination in our current laws, how much longer must we wait while our country again holds back equal rights to its citizens?

As I look back at my college career, I am glad that I have figured things out in time to really enjoy myself. My original intention to leave college without making much noise, without impacting people or leaving my mark, failed, and I am extremely happy about that. Through college, I met a few people who convinced me to do my own thing, and I know that I benefited from this advice. Now when I get the chance to talk to younger guys, guys who still have important decisions to make in their college years, I tell them to be themselves, do what matters to them, and their friends will be there. I hope they listen to me, and I hope their time in college is as rewarding as mine has been.

For many years I worried about how I was going to come out to family. Now my mother, father, sister, and brother are the most supportive people in my life. My parents continue to love me; my mother brags about my accomplishments to her friends and my father keeps pictures from my athletic career in his office. This past winter, Keith came with me on a family ski trip, joining my sister and her boyfriend, and my brother and his wife. Both of my siblings are older than me, both are in serious relationships, and, for a few years, I had felt a distance between us. Part of me wanted to show them that my relationship is no different; that our relationship can last as long as theirs. On that ski trip, it was clear that the distance no longer remained. We treat each other like we always have, only now we respect each other as adults.

In the end, I have learned that all romantic relationships are made up of the same components. There is intimacy. There is passion. There is love. Adam and I had all three of these. Keith and I are lucky because we are also best friends. Our relationship is not different from any other college relationship. We go on dates, go to dance parties together, go to formal occasions together, and we wake up in the morning after spending the night together. After college, we would like to share a life, a family. It might be a little more difficult to have children, but we will have them, and they will be loved as much as any children on this earth. For the rest of my life, I know that I will encounter people who do not understand me. I also know that I will continue to affect others, because I can change people's minds simply by being honest and by being true to myself.

ANDY: FIVE YEARS LATER

I am one of the lucky ones. I don't say those words often enough, but I know how true they are. At age 27, I haven't yet acquired enough experience to lecture about life's lessons learned, but if I look back a decade at the frightened 17-year-old that I was, I can tell him confidently that I have made it out the other side. I like to think about my life the way it is now—stable and full of happiness. The major issues I faced at 17 have been figured out or reduced to minor problems by 27. But the painful reality is that it wasn't always so perfect. It is hard to go back there, but it is important to remember what it was really like. It was scary, but I know now it was not the end of the story. I still don't know the end, but I do know that things are really good—great, in fact. I never could have predicted being here at the time I had so many doubts and worries.

At 17, I was certain of only one thing—I was different. At that age, being different really makes you just like everyone else, but you feel as if you are completely alone. I kept my secret to myself for a few more thought-filled, painful years. I occasionally dreamed of telling my close friends; I even wrote a letter to one friend explaining everything, but I never had the courage to take it out of my dresser and was afraid my mother would somehow discover it. So I kept it all inside and thought about ways to escape.

Sports ruled my life at that time, and I constantly feared that my teammates would figure out my secret and reject me. Writing that sentence is so much easier than living through it was. My friends and I spent time together every day. We hung out in the locker room, practiced for several hours, and grabbed dinner together. On weekends, we traveled to away games. We would sit together in a bus and then compete as a team. All of those shared experiences, all that trust necessary between teammates—and yet I was so afraid of what would happen if my teammates found out.

You know how guys are with girls that they like? They get a little nervous and their breathing is heavier—sometimes it is visibly noticeable. As I sat next to my teammates on the bus or in the locker room, I tried so hard to control my heart rate and my breathing because I feared they might somehow suspect my sexuality by the pace of my chest rising up and down. I acted as straight as humanly possible when I sensed any suspicion from my teammates. It was a ridiculous fear; each guy in that locker room probably had his own issues to worry about—whether it was about a girl, family, schoolwork, friends, etc.—but how could I have known that at the time? I lived in fear each moment.

I did not value my life. At first, taking my life was just a passing thought, but it became much more than that. It is no secret that gay and lesbian teenagers are the number-one risk group for committing suicide. Ending one's life becomes a realistic option for getting rid of the secret without having to go through the pain of coming out. It offers a way to avoid having to tell the truth to family, friends, or the world. I shudder at the thought of suicide entering the discussion at any level. Sometimes people throw it out as a threat to someone else, as if they might end their life and leave the other person with the guilt. But actually contemplating suicide—that is something far different, far scarier. Nobody can go to that dark place with you and bring you back to reality. I have never really admitted how real that felt until now. But with the confidence gained from how my life has turned out, I can go there now and remember the pain I struggled with. The best decision that I ever made was to ignore those dark thoughts.

Although as a teenager I could not have believed it possible, I came out while still a competitive athlete. Afterwards I continued to play sports successfully and even had a brief professional career. My teammates' support was crucial during the coming out process. They got past the gay issue so quickly that I never really had to deal with it. I came out one day, and the next time I saw them it was an accepted fact. They never resented me; instead they appreciated and loved me for my honesty. After all, I exposed them to something new, something that forced them to question their assumptions. After coming out, there was nothing holding us apart, and my sexuality actually ended up bringing me closer to my teammates. Would that 17-year-old believe me? I wish he could have known it would be okay, could have known that he would not have to give up any of his dreams in sports in order to be out. In fact, I eventually had the opportunity to make a huge impact on thousands of people by telling my story openly. I wish I had not worried so much that it would be revealed that I am gay and thus end my athletic career. Many people have taken the time to tell me that my courage in sharing my story made their life easier and relieved them of some of their own big worries.

FINDING HAPPINESS AT HOME AND AT WORK

When I was 17, I was so afraid of not fitting in that I tried to date and hook up with girls. It took careful planning to feign interest without getting found out. I always had an excuse for avoiding sex. I complained about my sports injuries or being tired or intoxicated—or worse, I would blame the girl for not turning me on enough. Inevitably you end up hurting the girls you pretend to go after, and I know I caused a lot of pain by continuing with these efforts, but what was I supposed to do? I can remember having a girlfriend over to my house and being so relieved to find out that she was having her period—an easy excuse for keeping things nonsexual. But she deserved a guy who genuinely wanted to be with her, not someone using her as a cover. Over time, it became more difficult to fool the girls, and each relationship had to end. I remember discussing life plans with one of my girlfriends who was probably smart enough to put all the pieces together, due to my continuous excuses for avoiding intimate moments. When I mentioned having kids—at some point in my life, not necessarily with her—she acted surprised that I saw them in my future. It struck me that she would question it, and it was something I never forgot. I still want kids, but I want to share them with a partner.

I have fallen in love, several times in fact. I have experienced the real emotions of love and jealousy and a broken heart. Keith and I continued to date for several years after I wrote my original story. Looking back at what I thought I wanted and what I liked about my relationship with Keith—the masculinity and the mystery—it couldn't be further from the way I now feel. Those things probably had more to do with my own insecurities. I enjoyed not being labeled gay, and I loved being perceived as a masculine homosexual. Today I no longer want a boyfriend I can go to a sports bar with and "blend in." I want a partnership based on love, mutual respect, trust, and caring. Each of us determines our own level of comfort, and if I want to kiss my boyfriend in the most masculine sports bar in the world, I will do so happily.

Today I have found a level of happiness that I never thought possible—like what you think occurs only in the movies. Three years ago, I became friends with a wonderfully creative, caring man named Jamie. When the timing was right, we found ourselves in each other's arms and we haven't looked back. We support and love each other, and we make decisions that benefit us as partners. We live together and we smile together and we experience the joys of life together. Jamie is not my boyfriend. He is my partner. I feel so completely fulfilled, and I want everyone to experience this feeling. Most importantly, I want to tell that 17-year-old that he should not worry about love because he will have it. He will have it all.

It is somewhat ironic that I questioned the importance of life at 17 and now am in the business of trying to save lives. After college, I discovered a passion for cancer research. I have almost completed a PhD in biology with a specialty in prostate cancer. I get to use my brain every day to tackle important issues—to challenge and to question and to innovate. Finding something positive that keeps you up at night thinking is rare in life. I love what I am doing, and I want to be a professor with a research lab and teaching responsibilities. In the world of graduate school, I am completely open about my sexuality, and Jamie attends lab events regularly. My friends at the school are proud of what I have accomplished in coming out.

Maybe things worked out the way they did for a reason. Maybe I had to experience what I did and reach a critical point inside of me before I could come out to the world. Maybe everything clicked at the right point for me. There is no way to know how my life would have turned out differently if I could have come out at 17. Each gay or lesbian teenager has different circumstances and different timing that works out for him or her. Some are able to come out early, and others wait until years after college to come to terms with being gay. Again, all I can say to my 17-year-old self is that things will work out. Things did work out!

LOVE AND SUPPORT OF FAMILY

Whether the path is rocky or smooth, every coming out story is by nature a success story. I know I am one of the lucky ones and that many aren't so lucky. Many never get to come out, never get to be themselves. Many don't get to come out in their own time or on their own terms. I am in the fortunate position of sitting here to reflect on my journey and draw from those factors that may be useful to others who are wondering how their story might turn out. Family is one such factor.

In my original story, I described coming out to my parents. It was difficult for me because, as all closeted people do, I feared being shunned by my family. At the very least, I worried that they would see me differently—not as the person I had always been but as the sexuality that would come to define me. This fear kept me up at night and caused me to be closed off from my parents and siblings. And yet, when it comes to family, I again am one of the lucky ones. Some of my friends have parents who do not believe in homosexuality and continue to set them up with the opposite sex or worse, send them to so-called ex-gay conversion therapists. At our college, the gay and lesbian alumni foundation has a scholarship fund to support students whose parents have refused to pay for their children's education after they come out. It is frightening that parents could be so misguided and completely fail to love and support their own children because of something beyond anyone's control.

This was certainly not the case for me. As I mentioned in the earlier story, my parents never wavered in their love and support. They were interested only in understanding where I was coming from and why I had hidden such a large part of my self from them. Today my mother is one of my biggest advocates. She e-mails me links about gay rights protests in her area, and she cried in front of my partner and his mother during the Jewish High Holidays when it was her turn to talk about what she was thankful for. She was so proud as a parent to watch her baby achieve the level of love and happiness I have with Jamie.

But in spite of their support, my family and I were not entirely comfortable around each other immediately after I came out. Eventually, however, when I talked to my siblings on the phone, we discussed my relationships openly. I took my various boyfriends home with me to meet the family, and we all went on ski trips or beach vacations together. My family had to get to know me with a partner in my life. In some cases, I needed to educate them. My brother-in-law once asked at a family gathering, "Don't gay men want to be women and that's why they date men?" He had no hatred for me or for gay or lesbian people, he simply had no education about homosexuality. That same brother-in-law is now one of my closest friends and one of my biggest advocates. It is not important what his previous knowledge was but where his intentions lay. He has told me he could sense that I was closed off when he first met me, and he just wanted to get to know the real me. We bonded over wiffle ball games in the backyard, over our opposing sides of the Red Sox-Yankees rivalry each summer, and over our similar, easily excitable, always positive personalities. He watched me grow up into a confident young adult, and I watched him become an amazing father and husband. We don't ignore my homosexuality now; we continue to discuss and learn about it in a supportive way, together. The same guy who once believed I wanted to be a woman now fully supports his wife, my sister, donating an egg to mix with my partner's sperm so we can create a child, through a surrogate, that has genes from both sides of the family. Most men would not be so giving or understanding. This is how far we all have come as a family. I know how truly fortunate I am.

Recently we had a mini-family reunion, and one of my cousin's sons, who is maybe eight years old, said to me, "Why did you just kiss that man?" I responded, "Because he is my boyfriend." The boy asked, "Does that mean you are gay?" I said "Yes, is that okay with you?" He replied, "Yup" and got back to playing his game. Later he asked his mother, my cousin, "Did you know that there are two gay people in your family?" and she replied, "Yes, I know." Her son heard the sureness in her voice and quickly realized it was a nonissue. This story shows how casual my family and I are about my being gay, and how comfortable I have become in that I am able to calmly communicate with my young cousin about an issue that is clearly not typical in his life.

Another great family experience was finally getting to see my gay uncles married in Massachusetts. My mother's brother and his partner have lived together for 30 years. When I was growing up, they were always forced to tone down their private lives in public, and my family ridiculed them for their sexuality behind their backs. It taught me very clearly that it was not okay to be openly gay. After I finally came out, things started to change. It almost seemed like it became cool to be gay, and my uncles suddenly received a great deal of interest. Everyone wanted to know about their lives and about their relationship. My family's earlier feelings about my uncles' sexuality kept everyone from really getting to know each other. Now that being gay no longer made someone an outcast, my family could begin to appreciate my uncles for who they really are—two wonderfully caring, colorful men with great taste. They are easy to talk to, throw the best parties, and seem a whole lot younger than my parents or anyone else in that generation. In June 2007, they shared an amazing evening with their families during which we celebrated their love—and the brave decision by the Massachusetts Supreme Court to allow loving couples like them to be legally married. After all they had to go through, it was a great feeling to watch them be the center of everyone's attention. The rest of us, including those who used to mock their "gay lifestyle," were just happy to see two people in love.

Having the support of my family was something I did not predict, but their support has allowed me to grow from where I was when I first came out to the person I am now. I also am extremely appreciative of the friends I have always surrounded myself with. So where do I see my life going from here? I hope to get married one day and enjoy the freedoms and rights that all humans deserve. The political climate is as unclear as ever. However, the simple fact is that as ever more people come out, their friends and families are realizing that denying basic rights to their loved ones is wrong. The world moves only in one direction, toward progress. As Dr. Martin Luther King Jr. said, "The arc of the moral universe is long but it bends towards justice." I believe that Dr. King knew what he was talking about.

I hope that 17-year-olds in the future will not have to experience the fears I have described. Teenagers have enough to deal with already. Over the past 5–10 years, I have heard about so many teenagers who have been able to come out in high school or even earlier. It warms my heart to know that they have the courage to be true to themselves, and I hope they also have the support of loved ones. But even if they aren't quite there yet, I know it will turn out okay for them. Everyone has a different path, and my story is just one of many. I am here to tell my 17-year-old self that all of the fears diminish over time, that he will get past it, that he will live his life the way it was meant to be lived.

IS THIS MY LIFE?

*In this case, Dorothy describes how her need to be "attractive and loveable"
leads her through a series of romantic relationships. In high school, she has
crushes on boys who, like her, are out of the mainstream—"loners and geeks"
whom she hopes will like her. In college, she becomes sexually active and then
has to deal with the impact of a sexual assault early in her college years. With
James she feels safe and loved; when faced with the decision to break up, they
choose to get engaged. Dorothy is happy with her pregnancy and the birth of
her son, though her desire for approval brings her to yet another
new relationship.*

My hands were shaking fiercely as I clutched the plastic handle of the test strip. I was
sure I had done it wrong—I think I got more urine on my hands than on the frustrat-
ingly small strip—but in less than the three minutes advertised, a placid blue plus
sign appeared in the circular window. I repeated the test, but three minutes later I was
still pregnant.

I was more exhilarated than scared—I can't even say I was especially
surprised. But as I sat on the floor of that tiny bathroom, my heart heavy and
empty at the same time, I felt full of life and yet horribly alone. I was in fact
alone—all my flatmates had gone out, and I had taken the opportunity to learn
if my suspicions were true. I had never had a late or missed period since I began
menstruating at the age of 13—"Aunt Flo," like a disagreeable distant relative,
usually arrived too soon and always overstayed her welcome. I called James
almost immediately after dragging myself from the bathroom. I longed to have
him hold me in his arms, to see his smile and receive a kiss of reassurance. I felt
an invisible cord connecting me with James as I listened to the tinny ring, waiting
for him to pick up the phone. During the contraceptive-free summer that led up
to this moment, James and I had a running joke—every four weeks I would tell
him, "I have good news and bad news. The good news is, I got my period. The

bad news is, I got my period." Now I held my breath and prepared my words. When he picked up, I told him that I had good news and bad news: "The good news is, I didn't get my period. The bad news is, I didn't get my period." James was happy, but I could tell that the possibility of our having a baby was too much to comprehend via telephone.

I called home some hours later. I wanted to get my mom alone, but she was running out the door and couldn't talk for long, so after being passed briefly from mother to father to brother, I still had not relayed my big news. After, amid my sobs and the concerned questions of my flatmates—I had told them almost immediately about my predicament—I composed this e-mail to my mother:

> Mom,
> Okay. Here goes. So…I didn't want to tell you this over email, but I couldn't get you alone on the phone just now, and it will take me a week to get up the courage again.
>
> I took a pregnancy test today and it came out positive. I'm happy and excited (and, of course, scared). But more than anything, I'm scared that you won't be as happy about it as I am, or that "people" will think I'm throwing my life and education away. I should be much more worried than I am, but deep down I believe that this is what I am really here to do—be a mother. Writing, theater, Latin…everything else I've been studying (except Astro this summer) sort of seems like details in comparison. I know this does not sound like the kind of thing a mature, ready adult would say…I'm really struggling to explain how I feel.
>
> To be fair, I had hoped this would happen a few years from now, after I'd gotten out of college—I don't think that being pregnant and in college is ideal… I talked to James earlier this evening—he is also very excited, and a little scared. He's been talking for months about how much he wants to be a father. He's going to try to find a job near Hanover/Boston so we can live together next year when I go back for my last two semesters (I'm still planning to take classes this winter, and will only need two terms after that).
>
> I don't see this as "the end," only as an alternate route. But you're probably furious with me. I don't blame you—I just wish you wouldn't be. I hope you can be happy, at least, that I am happy. I'm sorry for not doing things the way you would have hoped they'd be done. Who knows what the next several months will bring? In the meantime, I'm just going to try to take care of myself. Lots of iron and calcium.
>
> Love,
> Dorothy
> Your Happy Daughter

I did not receive my mother's reply until the next morning.

> I'm speechless. Cameron is very sad. Dad is going to go through the roof and blame it on me. My feelings are, as you might expect, mixed. There's a lot to think about and to grieve before being happy. And there's a lot to be angry or disbelieving

about before thinking that you can actually deal with this. I'm sure I will be happy and excited for you. And for James. And I will be helpful. Count on that. But count on my saying that I knew you needed to do other things before this.

Holy Shit (which may be a tiny bit better than just "shit")
xxo m.

I suppose this was the best I could have hoped for. What upset me the most about this e-mail was my mother saying that my brother Cameron was "very sad." I didn't expect my parents to be thrilled about this right out of the gate, but I hadn't thought about how my pregnancy would affect my relationship with my younger brother. The realization that becoming a mother would irreversibly distance me from him was, and still is, what affected me the most. My friendship with Cameron had been so pure, whereas my relationship with my parents had always been tainted by their expectations, so the loss of their esteem was easier to bear.

I was glad to be a continent away when I finally got my parents on the phone. Their first reaction was distress over how to break the news to their own parents, and their second was to suggest that I wasn't ready to have a baby. My parents have a habit of reminding me when I've disappointed them of all of the help they've given me—help that is often unasked for and unneeded and is rarely worth the price of later reproach. When I talked to my father later that week, he suggested I get an abortion and "wait to have a baby." Thus, it is no surprise that I did not ask my parents for help.

Self-reliance is very important to me; it is the key to freedom. In one of my favorite photographs of myself, a two-year-old girl marches down a long gravel driveway that is bordered by autumn-colored forest, her hand raised in the air. Fifteen feet behind follows her young, thin father. This image describes my feelings about and the reality of my childhood. I remember spending a great deal of time exploring on my own, although after looking at this photo I am sure that my parents were really just a few steps behind.

During high school I embraced what seemed to be my permanently icono-clastic state and took my isolation as a sign that I was too wise to make friends with people my age. I worked at increasing the divide by wearing strange clothes—scarves, petticoats, and Star Wars t-shirts—sometimes even cross-dressing and reading *Das Kapital* as I walked between classes. I developed a reputation as a sexually liberated pagan Marxist and loved the attention I received.

As you can imagine, this made it difficult to find a boyfriend, and I was desperate for one. I purposely cultivated crushes on boys I thought would be likely to date me—I would latch onto loners, geeks, and traditionally unattractive boys and hope they would take an interest in me. Each spring, with hormones raging, I would get close to achieving my goal, but I was usually clutching at shadows. I will catalogue my few conquests here.

Freshman year: I attracted a dangerously thin bipolar pianist, who on Tuesday would ask me to his junior prom, on Wednesday insist to his friends that we weren't dating, and on Thursday invite me to a movie. Our relationship ended with a phone call—he had thought I would put out, and although I was secretly willing to, he probably expected me to make the first move.

Sophomore year: I dated a manic-depressive actor who had a girlfriend I didn't know about. I almost gave him my virginity. We were making out beneath a covered bridge, and had I not had my period I would have responded to his inquiring "Yes?" with my own whispered "Yes!" We broke up when I became too involved in trying to help him with his cocaine addiction, but he insisted for years afterward that he still loved me.

Junior year: I spent a year masturbating and writing a sci-fi romance novella about a man I could truly love, Xern, the futuristic bounty hunter.

Senior year: I chased after Nate, a boy who had once had a crush on me. We parked by the lake one winter night and he told me not to tell anyone we had kissed. He said he didn't want to date me and that we should stay friends, but he liked to hear me say how much I loved him and then tell me it could never be. He made me feel exhausted and used. I eventually changed my phone number and stopped speaking to him altogether.

I insisted to myself that I was better off single, that I was going to an Ivy League college and would find boys there who would be interested in me, and if I didn't, I could still get pleasure out of reading and writing, and that as a feminist I shouldn't feel that my self-worth hinged upon having a boyfriend. But although I told myself this, I couldn't help but think I was deficient in some way, since my three best friends *always* had a real boyfriend whereas the boys I dated were ashamed of me. I was so desperate to seem and to be an adult, and in my mind having a romantic relationship was integral to adulthood.

It was unfortunate that I went to college with something to prove.

I wanted to prove to myself that I was attractive and loveable. I gave my virginity to the first guy who would have me. His name was John, and he was everything you could expect of a John—not a bad guy. I thought that because I was intellectually opposed to religious beliefs that sex is bad and virginity should be preserved as long as possible, being a sexually active woman was a sign of power and liberty.

Only a week after my first time having sex, my temple of sexual concepts crumbled. After two drinks at an excruciatingly dull party, I decided to go home and watch *Star Wars* and then go to bed. I was followed home by Amir, a friend of a friend, who said he had never seen *Star Wars*. I couldn't find a nice way to make him leave my room, to get off my bed, to take his hands off me. I kept repeating, "No, this isn't a good idea, this isn't a good idea," but the bond between my body and my mind was broken. I was too terrified to move.

Having been at college only two weeks, I decided to pretend it never happened—I didn't want rape to be what my college experience was about. This was a big mistake. Immediately after being assaulted, I tried to make the event insignificant by insisting to myself that my body was merely a chariot in which to transport my magnificent brain, and that what had happened to me didn't matter at all. Sex didn't mean anything at all. This is the mantra I would repeat to myself whenever I remembered that night, but it was impossible to shake my disappointment in myself. I had an image of myself as being strong, wild, and brave, and I could not forgive my cowardice. I should have died fighting Amir off—I couldn't understand why I hadn't.

I spent two weeks in Europe at the end of fall term, touring through Austria, Switzerland, and Italy with the Handel Society of Dartmouth College. The Handel Society is a community choir of adults and students, and the weekly rehearsal was the only thing that remained constant throughout my four years at college. I joined the choir because I realized during orientation week that I would go nuts if I didn't spend some time with adults. The Handel Society tour was by far the best experience I had in my four years at Dartmouth, and when I returned from it, I had almost completely forgotten the tragedy I had suffered only weeks before.

But my mother, who believes that happiness is impossible without absolute honesty, sensed that I was hiding things from her. She was horrified when I told her that I had lost my virginity. She said I shouldn't be so proud of myself and was furious at me for betraying all of the things she had taught me (I wasn't quite sure what those things were, as my parents and I had never had a sex talk). She said that if I couldn't handle being at college, then maybe I should stay home. In an effort to transform her anger into compassion, I told her I had been raped and that I was capable of handling my troubles. My mother, who is a minister, is the only person who can make me cry. She said that when you have sex with someone, you give a piece of yourself to your partner, a piece you can never get back. That was exactly what I had tried to protect myself from—the feeling that I had given away parts of myself that I could not get back—and the greatest pain I had ever felt crashed upon me. Mom was sorry for me, but also angry that I had been drinking before being raped. She demanded that I promise her not to consume any more alcohol and not to have sex with anyone without telling her. I said I would not make these promises, though I did make a promise to myself.

When I returned for the winter term, I braided a piece of yarn and tied it around my hips as a reminder that I only wanted to have sex with people I really loved. It was humbling to think that I needed a physical reminder to preserve my ideals.

I remained celibate from January until May.

Some time in the middle of that chaste period I met James. I was guarding instruments in the music department, a windowless labyrinth in the basement of the Hopkins Center (hardly conducive to romance); he approached and started a conversation. I told him more than he would ever care to know about the Petrarch text I was translating, making no effort to flirt. I was sure this gangly long-haired boy could only be interested in one thing, and I wasn't ready to get entangled. I continued to see James in the music department, where I worked and rehearsed for the Handel Society, but circumvented several offers to "hang out." Finally I accepted his invitation, after spending a day together at a theater festival—I had been impressed by his quietly comic performance and by his talent at the piano. He took me to see a local band, and I fell asleep with my head on his shoulder. When I woke, he kissed me gently. Everything about James was gentle. The first time he spent the night with me, he encountered the chastity cord. When I explained its purpose, he was more understanding than I would have expected any man to be, and he was glad that I wanted to wait.

This experience meant a great deal to me—not only James's sweetness but also that I had the courage to tell him I wanted to wait.

My relationship with James developed rapidly. About a month after we started sleeping together, he discovered I was not on birth control. Having sex was still relatively new to me, and when James didn't provide condoms, I didn't really know what to say. I was a little too head over heels to let practical things like protection get in the way of a romantic moment. Somehow, it didn't seem strange to me that after only a month of dating, James and I would be talking about what we would do if I became pregnant.

But I wasn't pregnant, and I did start taking birth control. In retrospect, it was kind of silly for me to start taking the pill that summer, since James and I spent less than a fortnight of it together. James was at Dartmouth over the summer, and I was traveling the globe. I spent five days in Wyoming, 10 days in Ireland, a week in Norway, a week in Myrtle Beach, and a week in Paris—and in between I flew to Hanover to visit James. I managed to visit him every three weeks, often enough to keep the relationship alive, but what really sustained it was the letters we wrote to each other. James had elegant handwriting, and his letters (and flowers, books, and other gifts) found me all over the world. It was unbelievably romantic.

During the following year—my sophomore, his senior year—my relationship with James continued to blossom and take root. We sang Handel's *Messiah* together in the Handel Society, and he was in the pit band for the theater department production of *Hair*, which I helped stage manage. We were well occupied and almost exclusively in each other's company. We had separate dorm rooms, but we slept in the same bed almost every night. We had only a few "rough patches" during that year, the first when he realized I had given him Herpes simplex (i.e., cold sores), and the second when I told him about my rape the previous year. James was very sympathetic—almost too sympathetic—and frustrated that a person who had hurt someone he loved so much could go unpunished.

James and I argued about what to do about it—I was still determined not to do anything. Then one day we saw an article in *The Dartmouth* saying that the guy who had raped me was currently spending an off term at an all women's college. The fact that *he* should be chosen to spend a term at Wellesley suddenly awakened me to the negligence of letting his crime remain a secret. How could I put a whole college of girls at risk?

Although James, my mother, and my own conscience had been unable to convince me to take action, my body eventually forced me to act. Since the assault, I had been having a reaction to cold water, aspartame, and caffeine. Every time I took a shower or drank a Coke, I broke out in hives all over my arms and legs. I already had a bad habit of scratching itchy bites, so soon my limbs were covered in scars. I felt disgusting, and my mother made me feel even worse. James was the only person who didn't judge me, and his sympathy brought me closer to him.

The doctors told me it was probably a stress reaction and that I shouldn't worry about it, but then I started having trouble breathing. Finally, on Christmas Day more than a year after the incident, I ended up at the hospital with breathing trouble, and I decided it was time to stop stressing my body and settle the score.

I resolved to call Amir on the phone—I still wasn't ready to pursue legal avenues. Shaking and full of tears, I told him that he had raped me and demanded that he apologize. He said, "I'm sorry you feel that way. Please don't cry. I hate it when girls cry." I didn't care that I hadn't gotten a real apology from him—what mattered was that I had made the call. I had been brave. I had taken back the piece of me that had been lost.

The following year I did give a statement to the police—I didn't think it was possible to sob as much as I did the afternoon I relived my rape. But there were no reliable witnesses and the case was dropped.

It may seem strange for me to weave back and forth between my flourishing relationship with James and the rather sad business of the violation of my body, but feelings about both were present in me for years. *Star Wars* was my favorite movie of all time, yet every time someone mentioned it, I was filled with remorse, anger, self-disgust, self-pity, and ugliness. Oddly, of all the consequences of my rape, this is what hurts the most—that a film that once resonated with the nostalgia of my childhood was now an irreversible reminder of my failure to defend myself. James, on the other hand, praised me each day for my thoughtfulness, cleverness, beauty, and sweetness, and I learned to love myself again.

You can see why I was loath to let James go.

I helped James find a summer job near Dartmouth so I could visit him while I was studying over the summer. He was working 14 hours daily at a summer-stock theater, but two or three times a week I would drive to see one of the shows, bring James back to my apartment for the night, then return him to the playhouse, and get back to Dartmouth for my 9 a.m. class. I shouldn't have been lonely—Cameron was staying with me, and we spent hours each day playing cribbage, eating nachos, and watching reruns of *The Office*—but I was. I was very lonely. As I walked home from class each day, I would hug myself and take deep breaths, dreaming of the next time I would see James. After more than a year of sharing a bed—in the months before his graduation we had actually shared a house, living out a domestic fantasy—it was excruciating to sleep alone. And although Cameron was great company, he could offer me little encouragement about my academic pursuits. I was beginning to feel that I was only a mediocre writer, a mediocre director, and in general a mediocre student. While feeling like the center of James's universe, I had failed to realize how short I was falling of my own expectations.

These alternating sensations of longing and failure, combined with feelings of despair at my own insignificance and the rainiest summer on record, created regular emotional breakdowns and consumption of pint after pint of sorbet.

I eventually realized that the reason for my hyperemotive state was probably the pill. I decided that since James and I saw each other only a few times a week and I would soon be going to London, I might as well stop taking it. James was skeptical and disappointed. He said that if I stopped taking the pill, we would have to go on the rhythm method, stop having sex, or just wing it and hope I didn't get pregnant. I asked about using condoms, but it seemed he would rather not have sex than use them—I don't blame him for this. We discussed what would happen if I became pregnant. I didn't think about the reality of what getting pregnant would actually mean. But I didn't have the "it can't happen to me" syndrome—as soon as I went off birth control, I sensed that this was what I was in for.

I admit that I could see being pregnant fitting in nicely with my iconoclastic image of myself. I also admit that my positive attitude about the idea was partly influenced by the thought that if I got pregnant, James would have to stay with me. James was good with his piano students, and I felt that despite his not having known his own father, he would be a great father himself. I believed I would be a good mother—in fact, I might be better at mothering than at any other thing I could do with my life. I never once considered that having a baby would interfere with my finishing college. The more I thought about it, the more desperate I became to nurture and care for something. I would rub my hand along my stomach and imagine a baby growing inside. I imagined a little girl who looked just like me but with James's blue eyes, sitting in my lap reading a book. I was certain that if I became pregnant, I would be the happiest woman in the world.

But two months went by, and a week before James and I were to go our separate ways—he home to Kansas City, I to London to study theater—I still was not pregnant. James and I were beginning to see the clouds gathering in the distance, which put some strain on our relationship. He tried to break up with me, but I talked him out of it. Then when my twentieth birthday came around, he forgot it. I tried not to let this bother me, but I realized this was another bead on a string of missed opportunities for him to show tenderness or indulge me the way he had when we first started dating.

I cut my hair—a symbol of a new chapter in my life—and drove over to break up with James. I didn't want to, but I sensed that he wasn't as excited about our relationship as he used to be. Our situation reminded me of the opera *Lakme*, and breaking up with James seemed like the noble thing to do, since I had stopped him when he had tried to end it.

But I really didn't want to lose James, and almost as soon as I started to speak, my words became tearful whispers. We decided that instead of breaking up, we would get engaged. It would be a two-year engagement, and if at the end of the two years we were still together and still loved each other, we would get married.

You may have noticed, dear reader, that James and I had a tendency to see only two roads at any intersection, when in fact we were "thru-hikers" who shouldn't have worried about the roads at all, but just which direction was north. Thus we saw two roads: break up or get engaged. And since we still loved each other and the relationship was mostly working, we could not break up. I think the fact that this was the first significant relationship either of us had had and that we both had relatively low self-esteem contributed to our decision to stay together. In fact, I think that most of my major life decisions have stemmed from a desire not to end up like my parents, who fought constantly while I was a child (and still do). Some part of me wanted to protect myself from the unhappy relationship I knew was possible. And frankly, another part of me wanted to stick it to my parents—to show them that I could do what they were unable to do: find a loving partner at a young age and have a perfect marriage.

My mother was furious when she found out I had gotten engaged. She said it was too soon, and perhaps she was right—but then again, perhaps not.

When I realized I was pregnant, I almost didn't believe it. I had gotten my period on my birthday and left James only eight days after that. We had made love the day I left, which according to my cycle would have been a barely fertile day. However, if we hadn't gotten engaged, we wouldn't have made love at all, and Luke, whom I now cherish above all else on earth, wouldn't have been conceived.

At this point in Luke's childhood, I am absolutely grateful that James and I decided to get engaged and make love on the 25th of August, although I was ambivalent about my pregnancy at first. We exchanged these e-mails shortly after my happy discovery:

Dearest James,
I've been thinking of you all day—thinking of us, and our immediate future. I talked to my mom on the phone again, and she told me that my dad is still hoping I'll reconsider giving up the baby. Mom warned me that, whatever choice we make, it will be very difficult for us.

I've assumed that you want to keep the baby without really asking you what you want. I realized that what both of us envisioned for our future has been shaken, and seeing the look on your face yesterday as we struggled to figure things out…I thought I should at least ask: Are you sorry that this happened? Would you rather it were easier?

I'm happy. I'm excited, for my sake, but my mom reminded me today that I was thinking only of myself, and I felt suddenly guilty for having let this happen to my family, but at the same time I think my parents should be able to suck it up and rejoice with me.

But I was in tears, afraid that this could make your ambitions impossible, or even just painfully difficult.

So please, tell me if you are having any worries or wishes. I am happy and excited for myself, and for you, and for us, but I want to make sure you get a chance to tell me how you feel, in case you feel trapped.

I love you. I think this baby will be wonderful and beautiful and bring joy. I think happily on your being a father, and my being a mother.

I love you. I'll talk to you soon!

Ardently Yours,
Dorothy

*   *   *   *   *

Dearest Dorothy,

Your Mom is right that no matter what is decided, we will face challenges that will tax our energies and frustrate our ambitions. She is also right that supporting our pregnancy puts unexpected strain on people who never asked for it, namely your family.

The birth of a child prevents me from obtaining a long-term job or graduate program in Music right now. But, I feel that you and your family are feeling much more of the immediate impact. This pregnancy is contemporaneous with Cameron's applications to college, and so I can imagine Cameron feeling some of the younger-sibling want of resources. I am at a flexible time in my life, but Cameron and your parents are not. I feel guilty too, for passively relying on their resources without ever consulting them in the matter.

You too, are not at a time when you have much time to spare. I must admit that I feel that nursing a baby while going to Dartmouth is unrealistic...If you go through with keeping the baby, you will have to keep your mind open to the workload being altogether too much. Of course, I do not want that to be true, and I offer my presence and support to ensure that we can make it together, but, it's possible that it's impossible to do both at the same time and do justice to what are both very worthy responsibilities. You know very well how little spare time a student at Dartmouth really has.

If we decide to give up the baby, then we both will have to agree that we have made a very costly and irresponsible mistake in not using birth control. That is what I will conclude, anyhow, that I have made an irresponsible and costly mistake, and have done you and your family wrong. I want to be able to admit it when I've made a mistake, and I'm prepared to do that.

At the same time, I have always been sincere in my attraction for Fatherhood. Also I know that you very genuinely want to be a Mother. What I have written above constitutes the facts of the situation as I see them, but the morality of the situation, i.e., what we should decide, depends on our aims. I can envision us as a small family together, happy and comfortable after the now inchoate struggles have passed. That vision requires that we put providing for the child first. I can envision you finishing your next two years of college with total freedom and us concentrating on our engagement and choice of apartments and kittens. That vision requires putting school first. My vision of putting both school/career and child first is somewhat less carefree. We would be risking doing both poorly. Trying to have everything risks everything.

The vision of you finishing school without (more) strain or worry, and of my being able to get an anchor into the world, makes me most happy. I do not feel trapped. If you decide to keep the baby, I will be there to help you and work for us, if it takes living and working in less than desirable circumstances, and find a way to be happy while doing so. After all, we'll have each other.

But again, the vision of you being able to finish school on schedule makes me happiest. We want to be able to enjoy having time with our baby. I imagine that if you have a child, you will want to be able to spend all day with it. Not only does it need that attention, but also I wouldn't want us to miss out on it.

What do you think?

Love,
James

James and I never seriously considered abortion as an option, although we were both pro-choice. I went to a counseling center in London to find out what steps I needed to take—foods to eat and avoid, medical appointments, and so on—but it turned out to be an abortion counseling service, and once I told them I was planning to keep the baby, they wished me luck and showed me the door. I am still pro-choice, but the choice I made was to keep my baby. I knew I would be able to handle it, and at the time I saw it merely as living my life out of order— what would it matter if I were married and had a family before I finished college instead of after?

Although I said before that I was ambivalent, I was sure I wanted to keep the baby—I was too proud and excited not to. I was, however, uncommitted to the survival of the fetus. I recall with shame my hope that I would miscarry so I could regain my pre-pregnancy freedom but not have to suffer the guilt of ending the pregnancy myself. Throughout my first trimester, I harbored these feelings of indifference toward the little life developing inside me. Granted, I was frustrated at being alone and in a foreign country, with bad food, bad weather, and medi-cal bills draining my bank account. My body also shut down each day at 7 p.m., making it difficult for me to engage fully in my theater studies—but I didn't share these ugly hopes of mine with anybody. Frankly, part of me was still uncertain that I was designed for motherhood at all. My mother had told me at a young age that I "lacked sweetness," and I had told her more than once that I never wanted to become a mother if it would mean being like her.

But pride got the better of me. I have never liked being told that I can't do something—I was determined to rise to the occasion of motherhood, regardless of my doubts about my poor financial situation, possible "lack of sweetness," and inexperience with children. I also looked forward to finally reaching adulthood and earning my parents' respect. The summer before I started college, my father and I had a terrible argument, which ended in my screaming at him, "I never listen to you, Dad, because you treat me like a child!" He yelled back at me, "You *are* a child!" If I excelled at being a mother, it would prove that I had, indeed, grown up.

I remember the moment I fell completely in love with my baby. In the mid-dle of the fourth month of my pregnancy, safe at home in Pennsylvania with James curled up behind me, I felt the first kick. James felt it too—our baby was suddenly more than a little fish visible only on an ultrasound. Our baby had a personality, revealed by his active feet. I curled my limbs around my belly, as if by doing so I could bring myself closer and completely embrace the little life inside me. From that moment on, I counted down the days until I would be able to meet my little boy.

The joy I felt in anticipating my son's arrival shielded me from the reactions of the Dartmouth community. I could tell that people looked at my huge belly and wondered how *I* could possibly be a Dartmouth student—I still encounter the same reaction when I push the stroller around campus. It's like wearing a scarlet letter, though the letter is so badly stitched that no one quite knows what it stands for. Some people see a "D" for "dumb"—the stereotype that girls who get pregnant while in school didn't care enough about their education to use birth control. Some people see an "S" for "slut"—as though a woman gets pregnant by having multiple partners. Some people see a "W" for "waste"—why would someone want to throw away their education by having a baby in her junior year? I am not dumb or a slut; I graduated cum laude with high honors and am on my way to graduate school.

But to return to my story, just as people now see baby Luke and refuse to believe I'm still a student, people refused to believe I was pregnant until I was in my third trimester—I guess they thought I was just fat or had a really impressive beer gut. Although I was due to deliver on May 21, I took classes in the spring semester. Each classroom presented problems related to my increasingly round body, usually an insufficient gap between desk and chair or the number of stairs I had to climb to get there. I had "daymares" of suddenly going into labor in the middle of a lecture about labor unions in the 1930s, of Professor Nelson serving as midwife as I screamed so loudly that everyone in Hanover could hear me. And all the while I was feeling my little boy's active feet.

In Professor Luxon's class we discussed the perception of the sexes during Milton's era: men were rational, strong, Godly, bright, and all about the brain; women were emotional, weak, Earthly, dark, and all about the body. On May 25th, when my water finally broke after I printed out my final papers in the basement of Baker Library, you can imagine how emotional, weak, and concerned with my body I was.

The six-word story of my childbirth experience: Stabbing pain. Epidural. Nap. Beautiful boy.

That was on Memorial Day. I went to class the following Monday, my episiotomy still healing, the loose folds of my post-pregnancy belly delicately tucked into jeans I had been unable to wear for months, my breasts huge and heavy with milk.

I have observed an interesting behavior among Dartmouth girls. They often stop me while I'm pushing the stroller, lean over my smiling boy—Luke is *such* a flirt—and sigh, "Oh, I want one!" I know they say this to display their appreciation for my son's friendly demeanor, but it bothers me. It is as if they are saying that they wish they could have a baby, but because they are planning to go to graduate school or have an internship lined up or are otherwise driven and hard-working, they can't have one now. I think this attitude is what makes people frown on having children young. My ambition has not waned since I embraced motherhood, although I have tempered my obsessive desire for fame with my appreciation for stability.

I have never been happier to be a woman than I was when I was pregnant, never happier to be human than I am now, as a mother. Luke is the first person in my life I haven't had to impress. I'm sure every Dartmouth student wishes they had someone who loved them as much as Luke and I love each other. I love my little boy and he loves me, body and soul, unconditionally, and no stereotypes or shocked looks could possibly diminish that joy.

But things don't always turn out as we plan. As I write this, I sit in my ready-to-rent-clean apartment, most of my furniture gone, ready to move back home with my parents. I am planning to pursue a PhD in English Literature. I applied for programs within driving distance of my parents with the thought that James would be coming with me and my parents could help out. But James is not coming with me. We got to the end of our two-year engagement and decided that we should end our relationship—it was not easy getting to that point.

For the first five months after Luke was born, I experienced an unparalleled degree of domestic bliss. James taught a few piano lessons every day, and then we would spend the rest of the day together, playing games and watching movies as we interacted with Luke. I started classes in the fall, and James spent the mornings with Luke.

We were sleeping in separate bedrooms by the time Luke was five months old. My parents have slept in separate bedrooms as long as I can remember. Until we stopped sleeping in the same bed, I never realized how important sex was in my relationship with James. Today I still wonder whether this was why, five months after Luke was born, James told me out of the blue that he no longer loved me. Something about our relationship, which I thought had been resurrected after our doubts the previous summer, had gone askew, and James was able to tell me serenely that he no longer loved me, that he didn't find me physically attractive, and that he wanted to have the option of seeing other people some day. I was horrified. I felt like someone had replaced all of my internal organs with dead fish. James seemed dispassionate and diplomatically apologetic about the new state of affairs, which made things worse. Things had been going so well! I was living out my domestic fantasy, sending out applications to graduate school so I could support James and Luke, and I was on the track to finish my BA on time—and suddenly James dropped this bomb on me.

I did not deal with this crisis in the way a responsible mother and dutiful fiancé should. Instead, I allowed myself to fall head over heels in love with someone else—someone who happened to be much older than I, and married. This man said more than once that it was "not a fair fight" between him and James, because James was young and suddenly unromantic whereas he, the "other man," had the advantage of not having to argue with me about whose turn it was to do the dishes. For four months I carried on the affair without James's knowledge, but as my lover and I became more careless about where we were seen, we eventually got caught. My parents already caught me writing some very sensual e-mails—my relationship with this older man relied heavily on love letters that were twice as passionate as the ones James and I wrote to each other. I was forced to spill the whole truth, and I clung proudly to my love for this older man despite my parents' disgust and insistence that I give him up. My mother considered my affair a betrayal of her trust and accused me of being selfish. She even said I possibly harbored secret desires for my father and was projecting them onto this older man. But I didn't go looking for older men; I happened to fall in love with this particular man despite his age and not because of it, and I have been happy with him for reasons that have nothing to do with either of my parents—although the reason I allowed myself to cheat on James does.

When James told me he did not love me, he said he just wasn't as romantic as I wanted him to be and that he would never be able to live up to my expectations.

I could see he was right, and my determination not to end up in a loveless relationship (like my parents) allowed me to cheat on him. Pressure from my family to marry James both before and after Luke was born also contributed to my weakness, especially because my parents had bent to the same pressure when they found out I was on the way. Once James told me he did not love me, I considered my relationship with him over.

My parents never said "I love you" to each other. They never kissed. They fought every day and talked about each other behind their backs. I spent my entire childhood wishing they would get a divorce. I suppose this is why I jumped ship at the first sign of trouble—I was determined not to get tied up in a loveless relationship that would drag on forever.

I had always believed that cheating was wrong—that a woman should at least dump one man before moving onto the next—but things with James were complicated. I couldn't break up with him because we had Luke and I needed his help, because we shared an apartment I couldn't afford on my own, and because I held out hope that James's unromantic attitude was due to lack of sleep or a passing mood. I continued to fall more in love with this other man as James continued to fall further out of love with me. James and I had rather ugly fights about who would be the primary caregiver if we lived apart. Even during these fights I didn't tell James about the other man because picturing the future without him was still too scary.

James is gone for now. I say "gone," although James is still planning to be part of Luke's life. And I say "for now" because I still hold out hope that he will return. I usually enjoy analyzing myself and trying to figure out my motivations and desires, but my head aches when I try to understand how I can be in love with someone older than my parents and yet still wish to have a normal suburban family with James. I've given up trying to understand the way my brain works. All I know is that I love James (like a brother or a friend) and that I would love him more if he came back to me and that I also love this older man, who loves me the way I need to be loved, but who inspires hatred in my parents and whom I cannot marry.

I have spent the last two weeks without James. I see my lover twice a day, but I spend most of the day playing with Luke. It is an echo of last summer, except with fewer naps. I enjoy motherhood as much when it is tiring and tedious as when it is exciting.

But I've discovered that I have an almost insatiable craving for approval. Luke can't give me this. James refused to. My lover can—because he too needs to be loved and approved of. My parents praise me, as does my brother occasionally, but somehow this still isn't enough. I am ashamed for wanting more than my fair share and for not being able to transcend this hunger for affection. I am lucky that motherhood came upon me because Luke is the only being I haven't felt the need to impress, and we can bestow endless affection on each other without keeping score.

PART III

CHALLENGES

THEORETICAL OVERVIEW

Within the field of adolescent research there exists a debate over whether adolescence is typically a period of storm and stress, of alienation and separation, or a more harmonious evolution in which positive feelings about self and family are extended into the larger realms of peers and society. Each of these perspectives has merit and accounts for the different individual circumstances and coping styles of a complex period of human development. One point of agreement in this debate is that adolescence is a period of radical transformation of the physical and psychological self. Even under the best of circumstances, adolescents travel an exquisitely poignant journey through difficult developmental terrain. Finding one's way would be challenge enough, but when the ground is continually shifting with the ongoing physical, emotional, and cognitive growth of this period, the journey becomes full-time work for most adolescents. When the ordinary stresses of adolescence are overlaid with extraordinary additional stresses, there emerge important risk factors for healthy development. The cases in this section explore both the dangers and strategies for coping with these challenges.

Our notion of "challenges" implies obstacles or special difficulties that must be negotiated in addition to all the more "typical" preoccupations and developmental tasks of adolescence. Challenges are important both because of what they tell us about adolescent coping strategies in general and because many adolescents face such circumstances at some point. If we add up all the adolescents who must deal with challenges such as physical disabilities; serious illness; divorce; the death of a parent, sibling, or close friend; physical or sexual abuse; mental illness; and so on, we can see that significant challenges, whether acute or chronic, represent, if not the norm, at least a sizable subsample of all adolescents. An autobiographical exploration of challenges also provides the reader a window into resilience. It allows us to learn which coping strategies and character traits appear to be most protective and even promotive of adolescent mental health.

Each of the five cases included in this section represents a distinct challenge to healthy psychological growth at multiple developmental periods: (1) a severe stutter and serious sexual abuse in early childhood, (2) the emotional crisis surrounding an abortion in adolescence, (3) a journey from war refugee to immigrant to the United States and gradual acculturation, (4) the problems presented by untreated attention deficit/hyperactivity disorder (ADHD) and of conflicts with a parent with serious substance abuse, and (5) the special obstacles faced along the adolescent journey posed by a significant physical disability. Taken as a whole, these cases highlight what is both unique and universal, at least for Western culture; unique, in terms of specialized issues these problems raise for adolescent development; universal, in that the cases highlight the way in which the tasks of adolescence remain relatively constant even in the face of powerfully destabilizing events and extraordinary stessors. The overlay of preexisting emotional, social, or physical problems to the already daunting tasks of adolescence can further complicate the transition to adulthood. At the same time, and more hopefully, the evolving ability throughout adolescence to engage in abstract, analytical thought in combination with increasing emotional and physical autonomy and separation can make it possible for the adolescent to overcome some of the more debilitating psychological effects of these issues.

Self-understanding is one of the more important aspects of emerging adolescent abilities for overcoming serious challenges. Prior to adolescence, childhood is characterized by the embeddedness of the child in his or her family and the profound tendency, whether for better or worse, to identify with important persons and norms within the family. The increasing importance of the peer world and the simultaneously evolving capacity to see parents as less powerful and more fallible are conducive to a loosening and diversification of earlier identifications. This evolving capacity for perspective can facilitate healing through important substitute relationships such as teachers, mentors, peers, families of friends, and others (Noam, Powers, Kilkenny, & Beedy, 1990). Such healing may be necessary when families have not been sufficiently nurturing, protective, or enhancing of self-esteem. While these relationships may also be important at earlier periods, the adolescent can increasingly see her *self* through the eyes of these important others. This fresh perspective allows the adolescent to take a more autonomous approach to creating a self of her own choosing. There has long been recognition that this emergent ability to gain self-knowledge and perspective through interaction with others—this "looking glass self" (Cooley, 1902; Mead, 1934)—helps explain why positive relationships can have such a restorative effect on the damage of earlier events. This "mirroring" becomes especially salient in peer and romantic relationships during this time (Erikson, 1968; Sullivan, 1953) as the adolescent learns to take a perspective on herself by means of gradually modifying the self she sees reflected in the eyes of peers.

Self-understanding has been shown to be an important "protective factor" (Beardslee, 1989) in ameliorating the risk to healthy psychological development from serious life stressors. Ideally, self-understanding should lead to action that transforms one's adaptation to circumstances or changes the circumstances themselves. It is only when insight leads to new and better means of coping with life's challenges that we can say the individual is rising to the challenge. Indeed, insight without action can reflect a profound sense of hopelessness. The cases presented here all reveal the adolescent biographers reacting to significant stress by first developing insight and then taking steps to make things better.

An important emerging field within developmental psychology is devoted to studying individuals who are resilient or seemingly invulnerable to serious risks and stresses that have been shown to affect negatively the mental health and long-term adjustment of many children. This relatively new field represents a significant historic shift from studying almost exclusively those individuals who succumb to developmental risks to studying those who are equally exposed but who overcome the risk and remain healthy. Among the factors shown to place children at risk are serious mental illness of a parent, physical or sexual abuse, serious marital discord, poverty, emotionally unsupportive relationships with parents, foster home placement, and parental alcoholism (Rutter, 1975, 1979; Werner, 1989). While different studies find differing degrees of relative risk for each of these and other factors, it is found that, when only a single risk factor was present, the probability that a child would suffer from a psychiatric disorder was no greater than for a child in a family without any of these risk factors. However, two risk factors produced a fourfold increase in the chances of a psychiatric disorder in the child; four risk factors produced a tenfold increase in risk. It would seem that most children can cope with a certain amount of stress stemming from these risks, but when overloaded with multiple stressors, they become exponentially more likely to succumb. Many children and adolescents, however, do not succumb even under such stress. Therein lies a hopeful avenue for understanding how some children are protected, or protect themselves, against the vicissitudes of serious stress. We might speculate that, whatever these protective coping mechanisms are, they appear to promote good mental health in general and could therefore be helpful even in low-risk individuals.

Three of the most important protective factors to emerge from research are (1) personality features, such as self-esteem, (2) family cohesion and lack of discord, and (3) external support systems that encourage and reinforce the child's efforts to cope (Garmezy, 1985; Masten & Garmezy, 1985). Protective factors are not fixed attributes; they are subject to development or reduction over time within the same individual, and those that may aid in coping at one time may not work at another. Thus these factors should be seen as dynamic; the resilient individual is one who can adapt his or her coping strategies to changing situations. In this sense, protective factors should not be seen as fixed traits of the individual or circumstance, but rather as interpersonal and interactive. This is what Rutter (1987) refers to as protective *mechanisms* or *processes* that the individual may apply or modify as needed.

The cases in Part III reveal a variety of risks and developmental vulnerabilities, as well as a number of protective coping mechanisms. These mechanisms are employed to secure important emotional needs, and with the dramatic emotional development during adolescence, these needs themselves undergo transformation.

In the case of a sexually abused adolescent, "The Simple Beauty of a Conversation," a severe stutter during childhood and adolescence (that may or may not have been related to his abuse) devastated his self-esteem and his relationship with his parents. This devastation had a profoundly negative impact on his social relations. But the functional needs and possibilities of adolescence propelled him into new relationships—warm mentors at work and an accepting and affirming girlfriend—which gave him belated self-confidence to overcome the more debilitating effects of his stutter and abuse. In this sense, the functional tasks of adolescence became for this young man more than merely something to be achieved on the road to adulthood; they became a crucial opportunity for redressing the developmental damage incurred in his childhood. Each phase of life, therefore, not only provides extra obstacles for adolescents with special challenges but also represents a fresh chance to redirect the inexorable movement that phase will require. His ability to seek and utilize the support and encouragement of adult mentors, as well as his self-understanding, is the protective mechanism that may account for his resilience against the vulnerabilities from his abuse and speech problem. These mechanisms and the developmental task of romantic intimacy that emerges in adolescence combine in a powerful protective partnership.

Case 15 represents a long-term challenge, whereas Case 17, concerning adolescent abortion, "Proud of the Strength I Had," involves an acute crisis that results in an extended period of depression, anxiety, and guilt feelings. The resulting effects on this autobiographer's self-esteem, attitude toward sexuality, and capacity for intimacy represent risks to her healthy transition to adulthood. A variety of studies find that many women who undergo abortions experience periods of depression, regret, and guilt (Cvejic, Lipper, Kinch, & Benjamin, 1977; Ford, Castelnuovo-Tedesco, & Long, 1971; Smith, 1973) but that these feelings are typically mild and abate in the short term without negatively affecting general functioning. Other studies have found that the primary response to abortion is relief (Adler, 1975; Ewing & Rouse, 1973; Monosour & Stewart, 1973) and that in the case of adolescent abortion in particular, it "is neither psychologically harmful nor in other ways damaging to the patient" (Olson, 1980, p. 440). And while another study showed that some women who underwent an abortion suffered from depression, prior mental health status was a stronger predictor of mental health after pregnancy than abortion or delivery (Gilchrist, Hanaford, Frank, & Kay, 1995; Russo & Zierk, 1992). A longitudinal follow-up study of young women who had abortions found that pregnancy termination was not directly related to an increase in clinically significant depression (Schmiege & Russo, 2005).

In comparison with adult women, adolescent females are found to have somewhat more negative emotional responses to abortion, though not severely worse (Adler, 1975; Bracken, Hachamovitch, & Grossman, 1974; Margolis, Davidson, Hanson, Loos, & Mikelson, 1971; Payne, Kravitz, Notman, & Anderson, 1976). This seems to reflect the experience of our autobiographer, who describes somewhat more lasting negative feelings, perhaps because as a middle adolescent at the time, she was unable to fully anticipate her sense of loss and to prepare for it psychologically as older adolescents appear better able to do (Hatcher, 1976). The sense of betrayal and isolation was intense—her former boyfriend offered no support other than to pay for the abortion, and she felt unable to tell her parents or even her twin sister.

She describes how this crisis led to her participation in a college support group for other students who had terminated pregnancies. Emotional catharsis and gradual understanding of her feelings led to active participation in reproductive rights events and close friendships with other women who shared the same experience. The integration of self-understanding and action is central to her eventual success in managing this stress and recovering from her depressed feelings. This emerging insight also brought into focus her family's inability to communicate emotionally and her determination to redress this constriction of her own emotional openness. When her younger sister thought she might be pregnant, our author took this opportunity to soothe her own feelings of isolation and abandonment by providing the type of support to her sister that she wishes she had had. Thus the opportunity to reflect on the linkage between how she became pregnant—"not being able to talk about sex and contraception" with her boyfriend—and her family's emotional silence—"I grew up in a family that stuffed their feelings and never talked about anything, including sex"—led to an important self-understanding about the ways she wanted to change. This crisis illuminated an underlying and ongoing challenge to her happiness: her family's dysfunctional emotional communication.

The developmental vulnerability of an unwanted pregnancy is itself reflective of the adolescent tasks of balancing intimacy, identity, and sexuality. In this case, we can witness the painful beginnings of learning how to develop and employ protective mechanisms—sharing intimate feelings with trusted friends, providing the type of support to others she now knows she needs, searching for an ideology that gives meaning and purpose to her experience, and actively identifying with other women who assert their feelings. Her moves in this direction are tentative, but she seems to have a solid understanding of the cause of much of her unhappiness and the means of redressing it. Similar to the lessons of the other cases, the challenge to her emotional development is met by interaction of protective mechanisms and developmental tasks.

In Case 18, "Seeking the Best of Both Worlds," the adolescent tasks related to separation and individuation become especially poignant in the context of an immigrant family having fled a war-ravaged Vietnam. The traumatic experience of emigrating under such circumstance can understandably have profound effects on both the individual and the nature of family relationships. The author describes feeling both great loyalty and respect for his mother's heroic role in rescuing the family from an impossible situation and feeling shame and contempt for her unwillingness to allow him to adapt to the U.S. culture to which she had exposed him. He wants acceptance and permission from his mother to live in both worlds—the Western world to which she brought him and the traditional world of his family. Even though he is willing to accept the dichotomy of worlds and to live according to the rules of family when at home and of society when outside, his mother seems unwilling to make any such accommodation for herself and thinks he should not either. The result is that he chooses to segment his self into "dutiful but resentful" son at home and "Americanized" adolescent in school and the larger world. He must resort to constant lying and other subterfuge to keep his mother from knowing his other self. This stress of a double life and the alienation from his mother leaves him emotionally isolated and increasingly depressed.

In addition to all the normal preoccupations of adolescence, and beyond the typical parent–child conflicts of the period, this author demonstrates how hard it can be for immigrant adolescents to integrate the best of both cultures if their family demands exclusive loyalty to the native culture. His strategy of alternating his behavior to whatever culture he finds himself in is often effective for immigrant adolescents (LaFromboise, Coleman, & Gerton, 1993) and is even associated with positive mental health (Rogler, Cortes, & Malgady, 1991). In this case, however, we can also see the tremendous emotional stress and developmental risk this form of adaptation can cause. At the same time, the case also illustrates how his increasing competence and validation in the larger culture gradually creates a new and respected role in his family as the intercultural go-between. By the time he writes his autobiography in college, he describes ways in which he has been able to influence his mother in rearing his two younger siblings so as to lessen some of the pain and conflict he experienced.

Finally, in his follow-up essay written nine years later, he describes how his two younger siblings have not fared as well as he and his older sister, both of whom are now physicians. Indeed his younger brother and sister, suffering from the effects of long-term emotional and physical abuse at the hands of his mother, are depressed and suicidal. He has now been granted legal custody of his younger sister, whom he is raising with his wife. Although he has now completed medical school and is married, his mother's harmful parenting still preoccupies him as he tries to nurture his younger siblings and thereby undo some of the damage their upbringing has wrought. His updated story raises interesting questions about differential resilience in a single family and how individuals can react to similar stressors in different ways.

The title of Case 14, "Bad," reveals how the author felt about herself from a young age. She describes constant behavior problems and poor academic performance throughout elementary school. In turn, these problems led to serious conflict with her mother, which further exacerbated her low self-esteem and feelings of shame, hopelessness, and guilt. It was not until eighth grade that she was finally diagnosed with ADHD, but even then neither medication nor environmental accommodations in school or home were prescribed. By mid-adolescence, the result of her untreated ADHD was depression and increasingly self-destructive behavior including serious substance abuse.

ADHD is a disorder of both childhood and adulthood, characterized by impulsive behavior, inattention, poor organizational skills, and often oppositional and disruptive behavior. It occurs in 3–6 percent of the school-age population. Our author is ambivalent about whether her diagnosis was taken seriously enough for treatment to be provided. On one hand, she wishes she had received help: "I now regret so much the way my parents and I let my diagnosis be pushed under the carpet. If I had had some help I could have accomplished so much more...." On the other hand, she states that she is afraid of the medications typically used to treat

ADHD because of bad experiences she had abusing them as recreational drugs. Yet her case is a classic example of the tragedy of undiagnosed and untreated ADHD. While girls represent only about 10–15 percent of diagnosed cases, the prevalence of ADHD in school-age females is shown to be approximately 33 percent in community-based population studies (Gaub & Carlson, 1997). There are many reasons for this underdiagnosis, including the tendency for girls to have the inattentive subtype of ADHD rather than the more obvious hyperactive form. Similarly, boys with ADHD are more likely to exhibit serious behavior problems including aggression and delinquency and therefore are referred for treatment by parents and school officials (Gershon, 2002).

One of the reasons parents often give for choosing not to allow medication to be administered to their child with ADHD is the fear that it will increase the likelihood that their child will grow up to use illegal drugs. There is, however, a substantial body of research that shows that the opposite is true: Children with untreated ADHD are significantly *more* likely to abuse drugs than those who take prescribed medication for the disorder (Biederman, Wilens, Mick, Spencer, & Faraone, 1999). It is important to note that our author feels that her Outward Bound experience transformed her, and she went on to have a successful college career without medication or other treatment. Similarly, we should note her emphatic embrace of her ADHD as a gift—an intense way of feeling and being that gives her certain advantages and a competitive edge. And while one should understand ADHD in the context of the whole person and not simply as a disorder or disability, it is also true that for many persons undiagnosed and untreated ADHD poses major challenges to successful performance in school, work, and relationships. This case highlights both the serious negative effects of ADHD while also providing a very hopeful outcome over the course of adolescence.

Case 16, "Forever an Awkward Adolescent," illustrates how physical disabilities can also pose additional challenges along the adolescent pathway. The physically challenged autobiographer describes how he used to experience closeness with his father by allowing him to do virtually everything for him, including helping him dress each morning up until high school. He states that as adolescence and his desire for independence emerged, better late than never, he began to insist that his father restrain "his legendary penchant for interfering." His need for independence, however, didn't obliterate his desire for closeness with his father; it caused him to redirect it along more age-appropriate lines, like shared ideas and interests. We can see how the developmental tasks of adolescence, here for greater autonomy, have similar transformative effects on parent–child relations for a severely disabled adolescent as they do for others. The difference is that it is adapted to those particular circumstances, and in the case of a physically disabled adolescent, the importance of the struggle for autonomy has special salience regarding how much independence he or she will be able to achieve as an adult. For another adolescent, the same autonomy task might lead to a demand for greater privacy or a right to choose his or her own clothes but with less long-lasting implications.

In addition to the press of developmental tasks, the autobiographer's coping is enhanced by the remarkable self-understanding he demonstrates in his attempts at adaptation. He repeatedly stresses his own responsibility for his adjustment and happiness, and the need to find some means of "fitting in" with his able-bodied peers lest they give up trying to relate to him and leave him to his " 'default' pigeonhole...of a short, oddly postured disabled kid." And he writes repeatedly of having to create "a persona I could live with" by mirroring himself in the eyes of his peers. This search for identity by means of acceptance and validation by his peers is another important task of adolescence. Thus he demonstrates the interaction of developmental tasks and protective factors, identity formation and self-under-standing, respectively, which together serve to compensate for the risks of isolation and dependence his physical disabilities represent.

"Forever an Awkward Adolescent" was originally published in the first two editions of this book. We brought it back in the fifth edition because the author had written a retrospective update, "Thirteen Years Later." Writing in his mid-thirties from the perspective of a successful executive in a disabilities advocacy organization, he reflects on his original perspective as a college student on what his future might hold. He writes about what has held true and consistent in his life, and what new challenges and opportunities for growth he has faced and anticipates in his future.

The five cases in Part III reveal much about the opportunities of adolescence for growing stronger through challenge. Unfortunately, not all such challenges are met so successfully. These autobiographers do, however, represent the fortunate fact that most adolescents who face such circumstances do somehow find a path to productive lives. The following cases tell stories of how such challenges can be met, and though the life stories could not be more different, their pathways to overcoming have much in common.

BAD

In this essay,* Gretchen, a 21-year-old white woman, tells the story of her eventual recovery from the psychological injury done to her by others' misunderstandings of her attention deficit/hyperactivity disorder (ADHD). Within her family, Gretchen was labeled a problem child: poorly organized, prone to school failure, and apt to become distracted. Perhaps as a result of her parents' marital difficulties—which destabilized the family generally—Gretchen was afforded little room for error, and as her problems persisted, she was subjected to escalating emotional and physical abuse by her mother. Finally, during her senior year of high school, Gretchen dropped out and ran away to live in the city with her boyfriend. After months in a drug rehabilitation center and a stint in an outdoor therapy program, she chose to return to high school. Writing as a college sophomore, Gretchen challenges the conventional belief that ADHD is nothing but a problem, a syndrome to be cured, and a disease to be eradicated. Instead, based on her own experience, Gretchen believes that ADHD can be a source of joy and life energy, a part of a person's cherished uniqueness. Accordingly, Gretchen advises her readers to adopt a more curious and open stance toward ADHD, warning that failure to do so can result in the misjudgment and abuse of persons like herself.

I woke to the sound of my mother's footsteps hammering down the stairs to the kitchen. Through sleepy eyes, I looked out at the glorious fall foliage, the bright sunshine warming my face as I sat up and stretched my small body, thinking, "It's finally Saturday!" I loved Saturdays in the fall; it was soccer season, and Saturday was the one day of the week I spent with my dad. As part of our Saturday ritual, Dad would always bring doughnuts for me and my sister, one chocolate and one honey dipped. The smells of coffee, doughnuts, and the newspaper surrounded him

---

*From Rodis, Garrod, & Boscardin, *Learning Disabilities and Life Stories*, published by Allyn and Bacon, Boston, MA. Copyright © 2000 by Pearson Education. Reprinted by permission of the publisher.

when he came to pick us up for my soccer game. I loved the way Dad looked on weekends, his hair messy and his face unshaven and salty from his early morning jog. Handing me the doughnut bag, Dad asked if I had my gear ready, and I realized I didn't know where my uniform, cleats, or shin guards were, though I did know where to look.

I darted upstairs to examine the heap of things on my bedroom floor. I first looked under the bed, where I found one shin guard and one cleat behind my Scrabble box. Beginning to feel frustrated, I scurried around my room, finding only two dirty soccer socks in my doll clothes drawer and a pair of soccer shorts from last year's uniform. Wanting to appear organized, I threw on the mismatched pieces of my uniform, just in time to hear my father's call up the stairs, "Ready, Gretchen?" As I ran down the stairs, I was something to behold wearing my wrinkled shirt, still dirty from my last game, a pair of shorts that were too small, and my dirty soccer socks, carrying one cleat, and one shin guard that had a doll hat stuck to the Velcro strap. I squirmed as my father examined me, his thick, dark eyebrows raised, his eyes squinting skeptically. I spotted my sister's gear stacked neatly in the corner; dropping mine, I scooped hers up and followed Dad out the front door, feeling somewhat relieved by the cool morning air. My very organized father followed with a shopping bag full of cookies and punch for the team; it was his turn to bring the postgame refreshments, and I thanked God for letting me remind him of that yesterday, and not on the way to the field.

We sat in silence as we drove to the field, but I was happy just to be with Dad. I loved watching his strong hands shift the car, which smelled just like his office: a mix of leather, paper, coffee, and new carpet. I liked to feel part of my father's world, and this for me, this time alone, was a bonding experience. I would often pretend I was one of his clients and that we were on our way to a meeting. I'd also pretend that the air of seriousness that surrounded my father was comfortable.

Before the game, I huddled with my team, shivering because I had forgotten my sweatshirt. When my coach shouted, "Get out there girls, let's hustle," I stared blankly, wondering why she hadn't put me in the lineup. Then I heard my dad yelling from the sidelines, "Weren't you listening? GO! Get out there, you're playing defense, pay attention! GO!" I ran onto the field, with my too-small shorts riding up my behind. My mind drifted as I watched my teammates dominate the game at the other end of the field, and I started mentally going over the moves I had learned in gymnastics that week. I started to do a cartwheel, and as my legs kicked over, I saw the ball heading straight toward me. My coach screamed from the sideline, "Gretchen, for Christ's sake, this isn't GYMNASTICS, it's SOCCER! Why are you doing flips in the middle of the game? PAY ATTENTION!" I glanced at the laughing parents standing on the sidelines, saw my father's embarrassed look of disgust. My coach took me out at halftime, and I sat with my back to my father for the rest of the game, hating myself for being so stupid, wondering why I could never be as organized as everyone else. The car ride home was silent. I was filled with shame and devastated that my day with Dad had been ruined. I was not, after all, his client, but merely his unreliable child whom he couldn't understand.

"I would hear my name being screamed from the front of the class."

When I think back on my years as a young student, I can laugh at some of my behaviors in class. I was constantly told to sit down, to stop talking; if the teacher gave instructions, I was always one step behind everyone; if we were supposed to hang up our coats, I would be easily distracted by something else. I was constantly yelled at for being disruptive, and I remember feeling very guilty, but, also confused: I did not mean to disrupt my class, and I often didn't even realize I was doing anything wrong. I realize now that I was not a child with a discipline problem, but a child with ADHD.

But, at that time, nobody knew what my real problem was, and at school embarrassing things would happen to me daily. I was constantly in trouble for taking too long when I went to the bathroom or to sharpen my pencil. I would look out the window and totally forget I was in class. Then I would hear my name being screamed from the front of the room. The thing was, I could not control my behavior. I felt I was not in control of my own mind and body. My frustrated teachers and my parents always wanted to know why I was not paying attention or why I was acting up in class, but I would only tell them, "I don't know, I just did." Often I couldn't even remember what I was in trouble for! But no one ever believed me, and soon I was pegged as a liar—a label that followed me for a long time. Every teacher at my school knew me because I was always in trouble. I was regularly kicked out of class, which bruised me emotionally because I could not explain my behavior. I felt like a really bad kid.

"There are days when I can actually feel my ADHD taking over my mind and body."

ADHD is not merely a part of me or an influence in my life. It is me. It is the main force that controls me mentally, physically, and socially; I cannot separate it from myself or keep it under control. It is hard for me to explain what it feels like to be driven by an inner force that is so powerful and primordial. There are days when I can actually feel ADHD taking over my mind and body. It's kind of like being on a ride at the fair that goes 'round and 'round in circles as it jolts up and down and side to side, and everything is a huge blur of lights, smells, and noises, and you try really hard to single out your friends down on the ground watching you, but you can't focus because it's spinning so fast. That is how hard ADHD can hit. Imagine that happening when you are in class trying to listen, or when you are trying to do your homework. In class, I often have the feeling that I am sitting in the middle of a drain, and I sit there at my desk, spinning furiously, trying to stop the motion. When the force erupts, my anxiety starts to take over, and I have to fight the urge to scream with frustration. My body reacts to this rush, and I have to move. There is nothing that can bring me back to the moment, and the only thing that helps me to relax is space and open air. An escape! This is an extremely complicated psychological state to have to describe when someone asks, "What's the matter?" or "Why can't you just sit still?" I feel that someone would think I was psychotic if I tried to describe the feeling.

The strangest thing about this state is that, though I know what I am sup-posed to be doing, I have absolutely no control. I can have a huge list of things I know I have to do, or else pay severe consequences, but I still will not do them. There is a force stronger than my own will controlling me. For example, if I have an important assignment to complete for school the next day, I'll go for a run or clean my room, all the time thinking, "I'm not doing my assignments." Then I≈might read the paper or go out with my friends, still conscious that I have this assignment, but still not doing it. I want to, but I really can't stop not doing it, can't stop doing something else. This also happens in class: I get the urge to do something else, like go for a hike, and I go. It does not matter what else I should be doing—I have to go. I'm driven.

"How come no one ever saw the fear in me?"

As a child, the hardest part of the day was the bus ride home. I always had a bag full of notes from my teachers, and I knew the school had already called my mother to tell her I had them. I would get off the bus scared to death and very sad. I would contemplate running away or wonder whether things would be better if I were dead. I would close the front door very quietly, knowing what I would get when my mom knew I was home. I always felt like I had worms in my stomach and would sometimes vomit from the anxiety. I'd develop a migraine, which my mother would say I was faking because I knew I was in trouble. I often felt like I was spinning out of control, and my parents would make me spin even harder, until finally I would just shut down and cry myself to sleep, feeling worthless and scared. I always felt very misunderstood.

My mother had a mean and violent temper when I was a kid. I know now that she was unhappily married and felt neglected by my father, and she would take out her anger on me and my sister. But as a child I just thought that this was how my mother was. I always got it worse than my sister—I added more stress because of school. When my mother got mad, she screamed so violently that I did not recognize her. She also hit. Instead of sitting and discussing why I was having trouble in school, she would usually beat me. This made me fearful; I started to lie to my teachers and hide my bad reports from my mother because it was my only defense from the abuse.

The first time I was caught forging my parents' names to a progress report was in the third grade, when I was eight years old. The consequences of lying were always worse than the bad report, but I could not stop. I had to protect myself somehow; nobody else understood what it was like for me. I felt that the only way for me to avoid punishment was to lie, and though I was often caught and punished, for some reason it didn't stop me. It became a habit, and I found myself lying even in situations where I did not have to. I never got in trouble at school for problems like fighting, but I was very dishonest, which gave me a bad reputation. My parents and my teachers overlooked my learning problems and focused on my behavior.

How come nobody ever saw the fear in me? Why did I have to be so deceitful so young? This overwhelming fear started very young, and stayed with me until recently, like a terrible weight I carried inside. I was a nervous child, and the stress caused migraine headaches and a nervous stomach. Stress can do many things to people, especially children, which I feel is one of the largest factors behind my failure in school.

As I got older, things only got worse. I was evaluated several times at my school, which only showed that I had deficiencies in copying from the board, work completion, math, and spelling. I was always off the charts on my vocabulary and comprehension abilities. They always told me that my testing scores were way above average and that I was capable of the work, but that I was careless and lazy.

I was often told that I didn't have my priorities in order, which was why I was doing so poorly in school. When I was in seventh grade, my parents decided to put me in private school, hoping that it would solve my problems. This may have been a good idea, but, in fact, it only brought on a new wave of problems. The private school had parent advisory slips—commonly known as PA slips— that would be sent home if you were disruptive in class, did not do homework, or if you were basically not doing well in a class. I probably hold the record at Cabot Academy for the most PA slips! As I explained, bringing home PA slips was not an option for me because I was so scared of my mother. So, once again I forged and lied daily. I would hand the forged slips to my teachers, but they usually found out my mother had not seen them and would then tell me I was caught. For the rest of the day, I would conjure up possible escapes, imagining myself living on the streets or in the woods, lonely and afraid. But I always went home. I would get home, where I would be verbally tormented by my mother. I would try to explain that I didn't know why these things were happening and that I was as confused as she was, but all she could say was, "You're lying," or "You're a lazy, stupid, self-ish child." I was called an "insensitive brat," a "lazy, fat ass," and I often heard my mother say, "I could fucking kill you!" As she screamed at me, she would twist my arm or smack me or push me, then send me to my room, saying, "I don't want to see your face for the rest of the night." I would wish that she could understand that acting that way was only hurting me and killing my self-esteem. I wanted her to realize that I was not doing these things because I was a bad person. I wanted her to realize that my problems in school were caused by something that I didn't understand. Instead, my mother only added to my problems.

Several incidents will never be erased from my memory. I hope that shar-ing one will help explain why I stayed in this pattern of lying, why I was just too scared to stop. I was in bed one night when I heard the phone ring. I thought it could be one of my teachers telling my parents that I had failed a math test. I heard my mother say, "Thank you very much for calling and letting me know." I knew I was right. I heard my mother scream from her bedroom and come flying down the hallway to my bedroom. The door burst open, and standing in the light of the hallway was my mother. She stormed into the room with a belt in her hand and started to whip me where I was lying in my bed. She was screaming cruel things at me and whacking whacking whacking me with the belt. Finally, my sister ran into my room and pulled my mother off me. It was total chaos. My sister and I were screaming and crying, and my mother was totally flipping out. I was confused and embarrassed that my sister had seen this. I know she felt bad for me, but I also know that she was angry at me for causing this. I put a chair in front of my door and huddled under my blanket, crying and getting sick to my stomach until, finally, I fell asleep. All this because I failed a math test. By the time my father got home from work, the house was silent and we were sleeping.

"I don't ever remember my parents getting along well."

It is amazing to me how much my family influenced how I see myself and shaped who I am. I will start with my parents. I believe that my parents' marriage was doomed to fail from the beginning. They were married at 25, and within two years they had my sister Meredith and me. My father started a job at an accounting firm in Boston, where he has worked for the last 21 years. My mother stayed at home for the first few years to take care of me and my sister. The main reason my parents are no longer together is that my father is married to his job; it's the reason they started fighting. My father worked 12–14 hours every day of the week. My mother thought it was unfair that she was left home all day with two babies to take care of and that she was totally alone all the time. When my father did come home, my sister and I were usually asleep; we never spent time with him. I believe that my mother felt neglected and that she felt bad that my sister and I never saw my dad either. My mother could not handle my father's work schedule, and she became very depressed and angry, and my parents fought regularly over the fact that my father was never home. I think my mother was so angry that she couldn't tell my father that the problem was that she really missed him and wanted to have a better marriage, so she would yell and scream and push him away even further. Eventually, their arguments became violent, and my mother would hit my father. The first time I witnessed this was horrific. It is hard to see your parents acting so irrationally. I was scared my parents would end up killing each other.

Looking back, I understand my mother's frustrations. I know she needed much more affection and communication than she was getting from my father. I know she tried to make their marriage work in many ways. She became an excellent cook and homemaker. She kept herself looking great, always beautifully dressed, and in great physical shape. She was envied by her friends for being so domestic and desirable. Only my father never recognized her efforts, never complimented her or gave her more time. That is why my mother became a very angry person.

My mother's temper became the thing that scared me the most. She would hit me and my sister when she became angry, often enraged over little things like spills or messes around the house. My mother treated every situation with violence. My father never really knew what was happening, and there was no one to help us. My mother's erratic behavior was confusing: After she hit me, she would give me a big hug and a kiss and tell me she loved me, but it never made me feel better. I wanted her to feel bad for what she had done, not kiss and make up. I often felt I was living in the middle of total chaos but was too small and powerless to stop it.

"The doctor told them I had ADHD."

When I was in eighth grade, my parents decided to take me to see a specialist. I had been evaluated many times throughout the years, but I was still not improving. My parents were desperate to get some help for my problems. I remember the ride to the hospital: It was no big deal for me, since I had become accustomed to being taken to psychologists and doctors. As I went through yet another series of testing—the ink blots, the puzzles, and the building blocks—I wondered how these simple games would tell these people anything about me. At the end of the testing, my parents and I met with a doctor, who told them that I had ADHD. He said the drug Ritalin was the latest treatment and told my parents how it was used. I had never heard of ADHD, and at the time, it did not mean much to me. I just figured, "Well, that's one more thing we can add to the list, so can we go home now?" That was the extent of my diagnosis; we never got any information about ADHD, and we never talked about it again. My parents never thought to seek any advice about my condition, and, for me, it was just another name of another syndrome that was not going to change who I was. It didn't really bother me that we never talked about it because the doctor didn't seem to think it was a big deal. By the end of that school year, I was kicked out of private school and went back to public school still without any mention of my ADHD.

I now regret so much the way my parents and I let my diagnosis be pushed under the carpet. If I had had some help, I could have accomplished so much more and been spared the humiliation I felt when I was expelled from school. The guilt was even worse; I was so tired of disappointing my parents. I knew I was doing poorly in school, but I never expected to be kicked out. I think this was a turning point for me in many ways. I think this is when my parents finally gave up on me and when I gave up on myself. I was tired of not being understood and of being hurt so much that eventually I stopped caring about myself. I became so afraid of failure and admonishment that I was unable to take a risk or try really hard for things. I became scared of conflict or even the possibility of conflict. I couldn't trust anything I believed, and I became a sponge for other people's opinions. I never told anyone my feelings because I was so embarrassed about myself all the time.

Yet all of this did lead to something positive: I became a listener! The one area of my life that gained something from my bad experiences was my ability to be a good friend. I have had the same friends for many years, some since the first grade. I always put a lot into my friendships. All my friends would come to me with their problems because I was a good listener. I wanted to make sure these people felt that their problems were significant and that they were being understood. I never wanted anyone to have their feelings misunderstood as I did. I would change plans for my friends, even if it meant missing the biggest events; I would never desert a friend. I never let myself be in a clique and made it a point to try never to hurt anyone's feelings. I stuck up for kids who were being picked on and felt good about helping people. I was so well liked that I never had to worry about being picked on like I was at home or by my teachers. I was never a victim. Many teenagers have a hard time socially because kids can be really mean, but I never experienced that. This was great for me, but it also became a problem. I became so involved with everyone else's lives that I totally ignored how I was really feeling. Helping other people did make me feel better, but it was not enough.

During my sophomore year in high school, I became involved with Rob, a boy I had known throughout my school years. Rob gravitated to me because he had a lot of emotional difficulties. In elementary school, he had cancer for seven years, but cancer was the least of his problems. When Rob was diagnosed with bladder cancer, his father took off, and Rob never heard from him again. After later bouts with lung cancer and a tumor on his spine, Rob went into full remission when he was 12. A week later, his mother announced that she had cervical cancer and that it was too far gone to help. She had never told anyone because she wanted Rob to be taken care of first. She died when Rob was a freshman in high school, and he blamed himself. This kid had major problems, and he became my new project.

I went out with Rob for five years, devoting myself mainly to his problems. I believe he'd be dead by now if not for me, but it sure didn't get me anywhere. He was a drug user, and I got into heavy drugs with him—acid, pills, coke. For two years straight, that was all we did. It was great: I was "helping" Rob, and I was too fucked up to feel my own pain. Rob hated school as much as I did, so we stopped going after a while, and if I did go, I was high. My parents separated the year I met Rob, so they were dealing with their own problems. My mother was such a wreck throughout her divorce that it was easy for me to get away with things.

But midway through my senior year when my mother had an emotional breakdown, I totally lost it. She wanted me to affirm her and comfort her, but I was so angry at her for what she had put me through that she made me sick. I could not even feel bad for her, and I let her suffer. My dad and sister were gone, so I was left alone with my irrational mother. And I just lost it. I quit school and ran away from home. I got an apartment with Rob and two of his friends in a part of the city surrounded by crack houses. This was the worst possible environment, but I did not care. I felt like I was losing my mind and just had to get out of my house. I have never been so depressed in my life; I totally hit rock bottom. I was still seeing my therapist through all this, and one day I showed up for a therapy appointment to find my dad waiting there with two guys in white coats. My father forced me to take a drug test, after which I was locked up in rehab for a few months.

"Those three months in Minnesota were a period of rebirth."

When I got out of rehab, I had a hard time motivating myself to do anything. The whole world felt dead to me. My relationship with my parents was not great, and my self-esteem was at the lowest place it had ever been. I couldn't pretend I was happy; I couldn't even smile. I was able to put a lot of effort into figuring out what I needed to do to be happy again, and the one thing I was sure of was that I needed to get away from my family, my friends, and my hometown. I needed to see myself in another setting, to cut myself off from the rest of my world and totally concentrate on myself. My father suggested that I try an Outward Bound course for the summer, and I instantly agreed with him. I knew a little about the philosophy behind Outward Bound, but I didn't know what to expect from my trip. I think the main reason I agreed to do the trip was because the distance and seclusion sounded so right.

I spent three months in the woods of northern Minnesota backpacking, kayaking, and canoeing. There is something so amazing about living without a clock or a schedule hanging over your head. Getting away from the noise, hustle, and stress of life, I was able to reflect and think. I found a calming silence in nature that soothed my mind and gave it the time to expand without unnecessary chatter and noise.

My Outward Bound course was the most significant experience I have had, the best choice I have made in my life. The changes I experienced during my trip were so strong and unbinding that I could feel them as they were occurring. I had moments of great clarity that allowed me to separate myself from the cloud I had been living in for years and to free myself from insignificant worries and fears that I had been holding on to my whole life. I think this was the first time I recognized myself as an individual person, rather than as a mere part in the lives of all the people I knew and all that I experienced. Before, I had absolutely no sense of who I was; I viewed myself according to what other people told me I was. Outward Bound gave me the personal freedom to explore inwardly and form an identity for myself. This freedom was the crucial aspect of my experience. I was in a group of seven strangers who did not have a clue about my past, and this was the first time that I could be the person I knew I was. I did not fear that these people would analyze my behaviors like my family did. I had lost the faith of all the people who were close to me and was used to getting few words of encouragement.

Those three months in Minnesota were a period of rebirth. I shed about 19 years of unwanted skin that was trapping my spirit. With every step I took, I sweated out the toxins in my body and mind. Every day, I struggled and cried, and I released and released all the pain inside me. For the first time my nerves settled, and the sick feeling I had in my body left. My stomach felt empty and happy without the butterflies that had lived in there for years. I smiled and I laughed out loud, and I was happy!

Equally important to my rebirth was that I gained a lot of insight into my family. I had had so much anger at them for so long that I could not distinguish the good in them. I know that I had an inner demon eating away at my spirit, and my family was that demon. In time, I was able to conquer the burdens they had placed on me and recognize my own faults and the ways I had contributed to the deterioration of my family. I had put so much emphasis on defending myself that I hadn't seen my role in the problem. I went home from my trip feeling settled and open to them. The trip also gave me time to decide what I wanted in the future, and I decided to go back to high school to get my diploma.

There is a part of me that would never want to change the fact that I have ADHD. I believe that this condition can be positive in many ways for the person who has it. The main setback for most people with ADHD, especially children, is that they are misunderstood. If I had been taught to believe that ADHD was a learning difference rather than a learning disability, I feel I would have had a more positive view of myself while growing up. ADHD has caused me problems as far as learning goes, but not because I cannot learn. I just do not learn the same way other people do. But then, everyone learns differently, not only people with ADHD. ADHD becomes a learning disability when teachers try to put many different kids together in one room and expect them all to learn the same way. I feel that a lot of the problem for children with ADHD lies within the education system. Most schools have a set curriculum and routine method of teaching, but it is ridiculous to believe that all children will be stimulated by the same things. The problem is that not all classroom settings incorporate a multimodal form of teaching. There are simple strategies that can be incorporated into the classroom that can greatly help all students learn more effectively according to methods that work best for them.

Many specialists believe that medication is the most effective treatment for students with ADHD. This is something that I am very afraid of. I have experimented with a few of the drugs that are prescribed, like Ritalin and Dexedrine. When under the influence of these medications, I am a completely different person. I lose all my energy and emotions. It is like the driving force behind who I am is sucked out of my body leaving me feeling like a hollow shell. My ADHD is the source of my energy, and it is vital for me to have that. I feel that my personality would not be what it is if I did not have ADHD. There are so many positive aspects of ADHD. For example, I can do many things at one time successfully. My mind is always in motion and always looking for something to do. My main goal is to be able to control my ADHD in certain settings, and to use my ADHD as an advantage, rather than taking drugs to suppress all my creative energy.

Although most people look at ADHD as a negative condition, I disagree. I believe that if you were to ask anyone that has a friend with ADHD, they would say that all of these crazy symptoms are what they love about that person. ADHD makes a person an individual unlike anyone else. I know that at times my erratic behavior and spontaneity aggravates my friends and family, but those are the qualities that make them laugh and appreciate me. The problem is that most of the literature about ADHD is written by people who do not have ADHD. They generalize ADHD and say that the symptoms are concrete. This is extremely offensive to me. I understand my symptoms, and I know how my ADHD affects me, but it's all personal. My situation can be totally different from another person with ADHD.

I am happy that I have the opportunity to write about my experiences. They are me, and they are real. I hope this essay will help some people see the importance of dealing with learning disabilities so that they or their child will get the help they need. I also hope people can learn from my story so that they will deal with this issue differently from the way my family did. I want people to understand that

ADHD should not be labeled a disability, that it only becomes a disability when it is not understood and when people fail to see the benefits and the positive aspects of it. I believe that my ADHD caused people to look down on me and tell me that there was something wrong with me. I had hundreds of tests for that reason alone; everyone wanted to know what was wrong with me rather than just seeing the energy and passion that I had for so many things. My teachers and parents overlooked all the areas in my life where I was succeeding and instead concentrated on my faults. If I had learned earlier how to turn my ADHD into an advantage, I would have had a better outlook on life and I would have had more respect for myself as a person. It has taken me a long time to be able to see the good in me. Because of all the people telling me there was something wrong with me, I was unable to recognize any part of myself as positive and "normal." All I wanted was for people to listen to me and to really see me, not what the doctors were seeing.

THE SIMPLE BEAUTY
OF A CONVERSATION

This author's shocking discovery of his speech impediment in first grade leads him to feel insecure and self-conscious regardless of academic and social accomplishments. Ray's "identity as a stutterer" makes him give up in school, because it is "easier not to attempt something than to fail at it." He plagiarizes and cheats his way through high school without being caught, as much a rebellion against his parents as a way of getting by. His religious faith, a close friendship, and his work in the library help him through some of the most difficult years, providing support and contributing to a growing sense of himself as a valued person. Ray experiences a setback when, early in college, his girlfriend is raped, an experience that causes memories of his own early sexual abuse to surface for the first time. He feels like a stronger person now, "standing on his own two feet." His stutter reappears only occasionally, reminding him of the difficulties each of us has in our lives.

As I started high school many teachers and friends held high hopes for me, but by the end of my senior year there was a question as to whether I was going to graduate or repeat the year. My academic problems did not all stem directly from my learning problems. The most accurate description would be to say that I was burned out. I desperately wanted someone to recognize that I was having problems and to offer help. That never happened, and I continually failed at all attempts to get myself on track. It became easier not to attempt something than to fail at it. I could see no future for myself. I never even tried to think about what I wanted to do after graduation. I couldn't handle the present, so trying to plan my future was an impossibility.

I got by the best that I could. High school was very painful and difficult for me, and as a way of protecting myself I pretended that I didn't care about the school or my classes. If I had let myself feel that high school could be a very positive experience for me if I was successful, then the pain would have just been worse. I did very little homework, cheated on almost every test, plagiarized all my critical papers, and skipped school as often as I could get away with it.

I need to go back to my early childhood to explain all the problems I had with school. At the age of five, I went through kindergarten. I enjoyed it, and as far as I knew, I was just like all the other kids. However, I found out that while all my other friends were going on to first grade, I was going to go to another kindergarten class. No one ever explained to me why I was repeating kindergarten. When I got to the new class I was with a bunch of other kids who were pretty normal. For one hour a day, however, I was taken aside with a special teacher who came to the class just to work with me. I didn't mind because I remember thinking she was pretty. She would show pictures and ask me to tell her what I saw. For example, she would show me a picture of a dog and I would say, "dog."

"No, that's not right. Try it again," she would often say.

I had no idea what I was doing wrong. The picture was very obviously a picture of a dog, and as far as I knew, I was saying the word "dog." This would happen with pictures of trees, cats, farm animals, and many other simple items. I would tell her what it was, and she would say, "No, try again." She never told me what I was doing wrong.

The other kids in class must have picked up on what was going on because pretty soon they all started calling me names like "retard" and "moron." I didn't understand this either. I went home crying to my mother one day and asked her why I was being called these names. I can remember the most pained expression I have ever seen come to her face and she said simply, "Because they're not very nice children."

I made it through that year in pretty good shape, all things considered. In first grade, the same teacher came to see me every day again. We would go to a small office in the basement and do the same things we did in kindergarten. I know it was unintentional, but one day she did one of the most cruel things I have ever experienced. I went to see her that day, and we went through the same routine. This time, however, she had a tape recorder. She recorded the answers I gave to the pictures. Then she rewound and played the tape back to me. I'm not even sure how to describe my reaction to the tape. I was about six and a half years old, and like every other little kid, I wasn't all that self-conscious or worried about the differences between myself and other kids. But that tape crushed me. The voice I heard was absolutely unintelligible. The voice was stuttering terribly, and all the pronunciation was completely off. I couldn't even recognize what it was saying. The voice didn't even sound human. I was sure that I had said "dog," but when the tape got to the point where the word should have come, something completely foreign, not even resembling "dog," came out. I started crying and screaming, "That isn't me! You put another tape in there! That isn't me!" She couldn't calm me down.

I guess everybody assumed I was aware of my speech problems because they were so severe. At the very least I must have been aware of my stutter. But

I wasn't aware of it at all. As I've said, no one, my parents included, had ever talked to me about it before.

That tape had an immediate effect on me. I became very withdrawn and would hardly talk to anybody. I particularly avoided talking to my parents, both because I didn't want them to hear me speak the way I did and also because I felt betrayed; I wanted to hurt them with my silence. That might sound like a lot for a six-year-old, but it is very true. Everything that had happened—staying back in kindergarten, the special teacher, and all the kids making fun of me—became clear to me, and I became very bitter toward my parents for having never talked with me about it. I really hated them. Over the next 10 or 11 years, I spent much of my time finding little ways that I could hurt them and get back at them for the way they had failed me.

My relationship with school didn't fare much better. Soon after the tape was played to me, the special teacher told me that she was transferring and that we wouldn't be working together anymore. I have no idea if the tape incident had anything to do with her decision, but I am sure now that it did play a part in my parents' decision not to get any more help for me. They couldn't deal with the pain, and I think they felt that the best thing to do was to ignore my problems and hope they would disappear with age. So I no longer went to any special classes. In the regular classes, I did everything I could to keep from having to speak in front of the class. I didn't want the other kids to hear how I talked. Through the rest of grade school, every teacher I had just about killed himself or herself trying to get me to apply myself more. They all felt I had great potential if I would be more out-going. I resisted all these efforts. While my pronunciation improved somewhat, my stutter had not improved at all by the time I entered junior high.

It is very difficult to discern how much my stutter affected my image of myself and how much it affected others' image of me. Trying to look back objec-tively, I would say that for the most part, it had its greatest influence on my own self-image. When I was growing up, it sometimes seemed that everybody was laughing at me and pointing me out, when in reality probably only a few did so. There are some events that make me realize now that my friends and classmates must have held me in fairly high regard. In the fourth grade, I was elected class president. In sixth, I was given awards for sportsmanship, leadership, and math ability. In the seventh grade, I was chosen as the "Most Intelligent" out of a class of about 150. Still, these did very little to raise my self-esteem, so sensitive was I about my stutter. The effect of these positive reinforcements was minimized to the extreme by my self-consciousness. The only identity I had for myself was as a stutterer. None of my other accomplishments came close to having the effect on me that the fear of stuttering and speaking incorrectly in front of others did. I felt that no one else knew who I really was because I had become so proficient at hiding my speech problems. I saw myself as hiding who I really was from others. To some extent this was true.

In junior high, my self-esteem reached its lowest point. My outlook on every-thing was dictated by my view of myself. I built a reputation at school for being able to get away with cheating, skipping classes, forgery, and other things like that. During lunch at school, a lot of kids would come to me looking for help. I'd make a cheat sheet, sell an essay, or do whatever the occasion called for. This was my first niche in junior high and freshman year. It was fun at first because it was novel and it got me a lot of attention. Sometimes it was more innocent, and sometimes it was of a much more serious nature. For example, I went through the honors English sequence in high school and plagiarized almost every critical essay I was assigned to write. Some other students were caught doing this but I never was. I learned how to choose obscure, yet valid, sources and how to change things around just enough so that there was very little chance of getting caught. I cheated on almost every test I took and spent a minimal amount of time on homework.

I was shy with girls and doing things like this created opportunities to talk with them. This was very important. I've been attracted to girls as long as I can remember. My first kiss was in kindergarten—the second year that is. I was embarrassed afterward and I was afraid the girl would start telling the other kids that I had kissed her, so a couple of days later I went back to her house and beat her up, which sounds worse than it was. I had my first opportunity to have sex when I was in the sixth grade. The girl was in the eighth grade, and I'm pretty sure she was drunk. We were behind some bushes in the church playground across from my house. She came over to me and took off all her clothes. She kept saying, "Come on over and lay me." I had never done more than kiss a girl at that point and I didn't know what "lay me" meant. I went over to her and she stuck her hand down my pants. I ejaculated as soon as she touched me. She laughed at me and said she wanted me to do that again but this time while I was "porking" her. I didn't know what that meant either. To be honest, I had no idea what to do at all. We fooled around for a while, but we didn't actually have sex because I didn't know what to do. She kept laughing at me the whole time. I put my clothes back on and left her lying in the bushes. Immediately after this experience and for the next few days, I felt awful. I was cold and shivering all the time and I couldn't stand to have anyone closer than a few feet away from me. I didn't understand why I felt this way but then I didn't understand anything to do with sex at that time.

I went through puberty at an early age. By the end of the sixth grade, I had had a couple of wet dreams and I was masturbating often. The incident with the first girl made me curious about and interested in girls. A friend and I used to climb trees in our backyards together. It started a few years earlier as an innocent childhood pastime, and we just kept on doing it. One late afternoon during the summer after sixth grade, we were sitting up in the tree talking quietly when we saw a light go on in my neighbor's house. It was the bedroom of a girl who was about a year older than we were and who was my sister's friend. My friend said to me half jokingly, "Wouldn't it be awesome if she changed and didn't pull her shade down?" I agreed, of course, but we really didn't expect anything. But then she did change into her bathrobe without pulling down the shade. We sat for a while without saying anything. I think we were both embarrassed to talk or to move because we both had erections and didn't want the other to know.

One day later in the summer the girl we spied on, Jean, stopped by to see if my sister was around. I was home alone that day and told her so. She came in for a while anyway and we started talking. I got an erection and since I was wearing my bathing suit it wasn't long before she noticed, although I tried to hide it as best I could. At first I was embarrassed, but pretty soon we started talking dirty. We kept daring each other to say dirtier and dirtier things and to shift our clothes around to reveal more. Eventually we went into the shower and I lost my virginity. I think it was her first time also, but I'm not sure.

The time in the shower felt pretty good to me, but I don't think Jean enjoyed it very much. She looked like she felt very guilty. Nevertheless she started coming over often when I was alone. We fooled around and tried a lot of things. She must have known more than I did because I really didn't understand how girls got pregnant, but after the first time in the shower she never let me penetrate again. Instead we did other things. At the time we did it I liked it, but I always felt dirty after she had left. Every time we fooled around, she would ask for a few of my father's beers to take back home (he never kept track of them). One day she came over with a *Penthouse* and read some of the letters to me. She said she would try those things if I could get her a full bottle of wine. My father had one and I gave it to her. I had heard about prostitutes in church and what it meant if you got into that stuff. I started thinking that what we were doing was almost the same thing. I had a terribly guilty conscience, but every time she came over the same thing would happen.

There was something more than just a guilty conscience though. I couldn't bear having people being physically close to me. If I ever was in a crowd, such as in a mall, I would get lightheaded and have dizzy spells. I also hated to have anyone stand behind me. If I was in any line, I would stand a little off to one side to prevent people from being directly behind me. I thought that maybe these feelings had something to do with what Jean and I were doing, but I didn't understand them.

When school started again, Jean stopped coming over. We never talked about what we had done again, and I think both of us really wanted to forget it. I have never bragged about these experiences to anyone. There are just too many painful feelings and too much confusion connected with it for me to be able to talk about it lightly. As a Catholic, I felt what I did was morally wrong, and then there were all those other feelings which I couldn't figure out. In college, I told the first girl I slept with that I was a virgin. She said she was, too (and she was probably telling the truth), and that it made it more special because it was the first time for both of us. I've only slept with one other girl since, and I told her that my only experience was with the other college girl. Right now I just don't feel comfortable letting anyone know about what happened.

After the summer with Jean I entered junior high school. That's when most kids start dating, but I became very shy with girls. I knew what sex was like, but I had a lot of trouble talking to girls. Each day I was becoming more and more self-conscious about my stutter; I felt that no girl would ever go on a date with a guy who talked like I did. As a result I didn't have any dates in junior high or high school, although I did begin to talk to girls more. I had other problems then as well. I've mentioned what my academics were like. My grades were respectable, but they were not earned honestly. My parents and I were moving farther apart. About the only time we ever talked was when we were fighting.

As a result of my problems with my family and in school, I needed to find a place I could find some solace and security. Actually, I found three areas: religion, friends, and work. I was raised in a fairly strict Catholic manner. My mother took me to church every Sunday, and we fasted before and after mass. I went to classes preparing me for all the sacraments and attended service on every holy day. Sometimes the tedium and monotony of these rites would get to me, but overall I have always been a religious person. Often prayer and hope for the future have been the only outlet I have had when times have been really bad. I have never had a serious question about my belief in God and the scriptures, and for most of my life I have prayed every day. While my religion is and always has been an important part of my life, I have often questioned the attitudes of the Catholic Church itself. Nevertheless, I do have strong faith, and I try to follow as best I can the teachings of forgiveness, forbearance, and humility. I take pride in my faith.

When I was a sophomore in high school, a priest in my parish, a person whom I really admired, came to me and tried to convince me to enter the priesthood. I actually considered this for a time. In the end I decided against it. But that is not the significance of that incident. This was the first time that someone I really admired let me know he saw some value in me. He was seeing good in me that I couldn't see myself. It had a profound effect on me. I didn't turn myself around in a day because of it, but I did have my first thoughts of where I was going and the person I was as opposed to the person I was capable of being. These were brief, very scattered thoughts, but the seed had been planted. It was the encouragement of other people like him that helped me learn that many people saw me in a better light than I saw myself. I had very little self-respect so I had to get it from others, most of whom have been very religious. At least they are religious in my estimation of how the religious should be; they practice their faith, and they show their belief in how they treat other people rather than by preaching to them. And they are secure enough in their faith that they can accept faiths that differ from their own. I have a lot of respect and admiration for these people. I learned from them that a strong belief in the self often goes hand in hand with a strong belief in a set of principles and precepts.

The Catholic Church requires public worship and professing of faith, but I was always very private about it. In that sense I made a poor Catholic. In fact, along with most of my friends, I denied holding any beliefs. I made jokes about the church and about older adults who were very religious. It's also true that I outwardly denied my faith because my mother was Catholic and worship was an integral part of her life. I didn't want to be anything like my parents, and it was a form of rebellion. But, still, inside I found it a source of comfort and hope. As I grew older, I started understanding the readings at mass more and saw that they could be applied to my life. I often looked at myself as a modern-day Job.

I suffered through trials and hardships as a test of my faith. Not only my faith in God but also my faith in myself and my ability to keep hope alive in my breast and work for something better. I had occasional thoughts of suicide, and three times I made concrete plans to go through with it, but there was always something inside that wouldn't let me give up on myself. Religion helped add to my sense of identity, but that still wasn't enough. There was only so much I could get through my private contemplations and beliefs; I needed experience on a more social level.

This leads to the other two areas—friends and work. I had enough friends that I didn't feel like an outcast, but I had only one really close friend, the one who was my peeping-Tom partner. The two of us had met when we were five and have been best friends ever since. The strength of our friendship cannot be overstated. We never pressured each other into doing anything (like trying drugs), and we could share our secrets and problems. My friend, Bill, had a much better relationship with his family than I did, so I adopted his family as my own in a way. I didn't look up to or respect my parents, but I did his. Their opinions had more weight with me than my own parents' opinions. I don't mean to imply that my mother and father were failures as parents, but I held hard feelings against them and looked to Bill's parents for guidance.

Bill and I did everything together. We liked the same shows and music and hung out together all the time. In fact, it wasn't uncommon for teachers and other kids to get the two of us mixed up. There was a great amount of security in that relationship for me. I felt that Bill accepted me for who I was; he was the only person who I wasn't afraid to stutter in front of. Bill and I were (and still are) blood brothers. When we were very young, probably seven or eight, we slit our thumbs with a knife and rubbed our bleeding fingers together. I assume that isn't done much today. We took everything from swimming lessons to guitar lessons together.

Our parents all worked, and much of the time we were left to ourselves. During the summer we spent most of every day unsupervised. Some of our activities were questionable. For example, there was the summer that a moose was spotted in our town. A moose had not been seen in our town for over a hundred years so the news stirred up some fear along with the curiosity and fascination. Only a handful of people had seen the animal, and it was assumed that it had just moved on out of town. One afternoon Bill and I came up with a brainstorm. Our local paper had carried a picture of the tracks left by the moose so we cut that out. Next we got some wood and cut out models that resembled the prints. We tied the models to the bottom of our sneakers and walked in the backyard. Sure enough, we left tracks in dirt that were very similar to those in the picture. The next few nights we snuck out of our houses and went to the swampier areas of town. We put the moose feet on the bottom of our sneakers and walked in the mud of several backyards. A couple of days later we read in the paper that the moose was back and, the paper said, it was possible now that there was more than one. The police had been placed on alert. Aside from our terror of being found out by the police, we loved the whole episode. We had fooled the adults again.

The two of us did everything together and continually made future plans. In the long run, this may have come close to hurting me; I relied too much on Bill's friendship and didn't try to be more outgoing and build my confidence. On the other hand, if I hadn't had Bill and the security of our friendship, I never would have learned how to function well socially.

The summer before high school, I got a job at the town library, and I was excited about starting work. I had spent a lot of time at the library (it was very close to my house), and I knew several of the librarians. My immediate boss, Mrs. Johnson, turned out to be one of the most special people I have ever met. She was kind, friendly, intelligent, always quick to praise but also ready to point out mistakes in a constructive way, and an all-around lovely person. She could discern everybody's personality. She must have known that I needed a place where I could feel I belonged because she soon gave me many important responsibilities that were within my capabilities. This helped my confidence tremendously. I felt everyone there wanted to see me succeed, and when I made mistakes they treated them as very minor in comparison to all the other things I had done right. It wasn't long before I was working very hard at my job. I would do everything they wanted done—and more if I could find other little jobs. If they needed someone at an awkward time on short notice, I always volunteered. At first it was simply that I wanted Mrs. Johnson and the others to keep giving me praise and because their good opinion was very important to me. Eventually, though, I began to realize the importance of doing a task with integrity and diligence, and that good work was its own reward. Before working at the library, I had never felt what it was like to accomplish something that I had spent much time and effort doing. There was great satisfaction in it. It was a long time before I applied this to schoolwork, but that would come.

I worked at the library for about six years. It's hard to summarize all I learned and all the feelings connected with the library and the staff, but there are a few key points. First is the dedication of the staff. Many of the full-time employees held a master's degree in Library Arts and yet were making under $22,000 a year. They unfailingly did their best to work for the community in what was often a shamefully thankless capacity. I admired their dedication. I felt I wanted to emulate that, and often now when I feel I'm unfairly overloaded with work and responsibilities I think of those people and remember that I should appreciate what I have going for me. The other staff—the part-timers, custodians, and such—were the same. They all did their jobs well and created an enjoyable atmosphere for everyone. Sometimes I wondered how so many good people could be concentrated in one small place. Maybe I'm a naïve optimist but I came to the conclusion that it was the atmosphere, the congenial and supportive feelings around us all, that was responsible for it. Most people have it in them to be their best but the circumstances surrounding them are not as favorable. And where did this atmosphere come from? I think it came from Mrs. Johnson and a couple of others there who were much like her. They were very supportive, generous, and kind to everyone, and so everyone else began to emulate and encourage this attitude. I don't know how well I have succeeded, but I have tried to hold this attitude and to project it to those I come into contact with. I've learned that how you treat people can really make a difference. Sometimes a kind word from the right person at a certain time can make all the difference in the world.

Another aspect of the library that was very important to me were the patrons, whose questions and requests for help had a great influence on me. I felt I held a certain power. If I knew the answer to a question, then I could solve a person's problem. Perhaps if a person was particularly nasty, I could purposely misdirect that person (I never did that but I was aware that I held the power). It really built my confidence. I was given certain responsibilities, and I was living up to them. This was something I couldn't find in school.

After a couple of years of working at the library, I noticed that many people recognized me outside of the library. For a very shy person, this really fed my ego. One of my favorite memories happened right in the library. A mother brought her little girl to check out some children's books. The girl was no more than three and a half years old. She could walk and talk only a little bit. Her mother sat her on the counter as I checked out her books. I was talking to the girl like I usually did with little children; I asked if she enjoyed reading or if her mother read her stories at night. When I was done checking out the books and the mother was taking her off the counter, she smiled and said, "He's a nice man, isn't he, Mommy?" Her mother agreed. I felt about 10 feet tall the rest of the day. I knew from my experience at the library that I wanted to work in some capacity with people.

The problem was always that I couldn't seem to apply myself to anything outside of working at the library. I matured a great deal while working there, but I needed to extend that to other areas. I continued cheating on tests and papers throughout all of high school, but after freshman year, I stopped advertising it. I quit helping my friends cheat and bragging about my crooked accomplishments. I wanted to become a more serious student, but I wasn't secure enough in my abilities to give up cheating. I felt I needed to cheat to get good grades. It was also partly force of habit; I was accustomed to cheating—not studying—and that was hard to break. I was still very withdrawn in class and did not participate. I avoided all high school social events. Overall, high school did not have a great effect on me because I put so little into it. What I did outside of class was of greater consequence.

When I wasn't working and my friend Bill wasn't around, I spent most of my time by myself feeling very lonely. Only those who have experienced extended periods of loneliness know what it can do to you. Fortunately, I had enough interests to occupy some of my time. For example, I was very interested in astronomy, and early in July there is a meteor shower that appears every year. One summer I decided to get up in the middle of the night to watch it. I had never seen a meteor shower before, and I was not expecting it to be anything too spectacular. I got up around one in the morning and went outside the house. It took a while before I could discover the section of the sky in which it was taking place, but when I first saw it, I was frozen in place. Every few seconds a bright streak would shoot across the sky and disappear. Each one couldn't have lasted more than a second, but the power they seemed to display left me awestruck. They sped over the sky so quickly that they were hard to follow, and I got dizzy from turning my head so quickly.

Then I decided I wanted to enjoy this more. I went inside and made a couple of sandwiches and got a drink. On leaving the house, I caught a glimpse of my father's old pipe. It was a big, awkward thing, but it seemed to match the moment perfectly. I had never smoked before—I had never even considered it— but I grabbed some tobacco and some matches and went outside with my little package. When I got outside, I wasn't satisfied with my view. My house is on a hill, but the house next to mine was taller and was blocking my line of sight. Nothing was going to get in my way of enjoying this show, so I decided to climb up my neighbor's roof. I had scaled the side of their house several times before a few years earlier (to peek in their windows), but I had never been on the roof. The house had a fairly sturdy drainpipe so I tied my things in a bundle around my waist and climbed up to the roof. It was an old house with a lot of nooks and crannies in it so I found a good comfortable spot which couldn't be seen from the ground and sat down to rest. Lighting up the pipe took a few tries, and when I did light it, at first I felt sick from the smoke. After a while I got used to it and started on the sandwiches. There was no moon that night, and the sky was very dark. I looked upward and watched the lights streak from one side to the other.

I was all alone. I could see no one, and no one could see me. The darkness of the sky was very soft and deep and the warm yellow streaks painting a path across the backdrop every few seconds were both magnificent and calming. My troubles were all below me, and the show I was watching seemed to put everything into its right place. This was so much larger than anything else I had ever seen. How many trillions of miles and billions of years had these meteors travelled only so I could watch them burn out in flame? Everything else seemed insignificant. There were no happy families, no unhappy families. No good students and no bad students. There were no words locked inside my head refusing to come out right. All of us were little and of no importance to what I was witnessing. A quote from Dickens floated over me and didn't seem as harsh as when I first read it: "The universe makes a rather indifferent parent." I stayed on the roof for a couple of hours, and for that time all was right in the world. Unfortunately, that was only a passing moment—no matter how good it made me feel, it didn't help me deal with everyday life.

After barely graduating from high school, Bill and I went together to a community college. It was something of a joke academically; my high school classes were more difficult. In spite of skipping a lot of classes, we ended up with As and Bs and decided to transfer to a technical college. A couple of weeks into the semester, I realized engineering was not for me and decided to transfer again in order to become an English major and live at school. It meant separating from Bill the next fall, but I felt it was time for me to try going out on my own.

That summer I met a girl named Ellen and soon started dating. Everything seemed perfect—almost too good to be true. We understood each other's feelings and problems and were able to give support to each other. For example, one day we were talking and I stuttered a little bit. She asked me directly about my stutter. No one had ever done that before. People had avoided mentioning it because they thought it would embarrass me. That attitude carries the implication that there is something wrong with having a stutter. Ellen asked me about it very straightforwardly. I realized that she accepted it as simply a part of me—just like my hair is brown and my eyes are blue. It had a great influence on me, and I felt myself falling for Ellen. I took her to her prom, and we saw a lot of each other during the summer.

So much happened that summer that it's hard, even in my own mind, to organize it all. Most was due to Ellen's influence and the nature of our relationship together. She was the first girl I ever developed an intimate and supportive relationship with. We shared our secret hopes and dreams and could rely on each other if we wanted to talk over problems we were experiencing in our lives. We each knew that we could depend on the other. We took things very slowly as far as a physical relationship went. When I think back to the time we shared, I think my favorite memories were when we went to the park and had a picnic. We would lie on the grass, sometimes I would lay my head on her lap, and talk or just sit quietly. There was something very special about being able to spend quiet time with someone as close to my heart as she was. All the days we spent together seemed to be sunny, happy, and fulfilling. I'm probably romanticizing our time together, but that is the quality of my memories of Ellen. Being able to build a relationship like that, particularly since Ellen and I were so well matched, resulted in my maturing a great deal.

I can't give a surefire explanation for it, but my stutter was decreasing markedly. By the end of the summer, stuttering had become a rare incident whereas before it had been the norm. Perhaps it was because I was at the age when men finally stop growing. My metabolism may have changed slightly. Maybe it was because I was maturing mentally and emotionally. By the end of the summer I was almost speaking normally. I am determined never to forget, however, what it was like having a problem such as that and what it was like to have people judge me and put me down for something over which I had no control. I'm very fortunate to have experienced that and to have had it corrected for whatever reason. I work with the mentally handicapped now, and it's always surprising to see how far they can go beyond what is expected of them. I've learned never to place restrictions on the abilities of other people, and more important, on my own abilities.

Ellen was going to a school about 1,500 miles away. We could have made a commitment at the end of the summer, but we both thought that we should go off to school with full freedom and then see how we felt. It was difficult because we were both very much in love by that point. It was a good decision though, and we promised to keep in touch. Without Ellen's support, I don't think I would have had the confidence to leave my home and all my established friends and go off to an unfamiliar environment. She was never even aware of that. It was one of the ways she helped me without knowing it.

We left for school and, as promised, we kept in touch. I wrote her every day, and she called me often. After three weeks we found it very hard to be apart. We kept on saying how much we missed each other. Toward the end of September, Ellen said that she was coming home in a couple of weekends. She wanted to get together and spend a day with me. I'm pretty sure we were both ready to make a commitment—we were going to become engaged, so to speak. Ellen hinted that she felt ready to begin a sexual relationship. We started talking on the phone more often, and Ellen began thinking about transferring to a school in my area so we could see more of each other. I was on top of the world.

Friday night around 11:00, about a week before Ellen was to come home, I was in my room studying when I heard the phone ring. It was Ellen and she sounded upset. She said she had been assaulted that afternoon and described what happened. When she had finished, I said, "Ellen, you keep saying that you were assaulted, but I think it's important that you admit outright that you've been raped."

It was a painful phone call for both of us. We talked for an hour or so; I said I knew a place I could call to get some information and I would call right back. I called a rape crisis hotline and found out all the medical, legal, and physical aspects I could. I called Ellen back, and we decided to fly her up here, take her to a hospital, and see what she wanted to do as far as pressing charges. She felt she couldn't tell her parents what happened, so I had to help her on my own. I did what I could for her, but I don't know how much help I was. I was very upset. It was an extremely difficult weekend. She went back to her school in a couple of days, which was probably the hardest thing of all. I wanted to keep her with me and protect her. But she had more courage than I did and went back to finish the semester.

I was in a bad state after she left. I didn't eat for a total of six days, and when I did start eating, it was only in little bits. I couldn't sleep, and when I did, I was having terrible nightmares. I would dream of people chasing me and then setting me on fire; people surrounded me and hacked at me with knives. The nightmares were bad, but I wondered why they were always about me. Ellen was never in any of these dreams. I felt very selfish, like I didn't really care about her. This brought on a tremendous feeling of guilt.

Soon the dreams started to change and seemed to reflect something that had actually happened. I couldn't put my finger on it, but each time I woke up I seemed to be close to recalling something I hadn't thought of in years. Bits and pieces started coming together, and it just got worse and worse. I began calling back memories in my waking hours. For over 13 years, my mind had withheld these incidents and blocked them from coming forward. However, now with Ellen's experience, it all came back. I remembered being a small child and a man I knew bringing me into a bedroom. I remembered him laying me on my stomach, and his hot breath on the back of my neck and the pain as he pushed down on me. It happened more than once; he did things that I didn't understand then but I understand now. I can't say how many times he did this because they are all blurred together. The experiences had been locked in my memory for years—I had never recalled or spoken about them to anyone before. I must have been afraid at the time to tell anybody, including my parents, what was going on.

By the end of the semester, I was a mess. I was in a crisis situation and my grades were horrible. I did pull through it, but the next semester I decided to get counseling. I started understanding a lot of things. I understood now why I hated crowds and having people stand behind me. I understood why the experience with sex brought up so many confusing emotions. What I have never learned to understand is why some people will use other people weaker than themselves to satisfy their own selfish wants. I still know the man who did the things to me, and it really seems he doesn't remember it at all. Maybe he does and is suffering with a terrible conscience, but I don't think so. I have been watching him since to find out if he has been doing it to any other child. I don't think he has. If I find out that he is, I'm not exactly sure what I would do. Most likely I will kill him if I think I can get away with it. I don't have violent feelings toward most people, but if someone like him keeps hurting innocent people in that way, I don't think he should live. I want people who do things like that to know that they are in a lot of danger.

The relationship between Ellen and me was never the same. We stopped dating. She wasn't able to continue a physical relationship with me, or start one with anyone else at that time. It wasn't a complete loss because we developed a very strong and supportive friendship. I eventually told her what had happened to me as a child, and we helped each other in many ways. Our friendship became something very important to each of us, and we have both benefited from it. I learned from her what love and generosity in the face of pain really is. Since then we have both gone on to date successfully and are both happy and contented people. We both had something horrible done to us, but neither of us is guilty of ever hurting another person.

I have found a role for myself. It was very painful growing up, but through the pain and all my mistakes I have learned a lot. I do very well in school, and I'm working my way toward studying counseling psychology in graduate school. I earn As and a few Bs now, and I'm finally the student that I've always wanted to be. In fact, I'm more successful in college than anyone else in my family. I'm not spiteful and bitter and don't rub it in my family's face, but I do like the feeling (and the place in the family) it gives me. I find that even now I tend not to participate in class discussions as much as I could, but that is more from old habits than from shyness. I date girls, but I haven't dated steadily since Ellen. I guess I'm guilty of comparing every girl to her and the quality of the relationship we had. A friend who is studying for her doctorate in psychology and knows my history with Ellen would like to see me get into counseling men who physically and sexually abuse women. I can't consider that right now because I still have very violent feelings toward these people, and I know that is wrong. Maybe sometime in the future I'll be able to think about it.

Some days I go through mood swings. In the morning, I can be the most cheerful optimist and yet come back in the evening seeing red with rage. However, it has been a long time since I've experienced any sort of depression, and

I think that is the important thing. I simply write off my mood swings to my Irish temperament. Besides, these mood swings are so minor compared to my former depths of depression that I can joke about them.

Recently, I became very ill and spent several days in the hospital confined to a bed and connected to an IV tube. For the next several weeks, I was very weak. During this time, my speech regressed terribly. It made me realize that my problems had not gone away, but rather that I had learned to compensate for them. When I was weak and fatigued, I didn't have the concentration necessary to maintain my methods of compensation. I was at first upset and felt once again rather that I was very different from others. Soon, however, I came to the conclusion that it was a good thing. It would come back every once in a while to make certain that I didn't forget where I came from and how far I've come. I would be reminded from time to time that we all have our strengths and our weaknesses, and it is important to accept both from all people. I would be reminded of the simple beauty of a conversation.

Altogether, I have been very fortunate in my life. Some terrible things have happened to me, but then I have also been lucky enough to come into contact with many wonderful people. These people have shown me what it means to be a caring and responsible person. They've allowed me to make all my mistakes without placing any judgments on me. I have learned from them that the way you treat other people can really make a difference for the better. Treat everyone with the dignity and respect they deserve, and it will always come back to you. Stand by others when they're in need because when you're in need, you'll find you have a lot more friends than you thought you had. But most of all, learn to stand on your own two feet. If you can't help yourself, there is little that others can do for you. Everyone is going to experience pain and hardship at some point in their life, and that is when we learn the depth of both our own strength and of our relationships with others. If we have planted strong roots, we should be able to withstand much of what comes our way. At the library, there was a saying on the bulletin board which I have always liked: *Be optimistic even when you feel desperate.*

CASE 16

FOREVER AN AWKWARD
ADOLESCENT

This is the story of a young man born with serious physical disabilities. David describes the tension between his parents over how high their expectations for his autonomy should be. His father's "legendary penchant for interfering" results in his doing everything for him, whereas his mother, having "less patience with incompetence," expects him to learn to do for himself. College becomes a new opportunity for forming close female friendships and for academic achievements, but these are tainted by doubts over whether he is held to the same standards as his peers. And he asks, "What is to become of my sexuality?" and envisions "a 35-year-old with the sexuality of a 14-year-old, and the prospect does not please me." As he plans to begin graduate school for a career in media, he will not accept society's narrow expectation that he should practice his profession as a representative of the disabled because, as he says, "I do not think of myself as a disabled person."

My first clear memory is from nursery school. When I was three years old, my parents sent me to a small nursery school for three or four hours about twice a week. It was in the basement of a local church, and I distinctly remember being carried down a long corridor past beautifully colored stained-glass windows. Someone was carrying me and pointed out the colored shapes that were on the opposite wall as the sun shone through the windows.

I should note that at this point I had not yet learned to walk. I still think of it as "learning" to walk, but this is not quite accurate. Because I was born with physical disabilities, the first three to five years of my life were interspersed with multiple operations, where the doctors tried to stretch my hamstrings surgically. After each of these operations, I was put in a plaster cast—at one point, both legs up to the waist. It was all in an effort to unclub my feet so that I might someday be able to walk. Everyone was very excited when I finally did, spontaneously, while waiting with my father in a doctor's waiting room. My parents and all their good friends were in tears, I guess, because the professionals had been about evenly divided on whether I'd ever walk at all. I don't remember this important occasion, however, which is one of my peculiar tricks of memory—I never seem to understand the full implications of various "remarkable" events in my life.

I don't have a lot of clear early memories of my parents. I always took them for granted, at least until I began to figure out ways that I might lose them. Like when I began to realize that their marriage wasn't that great. They really should have divorced 25 years ago. Except then, they wouldn't have had me! Even so, they are very unsuited to each other, and their arguments and periodic leavings and returnings were a bit of a cloud in my childhood.

I am sometimes embarrassed and worried about how little their sour relationship has seemed to affect me. I have had moments of tears and fear during particularly bad patches but, by and large, I have never had those self-blaming feelings that everyone says kids have when their parents have problems. I think it is a testament to my parents that despite their trials, life at our house always had a sense of security and permanence. I don't know if they did it on purpose; more likely it was their conservative view of how one conducted one's life that did it. Breakfast was always there. Dinner was always at 6:30. Everything was predictable. At the time, I came to envy my friends' younger, more adventurous parents (they went to movies—we never did), but now I think that it was better for me to have parents who took refuge in routine. I never really worried that I wouldn't be taken care of, that I wouldn't be loved.

I entered adolescence (and eighth grade) at about the time we made a cross-country move. Thinking back on that period, I am certain that the move was good for me. For one thing, my best friend had moved away the year before, at a time when our relationship was becoming difficult. We first became friends, at age five, because we shared a disdain for the crowd. We weren't joiners. For me, this trait was determined by my disabilities; I had had to learn how to entertain myself. The fun I had was sedentary: matchbox cars, model planes, books about WWII fliers, and TV—which spent a great deal of time catering to the imaginations of would-be fighter pilots and space travelers. My friend also liked these things, but more by choice. After a while, we reinforced our reclusive tendencies, and as we grew older, we grew farther and farther apart from our peers who were either getting into sports or getting into trouble.

Predictably, as puberty struck, my friend and I began to reevaluate (separately) where we stood. I suspect that my friend began to see that others his age were having a lot of physical fun, horsing around in ways that seemed impossible, or at least improbable, for me. Suddenly going over to each other's houses to play with Legos no longer sufficed to sustain our friendship. I, too, began to identify with other peers, people who also stood out, but who seemed to have made the transition from Legos to a kind of makeshift intellectualism. When a group of us began reading *The Lord of the Rings,* my best friend did not join in. Soon after this, he moved away.

For my family, the move across country was very traumatic, though they tried to act as though it was an adventure. My main concern was whether I would be able to survive in the new public school I would be entering. Having spent all my grade school years at an "experimental education" school on a college campus in my hometown, I was not used to a structured school environment. The realm of real schools was a mysterious and sinister one in the lore of this "campus school," and I'm afraid I bought into the horror stories of academic rigor and regimentation, which passed for information on public schools among my 12-year-old schoolmates. I think that entering middle school in the new town, far from any familiar people or places, was the best way for me to get into regular schooling; kind of like being thrown into a pool as a way of learning to swim. As it turned out, it was all right. I gained confidence in my academic abilities by having my intelligence confirmed for the first time by grades. The teachers there were every bit as human as in my other school, and the kids were far more numerous, so I could hide in anonymity. At least, that is what I thought. Actually, because of my disabilities I was almost instantly known, or known of, by everyone in the school. I was also treated with uniform kindness and curiosity from the first day, but even then I wondered, as I do now, how much of that kindness was actually pity for me because of my disability.

Since I have been physically disabled all of my life, I have managed to cope with the purely practical problems arising from this with a minimum of fuss on my part; I felt no loss, because I had no feelings of "normality" to compare with. One of my physical problems is that I am short, about four feet, two inches tall. Until I began growing whiskers on my face and driving a car, I was constantly mistaken by strangers as being a little kid. It's a hell of a pain for a 16-year-old boy to be handed a kiddie's menu every time he enters a restaurant. It is even worse when mere coherent speech is greeted with awe. If explaining to the old lady in church that I am taking five classes in high school provokes an assumption that I must be terribly smart, how am I supposed to know whether I really am or if everyone is just impressed that I don't drool on myself? I have high standards for myself, perhaps not as high as many straight-A college students, but I am always impressed when I witness, say, good writing and intelligent conversation in others, and I aspire to such standards of intelligence. During my teen years, it was a constant nagging irritation that everyone around me had what I felt were extremely low expectations. I never knew where I stood.

Almost everybody treats me well, whether or not they really know me. In fact, I gained a reputation among some of my high school peers for being really smart, even though plenty of students within my range of ability (such as those with whom I went through an Honors English program) had better grades and study habits than I did. After awhile, I began to realize that people were predisposed to treating disabled people with extra kindness. Perhaps, I thought, my "smart kid" reputation, which I considered to be disproportionate to my actual abilities, was part of this extra kindness. Supporting this notion was my observation that many people who had known me for a long time, even some members of my extended family, tended to express admiration for my accomplishments with an enthusiasm far beyond what I considered to be appropriate. I was able to gauge this by comparing my parents' response with that of my brother and certain close friends, all of whom had gotten used to the fact that, indeed, I had learned to walk and talk and go to school like any normal kid, and hence, responded in a more subdued fashion to what were, after all, fairly minor accomplishments on my part.

My desire to do well academically did not, oddly enough, compel me to become an especially studious student. My parents never really put the pressure on me to get straight As, and when I came home with report cards that were mixed As and Bs, they seemed to feel these were fairly wonderful. Either they were too old to understand grade inflation or they were falling into the same trap I already explained—being glad that I was still alive and walking and apparently intelligent. I tend to think that it was a little of both, which means that I have been guilty, on occasion, of taking advantage of the very tendency which I despise. I have often allowed myself to rest easy in others' low expectations. This is something that I continue to fight in myself. Still, it was terribly important to me that I never got less than a B. I constructed a sort of artificial line of performance, below which I told myself my parents would be disappointed. For some reason, I was never too concerned about what my teachers or my friends thought of my grades; I looked solely to my parents for approval on that score.

If, as I surmised, peoples' expressed admiration of me was exaggerated by the issue of my disabilities, then how could I be sure exactly how much of that praise and admiration had been earned and how much was phony or misplaced? Naturally, as I moved through adolescence, I cared more and more about where I stood in the grand scheme of things. Since the whole business of looks and sex appeal was entirely outside my league, my only arenas for competition and comparison were in academics and in "being likable." I tended to look to everyone I met for approval, and conversation was my weapon. At first, I was just naturally inclined to have an odd sense of humor, and to express both this humor and my interest in history and politics in conversations with adults and with as many interested friends as I could find. After a while, though, around my senior year in high school, I began to sense that being able to carry on a conversation about a wide range of topics was not just fun but an asset, too.

I have long thought that one of the real handicaps of having congenital disabilities is that one often grows up isolated from all the trivial things that adolescents banter about: music, girls, cars, clothes, films, TV, and magazines—the whole range of popular culture is a special language that the adult world too easily dismisses as unimportant. But for the teenager cut off from this language, relating to peers who are already leery of him or her because of a disability is doubly difficult. The goodwill most people have to "give it a try" with the disabled teen may be there at the beginning, but unless the teen is able to "run with the ball" and "fit in" at least by speaking the same language as his or her peers, the goodwill quickly turns to embarrassment, and then the disabled teen will be ignored. If it were up to me, people who counsel disabled kids and their parents would stress the importance, often denigrated in "normal" kids, of "fitting in."

In retrospect, I think that a lot of what I was doing in high school was constructing a character, a persona, I could live with. Most adolescents do this, but for me, it was doubly important because the character I had, my "default" pigeonhole in the eyes of others, was that of a short, oddly postured, disabled kid. I wasn't sure at the time, and I'm still not positive, just what kind of persona I want to have. This has made constructing myself an ad hoc process. For the most part, however, I think I have been able to impress others enough with images other than disability. When I get scared, though, when I think about it too much, I wonder if it's all my imagination. Does everybody still think of me as a disability, and not as a person? I don't know. I'll never really know for sure, because I am always suspicious of others' response to me. I guess that I function from day to day on a veneer of faith; I survive with happiness and pride by assuming that other people see me as I see myself.

My parents are two people whose reactions to me I have trusted. From my mother I get a cartload of political convictions, or perhaps prejudices, because at times I think that her convictions are as much prejudice as they are considered opinions. I count among the greatest gifts of my college years the ability to critique and analyze my own political and social beliefs. By and large, I inherit from Mom a respect for what good can be done by government, along with a profound and unquenchable skepticism which prevents me from ever being satisfied with what government or any other authority is doing. I realize, because I have seen it in my mother, that this is a frustrating way to approach the world. Always having to "bitch, bitch, bitch," not because it's right or good or a citizen's responsibility but because I can't contain myself, is a burden—especially in a society that frowns upon excess in expressing one's views.

Having lived for the most part away from my mother for four years, I have found that I still care deeply about what she thinks of my actions. I don't think I could ever pursue a career, for instance, that violated her standards of morality. This cancels out a lot of possibilities, but fortunately, I have no desire to become a stockbroker. Nevertheless, as I pursue graduate studies in mass media and popular culture, I find myself wondering about how she would feel about my being an advertising copywriter, or a television producer or network reporter. I tend to think that as long as I stay true to my own standards, I will not run afoul of hers, but sometimes I am not sure, and that worries me.

One of the peculiar dynamics of my relations with my parents has been growing up in an atmosphere thick with a history of Dad's legendary penchant for interfering. When I was much younger this didn't bother me, because I sought the security he provided. He was always the provider, the caretaker. In fact, he even helped dress me in the mornings right up till I entered high school. He was always looking for ways to make my life easier. Of course, the problem with this is that it retarded the development of my self-sufficiency. Mom was dead set against this. It wasn't that Mom was uncaring, it is just that she had less patience with incompetence.

In the long run, she was right; it was more help to me to force me into doing things myself than to smooth out any remotely rough areas of day-to-day life. As I got older, Mom became increasingly adamant that Dad was now an abnormally doting parent. She felt that perhaps it was more selfishness on his part—his need to feel needed and in charge—than a true concern for my welfare, which kept him so involved in my physical challenges. Eventually, she began to suggest to me that I ought to resent his "interference" as much as she did. In a way, this was good, because it finally caused me to increase and jealously guard my self-sufficiency. At first for Mom's benefit, but eventually for my own, I began to oppose my father's instinctive moves toward helping me dress, get in and out of cars, put on jackets, and so on. He knew that it all was for the best, and I no longer saw him as my guardian for life. Instead, I began to see him as a friend, a father, and sometimes a pain!

Our relationship has since changed for the better. We now have more arguments than we used to, but they are adult-type arguments. And on the whole, we share a mutual interest in each other's lives. I am sure that he harbors more than a little "controlling interest" in my life, but if he does, he at least is honest enough to admit it, and often interrupts himself midsentence, chuckling at his own tendency to criticize and worry the joy out of new adventures.

Other people, too, have influenced me in less vital, but no less enduring, ways. I think that I first got a taste of the joys of discussing politics from the high school librarian. He was a balding, middle-aged man with a bit of a paunch and a wonderfully dry sense of humor. A fan of George McGovern, he introduced me to the blessings of "Norwegian charisma" while we both watched Walter Mondale stumble through the 1984 campaign. I would come in after lunch and wander over to his office, where we would swap political stories we had heard or read about.

Here was a man, as well educated and articulate as my parents, and with similar political stripes, who actually enjoyed watching the "march of folly" that politics provides. It was a liberation for me. There were very few of my peers with whom I could talk about politics, either because they didn't care or because my views were hopelessly out of sync with theirs. For two years, then, I was able to spend at least an hour of every day just yakking away about anything that popped into my head. In fact, from testing my wings with him, I was finally able to spar with my parents on political topics.

I suspect that this kind of jabbering contributed as much as anything else to my interest in editorial journalism. When I approached the journalism advisor about taking the journalism class (thereby becoming a member of the paper staff), I remember that I had a goal in mind of writing a column. My work in his English class impressed him, so he helped me convince the editor that I should have my own column. In retrospect, I am sure that part of his admiration of me was that damnable tendency I mentioned earlier—to see any accomplishments by a disabled person as a miracle—but I guess I didn't really mind it that much if, in the end, I received recognition purely on my own merits.

I am sure that is one reason why I loved writing that column and the one I wrote for four years in college. In college, I began my column before very many people knew who I was. Consequently, when I got favorable comments from strangers, it was all the more special to me. For the first time in my life, I could be sure that I had earned every bit of the praise I got. I am a person who has never been short of expressions of approval from others, but anonymous praise is like gold to me. This is why I look forward to continue writing of this nature and then, hopefully, as a career.

There is one incident from my adolescence that has had perhaps the greatest impact on my outlook. During the long drive from the West Coast to what would be my college in the East, I became seriously ill. At this point, the most severe aspect of my disability stemmed from the effects of severe scoliosis on my lung functions. As I grew, my spine curved even more; the more it curved, the more it applied pressure on my lungs. Hence, my breathing capacity was getting progressively smaller. While a spinal fusion operation at age 10 prevented this from becoming fatal, as it turned out, the procedure left enough room for worsening to make it nearly so.

Knowing that the high altitude we would have to endure on the drive east would make me uncomfortable, my doctors prescribed an oxygen tank that I could use whenever I got too tired by the lack of oxygen. Unfortunately, this did not solve the physical problem of actual breathing, and the result was a potentially deadly spiral; the more oxygen I breathed in, the less my brain was induced to stimulate breathing—the less I breathed, the less I was able to expel carbon dioxide. By the time I had reached my destination, I was unable to sleep, because I would stop breathing and wake up.

At one point, I was told that I would never recover fully from this malady—as, in fact, I have not—and that I had about five years to live. The only alternative was to surgically install a permanent tracheostomy so that, in addition to using extra oxygen at night, I could have the help of a respirator in breathing. We waited a few weeks in the vain hope that somehow I would spontaneously pull out of this hole, and during this time, I continued to prepare for my first day of classes which was less than two weeks away.

Most of the people around me, my mother and father in particular, saw my entering college as a fantasy. After all, I did look pretty bad, and I could barely cross a room on foot, much less walk to class. Only my older brother seemed to think that they were all overreacting. For all of my life he had lived with the constant and recurrent threat that I would die, that I would never walk, and that I could never do thus and such. Every time I had taken a turn for the worse, he had been told that "you'd better come and see him, it could be the last time." Every time I had "proved them wrong," as he put it to me. While he was particularly worried with this incident, he still felt that as long as I was certain I would start college on time, there was hope.

To hear him tell it, I am some kind of brave hero for having kept my faith in my ability to recover. From my point of view, it wasn't bravery or faith. I never really realized how serious my condition was. All along, my mind refused to accept the gravity of the situation. Instead, I whiled away these "sick" hours thinking about how I'd decorate my dorm room, and what classes I would take. Finally, it got bad enough that it was decided to do the tracheostomy. Within a week I was going to my first class. To me it seemed natural. It was what I'd planned all along. I was feeling much better, the oxygen with the respirator at night left me quite healthy during the day, and I was doing what I wanted to do.

In a number of ways, this incident is typical of my outlook as I have grown up. First, it shows how I have generally dealt with adversity: I ignore it. I refuse to accept it. I do not think of myself as a disabled person. While this has helped me thus far, it may not continue to do so. Out there in the nonacademic "real" world, disabled people, like any minority group, have to organize and vocally assert their rights. I have always shied away from doing this. For one thing, my relatively privileged family background has to a large extent smoothed my path. I have not had to advocate strongly for myself because money and my father's position as a doctor have advocated for me. Besides that, though, I simply do not want to be labeled. I take no particular "pride" in being disabled, even though I have as much reason to do so as any disabled person. It all comes back to that nagging problem—how can I earn praise and self-esteem without having my disability in the equation?

But as I inch toward a career, perhaps in journalism, certainly in some kind of media, I am finding that I will have to fight society's tendency to view me primarily in terms of my disability. In my chosen field, there is a tendency to pigeonhole people. Blacks report on race issues. Women report on feminism. I don't really want to be a writer or producer of columns or programs about disability. I understand that people see me as a useful tool—articulate, intelligent, and poised disabled people are hard to come by because so many of them have social disabilities that come with their physical problems. Some would say that it is my duty to serve society in the most natural way possible to me, to become an advocate for disabled people. While I accept the logic and morality of this, I simply don't want that!

In addition to calling my attention to this desire in me to be seen in my own terms, my near-death episode also made me more aware than I had ever been before of how important my relationship with my brother is. He was 14 when I was born, and I am pretty sure that he got short shrift because of the all-consuming problems of my infancy. Although he may harbor some resentment toward me, he also has a devotion to me that I always find surprising. Most importantly, he has supported and challenged me consistently throughout my life—from the time he set out to teach me to get up after falling down, to the times he questioned my opinions and forced me to take steps toward independence and maturity that I was unwilling to take. While others let me grow up somewhat spoiled and lazy, he insisted that there was no reason why I couldn't do dishes or cook dinners. During my years at college, the longest time I have ever lived near him, my brother has had a major role in helping me grow up.

By far the richest time in my life has been my four years in college. The intellectual benefits have been enormous, not so much in the amount of stuff I have learned, but in the atmosphere. My college and I were peculiar matches. Traditionally a very athletic campus, it nevertheless fits my personality in that its students have tended to opt for a kind of athleticism that emphasizes the enjoyment of the sport over outright achievement. I, too, get most of my enjoyment out of activities that have no intrinsic value, no tabulation of results.

Socially, college would have been a waste for me had it not been for my fraternity. It is a cliché that fraternity members learn as well as party in the frat, but it really is true in my case. Of course, mine was an atypical one; for 15 years coeducational, it has for an even longer time been a contradiction, a fraternity for nonjoiners. Because some of the members had the courage to invite me to rush in the spring of my freshman year, I was able to live for two full years in a house with 18 men and women who considered themselves a true family. We cooked together, studied together, and fought with each other over how to take care of our family and the structure that housed it. Because I lived with these people, they had plenty of time to get to know me.

Far from shutting me up in a closed community, my fraternity experience gave me the confidence to branch out and become better acquainted with others on campus. When people met me, I was identified with my newspaper column and with my fraternity. Thus, I was more than just a disabled student; I had other identities to start me off. I used them as a launching pad from which to make other people understand who I was in a deeper way.

Before writing this meditation on my adolescence, I was asked, among other things, "What makes you want to get up in the morning?" I think that my first answer would be, "Whatever it is I have to do on that particular day." This illustrates an important tendency of mine. All my life I have done what's been put in front of me to do. Kids go to school, so I went to school. After that, in my family, you go to college, so I went to college. After college, you either get a job or continue your education, so I will attend graduate school. I pay my bills. I do my reading. I grade papers. I cope. I get along. At the same time, however, I am motivated by a need for approval from others.

Some aspects of adolescence are harder to cope with than others. I often wonder what is to become of my sexuality—I cannot envision (except in erotic dreams) a time when a woman would find me attractive enough to spark a long-term love relationship. I have read of other people far more disabled than I am who have found both love and sex with compatible, willing partners. Yet, a paraplegic is, if immobile, still normal in appearance. I am not. I am short, my back curves severely, and because of my rapid metabolism and restricted abdominal cavity, I am skinny to the point of being emaciated. I have had many female friends, but what could possibly provoke them to see me and be sexually attracted to me?

I have tried on two occasions to move closer to two different female friends. In both cases, this consisted of my acting as comforter and patient listener in time of crisis or stress. On both occasions, they appreciated it and the friendships deepened. But in both cases, I suspect, they had no idea that I had any other motive than a friend's concern. And in each instance, I felt like a beast, because I knew that I had ulterior motives. I know something of the dangers of a male–female relationship based on the weak and emotionally distressed woman and the strong "I'll take care of you" man, and I have no desire to become a "codependent"—with or without sex.

I look at the future of my sexuality, and I see a 35-year-old with the sexuality of a 14-year-old. In this area, I am likely to be forever an awkward adolescent—and the prospect does not please me. At the same time, I hope that the sense of humor, the curiosity, and the weightlessness of carefree adolescence can be preserved, to some extent. I look around me and see many people in both journalism and cultural studies who seem to have retained these characteristics. Perhaps I can, too. I hope, finally, that I do not ever really grow up.

In sum, I have come a long way. Because of me and those who have supported me, I have accomplished many things and done a lot of growing up. I am still an adolescent, though. Only an adolescent has the audacity to hope for what I hope for, which is—everything.

DAVID: THIRTEEN
YEARS LATER

Everyone likes to think of themselves as unique. Nobody likes to admit that they are subject to "textbook" psychology, the courses of their lives determined by recognized trends and phases. Reading what I wrote 13 years ago, I am struck by how typical I was and how predictable the changes in my life—and lack of changes—since then have been. My disabilities and life history may make me seem different to others, but I know just how common my life experiences have been. This doesn't bother me; in a way, it's even comforting.

In some ways, 13 years ago, I was at the tail end of adolescence. I had graduated from college and was halfway through graduate school. I had lived on my own for almost five years. I had distinct interests and a good idea of where my talent lay and had a coherent worldview. I knew (or thought I knew) who I was, what kind of person I was.

Looking back I realize that I was actually in the deep end of adolescence, and that I'm only now really leaving that period behind me. I was still very dependent on my parents, not physically, but emotionally and philosophically. I had little "real-world" work experience, and no real leadership experience. I had no sexual experience at all, at least none that involved other people. I had no strong, deep relationships with anyone, platonic or otherwise. I was like what has been called a "functional alcoholic," a person with a definite drinking problem, but one that doesn't interfere with most everyday life activities.

Yet I was a mess. Parts of me were fully developed, but others woefully underdeveloped. I didn't realize it, in fact, because my deficits didn't prevent me from living a seemingly normal life. I was happy and was either unaware of my problems or, because they hadn't caused anything bad to happen, figured they weren't anything to worry about. Remember my tendency to ignore my medical problems, and therefore be able to survive them? I think that the same held true for my emotional and developmental problems: I felt okay. People seemed to think I was okay, so, I thought, "If it ain't broke, don't fix it."

Before I get into these deeper, more troubling matters, I need to make a list of the ways I have changed in 13 years:

1. Thirteen years ago, I thought of myself as a politically radical, or at least a lefty dissenter. Today I am still left of center, but in other ways I am quite conservative, and think maybe I always have been. Growing up during the Reagan administration, I assumed that authority was always wrong, possibly corrupt, definitely stupid. I figured that I'd carry this attitude through all of my life, like my parents, who were never satisfied no matter who was running the country. During the Clinton administration, however, I discovered how restful it could be to sit back and be comfortable with the group in charge. I still enjoyed analyzing and sometimes disagreeing with the finer points of policy, but I quickly got used to feeling that, basically, people in government at all levels were good, smart people who thought mostly like I did about things. If they did stupid things or advocated policies I didn't like, the difference was more like that between Catholics and Episcopalians than between Hindus and Muslims. Lively debate was still possible, but I felt that those in authority and I were heading in the same direction. It was during this time, too, that I began to feel that a lot of what was wrong in the world was due to faulty systems, not faulty people. That's an idea that has played a major part in my professional life, but more about that later.

2. Thirteen years ago, I had rarely, if ever, experienced open hostility or competition from my peers. An Ivy League education is supposed to be "competitive." In my experience it was difficult, but not competitive in the personal sense. Nobody wanted me to fail so that they could prosper. Also, if people disliked me, they kept it to themselves for the most part. I don't know whether this was because my disability made them feel that it would be inappropriate to oppose me, or because I hadn't yet tried any activities that brought me into real conflict with people. The result is that I was totally unprepared emotionally for open interpersonal conflict. Also, I lacked even the most basic skills for competition and conflict—skills that most eight-year-olds acquire after their first few Little League games. I've come some distance since then, but I still avoid conflict, even when it is necessary, and several times I have missed the signs of serious interpersonal conflict until it was too late.

3. My parents separated, my father found another love in his life, and my mother died of cancer. These events had their impact, but that impact has been gradual. Even my mother's illness and death had less impact on me as they occurred than her absence has had in the six years since. I have missed her support and guidance greatly. At the same time, I have been able to make my own way in my hometown in a way that I couldn't have if she were still here. I feel bad saying so, but I know that my mother would understand. She was always the one who wanted more than anyone for me to be my own person. Meanwhile, my relationship with my father has improved in some ways and deteriorated in others. We now relate to each other as adults, and Dad has expressed pride in my accomplishments.

4. After graduate school, I settled in my hometown. I did so because there was a job available there, but my mother, who lived there, and the attractiveness of familiar territory also led me there. I still live there, and probably will for some years to come. While I often think about an alternative career, I have no strong desires to leave my home just for the sake of starting over in a new town.

5.   The most significant change in me over the past 13 years has been the complete turnaround in my attitude toward my disability and toward working in the disability services field. The job offered to me in 1991 was a position at a new nonprofit organization in my hometown, an organization serving people with disabilities, that was governed and staffed primarily by people with disabilities. I had never heard before of such an organization. Philosophically, it rejected most of the negatives I had come to associate with disabilities: pity, charity, narrow group self-interest, paternalism, and segregation. Instead, this organization was a practical service and advocacy offshoot of the disability rights movement—another thing I knew nothing about even though I had lived with a disability all of my life. I started off doing publicity work for the organization, which wasn't so far from what I thought my career path in writing and media would be. I figured I would spend a year or two gaining work experience, while attempting to do some writing for our local newspaper. I never did write for the paper, not counting letters to the editor and editorials on behalf of the organization for which I worked. One reason was that I didn't have the energy and motivation to pursue journalism while holding down a full-time job. The other reason was that, in the disability rights movement, I found an approach to disability that fits my personality and a mission I am uniquely qualified to serve.

The disability rights movement fits my personality in that it approaches individuals' problems by seeing systemic problems that are at their root. My organization not only helps individuals with disabilities deal with their specific concerns, we also identify ways in which the structures, policies, and practices of ordinary society make life more difficult for people with disabilities. For instance, we typically help an individual with disabilities deal with architectural barriers in a workplace, but we also work to remove such barriers wherever we find them. The disability rights movement has its roots in 1960s activism and political engagement. In other words, it views disability in the same way I view pretty much everything.

Most important, we work in this field not because we feel sorry for people with disabilities, but because we *are* people with disabilities, and because it is just. Previously, I avoided association with any kind of "disability community" because the only ways I'd seen such associations was in the context of charity, and that disgusted me. It also prevented me from truly seeing how my disability gives me a kinship and solidarity with others who have a disability. In a way, I denied myself an important source of support and pride. By working within the field as I do, I have reclaimed my membership in an exciting and vibrant community, rather than joined a sad and depressing begging crew.

The most important qualification for working in the disability rights movement is having a disability. I also bring a superior education and an analytical mind to the movement. I find that I am able to conceptualize disability issues in the abstract, while also emotionally connecting with them. There are many who can do one or the other, but relatively few who can do both. This transforms my choice to work in the field from a mere preference or convenience into a sort of mission. It also led to my taking on local leadership in the movement. I am now the executive director of the organization I joined in 1991.

One thing that hasn't changed in me is my wish to do something with my life that is both personally satisfying and useful. Finding and joining the disability rights movement has been the single most positive development in my life over the last 13 years.

Although I would have learned more about my strengths and weaknesses no matter what I'd done after graduate school, the fact is that the work I have chosen has brought both my strengths and weaknesses into much sharper focus. I have already mentioned the strengths I have discovered. However, the weaknesses I have discovered may be more important in the long run.

In my original reflection, I wrote about not being sure where I stood in other people's eyes because I felt that they might be taking my disability into account when assessing my personality or performance. I implied that I didn't want or like unearned praise and admiration. I have since discovered that, even though I don't agree with it intellectually, I have become used to people "cutting me some slack," most likely because of my disability. I believe this caused me to be too dependent on being liked, which has led to some of the more serious problems I have had in my working life.

When the executive director's position opened up, I applied for it. As I've said, I was probably the logical choice, based on my resumé, life experience, and ability to understand disability issues. However, in retrospect, I see that I was really not prepared for leadership and supervision. I had no previous experience of either and understood them only in the simplest terms. There were one or two people in the organization who, I think, knew this better than I did, and once I became director, they made it known in subtle ways that they didn't have much confidence in my abilities. Of course, this was a shock to me. It was the first time I had ever experienced real opposition—not to an idea or opinion, but to my actual abilities and personality. A vicious circle developed in which I was afraid to confront this opposition, which confirmed my weakness and encouraged bad behavior on the part of employees, which I failed to deal with because of my fear of being disliked and creating conflict, and on and on.

Finally, after several years of alternating bad times and good times, I have begun to get a handle on leadership. The biggest hurdle was finding out that if someone doesn't like me or is angry with me, the world doesn't end. My life doesn't collapse. At one point, I even discovered that two of my employees were complaining to the Board of Directors about my "inconsistency." I can't blame them, because, as I've said, I tended to let people get away with things I shouldn't have. This meant that less contentious employees often got better treatment than hard workers. Unfortunately, it took staff plotting and Board intervention to get me to face up to this and other related problems.

Gradually, though, I have changed the way I do my work and the way I relate to people, including those at work. I am more willing to confront people when needed. I procrastinate less. I have learned how to accommodate individuals' needs and strengths, while also holding them to a fair standard of performance.

The best thing about this experience, however, is that it has made me stronger. I always understood the idea that adversity makes you stronger, but never really believed it to be true. I had survived a lot of physical and medical adversity and didn't see myself as being especially strong. Now that I have experienced the much more difficult forms of adversity found in the workplace and between people, I realize what adversity really is—and that I can survive it. As I said before, the world didn't end just because I screwed up, and this has given me the confidence I need to change myself in ways that will actually improve my performance. So I guess you could say that I had to fail in order to learn how to succeed.

With all of this going on, it's a good thing that I am usually able to put it all aside and enjoy my free time at home.

I still don't feel completely comfortable saying that I like to watch television, but it happens to be true. I don't apologize for it, but I'm certainly aware of the image it presents: a lonely guy letting his mind rot by watching the "idiot box" every night. For me, though, television is not a passive medium. I've always "read" TV. That is, I process it the way serious readers read books. Maybe a better comparison would be to say that I watch TV the way Roger Ebert watches movies. Even the worst shows say something, and I'm interested in what TV shows say. It is both a relaxation and an intellectual exercise.

Music is one of the few things that instantly reaches me emotionally. It is also one of the areas of my life where I don't mind saying I'm still an adolescent. If anything, I prefer today's music to the music I grew up with. My tastes are fairly broad. I like any genre of music if it is performed with passion and animated with ideas. The ideas don't have to be intellectually sophisticated or even admirable, but if I feel that something genuine is being communicated, then the quality of the musicianship or the sophistication of the composition isn't important to me. Music may be the only form of expression that I enjoy on a completely gut level.

My other spare time obsession is my website and weblog or "blog." I taught myself some of the basics of website design and, using blog software, created my own site on the Internet, which I add to several times a week. The blog has turned into the diary I always told myself I should keep, but never did. It's almost three years old now, and looking through the archives, I'm amazed at how much I have written in small, unconnected nuggets, peppered with Web links to news stories, books, music, and other strange things I'm thinking or reading about. I don't get very personal with the blog, which probably makes it less interesting. I guess it's an indication that I am still too shy to share much of my inner self with the world, even though I'm pretty sure only a handful of people ever visit my site. Still, it's fun, and it will be easy to switch to more personal observations and thoughts if I ever resolve to do so.

I often spend hours working to make a single page on my site look the way I want it, but have to force myself to do the more difficult tasks. I know the professional work I do is more important than playing with my website. It helps real people live better lives. It improves my community. It's something I can do that most other people can't. My current work also has the advantage of being the status quo: As difficult as the road ahead may be, at least it's a familiar road. In addition, the idea of doing something for a living that I do for pleasure is very attractive to me.

Lately I've been thinking about picking up my old idea of writing for the local paper. Since I like to watch TV and to write short pieces (as in my blog), I'd like to try to write a television review column. One of the benefits of living in a small city is that it may not be that difficult to achieve. I wouldn't do it for the money or recognition, but as a way to find out if I can combine my two greatest pleasures into something like a job. I like what I'm doing now, but part of me is restless to try something new, something different, something less safe.

I wish I could say that I've solved all of the "intimacy" issues hinted at and referred to directly in my original essay. While I don't feel that I am still an "awkward adolescent," in regard to sexuality and deep interpersonal relationships, I haven't made much progress. Sometimes I feel that I missed out on a window of opportunity—a time when other life concerns were relatively minor and allowed space to pursue relationships. As a professional, and a single adult among adults with families and careers, I find few opportunities to explore relationships I should have explored when I was younger. I just don't have the time, and neither do most of my peers. Add to that the same old barriers, most of them in my mind, having to do with my disabilities, and I find myself still alone.

For the moment, I'm at peace with that. I have good friends—some of them coworkers, others people I have met through other associations, and still others people I have maintained contact with since college. There are people I can share my ideas and feelings with. It's of little importance to me that I'm not married, that I don't have kids. I miss the intimacy and strong devotion that these bring to my peers. However, I also know peers who, like me, have built their lives of other elements. In fact, I have lived as I do for so long now that I find it hard to imagine any other kind of life. That in itself may be the greatest barrier to forming deeper relationships. Cut through all the noble-sounding words, and it all boils down to what sounds like a sitcom cliché: I'm "afraid of commitment." Whatever. I'm certainly not going to go on some great self-conscious quest for love, connection, commitment. I can't think of any endeavor so dismal and boring. Either another cycle of my life will come about when new opportunities arise, or it won't. I'm keeping my eyes and ears open, but I'm not "holding my breath" for it, as the saying goes.

I'm finally finishing up this adolescence thing. It was delayed. Thirteen years ago, I was just beginning it when I thought I was finishing it. There are still more things to learn, more experiences I haven't had. It's possible that parts of me will always be 19 or 20 years old. I think I can live with that, and happily. On the other hand, I thought 13 years ago that I knew what my life was going to be like and have since been surprised in many ways. Thirteen years from now, will I be satisfied with my life? I don't know. But I'm pretty sure that whatever happens, I'll be a better person then than now, just as I think I am a better person now than I was 13 years ago.

PROUD OF THE STRENGTH I HAD

This writer describes her experience of teenage pregnancy and how she copes with its effects on her emotional and social development. Without the support of her former boyfriend or the knowledge of her parents, Connie decides alone to have an out-of-state abortion soon after her high school graduation. She shares her struggle to find meaning in her actions and to redefine her own identity. In college, Connie finds support from a campus women's group that helps her make sense of her experience and understand herself better. She begins to examine her family life and the impact of those relationships on her feelings about men and the coping styles she has developed. Connie also comes to acknowledge her own strength and courage in dealing with this extremely difficult adolescent experience.

It was a week or so after high school graduation. The air was musty and the cement floor was cold. I played nervously with the phone cord and traced its path to the door with my eyes. The garage was the safest place, but I prayed that no one could hear me. It's funny how you suddenly believe in God when you think something bad might happen.

The woman on the other end of the line finally found my records. "Let's see," she said, "Oh yes, your test came out positive!" She sounded excited. I wasn't. I almost dropped the phone. My stomach felt like lead. I couldn't believe her.

"Are you sure?" I barely managed to utter. "Yes, isn't that what you wanted to hear?" Was she stupid? She had to look up my name for the results, didn't she know I was only 17?

"No," I said. She gave me the name of some abortion clinics, and I hung up the phone.

On August 18th I had an abortion. In September I left for college. My grades were never affected; in fact, I got a 4.0 my first semester. Studying kept me from thinking too much. Six months after my abortion, I saw a sign for a support group for women who had had abortions. I knew that I needed to go. Shaking, I called the number, and they told me where and when it would be.

In this group I began to let out some of the feelings that I had kept bottled up for months. Listening to the other women taught me that I was not alone, although many told stories and expressed feelings that were different from my own. Sometimes I left the group aching with the pain I felt from reclaiming all those feelings I'd pushed to the back of my mind. Other times I was amazed at how well I connected with these women, how much I learned from them, and how much I looked forward to this meeting every week. In the journal I kept, things came out on paper that I never could have said aloud.

MARCH

My boyfriend and I had just broken up when I found out. He wouldn't even speak to me so that I could tell him, but eventually I cornered him. He didn't care, and he didn't want to help. All he could say was, "Jesus Christ, are you sure?" I reminded him that it was his problem too, and he said he would give me the money, but he wouldn't go with me. He assumed, as I did, that I would have an abortion. My Mom would hate me for it. She had always condemned abortion, saying that it was killing a baby. Maybe it is; maybe I did.

After a few phone calls, I found out that you have to be 18 to get an abortion in my state without parental consent. I was just four months too young. Eventually I made an appointment with a clinic in a nearby state. The woman I spoke to was very supportive, but I had to figure out how I would get there. A week went by before I asked a friend to take me. Then a few more weeks of wishing I could tell someone and trying to hide the hurt and tears. I guess I did a good job, because no one noticed. The worst part was when I saw my half-brother, an adorable three-month-old. I couldn't hold him or look at him without thinking that I might as well be killing him.

APRIL

I live constantly in two worlds. One is where I can talk or write about it and show my real emotion—when I'm alone and cry, when I'm with the few friends who know, or when I'm with the support group, the only people who really understand. The other world is all the other times. Then I have to pretend that I am okay. I have to conceal my feelings. If someone reminds me, I can't share the hurt inside. Nor can I when some guy makes a joke or comment about a girl who had an abortion, when Amy eats a peanut butter and banana sandwich and Jean asks if she's pregnant, or when everyone giggles at the jokes, even me, but they don't know what's going on in my head. The pain is when there is an editorial in the paper about abortion, and Mary says, "My friend at home had one—I'll never forgive her. She could have given it up for adoption; I was adopted." If only she knew. The pain is when I walk by a poster advocating reproductive rights that someone has scribbled "Fetus-Bashers" on in red magic marker. I want to scream at the persons who did it, but they aren't there. I want to rip the poster down, but I don't. I want to tell the person I'm walking with how upset I am, but she won't understand.

MAY

Mom,

I know you'd hate me if you knew. To you it's disgusting, it's killing. I'll never be able to tell you. Maybe I'm hurting myself or our relationship by not telling you. I would have liked your support. I needed your help, but I couldn't tell you, and I still can't. I never wanted to hurt you.

    Sometimes I wish you had guessed somehow. But you would have wanted me to have the baby; you wouldn't have let me make my own decision. Maybe it was a bad thing to do, maybe it wasn't the "right" thing to do. But I don't want a baby, and I don't want to give birth to one only to give it away. I wanted to go to school and learn and have fun, not be trapped in my own body for nine months. I didn't want to be stared at by mothers who warn their teenager at their side: "She can't be more than 16; I hope you never do a stupid thing like that!" I didn't want my sisters to be ashamed of me. I didn't want my friends and teachers to think I was a bad person. Because as we all know, girls who have sex are bad, and girls who get pregnant are stupid.

When I read these journals over again, I remember feeling so isolated and scared that everyone would hate me if they knew. When I did start telling people, I felt terrified of what they might think or say. But the more people I told, the less it hurt to retell and the more confident I felt that I was right. The decision I made was a good one, and it was mine to make. I felt proud of the strength that I had to make it through this crisis on my own and stick to what I really wanted to do.

Experiencing for myself the inaccessibility of abortion for teenagers and going to the support group both pushed me to explore feminism and identify with it. I joined a pro-choice group on campus, went to protests against Operation Rescue, and wrote an article for a women's newspaper. I told my closest friends and even some not so close. My experience with abortion was becoming an integrated part of my life. But I also felt disillusioned by "the feminist movement." The political group I joined talked about "rights," and I didn't feel comfortable talking about my abortion, or talking at all, for that matter. It was hard for me to talk about abortion without including my own experiences. But I continued going because I had to make sure that abortion didn't become illegal, or in my case, more illegal. Being involved politically made me feel like maybe I could make a difference.

The pro-choice group organized rides to Boston for the protest against Operation Rescue, which was trying to close down clinics there. I rode down the night before with Sarah, another woman in the group, and we stayed at my dad's house. I don't remember when exactly I met her, or if we knew before that ride that we'd both had abortions, but for two and a half hours, we talked about our experiences. It was amazing how close I felt to her; she made me feel even stronger. We found that we both felt alienated from the political group, and we talked about it a lot. She told me that she was in the support group that I had been in the semester before. I realized how much I missed talking about my abortion with women who understood.

It was an emotional weekend and maybe one of the best ones in my life. Talking with Sarah and being with her at the protest made it seem that much more important to me. I felt so good and real and so passionately involved. This was something I believed in like I never believed in something before. It was an incredible feeling facing, inches away from me, the people who believed I was a murderer and wanted to take away my right to control my own body.

After the protest, I saw little of Sarah outside the pro-choice meetings until a later semester. She called and asked if I wanted to help her start a support group, or what we later decided to call a consciousness-raising group, for women who had had abortions. We both missed and needed those discussions. We put signs up and met the people who answered in a café on campus. Soon we were a group of eight, and the first night we met, I found myself in tears, realizing how much I still needed to talk about it and how much was still left unresolved. I wanted to piece my life together. Why had all this happened to me? Can I go on hiding it from other people, from my family? At the fourth meeting, I decided to tell my whole story. I didn't just talk about my abortion, I talked about my whole life. I was trying to make sense of it all. I began to identify some reasons behind my getting pregnant. One was my family. I told the group; "No one ever talked about anything in my family. My dad left when I was 13 and my mom told us not to tell anyone. My twin sister and I never said a word to each other about it. When my dad told us he was leaving, we cried. Actually she cried, I didn't. I went upstairs to my room and closed the door. And that was the end of it, no one ever talked about it again."

The second explanation that I alluded to was my early sexual relationships with men. I described myself during that time as very insecure: "In school I wanted desperately to be liked, and boys actually seemed to like me. When some guy asked me out, I couldn't believe it. I'd say yes. I didn't know what else to say, even if I didn't like him. I dated a few guys, and each time one of us got scared off and then avoided each other. Then Rick asked me out." I had difficulty talking about him even with this group of women. I tried to describe him and our relationship. "God, I don't know why I ever went out with him. He was…so awful. And we had a nine-month 'relationship.' After the first month, I just wanted to break up with him, but I couldn't do it. I didn't want to hurt his feelings, and I was afraid of what he'd do. He was always trying to get me to sleep with him. I was only 15. He ended up basically raping me."

Rick said he wanted me to be his girlfriend. There were guys I liked a lot more than him, but no one had asked me out before like that. He was nice and funny and said he loved me. Though I soon found him annoying and pushy, I couldn't break up with him, even after he raped me. I was scared that he might kill himself. I was afraid he might freak out and hurt me. I was attached to him and the attention he gave me. And I didn't even know I had been raped. "I just thought I was a horrible person because I couldn't keep him from touching me. I felt horrible, but I didn't know why. I thought I'd done something wrong. I just cried. I didn't even think of saying anything to anyone; I wouldn't have known what to say. I couldn't believe that I'd just had sex with someone; I couldn't even say the word. My parents never talked about sex either, except my mother's little innuendos about it being bad. So I thought I was the worst person in the world."

I finally broke up with Rick, but I often felt pushed into later sexual experiences as well. I said to the group, "I slept with Chris, too, or he convinced me to sleep with him. That's what it always seemed like. I didn't want to do it, but I would give in. It was always like the guy was trying to convince me and I never really wanted to, but I always would." With Chris, part of me did really want to sleep with him, but I was unsure and I didn't know how to talk about it. I think most of the time I didn't want to because I was afraid of getting pregnant, and I didn't know how to talk about birth control either.

Chris and I broke up when he went to college, partly because he was going away, and partly because I was interested in someone else. I was 16, almost 17, and a senior in high school. Darren was a junior, but I thought he was the greatest. He drank a lot and did some drugs, and I hated both. But for the first time, I really felt comfortable sleeping with someone. To Sarah and the other women I said, "Birth control was just never an issue for us." It was the first time I had admitted it, but it wasn't completely true either. It was an issue, but we never talked about it. I didn't ask him about it, and he didn't ask me about it. It was really strange because I was terrified that I was going to get pregnant. I always thought about it, worried about it, but I couldn't do anything about it.

Although we didn't use contraception, and we didn't talk about it, I thought about it constantly, and I was scared. I even wrote a paper about teenage pregnancy for a psychology class. I remember working on it, thinking, "This could be you, you have to do something about this." I remember having this feeling that I HAD to talk to him about it, but I couldn't. It seemed easier not to say anything and put it out of my mind, to try to forget about it.

At one point I thought I was pregnant, and I told him. He couldn't believe it, and he said something about me being on the Pill. I said, "No, I'm not, where did you get that idea?" But inside I felt relieved that the subject finally came up. He said that he just figured that I must have been, since I never seemed worried about it. It seems almost funny now, but it wasn't then. How could he have thought that all this time, when for me it hurt so much to pretend it wasn't a problem?

It turned out that I wasn't pregnant. He was so happy, and I was relieved. We talked more after all that, we started using condoms "most of the time," and I worried about it less. Then he started to drink more and got more into drugs, and he wanted to be with his friends and not me. He tried to break up with me, but I took a fit. "You can't leave me, Darren," I cried, "I love you, I can't believe you are doing this to me, you said you loved me!" Finally he gave in and said he still did, but he kept away from me and finally he broke it off completely. I was still hurt, but I knew I didn't like the drinking and our disagreements around it, so I didn't argue this time. Two or three weeks later, I worried that I was pregnant again. I tried to call him. He was never home, and his brother once just said, "He doesn't want to talk to you." Finally, I got in touch with him and told him. He just said, "Jesus Christ, I can't believe this!"

My mother is totally anti-abortion. I knew if I said anything to her, I would be having a kid. I only told one of my girlfriends; she was the only person I thought I could trust. I did one of those home pregnancy tests; I hid it behind the books in my bookcase because you have to let it sit for a couple hours. I totally freaked out when I looked at it, and it came out positive. My friend was more clueless about what to do than I was. I turned to another close friend, this time a guy. I asked him to drive me to the hospital so that I could have a real test done. I didn't tell him why I was going, and he drove me, no questions asked. I was convinced that this test was going to be negative, that the first test was wrong. I was sure of it. The next day the woman on the phone told me it was positive.

Meanwhile I started getting involved with someone else. Todd and I started spending a lot of time together. We weren't going out yet, but we were close. One night I told him about it. He said he'd been through it with a girlfriend, but she turned out not to be pregnant. He said he'd take me for the abortion appointment. I was so relieved. I told my mom and my boss that we were going shopping for the day; Mom even let Todd take her car.

When we got there, he just dropped me off, he didn't come in with me. At the time it was exactly what I expected, but now it seems strange that I didn't want him there for support. It didn't even occur to me to ask him to come in with me. I think I felt that it wasn't his responsibility and it was something I wanted to do on my own. I am still in awe of the idea that I went through this all by myself.

I walked in alone with my $250 check from Darren. I was nervous, but I felt better once I was inside. The woman on the phone warned me that there might be picketers, but no one bothered me. Most of the people in the waiting room had someone with them, but it didn't bother me too much at the time. I was so relieved to actually be there. I started to get scared waiting, but I still couldn't believe that I had made it there and that I was going to be okay.

The first thing they did was counseling, or at least that's what they called it. It's just when they describe the procedure in detail. I went into this room with the counselor and a 30-year-old woman who was there for the same reason but seemed totally relaxed. The counselor started to explain to the two of us exactly what happens with the doctor and the instruments.

Suddenly I was terrified and I started to cry. I couldn't help it. I was scared of how much it would hurt, of what it would be like. The counselor and the other woman were like, "Oh my goodness, what's wrong?" as if there was no reason whatsoever for me to be the least bit upset.

What bothers me about the whole thing is that no one ever talked about it, I mean really talked about it. They were all robots, just doing their job, describing the procedure, taking blood, giving out pills, acting like it was no big deal. It seems like it wouldn't have been so scary if we could have talked about it more. If someone only said, "I've been through it, too. It's okay to be scared, but you will be okay."

Someone sent me to get changed and directed me to the next waiting room. I was there for two hours in my gown. Or maybe it was just an hour, or only 20 minutes, but it seemed like forever. There were around five other women there, and a woman came in to call a name once in a while. The chairs were arranged in a circle around the room. We sat there facing each other, and no one said anything. Everyone seemed scared except the older woman who flipped through a magazine and made comments here and there. But the person who really stuck out in my mind was a girl who looked no older than 13. I felt so terrible for her—she looked so scared. I just wanted to reach out to her, and tell her everything was going to be okay.

Finally, they called my name, and I followed a woman to another room. Another woman was there to talk to me and to hold my hand during the abortion if I wanted to. The doctor said, "So you are going to college in the fall? So what's your major?" I couldn't believe he was asking me about college; I could barely answer, I was so terrified. But I guess it was better than him not saying anything at all. It was so painful. I remember screaming and crying, literally. Afterward I wondered if anyone heard me. They said it would hurt some, but this was the most painful thing I had ever felt. It hurts to think about it.

Afterward I went into a room with other women who were recovering, lying down with blankets and eating slices of oranges and crackers. After about 15 minutes I felt a lot better, so they said I could leave even though you're supposed to stay for longer afterward. I started to get cramps after about 15 minutes driving home. We stopped and bought some pain reliever, but it kept getting worse. They said that cramps were normal, so I didn't really worry about it. I didn't realize how bad it was until the next day when I got up and got ready for work. I was still bleeding heavily. I knew I should call the clinic. According to the information sheet they gave me, I should have called them if this happened. I thought about it, but I knew they'd want me to see a doctor. I don't know if I was more scared that something was wrong with me or that my mother would find out. For three days, I was in agony, and then finally it stopped.

My experience with abortion and the support groups I've involved myself in have allowed me to experience a great level of intimacy with other women that I never felt before. But it also seemed to pull me away from my family. It was something I couldn't go talk to any of them about, something I hid from them. I hate that they can't really understand a part of me. The people I'm closest to don't know my deepest secret, my deepest hurts, and the greatest motivation for some of my interests. Sometimes I feel guilty about not sharing it with them. I'm afraid that one of my sisters may have to go through the same thing one day and she wouldn't tell me either. She would have to deal with the same silence I did. But last year I realized that I hadn't hidden everything from them. One day my

17-year-old sister called me at school. She was scared that she was pregnant and didn't know what to do. Even though she didn't know I'd had an abortion, she knew how I felt about it. She said, "I can't have it. School and field hockey, I just couldn't." I told her it was okay, and she didn't have to do anything she didn't want to do. I told her where she could go for a test and that she could call me anytime she wanted. If she was pregnant, I told her, "I'd know what to do, it's all right." I was scared for her, but I was happy that I could be there for her. It made me feel good that she wouldn't have to go through it alone.

I know I will never tell my mother, and that's okay now, but sometimes it still makes me sad. We are still very close, though. I'm probably closer to her than any of my sisters. We talk a lot about boyfriends (both of ours), school, jobs, and my dad. I know she's not the best listener in the world, but I like to be there for her. Sometimes she really surprises me and gives me good advice, but she has trouble just listening. One of my greatest fears is that she will find out, and it will ruin the relationship we have. I think she'd hate me for a while, and she'd feel guilty, too. I'm sure her love for me would overcome it, but I just don't want to put her or myself through it.

I want to tell my twin sister. It is absolutely bizarre to me that she doesn't know this about me. Although we fight and still compete, we've shared a lot more since we've been at school and I feel pretty close to her. I told her about being raped, and we talked about that often. But I can't seem to tell her about my abortion. I want to. I'm not afraid of what she will think of me anymore because I've had one, but I'm afraid of what she will think of me for not telling her. I'm afraid that she will really freak out. That she wouldn't believe me anymore, or she'd hate me for not telling her. I'm afraid of totally shocking her.

Recently, my mom said to me while looking at an old picture of the four of us kids, "You were always so happy as kids, laughing all the time, having fun." I had a really weird feeling when she said it. I never remember being happy as a kid. Scared of my own shadow might be a better description. I couldn't bear to tell her that; I just nodded and smiled.

I remember all of us kids fighting a lot. I remember my mom yelling a lot. I don't remember my dad being home much. I remember him coming home at 1:00 in the morning. I remember them yelling a lot on weekends. We bought a sailboat, but it was mostly just another place to fight. I remember a teacher who I loved in seventh grade. We wrote in journals in her class. Once I wrote about one of our boat trips, only I left out the bad parts, the fighting. When I got the journal back, she wrote, "Sounds wonderful!" I felt like she liked me and what I wrote, but I also felt horrified. I had a sick feeling in my stomach, like I knew it wasn't true; it wasn't wonderful.

In the autobiography I wrote my senior year in high school, I identified my dad leaving as one of the two events that had the greatest effect on me (the other was being a twin). The hurt was fresher then, and I was angry and jealous. Those feelings certainly haven't gone away, they just aren't so strong. Then it seemed I wanted so badly to believe that my family was perfect before the day he destroyed it all and left. Now I tend to think of the bad times, all of the fights, and I can't remember the good stuff. Now I see that something was very wrong with my family before he left. No one communicated, but everyone fought. I guess my dad just wasn't happy, and he spent less time at home and more at work, and then my mom became unhappy. Or maybe it was the other way around. I don't know how it really happened or whose fault it really was.

To me then it was all my dad's fault; he did everything that hurt me. But sometimes I think my mother's reactions, as well as our own, made things worse for us. No one in the house talked about it, except my mom, who was an emotional wreck. She'd try to pry information out of us after we'd been to my dad's. She told us, begged us, to ask him to come home and to tell him that we loved him. She said he'd come if we did. We couldn't tell him how much it was hurting us; we just went to see him and tried to be "good." But mom telling me this made me feel even more like it was all our fault. She also told us not to tell our friends; she didn't want anyone to know. Until we moved two years later, I told my friends he was on a business trip when they came over.

I don't blame my mother for any of these things, even though they hurt me. I feel thankful that she survived and didn't just give up. As for my dad, I try to see him as much as I can. We can have fun together, but I feel like he can't ever be there for me emotionally. It still makes me sad. For the most part, I'm not bitter anymore. But he still tries to get away with giving my mother as little money as possible, and he pays almost nothing toward our college bills. Though they've been divorced for years, the hurt still seems to drag on. Mom still makes comments about his wife and kid. I understand her hurt, but I'm still caught in the middle.

I have tried here to explain my inability to deal appropriately with sexual relationships as being the result of my not having been able to talk about sex and contraception. The feelings from the beginnings of my adolescent sexuality were of being scared, not having control, and not having a choice. I now know that this is related to having grown up in a family that stuffed their feelings and never talked about anything, including sex. My family always avoided subjects that were upsetting, embarrassing, or controversial. So when it came to talking about contraception with my boyfriend, I had no basis to deal with it and felt it was beyond my control. My way of coping with the inevitable crisis of a pregnancy was not to practice contraception, but to put it out of my mind. That was easy; I had practiced that all my life.

SEEKING THE BEST
OF BOTH WORLDS

This is the story of a harrowing emigration from Vietnam to the United States as part of the "boat people" crisis after the war. The author describes his struggle both to be a good son to his very traditional mother and to find a means to belong and succeed in the culture to which his family fled. As he enters adolescence, he begins to feel that his mother's many troubles and unbending ways are harming both him and his siblings. When he discovers that his stepfather is abusing his younger brother and that his mother will not intercede, he experiences a turmoil of shame, guilt, and powerlessness.

His mother's insistence on traditional child rearing forces him to live a double life as an increasingly "Americanized" teenager on the outside while playing the role of dutiful son at home in spite of numbing sadness and over- whelming rage toward his mother. Eventually, it is his success in the world outside his family that allows him to gain his mother's respect and thereby influence how she raises his younger siblings.

"Con không biết ma. đã trở qua bao nhiêu là nỗi khỗ để đem con qua nước Mỹ nay—You don't know how much I went through to bring you to this country," my mother said in a soft voice as she lay staring at the ceiling. A continuous stream of tears flowed from the outer corner of her eye down into her pillow. At times like this, I would sit next to my mother on our torn carpet while she recounted the tragedies that had happened to her in her previous life of misery, the life she left behind in Vietnam. My older sister Chau, on the other hand, could never stand to listen to our mother's repetitions. She would usually brush her teeth and go to bed or go to our other bedroom, close the door, and delve into the imaginary world of her romance novels. I remember praying at the start of the episodes that I wouldn't end up crying myself (because my mother instilled in me her belief that *"nam nhi đại trúóng phu đỗ máu không rói lệ*—real heroes never show tears even if they are

bleeding to death") as these painful stories entered my mind. However, no gods or spirits answered my prayers, and after each occurrence I would feel low and unmanly because I had let tears fall even though I wasn't bleeding to death.

"*Dạ mạ*—Yes, Mom (respectfully)," I said. In Vietnamese, a child must always acknowledge his or her parent with a polite "*Dạ*" (pronounced "ya"). It matters not that the parent did not ask the child a question; any less respectful response could very well lead to a beating! I learned this lesson soon after I learned how to talk (being polite was much better than being hit).

"When I was your age living in my village, I never had a full meal to eat," my mother continued. "Most days we would only be given one small bowl of rice and a dab of fish paste for flavor. I wasn't as lucky as you are today. I could never eat meat every day like you can." As far as I can remember, my mother would, without exception, start her stories by establishing that her youth was utterly miserable compared to my life of luxury. To this day, I still am not sure whether by stating this she merely wanted me to feel grateful that I had enough food to eat or whether she was actually pitying herself as she realized the vast contrast between her childhood and mine.

"I was cruelly beaten daily by your grandmother and often for no good reason. She had fourteen children, but I was the only one who ever got punished. I don't know why. She'd beat me if I didn't fetch enough firewood for cooking. Or if I didn't cut up enough food to feed the pigs. Or if I stopped fanning her during those scorching summer days because my hands felt like jello." As my mother went on, at this point in her talk I would have a difficult time understanding her because her nose was plugged up from crying so much. Sometimes I tried to pay closer attention so that I could catch everything she said; other times I would not bother since I more or less knew by heart all that she wanted to say.

"The worst period in my life was after I married your father. I had just given birth to your sister when your father disappeared without a trace. I tracked him down finally in Hanoi. I found that he was living with his first wife, a woman that he never told me about. I was more than shocked that the man I loved and trusted lied to me."

After hearing my mother describe my father's deceit, I simultaneously felt resentment, sympathy, guilt, vengefulness, incredible sadness, and, oddly, joy. I resented and even hated my father for ruining my mother's life. The anger I felt inside was so overwhelming that I would often tremble while gasping for air. Sometimes I sat there and wished that he were standing right in front of me so that I could pick him up by the throat and slam him against the wall as hard as I could. I'd scream at him, "You damn asshole! How could you treat your wife like that? Don't you have a conscience? Is this the model that you want your children to follow? I am ashamed to be your son! But don't worry, I won't turn out to be like you, you piece of shit!" At the same time, I felt sympathy for the incredible pain that my mother must have endured since that episode. She did not do anything wrong; her only mistake was falling in love with a lying womanizer. Yet mixed with my negative emotions was a slight ripple of joy. I felt happy to see that my mother was courageous enough to take her children and leave him behind in his poverty-stricken home. I was shamelessly content that he still has to live in filth with his first wife while our family, although poor compared to others in America, has enough to eat everyday.

Throughout my early childhood, occurrences like the one above were commonplace. Almost anything could provoke my mother into telling those stories: seeing happy couples walking together in the park, seeing my sister and me not doing our chores, watching television shows that depicted any aspect of Vietnam, and especially having her children do badly in school (i.e., not getting straight As). Those nights I would cry myself to sleep thinking of how much I should hate my father and how much I should love and respect my mother. I racked my brains wondering how my father could have consciously treated my mother with such inhumanity. "How could he? How could he?" I hollered silently to myself over and over. "There must be some reason for what he did. My mother must be leaving a lot of details out. I should not listen only to her side of the story." I convinced myself that I could not make final judgments about him until I heard what he had to say. Thus, for years I wondered what his story was.

My first memories are of escaping Vietnam and landing in Hong Kong on the way to our final destination, America. I only remember random scenes of our journey; the rest of what happened my mother has filled in through our conversations over the years. Thus, I have a fairly detailed knowledge of what happened in those few days that drastically altered our lives.

In the spring of 1981, my mother, then fairly wealthy thanks to a prospering business, decided that she wanted to give her two children educational opportunities that her country could not offer. I was only four years old and my sister just six when one ordinary night my mother told us to say good-bye forever to our homeland....

A blinding flash of light snatched me from my restful sleep. Five seconds later, the inevitable boom of thunder crashed on our little boat and sent everyone into a state of panic. When I peered out at the darkness, I saw rushing at us some of the largest waves I'd ever seen.

"*Mạ, con sọ' qúa*—Mommy, I'm so scared," I cried. However, the raindrops on my face camouflaged my tears, and the roaring thunder drowned my attempts to communicate with my mother. I finally caught her attention by pulling on her sleeve as hard as I could.

"*Con đừng sọ' nhe*—Don't be afraid, son," my mother comforted, "It's just a little storm. It'll be over real soon." She covered us with a plastic bag, and we huddled so close that I could feel her heart pounding against my cheek.

"*Chị Hong, Chị Hong*—Sister Hong, Sister Hong," my uncle Oanh approached us from out of nowhere and said in a disconcerting tone, "There's too much weight on this end of the boat. We need more people to move to the bow. If we don't do it fast, the waves'll flip us right over."

"What do you want us to do?" my mother answered calmly.

"You put Phuoc on your back and I'll put Chau on mine. Then we'll slowly walk up there."

"Okay, okay," my mother approved. I did not realize what was happening. All I knew was that I wanted to cling to my mother for dear life. "Phuoc," she spoke directly into my ear because at any other distance the thunder would drown out her voice, "We're moving to the front of the boat. I'm gonna give you a piggyback ride, so you grab on as tight as you can, okay?"

"*Dạ*," I acknowledged and quickly climbed onto her back while the storm blanketed my body with what felt like a thousand pebbles every second. Without thinking, I immediately locked my arms around my mother's neck and grabbed each of my wrists with the opposite hand. Just as instinctively, I wrapped my legs around her waist and also bolted them in place. As we began inching toward our destination just a few meters away, my awareness of the surroundings increased tenfold compared to when I was sitting with my mother. I saw every wave as it crashed on the boat's side, I anticipated the direction of impending thunder, and I felt the blowing raindrops on my skin as if they were needles piercing all parts of my body. Another acute awareness was of my body's position in space. Because I did not budge, it seemed as though I became an extension of my mother's body. When she lifted her left foot to take another step, I felt the entire left half of my frame move accordingly.

"*Gần tới rồi con à*—We're almost there, son," my mother said. "Don't worry." When I looked up, I saw the bow just a few steps away. However, I did not feel as though I could breathe a sigh of relief because a few steps is still a few steps. I kept my tight lock around my mother's neck and waist. It turned out that this choice saved my life, because just then a huge wave slammed into the side of our boat with such force that it threw her off her feet and sent us plunging into the freezing water of the South China Sea. I do not recall feeling scared. When I was under water, instinct made me hold onto my mother as tightly as I could, shut my eyes to avoid the stinging seawater, and close my mouth so that no saltwater entered my system. I do not know why I didn't panic. I just didn't. Fortunately, the two of us avoided staying in the water long enough for hypothermia to set in. My uncle, who was following closely behind us with my sister, dived in after us when he saw us fall.

Following our dramatic rescue, the heavens blessed us with sunshine and peaceful waters. The gods also bestowed another miracle on us. Several days after our departure, just when we had almost depleted all of our food supply, we came across a cargo ship headed in the same direction we wished to go: Hong Kong. A year later in April 1982, my mother realized her dreams of raising us in a land where more opportunities and fewer obstacles lay before us. What my mother did not realize was that she herself would become the major obstacle in her children's future.

Throughout my early adolescence, I wished I had a better, more understanding mother. To this day I still believe that most of my "growing pains" could have been alleviated or missed entirely if my mother had also experienced these same "pains" when she was an adolescent. She did not know how best to assist me through my tough times, because she had no understanding of the cultural and social pressures facing teens growing up in America. She was often insensitive and apathetic when I came to her with an adolescent issue such as schoolmates making fun of me.

Puberty started rather simply for me in the sixth grade; there was no big event that announced its arrival. I remember exactly when I knew that I had entered this period of change. One evening while I was showering, I noticed that I had started growing pubic hair. At first I felt confused. "What's this stuff?" I asked myself. Thinking that it was just dirt or something, I tried rubbing it off. After a few unsuccessful attempts, I realized, "Oh, yeah, this is what my sex education class last year taught us. I'm supposed to start this business at my age. Don't worry about it. It's just puberty." I thought about telling my mother to make sure it *was* just puberty, but after some thought I decided against the idea because these topics were not spoken of in our household. Subjects such as sex, love, human genitalia, and rape were taboo in my family because they were supposedly "impure" things to talk about. We were not to adulterate our minds and hearts by bringing them up in conversation. Consequently, many issues that "normal" families in America talk about were never brought up in our household. This lack of discussion forced me to learn about them from other sources, such as television.

At first I did not think that puberty was going to be the time of tremendous psychological change that the sex education videos at school had depicted. I felt like the same little kid I was before, going to class in the morning, coming home to do homework and watch television in the afternoon, talking to my mother before going to bed, and then repeating this same monotonous routine. The only other difference was that my voice started cracking when I spoke, but that did not bother me because I understood that was a natural part of human development.

Although I was only aware of my physical changes, I was also changing mentally. I remember my sudden self-consciousness, low self-esteem, newfound interest in girls, and awareness of my lack of peer relationships, all of which started in junior high. Now when I look back, it seems that my experience was nothing out of the ordinary for children of that age. Yet my life then had an additional *extra*ordinary factor. The conditions under which I interacted with others my own age were, culturally, American conditions, while at home I confronted a Vietnamese cultural environment. On the one hand, my mother did not understand American culture and disapproved of the American beliefs (such as gender and racial equality, free speech in the family, etc.) that I had adopted. On the other hand, the children at school who were not Vietnamese did not accept the culturally Vietnamese side of me, probably because they saw it as strange and not "normal." (Back then it was a dream of mine just to be normal like everyone else.) I shall illustrate my point with a few examples.

Before the sixth grade, I never thought about how physically different I looked. I knew that I was Vietnamese, but I never felt that I was an outsider in school because of my skin color. When I began adolescence, however, I became acutely aware of my bodily characteristics. In grade school I was your stereotypical skinny, short, brainy Asian kid with a bowl haircut. When kids made fun of me by calling me "chink" or "nerd," I usually never paid any attention to them. This was true until the day I received a disciplinary referral and was sent home. During music class, a Caucasian classmate of mine, Eugene, was getting upset because

Mr. Marmastein told him he was out of tune. The entire class giggled as Eugene squeaked the words to "Yankee Doodle Went to Town." I, being a wiseguy, said loudly, "No more, Eugene, please!" With a frustrated look, Eugene quickly turned to me and yelped, "Shut up, you damn *chink*!" The old me would have just laughed it off without giving it a second thought, but that day a rush of anger swept through me, and I wanted to beat him up right there on the spot. The only thing that restrained me from doing so was my music teacher. I did not want to disrespect him by disrupting the class; I decided to wait till later. When recess time came and we were all let out to the grass field to play kickball, I only had one thing on my mind. As soon as I caught sight of Eugene, I ran over and tackled him onto the ground with all the might that my 80-pound body could conjure up. We wrestled around on the grass throwing blind punches at each other until the recess supervisor pulled us apart and gave us both referrals. The principal sent me home because I was the one who started the fight. Eugene's words somehow triggered a highly reactive area inside me, an area that told me that I was not the same as everyone else, and this made me feel inferior. At the same time, though, the fight made me proud and confident because this time, unlike previous times, I had stood up for myself when others thought I would be weak and passive. However, my raised spirits received a powerful blow from my mother's reaction.

"What? You got in a fight because he said you were Asian? *Sau con ngu qúa vậy*—Why are you so stupid, son?" my mother said, as if she didn't believe that "chink" was a derogatory word. Maybe if I told her again, she would understand.

"But, Mom. That word is racist! He wasn't just saying that I was *Asian*," I repeated. "He had a different meaning."

"Who cares what he meant," she replied. "It's just a word. Those white people are all racist anyway. Next time he says that to you, just ignore him." Ignore him? *What?* How could I do that when Eugene insulted me? And how could my mother say that *all* Caucasians are racist? Didn't the fact that she uttered those words brand *her* a racist? "And they're bigger than you, you know. I don't want you to get hurt again. We're smaller than they are, so we just have to act our size. So next time he makes fun of you, just turn your head and laugh." I did not know how else to persuade her. My mother did not seem to understand that in America, equality is cherished and prejudice is not tolerated. Wasn't that why she decided to risk her life and the lives of her children to come here in the first place? My mother's words directly conflicted with what my teachers had taught me in school all these years. How could I reconcile this? I could not believe what she said nor do as she ordered, because the morals I had acquired in school were too strong. This incident posed yet another problem for me—when should I listen to my mother and when should I not? In the past, she had always taught me how to be a good person, including the dos and don'ts of life and the difference between right and wrong. It was simple—Mother was always right no matter what. Thus, I always listened and took her words to heart. Now that I recognized a flaw in her beliefs, I did not know what to do or who to go to.

Another example of my mother's lack of empathy was how she laughed at me when I told her that other kids made fun of my name. For as long as I can remember, almost everyone I met has mispronounced my name at least twice before getting it right. It was such an embarrassing scene whenever I met anyone new that it made me wish I did not have to meet new people at all. The worst part of it was the name-calling I endured all my life. Through elementary school and beyond high school, my name was the subject of a laundry list of teasings. It may be difficult for others to understand how my name can be so damaging to me psychologically. However, it was not as if I had a name like "Jaime," which everyone pronounced "Himee." People can easily turn my name into vulgar words if they want to (and I believed that everyone around me wanted to). Here are a few of those hurtful teasings: "Fok," "Foo-ok," "Pook," "Fuck," "Phuoc you!," "What the Phuoc!," "MotherPhuocer." In my high school junior yearbook, there is a picture of me playing volleyball (I was on the team). Underneath it the subheading reads, "Phuoc 'U' Nguyen spikes one!" Those kids did not realize that every time they poked fun at me, I wanted to crawl into a cave and not come out until everyone was mature enough to accept my name.

The only person who understood my agony was my sister because she too has an uncommon name, but hers had less potential to be the butt of everyone's jokes than mine. On occasion when she and I went somewhere together, we would temporarily change our names to make the experience a lot more pleasant for ourselves. For instance, when I was a sophomore in high school and Chau was a junior, she wanted me to accompany her to a meeting of students interested in applying to college. She was sure that no one we knew would be there, so we decided to become "normal" for the evening. When the hosts asked us to write our names on those "Hello, my name is…" stickers, we picked random "American" names. As it turned out, we both found it easier to meet people when we weren't feeling self-conscious.

Whenever I told my mother about people making fun of my name, she would usually laugh and say, "Fuck? Ha, ha…sn't that a bad word? Ha, ha…That's kinda funny." At times like those I thought my mother was the most insensitive and uncaring person in the world. How could she sit there and laugh at her son when he had just told her that everyone in school was already laughing at him? Did she think that it would make me feel better if she laughed as well? Of course, I did not voice those questions. Thinking about it now, I believe that my mother's concept of emotional pain was completely different from mine. The physical pain and agony she endured for most of her life in Vietnam was probably 10 times more intolerable than mine. That's probably why she couldn't understand the emotional pain I felt when kids made fun of me.

My mother also hindered my healthy adolescent development by refusing to let me associate with girls. I recall one incident in junior high when a seventh-grade girl wrote me a letter. Minh, a Vietnamese girl who played in the orchestra with me, sent me the first "I like you" letter I ever received; in it she expressed her admiration for me because I was smart and musically talented. Frankly, I did not have the slightest inkling what to think of the situation. No one had ever taught me how to initiate intimate relationships. The guy friends I had at school were all uncool "nerds" like myself who did not have any experience with girls either. I did not even consider asking them for help. I never had an older male role model to turn to with questions; the only older men I was in contact with were my uncles, and they were unlikely candidates because they did not grow up in America.

Asking for my mother's advice about girls would be tantamount to suicide. She always forbade my sister and me to date or see any members of the opposite sex until we were college graduates. One may think that she was just joking—no parent can be that strict, right?—but believe me, she wasn't. She strictly enforced her commands with severe actions. For instance, one day after school when I was waiting for my mother, one of my female acquaintances came up to chat with me. We were talking about how Mrs. Sloboda's world history test was too difficult. But when my mother drove up and saw us standing there together, she thought the subject of our conversation was something less than innocent. She immediately rolled down her window and screamed at the girl, "*Ây, đồ con quỷ sứ kia, mày làm chi với con tao rứa*—Hey, demon, what are you doing with my son?" My friend asked me whether my mother was yelling at her; I told her that she was just telling me to get in the car (this was one of the perks of having a mom who does not speak English). When I stepped into the car, my mother started chastising me for talking to the girl. She did not listen to my explanation and warned me that if she ever saw that scene again, I'd end up in an orphanage. That was the last time I stood next to girls after school.

There I was holding my first love letter in my hand, but I had absolutely no idea what to do with it. I did not understand my role as the male figure: Was I supposed to ask her out first or wait until she made the first move? Should I talk to her just as a friend or try to flirt with her? My mind was filled with confusion at the time. The only places I could think of to turn to for direction were Hong Kong mini-soap operas. These translated productions were usually set in ancient China, where a gentleman was one who followed the Confucian code of conduct and women were innocent and supportive. Honestly, I learned more about relationships from watching those shows than from any other source. They taught me that real men were brave, polite, chivalrous, confident, and independent, while women were caring, sensitive, nurturing, and passive. Of course I am much wiser now, but back then I embraced these ideals. However, even though I knew from those movies how I *should* have acted toward Minh—who I thought was pretty and intelligent—I did not put that knowledge into practice. Instead of initiating any type of conversation, I tried to avoid her. Whenever she walked up to me to talk, I would turn around and walk the other way. Finally, after realizing that I seemed repulsed by her, Minh gave up on me and started seeing someone else. Later on I felt like such an idiot for letting her go. "Why didn't I go for it?" I asked myself repeatedly. "Am I not a guy? She liked me! She really did, and I just let her go." I thought that I did not possess the qualities that a "real" man had, those qualities that the Hong Kong mini-soap operas presented to me. It was not until my last years in high school that I realized what "manly" qualities actually were. It was also then that my self-esteem gradually rose to a level where I was confident enough to look people in the face when I was talking to them. These changes came slowly and originated from an incident that was a milestone in my life. This incident served as the beginning of my long and successful struggle to break free from my mother's emotional influence.

The changes took place shortly after my mother allowed her ex-husband, my stepfather, back into our family. A few months following his return, I learned with horror what kind of man he really was. My half-brother Tai, a vibrant four-year-old, told me that his father liked to pinch and bite him just for fun; he also liked to fondle Tai's genitals for prolonged stretches of time.

Something like this was not easy to accept or deal with, especially for a 14-year-old. I trembled at the realization that this beast of a man, this perverse monster, sexually abused his own son, my innocent brother. And all of this occurred right beneath our unwitting noses for weeks on end. "This cannot continue," I resolved. "I will *not* allow him to hurt my brother any longer!" Never in my life had I been more sure of what the right thing to do was. Although I knew that this could potentially hurt everyone else in my family, particularly my mother, I did not falter for a moment. I was willing to destroy my mother's happiness to protect Tai.

My method of expressing my frustration was to slam doors. Every time I saw my stepfather touching Tai's genitals, I would walk to my room and slam the door behind me. Our home had only two bedrooms, so Tai's father definitely heard and understood my signal. He understood all right, but he did not change, and the abuse persisted. However, my stubborn-headedness kept me from giving up. I wanted to reach a standoff, a sudden-death situation. That day came about two weeks after my initial resolution to fight. Thoughts of me being courageous or honorable never entered my mind; everything I did was by gut instinct.

It was a windy Saturday afternoon, and everyone was at home except for Chau, who was at work. My mother and stepfather were talking in their room while Tai and I played *Civilization* on my computer. All of a sudden Tai's father summoned him to their room. The inevitable happened, and again a rush of rage crashed into my body. I breathed hard as my heartbeat shot up like a bottle rocket. Shoving my chair behind me, I stepped out into the living room and looked into their room as I walked by. The scene did not differ from the ones I had witnessed over the past few weeks. After standing in the living room for a moment, I went to my room taking loud, heavy steps along the way and, upon reaching my destination, slammed my door with as much force as I could conjure up. I did it! My mother had to say *something*. I wanted to confront him that very moment; I wished that deep inside me there was a courage that would manifest itself now by giving Tai's father the hardest punch on the jaw. I waited for them to come in.

"Phuoc, what the hell are you doing!" my mother screamed as she raced over to my room and gave me a slap on the left side of my cheek. I still vividly remember the physical and emotional pain I felt the instant her hand landed on my face. "He's his father, and he can do whatever he wants with him. It's not like he's killing him or anything, he's just playing. And besides, it's none of your business! Now if you don't want to live here anymore, then I can always put you into an orphanage!" I knew then that my mother cared more about her own selfish needs than about the welfare of her younger son. My respect for her started fading behind a curtain of disappointment. What could I do? Everyone around me could not see what I saw, and after trying fruitlessly to expose the truth to them, this was what I received. Fear and alarm overwhelmed me at that moment, and I did not, could not, fight any longer. I had already drained myself of all the fortitude I possessed, and no matter how deep I searched, my well of courage was dry. At that time, fear—the emotion I detested most and the emotion I constantly encountered—took control of my mind. I didn't want to end up in an orphanage, a ward of the state. I didn't want her to put me in a foster home. No. No. I couldn't let that happen. "It was the wind, Mom," I responded innocently. "The wind slammed the door." And that was that. I was tired. I didn't want to feel any more emotions. I just wanted to lie in bed and pretend that none of it had happened.

I had never been more disappointed with my mother in my life; the time she ignored my pleas for new shoes, the time she made fun of my name, could not begin to compare with this. I wished she was not my mother. I wished that I had never been born into this backward family.

Two months later my mother kicked her ex-husband out. Apparently, he emptied her bank account with his gambling habits. While he had been staying with us, he constantly took her money to play cards at the local casino. Eventually, my mother had no money left to pay the bills. This time his leaving was for good, she said. His departure left me with a feeling of relief for my brother because it released him from constant victimization. Yet I knew that what he went through might leave lasting psychological effects.

The problems between my mother and myself did not spontaneously disappear when my stepfather left. I remember not feeling anything at all for her; it was as if my stepfather had taken with him all of my emotions about my mother and left only a void. I did not speak with her for half a year following his separation from us. I constantly asked myself how my mother, whom I regarded so highly—a woman who had risked and sacrificed everything for the sake of her children—could ignore the obvious abuse of her child by her husband. This inner questioning led to my emotional isolation from her. Withdrawing from my mother's world allowed me to step back and reevaluate from a different perspective my perceptions of her and myself. With the help of this new vantage point, I painted a new picture of myself and my relationship with my mother.

"*Thúa mạ con đi học*—(Respectfully) Mother, I am going to school." "*Thúa mạ. con đi học về*—(Respectfully) Mother, I am home from school." These 11 words, which tradition forced me to utter every day, were the only words I remember saying to my mother during those silent six months. How did I do it? What did I feel? What did I use to replace my relationship with my mother?

My first few weeks of silence I attribute to hatred. I loathed being in my mother's presence. When we were together in the same room, I never looked at her face or even positioned my body toward hers. At the dinner table, I swallowed my food without tasting it as fast as I could to shorten the torture of sitting near her. When we had company over and she asked me to come out and greet them, I stayed only long enough for them to see my fake smile before returning to my room. I did not think she deserved to be a mother, thus I did not treat her like one. I regarded her like a distant relative—with respect, but with no warmth or emotion. At night when my mother slept with Tai in her arms, so much anger welled up inside me that one time I released my rage by biting on a pillow with all my strength. "How could she go on like nothing happened?" I asked myself. "How could she not feel guilty?" Those nights I stayed up until two or three in the morning feeling sorry for my brother, furious at my mother, and disappointed in myself. I did not talk to anyone about my problems. Chau had isolated herself from the rest of our family, so she and I did not communicate, and I did not feel close enough to any of my friends at school to share with them my inner emotions. I also felt too ashamed to tell anyone about the unhappy circumstances in my family. Consequently, I existed for weeks like a walking balloon full of negative emotions just waiting to burst when I could no longer contain them. But I did not burst. I needed to appear strong and stolid (like the heroes in the Hong Kong movies). I needed to show my mother and myself that I did not depend on her for my emotions. The way I subdued these feelings is similar to what happens when a chemist immerses a helium-filled balloon into a vat of liquid nitrogen. Like the helium in the balloon, my emotions underwent a condensation into a colder, less active state.

For the remaining months of my silence, hatred and anger no longer played a large role in my reluctance to communicate with my mother. I figured, "Why should I torture myself with all these bad feelings? They don't do any good. I can't go on living so miserably." Convinced that emotions only hurt rather than benefit me, I gradually suppressed them. Soon I replaced those gut-wrenching feelings of guilt, sadness, and animosity with apathy and insensitivity. I no longer felt uncomfortable sitting next to my mother, because I had no feelings for her. Although I still remembered the events that occurred several weeks prior, it ceased to cause pain and anguish. My indifference made it easier for me to sleep at night, increased my ability to concentrate in school, and lifted the midnight clouds that hovered over me. In retrospect, I can understand the attraction of this defense mechanism; it was an easy escape from emotional pain and dependence on my mother. The side effect of my remedy, however, was that I lost the ability to feel other types of emotions as well, such as sympathy, sadness, and joy. I felt like a machine. When I watched inspirational movies, I did not have warm, fuzzy sensations. When I was elected president of the sophomore class, my only reaction was, "Good, this'll look good on my college applications." When my friend Vu made a full recovery after undergoing chemotherapy for lymphatic cancer, I never felt ecstatic, just relieved for him. Now I realize the price of indifference, and I have been trying hard to gain back—with little success—my ability to feel deep emotions.

In the months following my isolation from my mother, I found numerous ways to convince myself that she had absolutely no influence on me and that I had completely and irreversibly broken away from her. I guess this was the rebellious stage of my adolescence. However, I did not rebel in the typical demonstrative fashion, like screaming "I hate you" to my mom or getting drunk. Instead, I rebelled in a passive way so that only *I* knew I rebelled, while everyone, including her, still thought I was the perfect son. One of my defiance strategies was to achieve top grades in my classes without putting in any effort. I cheated in almost every subject. After school, when my mother asked me if I had any homework, I always replied, "No, Mom, I'm already done." She never asked me to show her my completed work because she could not read a word of it. I also started lying a lot to my mother. One time I told her that my friends and I went to the library to study, but actually we drove to San Francisco and spent the day playing volleyball on the beach. I cannot count all the times that I lied to her and she never found out the truth. I felt much satisfaction knowing that I had some control over her; it raised my self-confidence and esteem and felt like sweet revenge for her dominance over me when I was younger. I simply wanted to believe that my mother had no part in my success in both academics and life. Yet I allowed her to continue assuming that I was the model son and that without her I would have been nothing. I figured she deserved at least that much because of the sacrifices she made in bringing me to America and raising me in a strange land.

What did I use to replace my mother's absence from my life? Certainly not other relationships! I found it difficult to make close friendships in high school for several reasons: my school environment, my inability to share feelings (mostly because I had no emotions), and the fact that I thought close friends were unessential for my well-being. The school I attended had the lowest SAT score averages in the country. Fifty percent of the student body was black, while about 90 percent of the faculty was white; the remaining students consisted mainly of Hispanics and Asians, with a few token white students. Almost everyone came from poor households; I once read an article about our school that revealed that over 70 percent of the students' families depended on welfare as their sole source of income. I witnessed gang fights almost every week, mostly between black gangs—the Bloods versus the Crips. But sometimes I also saw some action from the smaller Asian gangs like the Oriental Boyz. The extraordinarily high incidence of violence and drug abuse in my school forced the government to establish a gun- and drug-free zone around the school and the nearby housing complexes. Fortunately, I participated in the school's magnet program, called the Academy of Math, Science, and Engineering, that better prepared me for college. I limited the group of friends I hung out with mainly to other Vietnamese students from the Academy, and I stayed away from most of the black students because I was afraid of being associated with any of the gangs. My friends and I had lunch together, copied homework from one another, and joined the same clubs. However, outside of school we did not go out on a regular basis or call each other to have heart-to-heart conversations. Even when my friends did call me, we never discussed my family problems or feelings, probably because I didn't want to admit that I had any troubles at home. I also never developed strong companionships in high school because I did not feel that I needed them to make me content. I felt satisfied that I had friends to turn to when I wanted to copy homework from someone; other than that I had no burning desire to have best friends.

Relationships with girls also did not fill the void left by my mother's absence. In my high school years, a number of girls wrote me love letters, asked me out to proms, or tried to get to know me, but not once did I take the initiative to pursue a relationship with any of them. Sure, I went to their proms, but I only did it because I did not want to turn them down. It wasn't that I didn't find women attractive or that I didn't want a steady relationship; rather, I think that the combination of my mother's strict rules and a lack of male role models contributed to my nonaggressive behavior. As I stated before, my mother adamantly forbade me to have girlfriends, and although I wanted to establish my independence from her, I still needed to abide by her rules because I was living under her roof. The other reason I wasn't able to tell girls that I liked them was because I didn't know how. No one ever taught me the correct procedures for getting to know women, and what I saw on TV seemed too straightforward for my tastes. My closest male friend in high school, Vu, never had any experience with girls either. Thus, even if I wanted to go out with someone, I did not know how to approach her and ask.

I do not believe anything replaced my relationship with my mother. Her dominant presence simply disappeared as a result of my ability to suppress my emotions. How she felt no longer dictated how I felt. When she cried, I no longer cried; when she laughed, I no longer laughed with her; and when she told her disturbing childhood stories, they no longer affected me emotionally. It may seem heartless, but that was how I felt. I did not need anyone to take her place; what I *did* need, however, was to fill up the free time I had now that I wasn't spending it with my mother. I kept myself busy in high school by joining numerous clubs, volunteering at nursing homes and hospitals, playing on the tennis team, participating in math and science competitions, working, attending Vietnamese school on the weekends, and enrolling in night courses at the closest community college. I occupied my days with so many activities that on a typical day, I would not return home until eight or nine in the evening, and by that time my mother would be in bed.

In other ways, I came to understand my mother at a deeper level. In junior year, I had a history class in which we learned about ancient China; we discussed Confucius's philosophy and how his ideals still permeate East Asian culture. One of the most important aspects of Confucian theory is its emphasis on role-playing in the family and in society. I remember writing a report on Confucian influence on contemporary Vietnamese society and realizing that my family performed the parts that he outlined centuries ago. Observing my family as a source for my essay, I learned that Confucius dictated our lack of verbal and physical affection.

To this day I cannot say "I love you" to my mother, older sister, or younger brother. The only person whom I *do* verbally acknowledge my love for is Carol, my four-year-old half-sister. It may seem strange, but Carol is also the only one that I hug, kiss, or show any other form of affection to. The same is true for my mother, Chau, and Tai—from an outsider's perspective it may seem as though all of us love only Carol. I also hear Chau verbalizing her love for Vinh, her fiancé, and it seems perfectly natural. What would be completely *unnatural* and unprecedented is if she said "I love you" to me, my mother, or my brother.

During elementary school, my mother nurtured and cared for me as if I had just learned how to walk. One of the ways she made me state that I loved her was by asking, "Phuoc, where do you put your love for me?" My rehearsed answer was, "Mom, I put my love for you on my head!" (She considers the head the most important part of the body, so putting my love there meant that it was the most important love.) We kissed and hugged one another all the time and without reservation. By the time I started junior high school, however, we suddenly yet intuitively stopped being physically affectionate. Even though I missed my mother's touch, especially when I witnessed her affection for Carol, I knew that its cessation was appropriate for my age. Thinking back, the start of my adolescence and newfound need to break away from the nest, particularly when kids at school filled my head with the notion that kissing your mom was "sissy" and "gay," influenced the shift in our relationship. A change in my mother's attitude also contributed; she no longer asked me where I put my love for her. Instead, she asked Tai, who was two at the time, this question, which I thought she had reserved just for me. It was as if the game had age limits, and I had already passed them. My mother now expected me to show my love for her by obeying her and bringing home the As. Accordingly, she showed her love by feeding and clothing me.

"*Con không cha nhú nhà không nóc*—Children without a father are like houses without rooftops." My mother never failed to remind me of this Vietnamese proverb whenever she wanted to show off how she had disproved the old saying. She was correct in her claim, because we never grew up with a father, yet our house definitely has a "rooftop." My mother played the roles of breadwinner and caring mother at the same time. She disciplined us while bandaging our wounds, taught us how to ride a bike and then cleaned our scrapes and bruises, and encouraged us to succeed in the real world while wishing we would never leave her side. In December of my last year before entering college, I unwittingly replaced my mother as the rooftop and the foundation of my home.

The news jumped at me out of the blue. "I'm going to Vietnam next month to visit Grandpa and Grandma," was all my mother said. "I'll leave some money for you while I'm gone. I'll be there for a month." She never discussed with me the possibility that I did not want to take care of one-year-old Carol and eight-year-old Tai for an entire month, especially December, when I had so many things to do in my senior year. She never taught me how to cook dinner, potty train Carol, comfort her when she cried, and keep the house clean all in one day. Yet I never raised a single objection to her vacation plans. The only thing I recall telling her while we said good-bye at the airport was, "Have a safe trip, Mom. Don't let anyone con you over there, okay? Let me know when you want me to pick you up." For the next 31 days I enrolled in a crash course in parenting in which the teacher and student were one—me.

The most difficult part of the day came after Tai got home from school. During those few hours before bedtime, I ran around my two-bedroom home like a madman in nerve-racking attempts to prevent my hyperactive sister from hurting herself while also trying to complete multiple tasks. Within a two-hour stretch, I made dinner, did the laundry, mopped the floors, took out the garbage, changed Carol's diaper when I forgot to remind her about the mini-toilet, helped Tai with his fractions and long division, answered phone calls from friends seeking advice on how to fill out college applications, and played with Carol to keep her from wrecking the floors I had just mopped!

Every night I longed for nine o'clock to come around so that I could put the two children to sleep and actually attend to my own affairs. This was the time during my senior year when the college application deadlines loomed. In addition to completing seven or eight college applications, I worked on finishing nearly a dozen scholarship applications, all of which kept me up late every night. Luckily, I did not have trouble finding a topic for my personal essays; it was easy to write about my experiences performing the duties of a parent and how much I learned from them. This topic proved productive; the following spring I was accepted to a prestigious college and also won a full scholarship to the school of my choice.

Looking back on that month, I recognize now the richness of my experience and just how much it contributed to me as a person. During that time, I learned what qualities an ideal man and woman should possess. My firsthand knowledge replaced my archaic notions of men as chivalrous protectors of passive, caring women. Another new concept I developed was that there weren't any obvious differences between the required traits of a man and a woman. I no longer divided the genders and designated specific attributes each should acquire. It was as if I took my culture's gender role assignments and synthesized them into one person, and that was who I became. Whether it was hugging Carol to sleep when she cried in the middle of the night, explaining fractions to Tai, cooking, cleaning, or fixing the door handle, I did not feel as though I switched roles when I performed them. I never thought to myself, "No, I can't do this because I'm a man. That's not what I'm supposed to do. But, since Mom's not here, I *have* to do the woman's work." Those thoughts didn't cross my mind. What I did think, however, was, "Of course I'll do this. I'll do it because I love my sister and brother. No other reason."

Ever since my sister went away to college, my role and responsibility in my family has changed dramatically. I have much more say in household affairs than before. Now whenever I am at home I take care of all the bills and paperwork that my mother has accumulated over the months while I was in college. If there is a decision to be made, I usually make it and then tell my mother why I did so. I think she finally realized that I was old enough to make the right choices for our family. Along with my added responsibility, the weight of my word has increased markedly since high school. Again, I think my mother takes my opinion more seriously because I am old enough now to play the role of an influential person in our family. Knowing that what I say has a more profound influence on her than ever before, I have not wasted an opportunity to help my little brother and sister. Whenever I have a chance, I persuade her to change her ways toward Tai and little Carol so that they can have a smoother childhood than I did. By this I mean that I encourage her to allow them to make friends within and outside of the Vietnamese ethnicity, let Tai talk to girls his age because he can benefit from them and vice versa, and most importantly discipline them with words instead of whips. I believe my words have not gone unheard, especially those dealing with punishment, because since I started college I cannot recall ever hearing about her spanking Tai or Carol.

My years in college have allowed me to develop a new, more equal relationship with my mother. I think the time I spent at school three thousand miles away has made us both appreciate and respect one another (although she would never admit that she respects or appreciates me). She now sees me as an independent individual, and I see her as both a mother and a friend. I know that she takes much pride in seeing me succeed in my academic life, but even though I want to make her proud of me and hope that she gains the proper admiration she deserves from those in Vietnam, I do not base my goals and aspirations on pleasing her. If in the process of attaining my goals I also make her happy, then I will have lived up to both my American and Vietnamese ideals—doing things for myself and doing things to show respect for my parents. I praise my mother when I see the improvements in the way she is raising Tai and Carol compared to her raising of Chau and me. I think she knows that she cannot apply every aspect of Vietnamese culture to children she is raising in America. When I go home for vacations, I still function as the man in the house, the person who takes care of the bills, fixes doorknobs, and attends the parent–teacher conferences. At the same time, I am also the only male figure for my brother, which puts pressure on me to be the best role model I can. I play these roles willingly and with satisfaction.

As for my search for the culture that suits me best, I have come to the decision that neither Vietnamese nor American culture alone can fulfill my needs. Thus, I chose to pick out the best aspects of each culture and synthesize them into one. For instance, while I believe in the American ideal that every person is equal, I also disapprove of children not treating their elders with respect and proper manners. I do not consider myself Americanized or Vietnamized; rather, I'm enjoying the best of both worlds.

What are the issues that I am still struggling with? As I enter my senior year, I'm still trying to inflate the emotional balloon that I've suppressed for so long. Recently, my girlfriend Jennifer has been helping me recover my ability to feel strong emotions again. Last month she and I cried together, something I haven't done since my sophomore year in high school! However, I find it much more difficult to bring back the emotions than to tuck them away, and so far I haven't made much progress.

From the academic success my sister and I have earned, it may seem that our family is living out the American dream. We escaped from a war-scarred country that offered us few opportunities and arrived in a land we knew nothing about. My mother worked hard all her life to provide her children with a home that was conducive to learning. She created such an atmosphere by using the whip, along with guilt-provoking stories to encourage us to learn. Now that two of her children are excelling in their respective postsecondary institutions, my mother feels that she has done an admirable job of raising us. However, her feelings of pride come at a high cost to the relationships in our family. Maybe she did not know any other way to raise us than by using her native culture's means. She did not realize that most families who bring up successful children do not use the switch as their tool of support. I believe that practicing Confucian ideals in the family will lead to decreased communication and ultimately to feelings of isolation similar to those that Chau and I felt and are still experiencing. Fortunately, after seeing her family structure crumble because of her, my mother realized that her rearing methods needed improvement. She knows now that her children will inevitably become "Americanized" to some degree. Accordingly, she now allows Tai and Carol more freedom; hopefully, they will also live up to her ideals. I can sense that the relationships in my family are becoming more intimate. We all can hug and kiss each other now, and I am optimistic that in the near future my mother and I will be able to say "I love you" to one another.

PHUOC: NINE YEARS LATER

"Plea hep me. I don spea Englit very mut," uttered my mother softly into the microphone shortly after the middle-aged judge took her seat. "Okay Ms. Nguyen, the court will appoint a Vietnamese interpreter for you." With that, she thanked the judge and sat down to focus on the stack of documents she brought with her to contest the change in legal guardianship of her youngest daughter.

Mom wore a simple, body length, white business suit, decorated herself with make-up, gold, and jade, and styled her hair to highlight the tuft of gray that had appeared almost overnight. I stood not more than 10 feet to her right, with my wife, Erin, standing on one side of me while the attorney representing Carol, now 13 years old, on my left. We had been sitting in that probate and family courtroom for over an hour, yet neither my mother nor I had spoken to, or even looked at, one another. This scene took place seven months ago when we attended the final hearing that ultimately led the judge to grant Erin and me legal custody of my sister, Carol. This was also the last time I saw my mother.

When the editors of this book asked me to write a follow-up to "Seeking the Best of Both Worlds," they didn't realize that in these past months I have been facing the most challenging crises and transitions in my life. The portrait of me as an adolescent in my earlier essay will now be abruptly replaced by a portrait of me as a parent. I have also switched from being the filial child to the disavowed son who has broken his mother's heart and taken away all that she had been living for. If I had written this essay one year ago instead of now, the circumstances would have been drastically different. A year ago, I would have reported that our family was relatively intact, despite still working through years of deeply embedded emotional scars. A year ago I was nearing the end of medical school, having just completed a year of clinical rotations and graduated with a master's in public health from UC Berkeley. A year ago we were ecstatic to learn of the birth of our new baby niece, Kayla, my older sister, Chau's, first child. A year ago I was seeing my younger brother Tai regularly even though he was far away in college at UCLA. And a year ago, my younger sister, Carol, was finishing seventh grade, was living just 10 minutes away from Erin and me, and was becoming a teenager. In the span of just several months, the entire landscape of our family has been fundamentally and irreversibly altered. Yet, one element would have stayed unchanged: The consequences of my mother's abuse reverberate powerfully still in each of her children.

At the end of "Seeking the Best of Both Worlds," I described my newfound influence in the way my mother raised her two younger children, Tai and Carol. She no longer physically abused them; she gave them more freedom to make friends and did not expect perfect grades from either of them. I was proud of my mother for making these positive changes so that Tai and Carol could have more "normal" upbringings. Unfortunately, I learned not soon after that mom had replaced physical abuse with even more devastating forms of punishment: emotional and psychological abuse. That Tai and Carol proved more susceptible to these methods of mistreatment further compounded their distress, which manifested itself in broken family and social relationships, decreased academic performances, and even thoughts of suicide. This final consequence of my mother's words and actions compelled Erin and me to take the decisive step to protect Carol's health and well-being.

Shortly after writing "Seeking the Best of Both Worlds," I requested a yearlong leave of absence from college to study acupuncture and language in Beijing, China. Having declared a double major in biochemistry and Chinese, and not knowing whether I would pursue advanced studies or place myself in the market after graduation, I jumped at the chance to delay that decision while combining both my interests. This year of complete independence was instrumental in my decision to pursue a career in medicine and international public health, with a focus on health in China. Learning a traditional modality of healing and theory of disease broadened by a more culturally based scope of knowledge continues to serve me well today as I treat patients from varied ethnic and cultural backgrounds. The personal and academic growth I gained in China was well worth the price of not graduating with my original college classmates.

Despite times of loneliness at the start of my year in Beijing, I quickly made new Chinese friends and plugged myself into the small, but welcoming, Vietnamese expatriate community. The group of Vietnamese friends I made consisted of international graduate students from Ho Chi Minh City and several families from Europe, Australia, and the United States. They were the first ethnic Vietnamese families I had met since leaving California to start college. Indeed, they were the first Vietnamese families I had known that were not my close or distant relatives. My interactions with them over the course of the year provided a starkly different, and decidedly preferable, model of family dynamics compared to what I grew up knowing and resenting. Not unlike the struggles of my own family, my new friends were also refugees at one point, also spent years in camps in neighboring Southeast Asian host nations, also encountered discrimination and xenophobia after settling in our respective industrialized nations, and also somehow were able to succeed against the odds. Yet, unlike my mother in my own childhood experiences, these parents did not beat or emotionally abuse their children nor did they teach their children to embrace only Vietnamese culture. I remember one family that I still keep in touch with, the Phans, who came to Beijing from Paris because Mr. Phan was promoted to a managerial position in a French firm that operated in China. The Phans had a five-year-old son, Bathy, whom they treated with respect, as though his feelings and concerns were every bit as valid as their own. They didn't slap him when he interrupted conversations among the adults; neither did they laugh, shame, and criticize him for his short-comings. They made sure that he learned about and appreciated his heritage by only speaking Vietnamese in the household, exposing him to other Vietnamese children, and taking him on yearly trips to Saigon. At the same time, both parents were able to speak Chinese and emphasized to Bathy the importance of learning Chinese culture and language.

At first, I thought the Phans were a rare example of a "functional" immigrant Vietnamese family, to be admired only, and not to be expected. However, I soon met two other Vietnamese families in Beijing with similar backgrounds and child-rearing philosophies. In one family the father was Caucasian, yet he went out of his way to master Vietnamese so that his children would learn to embrace their mother's heritage. These model families, having *found* the best of both worlds, left a dramatic impact on the way I saw myself raising a family.

My year in Beijing also gave me new insights into romantic relationships with women. By the time I wrote "Seeking the Best of Both Worlds," I had already come a long way since my naïve idealization of the masculine role that I garnered from watching Hong Kong soap operas in high school. I had dated several women, and even had a yearlong serious relationship. Yet, it wasn't until I observed the model of healthy romantic relationships embodied in the Vietnamese couples I've just described that I realized what it means to have a long-term romance based on mutual respect and dependence. Since leaving China, these insights were reflected in two subsequent relationships, the latter of which continues and grows to this day.

On the eve of my return to the United States and my planned application to medical school, I called my mother for the first time in months. She sounded frantic, saying that Tai had stolen money from her to feed his "hoodlum" friends at school and that she was ready to go insane because of him. She recounted how she even tried to call the police to have 12-year-old Tai taken away and put into an orphanage before he became "*b_i__i*," the dust of life, and brought even more shame to the family. I asked to speak to Tai, and as soon as he picked up the phone, I could hear the torrent of tears rushing down his face. As we spoke, I readily recognized the similarities between what he was suffering and the difficulties I had at the start of my own adolescence. I shared in his desire to be a "normal" teenager with typical teenage problems. I decided then that I would postpone my graduation by yet another year to be close to home and to try to give my little brother a fighting chance at a "normal" adolescence.

Coming home I found a brother who was withdrawn, depressed, emotional, and mortally afraid of his mother's verbal violence against him. He related to me how much he hated to be yelled at by our mother and how this had escalated during my time abroad. My efforts at persuading mom to stop this emotional abuse were met only by Tai's rebukes. "You don't know what it's like after you tell her off," he protested, "after you leave she yells at me even more! You can easily go back to your apartment, but I have to stay here and listen to her yelling all the time. And she doesn't stop for days! She tells me how much pain she's in because of me and asks herself why I'm not getting good grades. She even says that she should've aborted me in Kansas when my dad found out she was pregnant. She calls me stupid all the time, and says I'll never be as good as you or Chi Chau. She blames everything on me!" My feeling of powerlessness then was similar to my helplessness at stopping Tai's father from molesting him years earlier. Besides entertaining the idea of calling Child Protective Services, I was at a loss for options at that point.

For the next year I lived only half an hour from my family, initially working two full-time jobs to pay off debt that I accumulated while in China, then enrolling at UC Davis to occupy my time with Japanese, Spanish, biology, and philosophy courses. I spent time with Tai and Carol weekly. I strategically picked times when mom was at work so as to give them a break from her. We dined out, watched movies, bowled, skated, fed ducks at the park, camped, and enjoyed activities of "normal" families. I even went as far as taking Tai on a two-week trip to Beijing during his winter vacation. This time together provided safe environments for Tai to voice his frustrations and fears about mom to someone who had lived through a similar situation. I shared with him some coping mechanisms to help him avoid mom's abuse as much as possible. By the time I prepared to return to college and finish my senior year, I felt relatively reassured that Tai was better off than when I had arrived a year earlier. However, it took little time at all for mom to unravel Tai's sense of self-worth and the gains he had made.

In his subsequent high-school years, Tai continued to be inhibited and introverted, but he always made sure he did enough to stay on mom's good side to avoid verbal punishment. Even during his senior year in high school, he would hug and kiss mom before and after school, gestures that I had rejected soon after I distanced myself from her emotionally in high school. Tai never had the good fortune of severing his emotional ties with and dependency on mom, however, and because of this, I believe he still suffers from these psychological wounds today.

Tai is now in his third year at a competitive university in California, where he is performing well academically and maintains many good friends. My older sister Chau, now a practicing physician in the Midwest, and I have been concerned over Tai's years-long struggle with clinical depression. We've urged him to see a therapist and have gone so far as to send him samples of an antidepressant. To our disappointment, however, and likely to his detriment, Tai decided to suffer through this illness alone. In the past several months, Tai's mental health has consumed the attention and time of our entire family. One evening a few months ago, Tai confided in Erin over the telephone of his intentions to end his life, saying that he wanted to tell her good-bye. Stunned by this news, she had no choice but to let me know and also involve our older sister. After driving through the night from our home and arriving at his apartment in the early hours of the morning, he sat with us in our car for an hour but was unmoved by our offers of alternatives. He even scolded us for coming down to see him, saying that it made things even worse for him. That morning we anxiously called the police to have him committed, as we did not know when he would carry out his plan. We were afraid that our visit would ironically hasten his decision. The scene of a half dozen police officers surrounding his apartment, blocking all exits by car or on foot, came straight out of a Hollywood action movie. Since then, Tai has been hospitalized twice for suicidal ideation. He reluctantly started taking antidepressants and antipsychotics, just to appease his psychiatrists, but he never had any intention of continuing his medication on a long-term basis. The only intervention he willingly accepted and actually appreciated was a PhD therapist who had experience with immigrant adolescent experiences, specifically those from Vietnam. In addition, he has made it clear that he needs time separated from his older siblings, and even Erin, whom he sees as those who betrayed him by committing him against his will. I don't know how long this voluntary isolation will last, but we have all honored his wishes, despite our deep sadness.

Looking back on this crisis, I remember mentally cursing my mother for what she had caused. I imagined how much more positive life for Tai would have been if he had been born into a different family and lamented the fact that he couldn't break away from her emotional stranglehold. I criticized myself for not acting on my earlier impulses to call Child Protective Services so that Tai could have a better chance at life, even if foster care were the only other option. I vowed that I would not let the same thing happen to Carol, my younger sister.

Our other major crisis in the past months, which has dramatically changed the course of our lives, has been over Carol's health and future. When Tai graduated from high school and left home for college, Erin and I encouraged my mom to move down to Palo Alto, where Carol could receive a better education and be closer to me, as I was at Stanford Medical School. The junior high school in which Carol was preparing to enroll was known as a particularly "ghetto" school filled with future gang members, high-school dropouts, and teenage mothers. Only after considerable discussion, and our offers to do all of the relocation work, did mom relent to uprooting her home of 18 years to start afresh. As the only child left living with mom, Carol bore the brunt of mom's frustrations about her new environment, about not having enough Vietnamese people around, and of course mom's unceasing criticisms of Carol's weight, poor grades, poor manners, laziness, impoliteness, and more. In the last year, since Carol turned 13, she often would spend weekends with Erin and me, to "get away from mom for a while." We would console her and dry her tears while doing our best to undo the damage that mom had inflicted on Carol's senses of self-esteem, self-worth, and self-image.

At the beginning of her eighth-grade year, Erin and I arranged for Carol to see her school counselor so that she would have another source of support. I remember Erin calling me during my clinical rotation in the neonatal intensive care unit to say that Carol's counselor had forbade her from going back home to mom's, that Carol was to stay with us for the time being, and that Child Protective Services had been called to investigate. This was the start of many weeks of anguish for Erin and me. Although we knew that Carol was still dealing with emotional abuse from mom, we did not recognize the extent of her suffering. Carol disclosed to her counselor that she occasionally had thoughts of hurting herself at times because of the guilt ingrained into her daily by her mother. These thoughts were deemed serious enough to warrant Carol's hospitalization in an adolescent psychiatric ward. At this point there was no doubt in my mind as to what I needed to do; Erin and I subsequently filed for legal custody, or guardianship, of Carol.

My final conversation with my mother occurred several weeks before the court hearing, while Carol was still hospitalized. She called me one evening and, speaking through her tears, asked me why I was out to destroy her family. She said that she gave everything to us, did nothing for herself, and even loved her daughter-in-law even though she isn't Vietnamese. She added that whatever I did, I should not spread word of this to the Vietnamese community as it would bring her too much loss of face. I could not comprehend how my mother could have uttered those sentences. With my sister suffering alone in a hospital bed, my brother still damaged seemingly beyond repair, that moment was a tipping point for me. I unleashed my fury at her like never before.

"If you were such a great mother, if you had no faults, then tell me, just tell me, why are three of your children seeing psychiatrists!" I screamed, not letting her interrupt me. "Why *is* it that two of your children were hospitalized for being suicidal? Why? Tell me, why?! Because you are *NOT* a great mother. Let me tell you right now, if any of my siblings dies because of you, my hate for you will be unending!" I can only imagine the shock my mother felt as these words landed on her ears, for I even surprised myself.

Her only response was, "I don't know what's wrong with them. I didn't do anything wrong. I just tried to love my kids and now you're trying to take them from me!" The last thing I said to her before hanging up was, "There's nothing more to say then. Let's just see how the judge decides what's right."

Carol's permanent entry into our home has cast Erin and me into the roles of parents of a teenager. The last eight months have brought countless challenges, from ordinary teenage needs like braces, school dances, tenuous friendships, Myspace.com, and classroom stressors to the *extra*-ordinary trials like antidepressants and psychiatry visits, uncontrollable bouts of guilt and crying, and Carol's nightmares about her mom coming after her. We have no illusions that the healing process will be fast and expect that therapy will continue for years to come. Carol has already amazed us with her resilience. Since ending her relationship with mom, she has blossomed into a more extroverted, social teenager, and her grades have shown further improvement. Along the way, Carol was blessed with caring teachers and counselors who have played important roles during this transition.

I sometimes ask myself what mom could do to reconcile with her children. At the very least, she must acknowledge and show heartfelt remorse for the role she played in the psychological trauma of her children. I doubt that day will come. For the past half year, she has not made any attempts to visit Carol, despite having the option to see Carol with our supervision. It would seem that she has made the ultimate sacrifice of losing her teenage daughter in the name of saving face. Currently, the only remaining child who is on speaking terms with our mother is

Tai. Rooted in feelings of guilt and sympathy, he now reluctantly plays the role of the "good son." However, this communication with mom has taken a toll on him, as his roommate has recounted to me that Tai has been more moody since he started talking to mom again. Recently, he has also been the only link between mom and the rest of the siblings. I don't believe that Tai's role as liaison has any positive impact on Carol, who still feels guilty for not wanting to see or speak with mom.

To this day, when I meet new people and tell them of how my family fled to the United States as part of the "boat people" in the early 1980s, they invariably comment on how brave and selfless my mother must have been to risk everything for her children. In response, I always say, "Yes, she most certainly was." My mother had a decades-long goal of one day moving back to Vietnam to bask in the glory of her "good works," returning to find admiration and respect among her family and peers in Hue. She often told me of her dream to build a four-story house, adorned with portraits of her successful children. "My two oldest ones are doctors," she would point out to guests. The house would be big enough to offer individual rooms for each of her four children and their families. Obviously, these dreams have been crushed literally overnight. She now has no "face" to return. How can she explain that her children, who outwardly are so successful in American society, do not talk to her, do not revere her, and would not visit her in Vietnam?

At the end of "Seeking the Best of Both Worlds," I described my effort to regain the ability to feel deep emotions, which I intentionally buried during my psychological "break" with mom in high school. Certainly, my loving wife of three years has helped me move forward in this regard. In addition, I found that the process of treating gravely ill patients in intensive care units has had a therapeutic effect on releasing my dormant ability to feel deep sadness. On the other hand, I have a disconcerting ability to transition to new environments without much hesitance. For example, just last week, as my wife and I were preparing to move from California to the East Coast to start my residency, Erin asked me, "I just don't get it. How come Carol and I are both torn apart and crying over moving to Boston, and yet you seem to have no problem with leaving after living here for five years?" I guess at this point I am still a "work in progress."

In the past, I readily attributed many of my mom's failures to her intractable adherence to cultural values that were maladapted to the environment in which she raised her children. I explained her severe physical abuse of me and Chau as common and accepted child-raising tools among uneducated villagers in Vietnam. I rationalized the reasons for her privileging males over females as deeply seated Confucian teachings that survive to this day in most of East and Southeast Asia. I even succumbed to her reasoning for why we should respect her and obey her to the end ("Even the eighty-year-old emperor has to kowtow to his one-hundred-year-old mother"). Only in the past few years, after considerable thought, have I come to the conclusion that mom's culture and upbringing cannot account for all the harm she has brought to us. Recently, Erin triggered a lengthy discussion by asking, "If you could imagine taking your mother and placing her, the way she is, back to her village in Vietnam, would she fit in? Would her treatment of you and your siblings be considered normal?" Armed now with experience treating patients with numerous psychiatric and psychological pathologies, my sister Chau and I strongly suspect that mom indeed has hidden a personality disorder under the guise of traditional values. Sadly, despite a court order mandating psychological therapy as a condition of visitation rights, mom stubbornly has decided that "face" is more important.

Nine years have passed since I wrote "Seeking the Best of Both Worlds." During these years, I was blessed with opportunities to study, volunteer, and work in many developing countries. Now that I am able to speak the languages and negotiate the traditions of many peoples, I feel uniquely suited for an eventual career caring for underserved populations in developing countries and partnering with local communities to implement public health interventions. Erin has encouraged me, and even joined me, in my pursuit of health care equity and justice for those who are marginalized and displaced. Like the husband I befriended in Beijing who learned Vietnamese so that his children will embrace their mother's cultural roots, Erin also sees us raising our children in a bilingual household. After residency, we hope to spend some time in Vietnam, where I can practice medicine and public health, and where Erin can master the language and follow her own career ambitions in child advocacy.

CONTRIBUTORS

Andrew Garrod is Professor Emeritus of Education and former Chair of the Education Department at Dartmouth College, where he taught courses in adolescence, moral development, and contemporary issues in U.S. education. He currently directs a teaching volunteer program in the Marshall Islands in the central Pacific and has conducted a research project in Bosnia and Herzegovina over a number of years. His recent publications include two coauthored articles: "Forgiveness After Genocide?: Perspectives from Bosnian Youth" and "Culture, Ethnic Conflict, and Moral Orientation in Bosnian Children," and the coedited books *Mi Voz, Mi Vida: Latino College Tell Their Life Stories* and *Balancing Two Worlds: Asian-American College Students Tell Their Life Stories*. With Robert Kilkenny, he is completing a manuscript for an edited anthology on growing up Muslim. He is twice winner of Dartmouth's Distinguished Teaching Award.

Robert Kilkenny is executive director of a children's mental health agency in Boston, Clinical Instructor in Social Work at Simmons College, and was formerly an instructor of psychology in the Department of Psychiatry at Harvard Medical School and a research child psychologist at McLean Hospital. He is coeditor of *Souls Looking Back: Life Stories of Growing Up Black* (with Andrew Garrod, Janie Ward, and Tracy Robinson), *Mi Voz, Mi Vida: Latino College Tell Their Life Stories*, and *Balancing Two Worlds: Asian-American College Students Tell Their Life Stories*. With Andrew Garrod and Christina Gomez, he is completing a manuscript for an edited anthology on growing up Muslim.

Sally Powers is Professor in the Department of Psychology and in the Neuroscience and Behavior Program and is Director of the Center for Research on Families at the University of Massachusetts, Amherst. She teaches a course on the neuroscience of social attachments. Her research, which has been supported by the National Science Foundation, the National Institute of Mental Health, and the National Cancer Institute, focuses on interpersonal, cognitive, personality, and endocrine factors that contribute to the development of adolescent depression and anxiety.

Lisa Smulyan is Associate Provost and Professor in the Department of Educational Studies at Swarthmore College, Swarthmore, Pennsylvania. She teaches courses in educational foundations, adolescence, gender and education, and comparative education. Her teaching, scholarship, and administrative work focus on how historical, social, and cultural contexts influence teachers, teaching, and learning. Her publications include recent articles on teacher education and the liberal arts and the personal and professional development of women teachers and doctors, and books including *Balancing Acts: Women Principals at Work*.

BIBLIOGRAPHY

Adams R., & Laursen, B. (2001). "The organization and dynamics of adolescent conflict with parents and friends." *Journal of Marriage and the Family* 63:97–101.

Adelson, J., & Douvan, E. (1975). "Adolescent friendships." In J. Conger, P. Mussen, & J. Kagan (eds.), *Basic and Contemporary Issues in Developmental Psychology*, 277–90. New York: Harper and Row.

Adler, N. (1975). "Emotional responses of women following therapeutic abortion." *American Journal of Orthopsychiatry* 45:446–56.

Allen, J., & Land, D. (1999). "Attachment in adolescence." In J. Cassidy, & P. R. Shaver (eds.), *Handbook of Attachment: Theory, Research, and Clinical Applications*, 319–35. New York: Guilford Press.

Allen, J. P., Hauser, S. T., Bell, K. L., & O'Conner, T. G. (1994). "Longitudinal assessment of autonomy and relatedness in adolescent-family interactions as predicators of adolescent ego development and self-esteem." *Child Development* 65:179–94.

Ames, N., & Miller, E. (1994). *Changing Middle Schools: How to Make Schools Work for Young Adolescents.* San Francisco, CA: Jossey-Bass.

Aristotle. (1941). *Rhetorica.* New York: Random House.

Arnett, J. (1987). "Development perspectives on adolescent risk-taking in contemporary America." In C. E. Irwin (ed.), *Adolescent Social Behavior and Health*, 93–125. San Francisco, CA: Jossey-Bass.

———. (2004). *Emerging Adulthood: The Winding Road from the Late Teens through the Twenties.* New York: Oxford University Press.

Baumrind, D. (1989). "Rearing competent children." In W. Damon (ed.), *Child Development Today and Tomorrow.* San Francisco, CA: Jossey-Bass.

———. (1989). "The role of self understanding in resilient individuals: The development of a perspective." *American Journal of Orthopsychiatry* 59(2):266–78.

Belsky J., Steinberg L., & Draper P. (1991). "Childhood experience, interpersonal development and reproductive strategy: An evolutionary theory of socialization." *Child Development* 62:647–70.

Benedict, R. (1950). *Patterns of Culture.* New York: New American Library.

Biederman, J., Wilens, T., Mick, E., Spencer, T., & Faraone, S. V. (1999). "Pharmacotherapy of attention-deficit/hyperactivity disorder reduces risk for substance use disorder." *Pediatrics* 104(20):104–20.

Blos, P. (1962). *On Adolescence: A Psychoanalytic Interpretation.* New York: Free Press.

———. (1972). "The child analyst looks at the young adolescent." In K. Kagan, & R. Coles (eds.), *Twelve to Sixteen: Early Adolescence.* New York: W. W. Norton.

———. (1979). *The Adolescent Passage.* New York: International Universities Press.

Bracken, M., Hachamovitch, M., & Grossman, A. (1974). "The decision to abort and psychological sequelae." *Journal of Nervous and Mental Disorders* 15:155–61.

Brown, B. B. (2004). "Adolescents' relationships with peers." In R. M. Lerner, & L. Steinberg (eds.), *Handbook of Adolescent Psychology*, 363–94. Hoboken, NJ: John Wiley & Sons, I.

Carter, P. (2006). "Intersecting identities: 'Acting white,' gender, and academic achievement." In E. Horvat, & C. O'Connor (eds.), *Beyond Acting White: Reframing the Debate on Black Student Achievement*, 111–32. Lanham, MD: Rowman and Littlefield.

Chodorow, N. (1989). *Feminism and Psychoanalysis*. New Haven, CT: Yale University Press.

Chu, J. (2004). "A relational perspective on boys' identity development." In N. Way, & J. Chu (eds.), *Adolescent Boys*, 78–106. New York: NYU Press.

Clark, R. (1983). *Family Life and School Achievement: Why Poor Black Children Succeed or Fail*. Chicago, IL: University of Chicago Press.

Collins, W. A. (1995). "Relationships and development: Family adaptation to individual change." In S. Shulman (ed.), *Close Relationships and Socioemotional Development*, 128–54. New York: Ablex.

Collins, W. A., & Laursen, B. (2004). "Parent-adolescent relationship and influences." In R. M. Lerner, & L. Steinberg (eds.), *Handbook of Adolescent Psychology*, 331–36. Hoboken, NJ: John Wiley & Sons.

Collins, W. A., & Repinski, D. J. (2001). "Parents and adolescents as transformers of relationships: Dyadic adaptations to developmental change." In J. R. M. Gerris (ed.), *Dynamics of Parenting: International Perspectives on Nature and Sources of Parenting*, 429–43. Leuven, Netherlands: Garant.

Collins, W. A., & Russell, G. (1991). "Mother-child and father-child relationships in middle childhood and adolescence: A developmental analysis." *Developmental Review* 11:99–136.

Connell, R. W. (2000). *The Men and the Boys*. Berkeley, CA: University of California Press.

Connolly, J., Furman, W., & Konarski, R. (2000). "The role of peers in the emergence of heterosexual romantic relationships in adolescence." *Child Development* 71:1395–408.

Cooley, C. H. (1902). *Human Nature and the Social Order*. New York: Scribners.

Cooper, C. R. (1994). "Cultural perspectives on continuity and change in adolescents' relationships." In R. Montemayor, & G. R. Adams (eds.), *Personal Relationships during Adolescence*, 78–100. Thousand Oaks, CA: Sage.

Côté, J., & Levine, C. (1987). "A formulation of Erikson's theory of ego identity formation." *Developmental Review* 7:273–325.

Cross, W. (1991). *Shades of Black: Diversity in African-American Identity*. Philadelphia, PA: Temple University Press.

Csikszentmihalyi, M., & Larson, R. (1984). *Being Adolescent*. New York: Basic Books.

Cvejic, H., Lipper, I., Kinch, R. A., & Benjamin, P. (1977). "Follow-up of 50 adolescent girls two years after abortion." *Canadian Medical Association Journal* 116:44–46.

Darwin, C. (1936). *The Origin of the Species by Means of Natural Selection*. New York: Modern Library.

Eder, D. (1985). "The cycle of popularity: Interpersonal relations among female adolescence." *Sociology of Education* 58:154–65.

Elder, G. (1980). "Adolescence in historical perspective." In J. Adelson (ed.), *Handbook of Adolescent Psychology*, 3–46. New York: John Wiley and Sons.

Erikson, E. H. (1959). "Identity and the life cycle." *Psychological Issues* 1:1–171.

———. (1964). *Insight and Responsibility*. New York: W. W. Norton.

———. (1966). *The Challenge of Youth*. New York: Anchor Paperback.

———. (1968). *Identity: Youth and Crisis*. New York: Norton.

———. (1975). *Life History and the Historical Moment*. New York: W. W. Norton.

———. (1980). *Identity and the Life Cycle: A Reissue*. New York: W. W. Norton.

Ewing, J. A., & Rouse, B. A. (1973). "Therapeutic abortion and a prior psychiatric history." *American Journal of Psychiatry* 130:37–40.

Feiring, C. (1999). "Other-sex friendship networks and the development of romantic relationships in adolescence." *Journal of Youth and Adolescence* 28:495–512.

Feldman, S., & Elliott, G. (1990). *At the Threshold: The Developing Adolescent*. Cambridge, MA: Harvard University Press.

Ferguson, A. (2000). *Bad Boys: Public Schools in the Making of Black Masculinity*. Ann Arbor, MI: University of Michigan Press.

Finkelhor, D. (1984). *Child Sexual Abuse: New Theory and Research*. New York: Free Press.

Flores-Gonzáles, N. (2002). *School Kids, Street Kids: Identity Development in Latino Students*. New York: Teachers College Press.

Ford, C., Castelnuovo-Tedesco, P., & Long, K. (1971). "Abortion: Is it a therapeutic procedure in psychiatry?" *Journal of the American Medical Association* 218:1173.

Fordham, S. (1988). "Racelessness as a factor in Black students' school success: Pragmatic strategy or pyrrhic victory?" *Harvard Educational Review* 58(1):54–84.

Freud, A. (1946). *The Ego and Mechanisms of Defense* (C. Baines, trans.). New York: International Universities Press.

———. (1958). "Adolescence." In *Psychoanalytic Study of the Child*. New York: International Universities Press.

Freud, S. (1953). *Three Essays on Sexuality*. London: Hogarth Press.

———. (1962). "The transformations of puberty." In *Three Essays on the Theory of Sexuality*, 73–74, 85–96. New York: Basic Books.

Furman, W. (1999). "Friends and lovers: The role of peer relationships in adolescent romantic relationships." In W. A. Collins, & B. Laursen (eds.), *Relationships as Developmental Contexts* (vol. 30), 89–103. Mahwah, NJ: Erlbaum.

Furman, W., Simon, V. A., Schaffer, L., & Bouchey, H. A. (2002). "Adolescents' working models and styles for relationships with parents, friends, and romantic partners." *Child Development* 73:241–55.

Galliher, R. V., Rostosky, S. S., Welsh, D. P., & Kawaguchi, M. C. (1999). "Power and psychological well-being in late adolescent romantic relationships." *Sex Roles* 40(9):689–710.

Garmezy, N. (1985). "Stress-resistant children: The search for protective factors." In J. E. Stevenson (ed.), *Recent Research in Developmental Psychopathology*, 213–33. Oxford: Pergamon Press.

Gaub, M., & Carlson, C. L. (1997). "Gender differences in ADHD: A meta-analysis and critical review." *Journal of the American Academy of Child and Adolescent Psychiatry* 36:1036–45.

Gershon, J. (2002). "A meta-analytic review of gender differences in ADHD." *Journal of Attention Disorders* 5:143–54.

Gibbs, J. T. (1984). "Black adolescents and youth: An endangered species." *American Journal of Orthopsychiatry* 54(1):6–23.

Gilchrist, A. C., Hanaford, P. C., Frank, P., & Kay, C. R. (1995). "Termination of pregnancy and psychiatric morbidity." *British Journal of Psychology* 167:243–48.

Gilligan, C. (1982). *In a Different Voice*. Cambridge, MA: Harvard University Press.

Gilligan, C., Lyons, N., & Hanmer, T. (eds.) (1989). *Making Connections: The Relational Worlds of Adolescent Girls at Emma Willard School*. Troy, NY: Emma Willard School.

Goethals, G. W., & Klos, D. S. (1976). *Experiencing Youth: First Person Accounts*. Boston, MA: Little Brown.

Gold, M., & Yanof, D. (1985). "Mothers, daughters and girlfriends." *Journal of Personality and Social Psychology* 49:654–89.

Gonzales, N., & Cauce, A. M. (1995). "Ethnic identity and multicultural competence: Dilemmas and challenges for minority youth." In W. D. Hawley, & A. W. Jackson (eds.), *Toward a Common Destiny*, 131–62. San Francisco, CA: Jossey-Bass.

Gray, M., & Steinberg, L. (1999). "Unpacking authoritative parenting: Reassessing a multidimensional construct." *Journal of Marriage and the Family* 61:574–87.

Grello, C. M., Welsh, D. P., Harper, M. S., & Dickson, J. W. (2003). "Dating and sexual relationship trajectories and adolescent functioning." *Adolescent & Family Health* 3(3):103–12.

Grotevant, H. D. (1998). "Adolescent development in family contexts." In W. Damon, & N. Eisenberg (eds.), *Handbook of Child Psychology (vol. 3): Social, Emotional, and Personality Development*, 1097–150. New York: Wiley.

Grotevant, H. D., & Cooper, C. R. (1986). "Individuation in family relationships." *Human Development* 29:82–100.

Hall, G. S. (1904). *Adolescence: Its Psychology and Its Relations to Physiology, Anthropology, Sociology, Sex, Crime, Religion, and Education.* New York: Appleton-Century-Crofts.

Hartup, W. W., & Laursen, B. (1991). "Relationships as developmental contexts." In R. Cohen, & A. W. Siegel (eds.), *Context and Development*, 253–80. Hillsdale, NJ: Erlbaum.

Hatcher, S. (1976). "Understanding adolescent pregnancy and abortion." *Primary Care* 3:407–25.

Hauser, S., Powers, S., & Noam, G. (1991). *Adolescents and Their Families: Paths of Ego Development.* New York: Free Press.

Hauser, S. T., Houlihan, J., Powers, S. I., Jacobson, A. M., Noam, G., Weiss-Perry, B., & Follansbee, D. (1987). "Interaction sequences in families of psychiatrically hospitalized and non-patient adolescents." *Psychiatry* 50:308–19.

Hauser, S. T., Powers, S. I., Noam, G., Jacobson, A. M., Weiss, B., & Follansbee, D. (1984). "Familial contexts of adolescent ego development." *Child Development* 55:195–213.

Havighurst, R. J., Bosman, P. H., Liddle, G., Mathews, C. V., & Pierce, J. V. (1962). *Growing Up in River City.* New York: Wiley.

Heath, S. B. (1995). "Race, ethnicity and the defiance of categories." In W. Hawley, & A. Jackson (eds.), *Toward a Common Destiny*, 39–70. San Francisco, CA: Jossey Bass.

Hemmings, A. (2006). "Shifting images of blackness: coming of age as black students in urban and suburban high schools." In E. Horvat, & C. O'Connor (eds.), *Beyond Acting White: Reframing the Debate on Black Student Achievement.* Lanham, MD: Rowman and Littlefield.

Hetherington, E. M., & Stanley-Hagan, M. (2002). "Parenting in divorced and remarried families." In M. H. Bornstein (ed.), *Handbook of Parenting* (vol. 3), 287–315. Mahwah, NJ: Erlbaum.

Hill, J. P. (1987). "Research on adolescents and their families: Past and prospect." In C. E. Irwin (ed.), *Adolescent Social Behavior and Health*, 13–31. San Francisco, CA: Jossey-Bass.

Hollingshead, A. B. (1949). *Elmstown's Youth.* New York: Wiley.

Jackson, J. S., McCullough, W. R., & Gurin, G. (1981). "Group identity development within black families." In H. McAdoo (ed.), *Black Families*, 252–63. Beverly Hills, CA: Sage.

Jordan, D. (1971). "Parental antecedents and personality characteristics of ego identity statuses." Unpublished doctoral dissertation. State University of New York at Buffalo.

Kimmel, M. (1994). "Masculinity as homophobia." In H. Brod, & M. Kaufman (eds.), *Theorizing Masculinities*, 119–41. Thousand Oaks, CA: Sage Publications.

Kohlberg, L. (1969). "Stage and sequence: The cognitive-developmental approach to socialization." In D. A. Goslin (ed.), *Handbook of Socialization Theory and Research*, 347–480. Skokie, IL: Rand-McNally.

Kohlberg, L., & Gilligan, C. (1972). "The adolescent as philosopher: The discovery of the self in a postconventional world." In J. Kagan, & R. Coles (eds.), *Twelve to Sixteen: Early Adolescence*. New York: Norton.

LaFromboise, T., Coleman, H., & Gerton, J. (1993). "Psychology impact of biculturalism: Evidence and theory." *Psychology Bulletin* 114(3):395–412.

Laursen, B., Coy, K. C., & Collins, W. A. (1998). "Reconsidering changes in parent-child conflict across adolescence: A meta-analysis." *Child Development* 69:817–32.

Leadbeater, B., & Way, N. (1996). *Urban Girls: Resisting Stereotypes, Creating Identities*. New York: NYU Press.

Lee, S. (1996). *Unraveling the "Model Minority" Stereotype: Listening to Asian American Youth*. New York: Teachers College Press.

Lesko, N. (2001). *Act Your Age!: A Cultural Construction of Adolescence*. New York: Routledge/Falmer.

Lewin, K. (1939). "Field theory and experiment in social psychology: Concepts and methods." *The American Journal of Sociology* 44:868–97.

Manaster, G. J. (1989). *Adolescent Development: A Psychological Interpretation*. Itasca, IL: F. E. Peacock.

Marcia, J. (1966). "Development and validation of ego—identity status." *Journal of Personality and Social Psychology* 3:551–58.

———. (1967). "Ego identity status: Relationship to change in self-esteem." *Journal of Personality* 35:118–33.

———. (1980). "Identity in adolescence." In J. Adelson (ed.), *Handbook of Adolescent Psychology*. New York: Wiley.

Margolis, A. J., Davidson, L. A., Hanson, D. H., Loos, S. A., & Mikelson, C. A. (1971). "Therapeutic abortion: Follow-up study." *American Journal of Obstetrical Gynecology* 110:243–49.

Martin, J. R. (1981). "Sophie and Emile: A case study of sex bias in the history of educational thought." *Harvard Educational Review* 51(3):357–72.

Martin, K. (1996). *Puberty, Sexuality and the Self: Girls and Boys at Adolescence*. New York: Routledge.

Masten, A. S., & Garmezy, N. (1985). "Risk, vulnerability and protective factors in developmental psychopathology." In B. B. Lahey, & A. E. Kazdin (eds.), *Advances in Clinical Child Psychology* (vol. 8), 1–51. New York: Plenum.

McLaughlin, M., & Heath, S. (eds.). (1993). *Inner City Youth: Beyond Ethnicity and Gender*. New York: Teachers College Press.

Mead, G. H. (1934). *Mind, Self and Society*. Chicago, IL: University of Chicago Press.

Mead, M. (1958). "Adolescence in primitive and modern society." In E. Maccoby, T. Newcomb, & E. Hartley (eds.), *Readings in Social Psychology*, 341–50. New York: Norton.

Mickelson, R., & Velasco, A. (2006). "Bring it on! Diverse responses to 'acting white' among academically able Black adolescents." In E. Horvat, & C. O'Connor (eds.), *Beyond Acting White: Reframing the Debate on Black Student Achievement*. Lanham, MD: Rowman and Littlefield.

Miller, A. (1983). *The Drama of the Gifted Child*. New York: Basic Books.

Miller, J. B. (1976). *Toward a New Psychology of Women*. Boston, MA: Beacon Press.

———. (1991). "The Development of Women's Sense of Self." In J. V. Jordan, A. G. Kaplan, J. Baker Miller, I. P. Stiver, & J. L. Surrey (eds.), *Women's Growth in Connection,* 11–26. New York: Guilford Press.

Modell, J., & Goodman, M. (1990). "Historical perspectives." In S. S. Feldman, & G. R. Elliott (eds.), *At the Threshold,* 93–122. Cambridge, MA: Harvard University Press.

Monosour, K., & Stewart, B. (1973). "Abortion and sexual behavior in college women." *American Journal of Orthopsychiatry* 43:803–14.

Montemayor, R. (1983). "Parents and adolescents in conflict: All families some of the time and some families most of the time." *Journal of Early Adolescence* 3:83–103.

Moran, J. (2000). *Teaching Sex: The Shaping of Adolescence in the 20th Century.* Cambridge, MA: Harvard University Press.

Mosley, D. T., Follingshead, D. R., Harley, H., & Heckel, R. V. (1981). "Psychological factors that predict reaction to abortion." *Journal of Clinical Psychology* 37:276–79.

Muuss, R. (1996). *Theories of Adolescence,* 6th ed. New York: McGraw-Hill.

Noam, G., Powers, S., Kilkenny, R., & Beedy, J. (1990). "The interpersonal self in life-span developmental perspective: Theory, measurement and longitudinal case analysis." In M. Perlmutter, D. L. Featherman, & R. M. Learner (eds.), *Life-span Development and Behavior* (vol. 10), 60–101. Hillsdale, NJ: Lawrence Erlbaum Associates.

Olson, L. (1980). "Social and psychological correlates of pregnancy resolution among adolescent women: A review." *American Journal of Orthopsychiatry* 50:432–45.

Parker, J. G., & Gottman, J. M. (1989). "Social and emotional development in a relational context: Friendship interaction from early childhood to adolescence." In T. J. Berndt, & G. W. Ladd (eds.), *Peer Relations in Child Development.* New York: Wiley.

Payne, E. C., Kravitz, A. R., Notman, M. T., & Anderson, J. V. (1976). "Outcome following therapeutic abortion." *Archives of General Psychiatry* 33:725–33.

Piaget, J. (1972). "Intellectual evolution from adolescence to adulthood." *Human Development* 15:1–12.

Plato. (1921). *Republic.* Oxford: Clarendon Press.

Ponterotto, J., & Pederson, P. (1993). *Preventing Prejudice: A Guide for Counselors and Educators.* Newbury Park, CA: Sage.

Powers, S. I. (1988). "Moral judgment in the family." *Journal of Moral Education* 17:209–19.

Powers, S. I., Hauser, S. T., Schwartz, J., Noam, G., & Jacobson, A. M. (1983). "Adolescent ego development and family interaction: A structural-developmental perspective." In H. D. Grotevant, & C. R. Cooper (eds.), *Adolescent Development within the Family,* 5–25. San Francisco, CA: Jossey-Bass.

Pritchett, V. S. (1971). *Midnight Oil.* London: Chatto and Windus Ltd.

Rogler, L. H., Cortes, D. E., & Malgady, R. G. (1991). "Acculturation and mental health status among Hispanics: Convergence and new directions for research." *American Psychologist* 46:585–97.

Root, M. (1999). "Multiracial Asians: Models of ethnic identity." In R. Torres, L. Mirón, & J. Inda (eds.), *Race Identity and Citizenship,* 158–68. Malden, MA: Blackwell Publishers.

Russo, N. F., & Zierk, K. (1992). "Abortion, childbearing, and women's well-being." *Professional Psychology Research and Practice* 23: 269–80.

Rutter, M. (1975). "Attainment and adjustment in two geographical areas. I: The prevalence of psychiatric disorder." *British Journal of Psychiatry* 126:493–509.

———. (1979). "Protective factors in children's responses to stress and disadvantage." In M. W. Kent, & J. Rolf (eds.), *Primary Prevention of Psychopathology: III: Social Competence in Children,* 49–74. Hanover, NH: University Press of New England.

————. (1987). "Psychosocial resilience and protective mechanisms." *American Journal of Orthopsychiatry* 57(3):316–31.

Rutter, M., Graham, P., Chadwick, O., & Yule, W. (1976). "Adolescent turmoil: Fact or fiction?" *Journal of Child Psychology and Psychiatry* 17:35–56.

Santrock, J. W. (1990). *Adolescence*, 4th ed. Dubuque, IA: William C. Brown.

Savin-Williams, R. (2005). *The New Gay Teenager*. Cambridge, MA: Harvard University Press.

Savin-Williams, R., & Berndt, T. (1990). "Friendship and peer relations." In S. Feldman, & G. Elliott (eds.), *At the Threshold*, 277–307. Cambridge, MA: Harvard University Press.

Schmiege, S., & Russo, N. F. (2005). 'Depression and unwanted first pregnancy: longitudinal cohort study.' *British Medical Journal* 331:1303.

Sears, J. (1996). "Black-Gay or Gay-Black? Choosing identities and identifying choices." In G. Unks (ed.), *The Gay Teen*, 135–57. New York: Routledge.

Selman, R. (1979). "A structural-developmental model of social cognition: Implications for intervention research." In R. L. Mosher (ed.), *Adolescents' Development and Education*, 123–32. Berkeley, CA: McCutchan.

————. (1980). *The Growth of Interpersonal Understanding*. New York: Academic Press.

Sisson, L., Hersen, M., & Van Hasselt, V. (1987). "Historical perspectives." In V. Van Hasselt, & M. Hersen (eds.), *Handbook of Adolescent Psychology*, 3–10. New York: Pergamon Press.

Slaughter, D. (1972). "Becoming an African-American woman." *School Review* 299–318.

Smetana, J. (1988). "Adolescents' and parents' conceptions of parental authority." *Child Development* 59:321–35.

————. (1989). "Adolescents' and parents' reasoning about actual family conflict." *Child Development* 60:1052–67.

————. (1996). "Adolescent-parent conflict: Implications for adaptive and maladaptive development." In D. Cicchetti, & S. L. Toth (eds.), *Adolescence: Opportunities and Challenges* (vol. 7), 1–46. Rochester, NY: University of Rochester.

Smith, E. M. (1973). "A follow-up study of women who request abortion." *American Journal of Orthopsychiatry* 43:574–85.

Spracklen, K., Andrews, D., Patterson, G., & Dishion, G. (1996). "Deviancy training in male adolescent friendships." *Behavior Theory* 27(3): 373–91.

Steinberg, L. (2001). "We know some things: Adolescent-parent relationships in retrospect and prospect." *Journal of Research on Adolescence* 11:1–19.

Steinberg, L., & Silk, J. S. (2002). "Parenting adolescents." In M. H. Bornstein (ed.), *Handbook of Parenting* (vol. 1), 103–34. Mahwah, NJ: Erlbaum.

Stern, L. (1989). "Conceptions of separation and connection in female adolescents." In C. Gilligan, N. Lyons, & T. Hanmer (eds.), *Making Connections*, 73–87. New York: Emma Willard School.

Strouse, D. L. (1999). "Adolescent crowd orientations: A social and temporal analysis." In J. A. McLellan, & M. J. B. Pugh (eds.), *The Role of Peer Groups in Adolescent Social Identity: Exploring the Importance of Stability and Change*, 37–54. San Francisco, CA: Jossey-Bass.

Sullivan, H. S. (1953). *The Interpersonal Theory of Psychiatry*. New York: W. W. Norton.

Surrey, J. (1984). "The self-in-relation." In *Work in Progress*. Wellesley, MA: Stone Center for Developmental Services and Studies.

Taylor, J. (1996). "Cultural stories: Latina and Portuguese daughters and mothers." In B. Leadbetter, & N. Way (eds.), *Urban Girls*, 117–31. New York: NYU Press.

Troiden, R. (1998). "A model of homosexual identity formation." In P. M. Nardi, & B. E. Schneider (eds.), *Social Perspectives in Lesbian and Gay Studies: A Reader*, 261–79. London, New York: Routledge.

Tyson, K. (2006). "Shifting images of blackness: Coming of age as Black students in urban and suburban high schools." In E. Horvat, & C. O'Connor (eds.), *Beyond Acting White: Reframing the Debate on Black Student Achievement*. Lanham, MD: Rowman and Littlefield.

Walkerdine, V., Lucey, H., & Melody, J. (2001). *Growing Up Girl*. New York: NYU Press.

Ward, J. (2005). "Racial identity formation and transformation." In E. Brown, & K. Saltman (eds.), *The Critical Middle School Reader*, 259–70. NY: Routledge.

———. (1996). "Raising resisters: The role of truth telling in the psychological development of African American girls." In B. Leadbetter, & N. Way (eds.), *Urban Girls*, 85–99. New York: NYU Press.

Waters, M. (1996). "The intersection of gender, race, and ethnicity in identity development of Caribbean American teens." In B. Leadbeater, & N. Way (eds.), *Urban Girls*, 65–81. New York: NYU Press.

Way, N., & Chu, J. (eds.) (2004). *Adolescent Boys*. New York: NYU Press.

Welsh, D. P., Galliher, R. V., Kawaguchi, M. C., & Rostosky, S. S. (1999). "Discrepancies in adolescent romantic couples' and observers' perceptions of couple interaction and their relationship to depressive symptoms." *Journal of Youth and Adolescence* 28(6):645–66.

Welsh, D. P., Grello, C. M., & Harper, M. S. (2003). "When love hurts: Depression and adolescent romantic relationships." In P. Florsheim (ed.), *Adolescent Romantic Relations and Sexual Behavior: Theory, Research, and Practical Implications*, 185–211. Mahwah, NJ: Lawrence Erlbaum Associates.

Werner, E. (1989). "High-risk children in young adulthood: A longitudinal study from birth to 32 years." *American Journal of Orthopsychiatry* 59(1):72–81.

Williams, T. K. (1996). "Race as a process: Reassessing the 'What are you?' encounters of biracial individuals." In M. Root (ed.), *The Multiracial Experience*, 191–210. Thousand Oaks, CA: Sage.

Wilson, A. (1996). "How we find ourselves: Identity development and two-spirit people." *Harvard Educational Review* 66(2):303–17.